POLITICAL CULTURE AND POLITICAL
CHANGE IN COMMUNIST STATES

# POLITICAL CULTURE AND POLITICAL CHANGE IN COMMUNIST STATES

edited by
ARCHIE BROWN
and
JACK GRAY

HOLMES & MEIER PUBLISHERS
New York

Selection and editorial matter © Archie Brown and Jack Gray 1977
Chapter 1 © Archie Brown 1977
Chapter 2 © Stephen White 1977
Chapter 3 © David A. Dyker 1977
Chapter 4 © George Kolankiewicz and Ray Taras 1977
Chapter 5 © George Schöpflin 1977
Chapter 6 © Archie Brown and Gordon Wightman 1977
Chapter 7 © Jack Gray 1977
Chapter 8 © Francis Lambert 1977
Chapter 9 © Jack Gray 1977

First published in the United States of America 1977 by
Holmes & Meier Publishers, Inc.
101 Fifth Avenue
New York, New York 10003

**Library of Congress Cataloging in Publication Data**

Main entry under title:

Political culture and political change in Communist States.

Includes index.
1. Communist state.    2. Communist countries – Politics
and government.    I.  Brown, Archibald Haworth.
II.  Gray, Jack, 1926–

JC474.P59   1977        301.5'92'091717        76–41832

ISBN 0–8419–0289–5

PRINTED IN GREAT BRITAIN

# Contents

# Contributors

ARCHIE BROWN, who was born in Annan, Scotland, in 1938, is a Fellow of St Antony's College and Lecturer in Soviet Institutions at the University of Oxford. After studying as an undergraduate and graduate student at the London School of Economics and Political Science (University of London), he was a lecturer in politics for seven years at Glasgow University before moving to Oxford in 1971. He has spent fifteen months at Moscow and Leningrad Universities in the course of three cultural exchange visits to the Soviet Union, and has visited Czechoslovakia four times since 1965. Archie Brown is the author of *Soviet Politics and Political Science* (London, 1974, and New York, 1976), co-editor (with Michael Kaser) and part-author of *The Soviet Union since the Fall of Khrushchev* (London, 1975, and New York, 1976), and co-author (with Gordon Wightman) of *The Communist Party of Czechoslovakia* (London, forthcoming). He has also published numerous articles on politics and intellectual history in academic journals and symposia.

DAVID A. DYKER was born in Aberdeen in 1944. After studying Political Economy and History as an undergraduate at Glasgow University, he took the postgraduate Diploma of the Institute of Soviet and East European Studies at Glasgow. He spent the 1967–68 academic year on an exchange scholarship at the Institute of National Economy in Tashkent (USSR) and he has made two study visits to Yugoslavia. Since 1968 he has taught at the University of Sussex where he is a lecturer in economics in the School of European Studies. He is the author of *The Soviet Economy* (London and New York, 1976) and of a number of articles in academic journals.

JACK GRAY, who was born in Glasgow in 1926, has been Senior Lecturer in Far Eastern History at the University of Glasgow since 1964. After graduating from Glasgow University in 1951, he spent two years as a postgraduate student at the School of Oriental and African Studies (University of London). From 1953 to 1956 he lectured on history at the University of Hong Kong and from 1956 to 1964 he was successively Lecturer in Far East History and Lecturer in Politics (China) at the School of Oriental and African Studies in London.

He made study visits to China in 1955 and 1975. From 1963 to 1968 he was Chairman of the Chatham House Working Group on 'China and the World'. Jack Gray is the co-author (with Patrick Cavendish) of *Chinese Communism in Crisis: Maoism and the Cultural Revolution* (London and New York, 1968), editor of and contributor to *Modern China's Search for a Political Form* (London, 1969) and author of *Mao Tse-tung in Power: Theory and Practice since 1949* (Chicago, forthcoming). He has also contributed numerous articles on Chinese politics and modern history to scholarly journals and books.

GEORGE KOLANKIEWICZ, who was born in Trani, Italy, in 1946, is a sociology graduate of Leeds University and at present Lecturer in Sociology at the University of Essex. Previously he held a research fellowship at Essex and a lectureship at University College, Swansea. He co-edited (with David Lane) and contributed to *Social Groups in Polish Society* (London and New York, 1973). He has made a number of study visits to Poland and is currently working on a study of social stratification in Polish society with particular reference to the working class and the intelligentsia.

FRANCIS LAMBERT was born in Penrith, Cumbria, in 1942. After studying history as an undergraduate (and open scholar) at New College, Oxford, he continued his postgraduate studies in Oxford and was awarded a doctorate for his thesis on the Cuban question in Spanish Restoration politics. Between 1966 and 1968 he was Junior Research Fellow in Politics at the Institute of Latin-American Studies of the University of London, and since 1968 has been a lecturer in history at the Institute of Latin-American Studies of the University of Glasgow. He is the author of several articles on Latin American politics in scholarly journals.

GEORGE SCHÖPFLIN was born in Budapest in 1939. From 1957 to 1962 he studied at Glasgow University, where he graduated with M.A. and LL.B degrees. After pursuing his studies at the College of Europe in Bruges, he joined the Royal Institute of International Affairs in London, moving to work at the Central Research Unit of the BBC External Services in 1967. During 1973–74, he was Hayter Fellow at the School of Slavonic and East European Studies (University of London). At the time of writing his chapter he was Research Officer with the BBC External Services and is currently Lecturer in East European Political Institutions at the University of London. Since becoming a British citizen, he has been a regular visitor to Hungary. He is the editor of *The Soviet Union and Eastern Europe: a handbook* (London, 1970) and has contributed a number of articles to scholarly journals and symposia.

RAY TARAS was born in Montreal in 1946. After studying at the Universities of Montreal, Sussex and Essex, he carried out research in Poland during the 1970–71 academic year before taking up a lectureship in politics at Lanchester Polytechnic (Coventry). He is the author of several articles on Polish politics, including chapters in David Lane and George Kolankiewicz (eds), *Social Groups in Polish Society* (London and New York, 1973), and J. Schapiro and P. Potichnyj (eds), *Change and Adaptation in Soviet and East European Politics* (New York, 1976).

STEPHEN WHITE was born in Dublin in 1945. After graduating from Trinity College Dublin, in 1968, he was a postgraduate student at the Institute of Soviet and East European Studies of Glasgow University, where he took his doctorate. He has made regular study visits to the Soviet Union and spent the 1970–71 academic year at Moscow University on a cultural exchange scholarship. Since 1971 he has been a lecturer in politics at Glasgow University. He is the author of a number of scholarly articles in the fields of political science and modern history, and is currently working on a book-length study of Soviet political culture.

GORDON WIGHTMAN, who was born in Edinburgh in 1943, is a lecturer in politics at the University of Liverpool. After graduating from Glasgow University in 1966 he was successively a postgraduate student in the Institute of Soviet and East European Studies and a research assistant and temporary lecturer in the Department of Politics at Glasgow, before moving to Liverpool University in 1972. He spent eighteen months in Czechoslovakia between September 1967 and April 1969 and made a number of shorter visits between 1963 and 1970. He has written on the changing composition of the Czechoslovak Communist Party and is co-author (with Archie Brown) of *The Communist Party of Czechoslovakia* (London, forthcoming).

# Preface

The idea of a collaborative work on 'political culture and political change' in a variety of Communist states was first discussed by the editors of this book in 1969 when they were colleagues at Glasgow University, and between then and 1971 when Archie Brown moved to Oxford a number of discussions took place within a small group of scholars interested in the study of comparative communism.

By 1972 most of the contributors to the present volume had agreed to join the inter-disciplinary working group and the project of *Political Culture and Political Change in Communist States* was formulated in detail. The present volume could not, however, have been produced without the financial support which enabled the authors (who teach in various British universities) to come together for co-ordinating meetings. Formal working group sessions were held in St Antony's College, Oxford, in September 1974 and in Glasgow University in May 1975, and they were followed by a final conference at St Antony's in December 1975 at which the authors had the opportunity to present their chapters (by this time in second or third draft) to an exceptionally well-informed and constructively critical audience and to benefit from much stimulating discussion. For making these meetings and the conference possible the editors and other authors are greatly indebted to the Nuffield Foundation. It was their decision in 1973 to support the project financially which turned aspiration into reality. The grant was made to Archie Brown and he and Jack Gray jointly co-ordinated the project and served as co-chairmen of the 1975 conference.

At this conference, particularly important contributions were made by those who acted as official discussants of the various papers and who, apart from their remarks at formal sessions, in a number of cases gave the individual authors the benefit of their further extensive comments. While the discussants cannot in any way be held responsible for the views espoused in the authors' final drafts which are presented in the chapters which follow, the contributors are conscious of the benefit they derive from this criticism. The following scholars were the discussants: Professor Rudolf L. Tőkés, University of Connecticut (Chapter 1); Dr T. H. Rigby, Australian National University, Canberra (Chapter 2); Dr Stevan Pavlowitch, University of Southampton Chapter 3); Dr Maria Hirszowicz, University of Reading (Chapter 4); Professor Ivan Szelenyi, Flinders University of South Australia, Adelaide (Chapter 5);

Dr Vladimir V. Kusin, University of Glasgow (Chapter 6); Dr John
Gardner, University of Manchester (Chapter 7); Professor Alistair
Hennessy, University of Warwick (Chapter 8); and Professor Hugh
Seton-Watson, School of Slavonic and East European Studies, University
of London (Chapter 9).

The other participants who helped to make the conference so extremely valuable (and who in several cases offered additional written
comments on particular chapters) were: Professor Włodzimierz Brus,
St Antony's College, Oxford; Miss April Carter, Somerville College,
Oxford; Dr Mark Elvin, St Antony's College; Professor S. E. Finer, All
Souls College, Oxford; Dr J. Goldberg, Hebrew University of Jeru-
salem; Professor Ghiţa Ionescu, University of Manchester; Mr Michael
Kaser, St Antony's College; Dr Dennis Kavanagh, University of Man-
chester; Dr David Lane, Emmanuel College, Cambridge; Dr Steven
Lukes, Balliol College, Oxford; Professor Alexander Matejko, Univer-
sity of Alberta, Edmonton; Mr John Miller, La Trobe University,
Melbourne; Mr Richard Newnham, St Antony's College; Dr Frank
Parkin, Magdalen College, Oxford; Dr Alex Pravda, University of
Reading; Dr Z. A. Pelczynski, Pembroke College, Oxford; Dr Harold
Shukman, St Antony's College; Miss Patricia Thomas, Assistant
Director, Nuffield Foundation; and Mr Michael Waller, University of
Manchester.

Since political culture is a concept which cuts across disciplinary
boundaries, the decision to gather together an inter-disciplinary team
of authors was a deliberate one. To the editors and contributors it
appears that there have been great advantages in having the disciplines
of history, sociology and economics as well as political science (the core
discipline so far as this particular study is concerned) represented in the
working group.

Within the group a high level of agreement in principle on a
particular common approach to the study of political cultures of
Communist societies was achieved. That it was not always possible to
apply this as fully in practice as we would have wished can only to a
limited degree be related to differences in disciplinary background and
of personal emphasis among the individual authors. It is, to a greater
extent, the result of variations from one Communist society to another
in the range and type of data which are accessible to the outside investigator. From the beginning it was abundantly clear that certain
types of source would bulk larger in some studies than in others. What,
as it seems to us, remains important is the effort which the various
authors have made to address themselves to an agreed set of questions
within a common framework of analysis.

It should be stressed that we are fully aware that this book is not a
*comprehensive* analysis of political change within Communist states.
No account which concentrated mainly upon political culture and

paid, of necessity, little attention to other approaches to the study of Communist politics could hope to be that. We are aware, too, of how much remains to be done even in the sphere of study of Communist political cultures. The limitations imposed by writing about such a broad theme as that of the political culture of a society at chapter length obviously mean that many problems cannot receive detailed attention. We hope, however, that we have at least done enough to show how important is the political culture dimension if a fuller understanding of continuity and change within Communist states is to be achieved.

*Oxford and Glasgow, 1976*                                 ARCHIE BROWN
                                                          JACK GRAY

# 1 Introduction

ARCHIE BROWN

The peculiar relevance of the study of 'political culture' in relation to change and continuity in Communist states lies in the fact that the goals of total political, economic and cultural transformation have been pursued by ruling Communist Parties in societies with the most diverse historical and cultural traditions. Before taking the discussion any further, it will be as well to make clear at the outset what the authors of the present work take 'political culture' to mean, since this term, like 'culture' itself, has been defined in all too great a variety of ways. It will be understood as the subjective perception of history and politics, the fundamental beliefs and values, the foci of identification and loyalty, and the political knowledge and expectations which are the product of the specific historical experience of nations and groups. 'Political culture', it should be added, is not divorced from a 'culture' in the widest social sense. On the contrary, it is closely related to cultural values and orientations more generally. It focuses attention, however, on that part of a culture which bears relevance to politics.

The seven Communist societies included in the present study have been chosen partly because of the great diversity in pre-Communist experience which they represent and partly because they embrace all of the distinctive 'models' of Communism which have been produced in recent times. (This naturally raises the question of the possible relevance of the former fact to the latter.) The countries selected are: the Soviet Union, China, Cuba, Poland, Hungary, Czechoslovakia and Yugoslavia. The first two have in common the fact that they were great imperial states, but in religious and cultural tradition they could scarcely have been further apart, the one being the centre of Eastern Orthodoxy[1] and the other the upholder of Confucianism. Cuba is utterly different again, in historical experience as well as size, having been part of the Spanish empire and later coming under strong North American influence. Among the East European countries, the re-drawing of boundaries after two World Wars has been such that even within the same state (and in some cases the same nation) the peoples

---

I am very grateful to Michael Lessnoff and Alan Angell for their valuable and constructive criticism of a previous draft of this chapter.

have been subjected to diverse influences and have belonged to different political and religious traditions. In some cases the environment
was Moslem and Turkish, in others Habsburg and Catholic; in some
the influence was Russian and Orthodox, in others Prussian and
Protestant. In addition to these cultural milieux, there was the distinctive Magyar tradition (though the Hungarians were themselves influenced by Austria) and the case of the Croats, some of whom (on the
Dalmatian coast) were for long under Italian influence.[2]

Though no individual scholar (or group of scholars) has up to
the present attempted to apply the concept of political culture to the
comparative study of Communist states, there are already in existence several studies of the political cultures of particular Communist
societies.[3] There is also a growing realisation among scholars interested
in comparative Communism that political culture can make an important contribution to knowledge and understanding in this field.[4]

That is not to say that there is general agreement among students of
politics on the value of the concept of political culture. Indeed, even
among those who are willing to accept in principle that the concept is
a useful one, there are some who would deny the possibility of applying
it in the study of Communist systems. And there is the additional
problem that scholars who have discussed sympathetically the possibility of political cultural studies of Communist societies have not as
yet reached a consensus on how the concept should be defined and
'operationalised'. The purpose of this brief introduction becomes,
therefore, threefold: (i) to consider some of the general criticisms which
have been made of 'political culture' and to suggest how the term may
most usefully be conceptualised; (ii) to consider the difficulties of employing the concept in the political analysis of Communist states and
to note the advantages, as well as the disadvantages, of so doing; and
(iii) to elaborate the framework of analysis adopted in this particular
collective work, setting out the themes and questions to which contributors address themselves in the chapters on individual countries
which follow.

THE CONCEPT AND ITS CRITICS

The term 'political culture' was in use sporadically for years before a
serious attempt was made to discuss and develop it as a specific concept
in the social sciences. The terminology, as Stephen White notes in
Chapter 2, was sometimes employed by Lenin, and it was first used in
English by Sidney and Beatrice Webb in the mid-thirties.[5] Under this
heading the Webbs discuss political education and the role of the mass
media in the Soviet Union. In modern political science, however, the
concept has developed into something considerably broader and richer,
the origins of which are to be found in the works of anthropologists

such as Margaret Mead, Ruth Benedict and Clyde Kluckhohn and the sociology of Max Weber and Talcott Parsons. An important stimulus was provided by political events in the 'Third World' when constitutions and institutions with which newly-independent states had been endowed fairly rapidly began to function in ways which surprised, and sometimes dismayed, their former political mentors. A pioneering article which assisted the development of the concept was published by Gabriel Almond in 1956[6] and others who have made significant contributions to the field include Lucian Pye and Sidney Verba.[7] Though the contributors to the present volume would, in varying degree, dissent from a number of the methodological and ideological assumptions of these political scientists, their debt to them should be acknowledged at the outset.[8] Indeed, the work which (by its perception and suggestiveness) perhaps provided the greatest initial stimulus to the present collective enterprise was Sidney Verba's important essay, 'Comparative Political Culture'.[9]

One criticism which the authors of the present study would, however, make of the way the concept of political culture has been applied up to now is the manner in which its elaboration has been intertwined with dubious theories of 'political development'[10] and with 'systems analysis'.[11] In this literature the characteristics of a developed political system have frequently borne an uncanny resemblance to the principal features of the American political system (often in a somewhat idealised form) and, on the whole, the western literature on political development and modernisation shares with much Marxist literature a tendency to disguise political and moral judgements in quasi-theoretical language. The intellectual context in which 'political culture' has generally been employed has undoubtedly been a factor in leading some critics to a precipitate rejection of the utility of the concept.

In the present work an attempt has been made to relate political culture to political *change* or *continuity* rather than to the more dubious and value-laden notion of *political development*,[12] and the authors of this volume have followed neither Almond nor Easton in their definitions of *political system*, taking this term to mean, rather, the network of political institutions and the pattern of political behaviour within a given state. The relationship between the political culture and the political system (as defined above), on the one hand, and *economic development*, on the other, is quite a different matter, for *economic* development is subject to measurement and largely free of the evaluative connotations of 'political development'. This latter relationship is, indeed, a problem of major importance both for the rulers of Communist states and for the scholarly investigator. Space does not permit anything like a full examination in this book of the relationship between social structure, economic development and political culture. That is a theme for another, and larger, book. But some basic socio-economic data were collected in the course of the research undertaken by the present team of authors with a view to casting light on the question. It is a reasonable initial hypothesis that there is a significant connection between social structure and political culture. To take an extreme case, social change over time in the course of which peasants as a proportion of the population drop from 80 per cent to 20 per cent would be unlikely *not* to be accompanied by changes in political culture. But on the evidence available we are not able to conclude that the social structure conditions political culture to a greater extent than the specific historical experience of a people. Whether we are dealing with East or West, it is possible to find societies of a similar level of economic development and of broadly similar class structures with, nevertheless, striking differences of political culture.

One of the most influential criticisms of explanation in terms of 'culture' and 'values' has come from Barrington Moore. His objection is to attempts to accord culture any independent status in explanation of political behaviour when the former, it is implied, is a secondary phenomenon, dependent on and moulded by institutions and interests.[13] As Moore eloquently puts it:

> To maintain and transmit a value system, human beings are punched, bullied, sent to jail, thrown into concentration camps, cajoled, bribed, made into heroes, encouraged to read newspapers, stood up against a wall and shot, and sometimes even taught sociology.[14]

But if *all that* and more is done to human beings with the aim of *changing* a value system, and yet the official values are not 'internalised' by a majority of the population (as would appear to be the case in most of the societies studied in the present project), some scepticism about the malleability of political culture is in order. It is, of course, important to explain how a political culture has evolved and to note how, in the process of interaction between political institutions and political culture, experience with particular types of institution has helped to determine aspects of the culture. But the dimension of time is crucial here. It would seem to be the case that institutional structures and even overt patterns of political behaviour can be changed much more quickly than political cultures, so that a revolutionary change in the political system opens up the possibility of dissonance between the political culture and the political system. Whether the new institutions can then create a 'new' political culture or whether the functioning of the new institutions becomes modified or significantly changed by the 'old' political culture is an open question, and an important matter for empirical investigation. At any given period of time – and this may mean many years and not merely weeks or months – there can be dissonance between the political culture and the political system. That is to say, there may be a prolonged failure on the part of the controllers of institutional power to socialise the population into acceptance of the official political culture. In such a case, a crisis triggered off by other stimuli (frequently but by no means always economic) may produce a more open political situation in which the strength and direction of political change may be strongly influenced by the dominant – and no longer dormant – political culture. In a situation of this type (Czechoslovakia in the mid-sixties serves as a good example), part of an adequate *explanation* of particular political conduct is likely to be in political cultural terms, and explanations in terms of institutional power or of interest alone will simply not be enough. This is not to deny for a moment the generally important part which interests and institutions have to play in the explanation of political behaviour, nor – obviously – to quarrel with Barrington Moore's remark that 'cultural values do not descend from heaven to influence the course of history'.[15]

Though at one point in his argument, Moore bluntly asserts that 'to explain behaviour in terms of cultural values is to engage in circular reasoning',[16] he does not in fact rule out of court *all* cultural explanation, despite his concern to deny to culture any *independent* status. Indeed, some of his hostility to any *emphasis* on the importance of culture would appear to rest upon the *way* in which certain scholars have used cultural themes to (unconciously) impart a *conservative bias* to their explanations.[17] This perhaps leads Moore to stress the negative part of his criticism of the use of culture in explanation, even though he does not in fact wish to exclude 'ideas or cultural themes' from explanations of political change and continuity, holding that 'there is a significant residue of truth in such explanations'.[18] Having accepted this much, he goes on to suggest that culture can never be more than an 'intervening variable', a filter 'between people and an "objective" situation, made up from all sorts of wants, expectations, and other ideas derived from the past' which 'screens out certain parts of the objective situation and emphasizes other parts'.[19] In saying this, he apparently accepts that culture, *independently* of the current 'objective situation', affects people's political perception. Furthermore, in discussing the 'residue of truth in cultural explanation', he goes so far as to note that this subjective orientation affects people's political behaviour when he writes that 'what looks like an opportunity or a temptation to one group of people will not necessarily seem so to another group with a different historical experience and living in a different form of society.'[20] It may be concluded that not only is Moore less opposed to explanation in terms of culture than some of his hastier readers have assumed, but that he comes closer to recognising culture as an independent causal factor in explaining what people do than he himself has fully recognised.

Another writer who is sometimes assumed (wrongly) to have dealt a devastating blow to the concept of political culture and who must also rank among the weightier critics of work in this field is Brian Barry. But to a much greater extent than Moore, Barry makes clear the distinction between attacking specific weaknesses in the way in which the concept of political culture has been used (in Barry's case, this refers to its use by Almond, Verba, Eckstein and Lipset) and attacking the idea that values and cultures as such can never have any separate explanatory force. Barry readily agrees that ' "values" or "culture" [are] themselves capable, at least in principle, of explanation'. This however, 'does not mean that they are therefore bogus explanations'.[21] While agreeing with Moore that it is inadequate to explain cultural continuity in terms of cultural 'inertia', since this is merely to redescribe the phenomenon, he notes the importance of the *family* in the process of political socialisation and how, therefore, 'something humdrum like the tendency of parents to bring up children with the same outlook as themselves' can assume explanatory significance. So far as agencies of socialisation such as schools are concerned, he appositely observes that 'there seem to be limits to what, in most societies, they can achieve without support from parents, and in any case such institutions often achieve some autonomy from pressures by the powerful.'[22] For Brian Barry, therefore, political culture can amount to more than Barrington Moore's 'intervening variable' argument, the view that 'values are at best the last link in the chain of causation before behaviour itself'.[23] He makes explicit what is at best implicit in Moore's account, namely, 'that "values" and "culture" are worth separate treatment as causal factors in any attempt to explain what people do. This is so even though it always makes sense to ask how these values came to take the form they do, and even though the answer will often involve a reference to the interests of those in a position to exert influence on them.'[24]

Another influential argument (which has some affinity with Barrington Moore's) against the concept of political culture as a variable which may be sometimes relatively independent of the existing structure of institutional power and of economic interests is to be found in Frank Parkin's elaboration of his criticism of 'contemporary political theorists' who have 'been prone to focus on the extent of normative consensus in the "stable democracies" '.[25] Parkin goes on to observe:

> . . . the extent to which values are legitimized in society is largely a function of institutional power. Values are much more likely to flow in a 'downward' than an 'upward' direction; consequently moral assumptions which originate within the subordinate class tend to win little acceptance among the dominant class. The reverse process, however, is much more marked, so that normative consensus is better understood in terms of the socialization of one class by another,

rather than as independent class agreement or convergence of values.[26]

Parkin argues that 'those groups in society which occupy positions of the greatest power and privilege will also tend to have the greatest access to the means of legitimation'.[27] This particular 'concept of a dominant value system', as he notes, 'derives from Marx's celebrated statement that "the ideas of the ruling class are, in every age, the ruling ideas" '.[28]

We may accept at once that institutional power confers great advantages on its holders in terms of their ability to influence the process of political socialisation, including the aquisition of values. This is perhaps particularly so in the case of Communist states where 'the power of power' is especially great. If we consider the family, school, experience at work, the role of the mass media, literature and the arts, and the individual's experience of politics in a narrower sense (what the political and economic system has done for him or to him) to be the major agencies of political socialisation, there can be no doubt that the holders of institutional power in Communist states have attempted (quite overtly) to influence every one of these agencies of socialisation and have generally had a decisive influence over almost all of them – though with the frequent and significant exception of the first.

It is not, however, possible simply to accept *a priori* that values are much more likely to flow in a 'downward' than an 'upward' direction. The changes which took place in the Bolshevik political culture in Russia after the Bolsheviks had embarked upon the serious business of government are instructive. While the coercive instruments of institutional power were certainly used to the full, it is also the case that a number of previously popular political symbols and widely-held values were gradually reinstated into the official political culture. The strong tsars who had been revered as well as feared at the time and admired by later generations of Russians – notably, Ivan the Terrible and Peter the Great – were 'rehabilitated' by Soviet historians at the behest of Stalin. Similarly, the emotional attraction for Russians of the 'motherland' was sufficiently strong for Stalin to find it expedient to reinstate the word (*rodina*) and concept of the motherland. At other times, the situation may be not so much one of values flowing 'upwards' or 'downwards', but of minimal influence of one value system over another. Thus, in pre-revolutionary Russia, notwithstanding the state's impressive panoply of institutional power, the lack of communication between the cultures of different social groups would seem to have been a more prominent feature of the society than the socialisation of one class by another or the achievement of a normative consensus.

It may be useful at this point to draw attention to an analytical distinction which has already been employed here, but which should be stated explicitly. That distinction is between the *dominant* political

culture and the *official* political culture. In Communist states, in particular, the *official* political culture is promoted incessantly through the
mass media, in educational establishments, and through other agencies
of socialisation. But do the *official* values, orientations and perceptions
actually *dominate* the minds of the majority of the citizens? Are they,
in that sense, the 'ruling ideas' or are they *merely* 'the ideas of the
ruling class'? This is surely a matter for empirical investigation. The
official political culture and the dominant political culture may coincide,
substantially overlap, or be at considerable variance from one another,
and the precise nature of the relationship is one of the problems which
students of political culture should be tackling. Frederick Barghoorn,
perhaps the most prominent of writers on Soviet political culture,
devotes a chapter of his latest book to what he calls 'The Dominant
Political Culture' and in it he uses the adjective 'official' synonymously
with 'dominant'.[29] But this all too frequent assumption that *official*
equals *dominant* is both unfortunate and question-begging.

In addition to stressing the problematical relationship of the official
to the dominant political culture, it must be added that it is wrong to
assume *a priori* that there is a dominant political culture in every
society. If we are to classify the possible configurations of political
culture, it may be suggested that, in principle, four different types exist.
These are: (*a*) a unified political culture; (*b*) a dominant political
culture which coexists with various political sub-cultures; (*c*) a dichoto-
mous political culture; and (*d*) a fragmented political culture, i.e. one
in which no state-wide political culture has emerged to dominate the
numerous political cultures or sub-cultures based upon tribe, locality,
or social or national group.

In practice some of these configurations are to be found much more
often than others. Configuration (*a*) is undoubtedly a *goal* of almost all
of the official political cultures of the societies included in the present
study, but in none of them has it been realised. (The leadership of the
League of Communists of Yugoslavia would probably happily settle for
(*b*), whereas in this multi-national state the real situation is rather closer
to (*d*).) There may be societies in which the only division of significance
is between two political cultures – for example, an 'élite' political
culture and a 'mass' political culture (as may be the case in certain
'Third World' countries) and these societies would be classified under
(*c*). In such a situation it would not be correct to describe either of the
cultures as 'dominant' in the sense in which that term has been used
here. (It is perhaps worth noting that an 'élite' political culture should
not necessarily be assumed to be the same as the 'official' political
culture. The *dominant* political culture may contain many elements
that deviate from the *official* – party-sponsored – political culture and
yet permeate social groupings within the élite.) To speak of *the* political
culture of a society is almost always an oversimplification – justi-

fiable only if it is a *conscious* oversimplification. While seeking to specify whatever wide-ranging consensus on fundamental political beliefs and values may exist – to identify, that is to say, a dominant political culture and to describe its relationship to the official political culture – it is important also to be alert to the probable existence of significant sub-cultures and to focus attention on different levels and groups within society.

One of the major disagreements on how 'political culture' may most usefully be conceptualised is between those scholars who believe that the term should subsume what people actually do and those who would exclude this. Should the concept embrace patterns of behaviour as well as psychological orientations to the political process, objective as well as subjective factors, or should an analytical distinction be made between political culture, on the one hand, and political behaviour, on the other, in order to see what part, if any, the former may play in explanation of the latter? The risk of tautology would certainly seem to be less if behaviour is *not* subsumed under political culture, though even writers who view political culture as 'the subjective orientation to politics'[30] have not always avoided the danger of circularity inherent in making inferences about values from behaviour and then using values to explain behaviour.[31]

The consensus among the present authors is that political culture may best be 'operationalised' in the study of Communist politics if its scope is defined in terms of subjective orientation and if its characteristics are not derived by generalising from observed behaviour. Robert C. Tucker, in a fairly recent article,[32] takes the opposite view from this (in common with Richard R. Fagen[33]) and argues for a more anthropological approach to the study of culture whereby the concept would embrace both beliefs and behaviour. Tucker, following Ralph Linton,[34] also urges a distinction between 'real cultural patterns' and 'ideal cultural patterns', the latter being 'consensuses of opinion on the part of the society's members as to how people *should* behave in particular situations' which may be quite different from how they actually behave.[35] Faced by a gulf between beliefs and actions, Tucker prefers to regard this as 'a discrepancy *within* the political culture rather than one between political culture and conduct'.[36] He tacitly admits, however, that the potential explanatory value of political culture may suffer when political behavioural patterns are absorbed in the concept, but questions whether the scholarly value of political culture as a concept depends 'on its explanatory potency'.[37] 'Might not', he asks, 'the central importance of a concept like that of political culture be that it assists us to take our bearings in the study of the political life of a society . . . to describe and analyse and order many significant data, and to raise fruitful questions for thought and research – *without explaining anything*?'[38] It is diffi-cult to see, however, why at least this modest goal may not be achieved by studying political culture *and* political behaviour without subsuming the latter in the former and why then we should jettison an analytical distinction which is useful if political culture is ever to play a part in the explanation of political behaviour. In the present study, therefore, political culture will be viewed (as already mentioned on p. 1) in terms of subjective orientation to history and politics, of fundamental beliefs and values, of foci of identification and loyalty, and of political knowledge and expectations.

POLITICAL CULTURE AND COMPARATIVE COMMUNIST STUDIES

A major objection to the application of the concept of political culture to the study of Communist politics has been the problem of obtaining evidence. The sample survey method, so far as the possibilty of the outside investigator conducting it is concerned, is ruled out and, in the absence of this, there is a definite danger of the study becoming excessively impressionistic. To counteract this, it is essential to use a variety of sources for the study of political cultures in Communist societies (though to use them to the full would require book-length, rather than chapter-length, studies of particular Communist countries).[39] These sources will include the discriminating use of *survey data collected within Communist states* themselves by citizens of those states. In some cases (as, for example, China) such data are unavailable to foreigners. In other cases (for instance, that of Poland) they are particularly rich and plentiful. Though there is a great variation in the quality and quantity of survey research between Communist countries (and considerable *qualitative* variations within any particular country) this is too important a source to be ignored. There is, it must be acknowledged, the constant danger that published survey data will be more flattering to régime values (or the official political culture) than is reality, both because of the pressures and constraints upon publication in the social sciences in these countries and because even the 'raw data' may be unreliable, inasmuch as respondents to questionnaires or interviewers may opt for the safe course of saying what they think the authorities would like to hear. Yet, even in the Soviet case, where the constraints upon social scientists are more severe than in, say, Yugoslavia, Poland, or (for a time) Czechoslovakia, and where the political caution of citizens may, with good reason, be greater than in some of the other countries included in our study, many surveys have produced data which deviate too much from the official values and ideals for them to be dismissed as propaganda.[40]

In a number of cases empirical sociological data gathered within Communist states can be supplemented by the *systematic interviewing of emigrés*. This has been done on a small scale by Solomon in the case of the Chinese[41] and on a much larger, and statistically significant, scale by Alex Inkeles and others in the Harvard Project on the Soviet Social System.[42] On their own, the views of emigrés may be an unreliable guide to the beliefs and values held in the society which they have left, in spite of their diverse reasons for leaving it, and so one should attach weight only to those findings which correlate strongly with views expressed in other sources. (It is worth noting in passing that emigration from the Soviet Union in the nineteen-seventies has been on a sufficient scale to make possible in principle a follow-up survey to the Harvard Project of the nineteen-fifties.)

The other sources for the study of values and beliefs, political knowledge, and foci of identification and loyalty within Communist societies are not so negligible as is sometimes imagined. *Creative literature*, for example, gains in importance in any state which operates a literary censorship, since it is frequently easier to include social observation of popular beliefs, values and knowledge in the form of 'fiction', where the author's personal attitudes to the views expressed are less easily identified than in more overtly socio-political writings. *Memoirs*, if read with discrimination, are also valuable. In the Soviet case, for example, there is now a fairly substantial body of memoir literature, which may be divided into three categories – that published in the Soviet Union, that written in the Soviet Union (as *samizdat*) and published in foreign countries, and that written by former Soviet citizens now abroad. The accounts of life and thought in Communist countries by *long term foreign residents* are also well worth study. Where survey data are scarce, as in the cases of China and Cuba, the need to use such sources becomes greater. *Historiography* within Communist countries may throw some light upon political culture, though it is necessary to be aware of the danger that it is a source which may disproportionately reflect the views of the holders of institutional power and thus be a guide to 'élite political culture' rather than to the 'mass political culture', should these happen to be at variance. The literature within these states on the problems of creating the *new man* and a *Communist consciousness* is also of significance. Its study is important not only for the insights which it provides into the official political culture (into the values which it is deemed appropriate for citizens to possess), but also for the light cast upon existing 'shortcomings' (or deviant values and attitudes).

These are among the sources which the participants in this present study have drawn upon. In no chapter have survey data *alone* been relied on. In some cases, the possibility of using such materials scarcely arose because of the paucity of published survey research. There are dangers both in using survey data in studies of political culture and in not using them. On the one hand, though it is possible to quantify attitudes, it is much harder to determine whether these are deeply held beliefs. There is thus a particular value in the type of survey which replicates questions asked in previous surveys – to test for ephemerality or persistence of particular orientations and beliefs. On the other hand, the danger of ignoring available survey data is that of an excessive subjectivity, for it is obviously a risky business to attribute values and beliefs to citizens of a foreign country (or even of one's own) without any objective check on the statements such as the careful use of quantitative methods may provide. Given that the range of sources and scope and reliability of the data are of uneven quality between one Communist country and another, one either renounces the possibility of studying the political cultures of certain Communist societies (and accordingly of including them in comparisons) or one tries to reduce the dangers to a minimum by not putting too much weight upon results achieved by any one technique of investigation alone and by looking for correspondences between the results obtained by one technique of analysis and one type of source and those obtained by other techniques and from other sources. Where there is a strong correspondence among various sources of information, one may begin to generalise, however diffidently, about the political cultures of particular Communist societies and, more diffidently still, attempt to make cross-national comparisons.

If there are methodological disadvantages in applying the concept of political culture to the study of Communist states, on account of the degree of secrecy which in varying measure prevails and the strict institutional controls maintained over the dissemination of information which may be politically inconvenient, there are actually some advantages in looking at societies of this type rather than at the more open and pluralistic democracies of western Europe or North America. Commenting on studies of Britain and the United States, Kavanagh has noted: 'The actual relationship between the values and structures is likely to be one of mutual reinforcement over time, and the fact that they interact in this way makes it wellnigh impossible to separate the values from the performance of the political structure'.[48] The possibilities of discussing sensibly the harmony or dissonance between values, on the one hand, and political structures, on the other, are perhaps greater in the case of Communist societies where there have been (a) a radical break in the continuity of political institutions, and (b) an unusually overt and conscious attempt to create new political values and to supplant the old. Indeed, the validity of the concept of political culture cannot be said to have been fully tested until it has been used in a comparative study of Communist states, for if the political cultures of societies which have become Communist can be readily moulded into a new shape with old values cast aside, the explanatory value of political culture may reasonably be regarded as marginal.

Criticising Almond and Verba's over-simple concept of the 'civic culture', Brian Barry has noted that at best these authors demonstrate a *correlation* between the 'civic culture' and 'democracy' rather than any causal relationship of the former to the latter. 'The naturally-occurring "crucial experiment"' is, as he suggests, a change of régime:

> If the 'political culture' alters *afterwards* (e.g. in Germany after 1945, towards a 'civic culture' type), this strongly supports the view that it is a more or less accurate reflection of the current political reality. If, on the other hand, it does not change, then this interpretation of the basis of 'political culture' collapses; and if, some time *before* the change in régime, a change in 'political culture' in the right direction were observed, this would provide good evidence for the view which attributes to it causal efficacy. To acquire information for answering these questions, it would be necessary to pick the cases for study in the light of their relevance to the questions – an obvious point but too often overlooked. . . . It would be difficult to get systematic data for the past about 'political culture', and there is always the difficulty that undemocratic régimes may be hostile to surveys which ask people what they think of their rulers, but whatever could be established would at any rate have a direct bearing on a major theoretical question.[44]

While the study of the political cultures of Communist societies is not likely to establish the causal efficacy of political culture in relation to political behaviour in such 'either/or' terms as Barry here implies (and not only on account of the practical methodological problems which he rightly touches on), his central point holds good. Whatever can be established about the political cultures of Communist societies is of importance not only for what it adds to knowledge and understanding of the countries in question, but for the extent to which it may illuminate a significant theoretical issue.

In addition to its bearing on this general issue of political science and its intended illumination of particular Communist societies, the present study has also been conceived with the aim of making a contribution to that branch of political science known as *comparative Communism*. This is quite a recent area of study and one which only began to develop when a number of scholars realised that not all Communist states presented a carbon copy of the Soviet model.[45] One of its primary concerns has been to explain the differences from, as well as the similarities to, the Soviet paradigm in the various states ruled by Communist parties. It has been one of the major hypotheses of the authors of the present study that analysis of political culture can make a contribution to such an explanation. In spite of the acknowledged difficulties involved in the study of political cultures of Communist societies, from a comparative point of view there is a major advantage (in addition to those mentioned earlier) in comparing Communist, as distinct from non-Communist, societies: namely, that it allows us to hold certain variables relatively constant. Important similarities are to be found in three vital aspects of socio-economic life. Firstly, the official ideology of all these states is Marxism-Leninism. Secondly, all (with the substantial and significant exception of Yugoslavia) maintain a form of state ownership of the means of production and their economic relations are of a state socialist (or, at any rate, non-capitalist) type. Thirdly, all have made use, to a greater or lesser degree, of the Soviet model of political organisation, including recognition of the 'leading role' of the Communist Party and of centralisation of power within it.[46]

Moreover, it would not be going too far to say that the principal features of the *official Soviet political culture* have, at one time or another (and, in most cases, *at all times*) formed the major component parts of the official political culture in all other Communist countries. There is, in a significant sense, an *official Communist* political culture which is international, though this is not the same thing as saying that it is the *dominant* political culture within particular Communist societies. Benjamin Schwartz has made the point that a major difference between Communist movements and societies, on the one hand, and the non-Communist, on the other, is that:

> the former adheres to the *ideal* of a centralized ideological identity in international politics. This ideal bears little resemblance to actuality today, of course, but the myth of socialist internationalism nevertheless exerts some important constraints upon adherents' goals and policies. Their rhetoric is similar, despite significant ideological divergencies, and there is a more or less finite limit to the scope of applicable approaches to the transformation of society. Communist leaders, moreover, feel themselves to be in a relationship to an international movement – amorphous as it is – and in terms of political culture, such orientations must be considered relevant. Finally, the ultimate goal of a world communist society, a sort of latter-day imperial ideal, has by no means been discarded by Communist theoreticians, even though the ideal does indeed seem farther away than ever.[47]

A number of important aspects of the official Soviet political culture are discussed by White in Chapter 2 and they can be taken to hold good for other Communist societies discussed in the present study except where the authors of these chapters draw attention to specific national deviations. To a considerable extent, adoption of the official Soviet political culture on the part of other national Communist élites has been a voluntary act. From the point of view of the latter, in so far as this culture seems to have played a part in consolidating the authority of the Soviet Communist Party, it makes sense to seek a similar control over political information and to try to instil the same values and beliefs.

This is not the whole story, however. The extent to which a political culture corresponding exactly to the Soviet one is officially promoted within the various Communist states has varied over time, as has the closeness of relations between particular Communist states and the Soviet Union. There is also the geopolitical aspect. The Soviet Union has generally been able to exercise stronger control over geographically contiguous Communist states than over those states which do not have a common border with it. Yugoslavia and Cuba, for example, have found a greater scope for proclaiming an official political culture which in some respects deviates from the Soviet one. China, which does share a common border with the Soviet Union, is sufficiently large and populous to show at least as great a degree of independence.

The other important feature that these three countries have in common is that they 'made their own revolutions', whereas throughout most of East Europe Communist Parties could not have come to power without the backing of the Red Army. This gives the Chinese, Yugoslav and Cuban leaders a greater measure of self-confidence than their counterparts in Poland, Hungary or Bulgaria can possess. This line of argument might also be supported by the example of Albania, though it does not belong to the group of states included in the present study. It is worth considering in the same context the most marginal case in terms of indigenous revolution among the countries included in our study, that of Czechoslovakia. The Czechoslovak Communist Party seized power in February 1948 without any participation by the Soviet armed forces, though it can be argued that the fact that Czechoslovakia had been decreed at the end of the Second World War to be within the Soviet sphere of influence tilted the balance of forces decisively in favour of the Communists. At any rate, Czechoslovakia came much closer to 'indigenous revolution' in the early post-war period than did either Poland or Hungary and in more recent years it has also come closer than either to producing an official political culture quite distinctive from the Soviet one.

Too much store should not be set upon the positive correlation between 'indigenous revolution' and non-Soviet type official political culture. After all, it is possible to argue that Czechoslovakia in 1968 was well on the way to producing the *most distinctive* official political culture of all in terms of deviation from the Soviet prototype, while, as noted above, it was the *most marginal* case in respect of indigenous revolution. This much, however, can be said for the relevance of the quasi-indigenous revolution (and the point applies *a fortiori* to the Chinese, Yugoslav and even Cuban political leaderships) – that there were reformist members of the Czechoslovak political élite who felt that they were masters of their own destiny and not clients of a Soviet patron. They thought that 'all' they had to do was to change the policies and orientations of the Czechoslovak Communist Party. They did not conclude (until after August 1968) that it was necessary to change the Soviet Union as well. The two general points to be drawn from this are, then, the psychological one that the self-confidence of national political élites and willingness to redefine their official political cultures and make them more distinctive from the Soviet culture will be affected by the degree to which they seized power indigenously, and the political-strategic one that the variations according to time and place in Soviet detailed surveillance of, and control over, other Communist states must be seen as an important factor determining the official political cultures as well as the institutional structures of these countries.

ANALYTICAL FRAMEWORK OF THE STUDY

Though the various contributors to the present study have naturally been free to include themes of special importance to the particular societies which they have been studying, they have agreed on a common framework of analysis, consisting of what they take to be the four major component parts of political culture, with additional attention being paid to several other especially significant themes related to political culture. Though not all the chapters deal with these points in the precise order in which they are taken here, they are listed numerically in the paragraphs which follow in order to outline as clearly as possible the analytical framework which has been adopted.

(i) *Previous political experience*

Though only popular *perception of previous political experience, subjective* rather than *objective* history, may be taken as a component part of political culture (as defined earlier), all the authors of the chapters on particular countries which follow have a brief historical section on those parts of the nation's (or, in some cases, nations') history which appear to them to be the most relevant to the formation of the political culture of the society with which they are concerned. The importance of not overlooking objective political experience lies in the fact that political cultures are historically conditioned, and so historical accounts, however compressed they may be, are necessary to an understanding of how a particular political culture has evolved. There is also likely to be at the least a very substantial overlap between objective and subjective political experience, and where hard information on subjective perception of recent and more distant history (for example, in the form of survey data) is missing, historical interpretation by the academic observer becomes all the more important. In so far as data can be obtained, however, greater attention is paid to popular perception of previous political experience since this is not only a component of political culture but, unlike the professional history of historians, likely to have a bearing on subsequent political behaviour.

## (ii) *Values and fundamental political beliefs*

What the important values and fundamental political beliefs are in any society is a matter for empirical investigation, but it should be stressed that the concern here is with values and beliefs at a deeper level than attitudes towards current political issues.[48] Fortunately, whereas in Western societies the latter type of data is more readily found because such data are in principle more easily ascertainable, in Communist societies survey research has generally had to avoid the sensitive zone of contemporary political issues and has in consequence not infrequently had recourse to areas of investigation which have a rather greater bearing on political culture. In so far as attitudes towards current issues may *reflect* more deeply-held beliefs, they too, of course, are of interest. Among the examples of values and beliefs which are discussed in the chapters which follow are the degree of attachment to security, liberty, independence, egalitarianism, individualism, collectivism, or paternalism, as well as beliefs concerning the *efficacy* of the individual in relation to the political process. *Beliefs* may also include myths. Thus, for instance, one of the more significant myths in a number of the countries discussed in this work is that of a *partisan movement* during the Second World War, though in some cases this belief corresponds much more closely with reality than in others.

## (iii) *Foci of identification and loyalty*

Among the various possible foci of identification are those with ethnic group, religious group, social class, party, village and family. The data available on these foci of identification and loyalty are again of uneven quality and of greatly varying quantity between one Communist society and another, but the issue is too central to political culture to be ignored. The *sense of national identity* which citizens of these various societies have receives consideration among the *foci of identification and loyalty*; and *political symbols* are also subsumed in this category. Both people and objects may assume a symbolic importance within a political culture. For examples of the former we need look no further than Lenin in the Soviet Union and Masaryk in Czechoslovakia, and of the latter to the symbolic significance in Hungary of the flag and the lost crown and in Poland of Warsaw Castle.

### (iv) *Political knowledge and expectations*

This component of political culture includes what people know (or perceive) of their own political system and its policy outputs and what they know of alternative political systems. The extent to which there is variety within the educational system and the nature and extent of diffusion by educational institutions of knowledge and information 'inconvenient' from the standpoint of the official political culture is relevant here, as, of course, is the degree of freedom of expression permitted to the mass media. The extensiveness of contact with other societies – for example, through tourism or by means of workers travelling abroad for employment – is significant, as is the extent to which foreign broadcasts are listened to, since these provide alternative sources of information to the state-sponsored ones. Expectations are likely to be related to knowledge and under this heading we may include, for example, expectations of certain norms of political behaviour, of the decision-making process, and of policy outcomes.

In addition to these four major components of political culture, several other particularly important themes deserve mention. They are taken up, to a greater or lesser degree, in the chapters which follow, but are worth a still fuller treatment than could be accorded them in the present volume.

They may be summarised as follows:

(*a*) *The relationship between the process of political socialisation and political culture.* This involves consideration of what are the major components of the *official* political culture, whereas the four points outlined above relate, rather, to the *dominant* political culture. The *efficacy* of socialisation into the official political culture is a major concern here, and ideally (lack of data for some countries makes this ideal difficult to achieve) a distinction should be made between its efficacy for different social groups. The large and important question which follows on from this is: how successful have the holders of institutional power been in *changing* the political culture – in replacing traditional values and creating a 'new man'?[49]

(*b*) *The relationship between political culture and political sub-cultures.* Of the four possible configurations of political culture mentioned on p. 8 of this chapter, that to be found in almost all of the Communist societies with which we have been concerned is the case of the *dominant political culture which co-exists* (peacefully or otherwise) with *various political sub-cultures.* Beyond specifying the dominant political culture and the most significant of the sub-cultures, the more difficult task is to *explain* why there should be a particular dominant political culture and why it (in so far as it differs from the official political culture) and certain sub-cultures should persist. It is also relevant to explore the extent to which the political sub-cultures correspond with differences of social class, ethnic group, or generational group.

(c) *The relationship between level of socio-economic development and political culture.* The problem of this relationship has already been touched upon in the first section of this Introduction (on the *concept* of political culture). A certain number of basic socio-economic data are provided in the chapters which follow, but our earlier hope of providing information on a series of important socio-economic indicators (which would be comparative both over time – the years we had in mind were 1938, 1950, 1960 and 1970 – and across national boundaries) had to be abandoned mainly because of lack of certain key statistics in some of the countries with which we are concerned and partly because the problems of comparability even where such data exist are such as to require separate and more specialised treatment. If the problems of comparability are great when one is dealing with the Soviet Union and East Europe alone,[50] they are compounded when China and Cuba are added. Indeed, in the case of China almost no worthwhile national economic statistics have been made available since 1959. The socio-economic data gathered have served as background information for the authors of this book and in some chapters are presented as such to the reader, but we have, of necessity, refrained from making across-the-board economic comparisons. It is important to be aware of the comparative levels of economic development in very broad outline, but to attempt to put figures to this would in most cases be to convey a spurious precision. (To illustrate the point with an extreme example, China specialists disagree as to whether the *population* of China is 700 million or 900 million or some figure within this remarkably broad margin of error.)

(d) *The relationship between political culture and political change.* Though to do anything like justice to analysis of the political cultures of Communist societies in the chapters which follow leaves relatively little space for discussion of political change in a descriptive sense, the *relationship* between political culture and political change is the major subject of our inquiry. The problem of *changing* the political culture has already been touched upon in (a) above, but there is also the question of the relationship between political culture, on the one hand, and change in political institutions, political processes and (to a lesser extent) particular policies, on the other. It is in this context of political change or continuity that it is, perhaps, most appropriate to consider the degree of *harmony* or *dissonance* between the political culture and the political system.

In choosing to ask big questions and to accept the constraints of space involved in writing about them at chapter-length, we are aware that this work can be no more than a preliminary essay into the problematical field of comparative Communist political culture. The themes are big enough (and in some cases the data are sufficiently plentiful, if one looks hard enough) to make possible the writing of a number of books rather than chapters on them in the context of *each* of the Communist societies with which we have been concerned (as well, needless to say, as in that of other Communist societies).[51] It is to be hoped that the present collective work – with all its limitations – will stimulate further research and publication both on particular Communist societies and on the comparison of Communist political cultures.

NOTES

1   This is to speak primarily of pre-revolutionary *Russia*. The USSR contains well over a hundred ethnic groups, ranging in religious and cultural tradition from Protestant Estonians to Moslem Tadzhiks.

2   See H. Gordon Skilling, *The Governments of Communist East Europe* (New York, 1966) p. 24. Skilling provides an admirable and concise discussion of the diversity of East European political and cultural traditions in his ch. 3, pp. 19–29.

3   The various attempts to study the political culture of the Soviet Union – most of which leave a good deal to be desired – are discussed in my *Soviet Politics and Political Science* (London, 1974) ch. 4, 'Political Culture', pp. 89–104, though it is worth noting that there is as yet no book-length study of Soviet political culture. There is, however, a growing literature on other particular Communist political cultures. Book-length works include: Richard R. Fagen, *The Transformation of Political Culture in Cuba* (Stanford, 1969); Lucian W. Pye, *The Spirit of Chinese Politics: A Psychocultural Study of the Authority Crisis in Political Development* (Cambridge, Mass., 1968); Richard H. Solomon, *Mao's Revolution and the Chinese Political Culture* (Berkeley, 1971); and David W. Paul: 'Nationalism, Pluralism and Schweikism in Czechoslovakia's Political Culture' (unpublished Ph.D. thesis, Princeton, 1973).

4   See the 'Digest of the Conference on Political Culture and Comparative Communist Studies' (held at Arden House, New York State, during November 1971, under the chairmanship of Robert C. Tucker) published by Dorothy Knapp, David W. Paul and Gerson Sher in *Newsletter on Comparative Studies of Communism*, vol. V, no. 3 (May 1972) pp. 2–17.

5   In the Webbs' *Soviet Communism: A New Civilization* (3rd ed., London, 1944) pp. 736–9. (The first edition of this work – for the most part, a monument to human gullibility – was published in 1935.)

6   Gabriel Almond, 'Comparative Political Systems', in *Journal of Politics*, vol. 18, no. 3 (August 1956) pp. 391–409.

7   See, most notably, Gabriel A. Almond and Sidney Verba, *The Civic Culture* (Princeton, 1963); Lucian W. Pye and Sidney Verba, *Political Culture and Political Development* (Princeton, 1965); and Lucian W. Pye, 'Culture and Political Science: Problems in the Evaluation of the Concept of Political Culture' in Louis Schneider and Charles M. Bonjean

(eds), *The Idea of Culture in the Social Sciences* (Cambridge, 1973) pp. 65–76.

8  For valuable discussion of some of the conceptual and methodological issues raised by the writings of Almond, Verba, Pye, Eckstein and others on political culture, see Dennis Kavanagh, *Political Culture* (London, 1972) and Brian Barry, *Sociologists, Economists and Democracy* (London, 1970) esp. ch. 3, 'Values and Stable Democracy: Three Theories', pp. 47–74.

9  This constitutes the final chapter, pp. 512–60, of Pye and Verba, *Political Culture and Political Development*.

10  See, e.g., Almond and Verba, *The Civic Culture;* Pye and Verba, *Political Culture and Political Development*; and Almond and Powell, *Comparative Politics: A Developmental Approach* (Boston, 1966).

11  See e.g., Almond and Powell, ibid. David Easton, in his approach to systems analysis, makes less use of the concept of political culture, but see his *A Systems Analysis of Political Life* (Chicago, 1965) ch. 7, 'Regulation of Want Conversion: Cultural Mechanisms', pp. 100–16. For an incisive criticism of Almond's notion of political system, see S. E. Finer, 'Almond's Concept of "Political System": A Textual Critique' in *Government and Opposition*, vol. 5, no. 1 (winter 1969–1970) pp. 3–21.

12  For an exceptionally valuable and lucid discussion of the fact and value controversy in the social sciences, see Michael H. Lessnoff, *The Structure of Social Science* (London, 1974), esp. ch. 6, 'Value-judgements and Social Science', pp. 131–65. (After briefly examining (pp. 135–6) Almond's 'functional model', Lessnoff concludes that it 'is to a large degree evaluative but not explicitly so'.)

13  Barrington Moore, Jr., *Social Origins of Dictatorship and Democracy: Lord and Peasant in the Making of the Modern World* (Peregrine ed., Harmondsworth, 1969), esp. pp. 484–7.

14  Ibid., p. 486.

15  Ibid.

16  Ibid.

17  Ibid., esp. p. 485.

18  Ibid., p. 485.

19  Ibid.

20  Ibid.

21  Barry, *Sociologists, Economists and Democracy*, p. 97.

22  Ibid., p. 98.

23  This is Barry's paraphrase of Moore's position, ibid. p. 96.

24  Ibid., p. 98.

25  Frank Parkin, *Class Inequality and Political Order: Social Stratification in Capitalist and Communist Societies* (London, 1971) p. 80.

26  Ibid., p. 81.

27  Ibid., p. 83.

28  Ibid., p. 82.

29  Frederick C. Barghoorn, *Politics in the USSR* (2nd ed., Boston, 1972) pp. 20–47.

30  Sidney Verba, op. cit., p. 199.

31    Such circularity may not, however, be a necessary concomitant of all
      attempts to infer beliefs from behaviour. Kavanagh suggests: 'We might
      infer beliefs *only from some types of behaviour*, e.g. voting . . . and use
      these beliefs to explain *other behaviour*, e.g. compliance with laws. An
      alternative approach is to infer beliefs from behaviour during a certain
      time period and draw on these beliefs to explain behaviour in subsequent
      periods.' (*Political Culture*, op. cit., p. 49.)

32    Robert C. Tucker, 'Culture, Political Culture and Communist Society',
      in *Political Science Quarterly*, vol. 88, no. 2 (June 1973) pp. 173–90.

33    Richard R. Fagen, *The Transformation of Political Culture in Cuba*
      (Stanford, 1969).

34    Ralph Linton, *The Cultural Background of Personality* (New York,
      1945).

35    Tucker, op. cit., p. 177.

36    Ibid., p. 178.

37    Ibid., p. 179.

38    Ibid.

39    The possible sources which could be employed in larger-scale studies of
      the political cultures of particular Communist societies are discussed
      more fully than here (with special reference to the Soviet Union) in my
      *Soviet Politics and Political Science*, ch. 4, esp. pp. 95–100.

40    See Stephen White, 'Communist Political Culture: An Empirical Note',
      in *Newsletter on Comparative Studies of Communism*, vol. VI, no. 2
      (February 1973) pp. 41–4, as well as White's contribution to the present
      book.

41    Richard H. Solomon, *Mao's Revolution and the Chinese Political Cul-
      ture*, op. cit.

42    Of the several books which emerged from the Harvard Project, the most
      valuable from the standpoint of the student of political culture is Alex
      Inkeles and Raymond A. Bauer, *The Soviet Citizen: Daily Life in Totali-
      tarian Society* (Cambridge, Mass., 1961).

43    Kavanagh, op. cit., p. 66.

44    Barry, op. cit., p. 52.

45    The first books in the field began to appear in the mid-sixties. Worthy of
      note among the earliest of such works are: H. Gordon Skilling, *Com-
      munism National and International* (Toronto, 1964); Adam Bromke (ed.),
      *The Communist States at the Crossroads* (New York, 1965); Milorad M.
      Drachkovitch, *Marxism in the Modern World* (Stanford, 1965); Ghiţa
      Ionescu, *The Politics of the European Communist States* (London, 1966);
      H. Gordon Skilling, *The Governments of Communist East Europe* (New
      York, 1966); and Donald W. Treadgold (ed.), *Soviet and Chinese Com-
      munism: Similarities and Differences* (Seattle, 1967).

46    It follows that I cannot accept the argument of John H. Kautsky – in a
      stimulating review article ('Comparative Communism Versus Compara-
      tive Politics', *Studies in Comparative Communism*, VI, nos. 1 and 2
      (spring–summer 1973) pp. 135–70) discussing a notable contribution to
      the literature on comparative communism (Chalmers Johnson, ed.,
      *Change in Communist Systems*, Stanford, 1970) – that there is nothing
      really distinctive about Communist systems. It is good that we are be-

coming increasingly aware of the differences *among* Communist systems, but the study of these very significant differences is all the more interesting because of the existence of important common features. Kautsky is wrong in seeing a tension between 'comparative politics' and 'comparative Communism'. The latter is a sub-division of the former and to stress the usefulness of comparing Communist polities and societies does not imply hostility to the comparison of Communist with non-Communist states whenever what one is wishing to compare provides good reasons for doing so. Joseph LaPalombara has written illuminatingly on (*inter alia*) the problem of the 'uniqueness' of Communist systems in a recent article: 'Monoliths or Plural Systems: Through Conceptual Lenses Darkly', *Studies in Comparative Communism*, vol. VIII, no. 3 (autumn 1975, pp. 304–32) esp. pp. 312, 313 and 332.

47  This summary of one of Benjamin I. Schwartz's contributions to the Arden House Conference on Political Culture and Comparative Communist Studies is provided by Knapp, Paul and Sher, op. cit., p. 14.

48  See Verba, in Pye and Verba, op. cit., p. 516.

49  In a more detailed study of the process of political socialisation than constrictions of space permit in the chapters which follow, one would wish to see the data from Communist societies compared with Western data on political socialisation. The benefits might be at least as great for social scientists attempting to theorise about the socialisation process as for students of Communist systems. For an invaluable guide to the political socialisation literature, see Jack Dennis, *Political Socialization Research: A Bibliography* (Sage American Politics Series, Beverly Hills, 1973). Among particularly suggestive works are: Fred I. Greenstein, *Personality and Politics: Problems of Evidence, Inference and Conceptualization* (Chicago, 1969); Fred I. Greenstein and Sidney Tarrow, *Political Orientations of Children: The Use of a Semi-Projective Technique in Three Nations* (Sage Comparative Politics Series, Beverly Hills, 1970); and David Easton and Jack Dennis, *Children in the Political System: The Origins of Political Legitimacy* (New York, 1969). The relationship in Communist societies of the process of political socialisation to the acquisition, growth or decline of régime legitimacy would make an important subject for a large-scale study. Though they are lacking in concrete data, several interesting 'thinkpieces' on the legitimacy problem are to be found in the contributions of Alfred Meyer, Oskar Anweiler, W. Harriet Critchley, George L. Kline and Rudolf L. Tőkés to Sylva Sinanian, Istvan Deak and Peter C. Ludz (eds), *Eastern Europe in the 1970s* (New York, 1972) ch. 3, 'Legitimacy of Power in East Central Europe', pp. 45–86.

50  Some comparative economic statistics for East Europe are provided in C. Gati (ed.), *The Politics of Modernization in Eastern Europe* (New York, 1974). Much fuller information will become available in a forthcoming three-volume work, *The Economic History of Eastern Europe, 1919–1975* (Oxford) under the general editorship of Michael Kaser (whose *Health Care in the Soviet Union and East Europe*, London and Boulder, Colorado, 1976, already provides a comparative analysis of one specific sector).

51  Cf. n.3 for references to the few book-length works to be completed thus far which are explicitly devoted to study of the political cultures of Communist societies. None of them concern themselves with the full range of issues which have been raised here and their approach differs from that adopted by the contributors to this book.

# 2 The USSR: Patterns of Autocracy and Industrialism

## STEPHEN WHITE

Soviet political culture is rooted in the historical experience of centuries of autocracy.[1] Isolated from the major trade routes and located in a territory which offered little potential for agricultural development, the early Russian state was not one in which powerful and autonomous social formations were likely to take root; and at least since medieval times the country has typically been ruled by a strong, autocratic monarch, with countervailing institutions – parliamentary, legal or whatever – remaining weak and undeveloped. 'If there is one single factor which dominates the course of Russian history, at any rate since the Tartar conquest', writes Professor Seton-Watson, 'it is the principle of autocracy.'[2] It would be a mistake to suppose that the country's pattern of political development held no other potential. The early Russian state, on the contrary, was characterised by the emergence of popular assemblies (the *veche*) which were similar in character to city governments elsewhere in Europe at this time and which similarly exercised important prerogatives with respect to the choice of a ruler, legislation, the imposition of taxes, and questions of war and peace.[3] But in most Russian towns the Tartar invasion of the thirteenth century brought this pattern of development to an abrupt end; and the expansion of the Muscovite principate in the fifteenth and sixteenth centuries led to the termination of city self-government in its last remaining outposts, Novgorod (in 1478) and Pskov (in 1510).[4] The basis had thus been laid for that impress of autocratic institutions upon the structure of social life which forms so central and distinctive an element in the country's political culture. The first part of this chapter will deal with that inheritance under three broad headings: the structures of government; perceptions of politics and the scope of government.[5]

### THE AUTOCRATIC INHERITANCE

*Structures of government*

A characteristic of the Muscovite state was the absence of political institutions in any way constraining the exercise of monarchical power.

The monarch (called, from 1547, the tsar), it was true, did discuss major matters of legislation and taxation with the boyar aristocracy in an institution known as the Boyar Duma. The Duma controlled the local administration, took decisions on the organisation of the army and landholding, and received foreign consuls. A legal code of 1550, indeed, regarded the Duma's authorisation as an essential part of the law-making process. The growing authority of the tsar, however, allowed him to reduce its influence. From the middle of the sixteenth century an 'inner Duma' evolved, composed of the more amenable of the tsar's courtiers, to which important matters of state were increasingly directed; and the tsar himself began to legislate in his own name. Although the Duma survived until the end of the seventeenth century, it was as a body much reduced in influence and dwindling in numbers. Even at the height of its powers, moreover, the Duma had been no more than an agency for the execution of the instructions of the sovereign. It had no area of competence of its own; its composition and size were extremely unstable; and it maintained no records.[6]

The *Zemskii Sobor*, which met from the mid-sixteenth until the mid-seventeenth century, more closely resembled an embryonic parliamentary institution. Its membership was broader than that of the Boyar Duma, and in principle elective; and in full session it was a body of by no means inconsiderable dimensions. Some four hundred representatives attended the *Sobor* of 1598, while that of 1613, at which Alexis Romanov was elected tsar, had as many as seven or eight hundred members. This was the period in which the *Zemskii Sobor* had its greatest degree of influence; and for the first decade of the new dynasty its sessions were almost continuous. Thereafter, however, it began to be summoned more rarely, and to concern itself principally with foreign policy questions; and in 1722 it was deprived of its right to elect the tsar. Even before this reduction in its powers, however, the *Zemskii Sobor* was in no sense a body which exercised a constitutional check upon the the prerogatives of the sovereign. The tsar, on the contrary, determined when assemblies were to be convened, and in what manner representatives were to be elected to it (in some cases simply nominating them himself).[7] The *Zemskii Sobor*'s decisions, moreover, were effective only when the sovereign chose to agree with them. Klyuchevsky's conclusion that the *Sobor* of 1566 was a 'consultation of the government with its own agents', it has been argued, may fairly be appplied to its other sessions as well.[8]

It was not, in fact, until the early twentieth century that Russian political institutions of an even remotely 'parliamentary' character made their appearance. Wrung during the course of the revolutionary events of 1905–6 from a reluctant tsar, the State Duma was always a vulnerable body whose powers were constantly in danger of curtailment by a jealous monarch. Formally, however, its powers were extremely extensive. It had the right to enact and amend legislation; it could appoint and dismiss government officials; it had the right to consider the national and departmental budgets; and it had general supervisory rights over the apparatus of state control. It had the right, moreover, to address questions to the chairman of the Council of Ministers (the re-established 'Cabinet'), and to individual ministers; it supervised the administration of the state railways and private companies; and it could examine in addition any question which the tsar might invite it to consider. Without the consent of the Duma, promised the tsar's manifesto of 17 October 1905, 'no law can come into force'.[9]

The Duma's powers, as defined by subsequent legislation, proved in fact to be rather more modest. The Duma's rejection of a budgetary proposal, it emerged on 8 March 1906, would not in fact prevent its enactment. The Duma, moreover, had no right to alter expenditure connected with the army and navy, foreign loans, the affairs of the imperial household, or many matters within the competence of the Minister of Internal Affairs. Some two-thirds of government expenditure was thus removed from its control. The Basic Laws of the state were likewise outside the Duma's competence; their review, extension or amendment was the prerogative of the tsar alone. The Duma's control over the executive was also extremely limited. Ministers were responsible to the tsar, not to the Duma, and the tsar alone had the right to appoint and dismiss them.[10]

The tsar, moreover, nominated just over half of the members of the second legislative chamber, the State Council, which had the right of veto over all the proposals which the Duma submitted to it (the remainder of its members were elected by the landed nobility, the Holy Synod, educational institutions and traders); and under the terms of the Basic Laws of the Russian Empire he remained the ultimate source of legislative authority. The tsar, for instance, could confirm or reject legislative proposals, determine when the Duma should sit and when it should be dissolved, and, if he chose to do so, promulgate decrees on his own authority which had the force of law. Legislation of this kind was supposed to take place only in 'extraordinary' circumstances, and it had subsequently to be presented to the Duma and State Council for the consideration. It became general practice, however, to resort to procedures of this kind, especially for particularly reactionary pieces of legislation, and Duma sessions were sometimes arbitrarily terminated in order to provide for it.[11]

The Duma's influence over the conduct of the government, these restrictions notwithstanding, appears to have increased steadily in the years before the First World War. Norms and procedures of a more or less parliamentary form were gradually taking form (it was Duma pressure, for instance, which led to the dismissal of four ministers in 1915, the most notable success which the Duma had yet achieved), and it is arguable that these powers of influence might have developed into full-blown legislative supremacy had war and revolution not super-vened.[12] This, however, must remain a matter for conjecture. So far as the facts are concerned, it is clear that the Russian Empire was governed, as late as the early twentieth century, by a scarcely-modified autocracy, and that it was the only major European country of which this could still be said.

The point, however, is not simply, or even mainly, the absence of con-stitutional checks upon central authority (the Queen, after all, to this day retains impressive *formal* powers in Britain). It is more important for our purposes to note that *popular links with such representative institutions* as existed were extremely tenuous, both in terms of levels of participation in the political process and, more 'subjectively', in terms of knowledge of and attachment to those institutions among the mass of the citizen body. The franchise, in the first place, was a restricted and highly unequal one. The right to vote was confined to males over the age of twenty-five; and within that category there were further exclu-sions in respect of the armed forces, students and foreigners. Provision was also made for further, more or less arbitrary, individual exclusions. Those who remained eligible to vote were divided into three (later four) electoral colleges, at which point a further series of biases came into operation. The result was to accord representation as follows: major landowners (0.3 per cent of the total population) received 32 per cent of electoral college votes; peasants received 42.2 per cent; and workers received 2.7 per cent (out of some 20.8 million workers and their families in European Russia in 1906, not more than one million had the right to vote).[13] In all, only about three-and-a-half million citizens were admitted to the franchise, a proportion of the total population no greater than in Britain a century earlier, and an extremely low one in comparative terms.

The results, in terms of the representation of social groups within the institutions of state, were as might have been expected. Under the revised electoral legislation of 1907, the landed gentry provided 51 per cent of the Duma's membership, the peasantry provided another 22.4 per cent, and working-men deputies were 2.3 per cent of the total.[14] Liberals and moderates, who were enlarging their share of the political power elsewhere, were notably under-represented. The 'liberal bour-geoisie', indeed, tended on the whole to regard the Duma with in-difference or even suspicion. The Duma, in their view, was composed of landed notables who were poorly informed of the needs of trading and manufacture, and had little awareness of their importance to the national economy. Russian business circles, accordingly, were generally more inclined to establish strong and autonomous economic associations outside the representative system altogether than to increase their influ-ence within it. The business world took a somewhat greater interest in the Third and Fourth Dumas; but the longer they continued to meet, the more it became apparent that landlord-reactionary rather than liberal-bourgeois views predominated within them, and the greater became their disillusionment.[15] The result was that representative institutions in Russia lacked not simply the constitutional powers of corresponding bodies in Western Europe; more crucially, they drew upon an altogether more restricted range of social support.

## Perceptions of politics

One consequence of the weak articulation of representative institutions was a highly *personalised attachment to political authority*, in particular to the person of the tsar. It has frequently been noted, for instance, that the popular uprisings which periodically convulsed Russian society in the seventeenth and eighteenth centuries were almost never directed against the tsar as such. Their target was much more frequently the boyar aristocracy, who were typically supposed to have removed the tsar from effective control of the nation's destinies and from whose maleficent labours the rebels generally proposed to deliver him. In Stenka Razin's rising of 1667–71, for instance, a careful distinction was always drawn between the boyars, who were massacred as traitors to the tsar, and the tsar himself, to whom the rebels offered to submit after every reverse. The rebels even went so far as to claim that the Tsarevich Alexis, the tsar's eldest son and the heir to the throne, was marching with them, though the tsarevich had died in 1670.[16] Pugachev, a century later, more boldly declared that he was himself the rightful sovereign. There were more than twenty such pretenders in Russia during the seventeenth century, and more than forty during the eighteenth century (the unfortunate Peter III was rescued from the dead on at least sixteen occasions). The myth of the 'just tsar', as Avrich has noted, played a major part in virtually every popular uprising during this period, and it was clearly deeply ingrained upon the popular consciousness. As late as 1917 Sir George Buchanan, the British Ambassador to Russia, was convinced that it was not the Emperor but the régime of which the nation had grown weary. 'Oh yes, we must have a Republic', a soldier told him, 'but we must have a good Tsar at its head.'[17]

The tendency to conceive of political authority in personalised terms was reflected also in the widely-used term 'Batyushka Tsar' (or 'little father tsar'), emphasising the personal nature of the bond between the tsar and his subjects, and in popular proverb and folklore. Some of the proverbs which were collected by Dal' in the middle of the nineteenth century ran as follows: 'without the Tsar the land cannot be ruled'; 'God in the sky, the Tsar on earth'; 'without the Tsar, the land is a widow'; 'the people are the body, and the Tsar is the head'; and 'no one is against God or against the Tsar'. Popular folk-tales emphasised different but related aspects of his political authority: the tsar, it was said, used to travel around *incognito* among his people, working beside them in farm and workshop and learning of their needs at first hand. Many saw him as the 'godfather of the peasant', christening their children and supporting the poorest among them (it was sometimes said that the tsar was himself of humble origin).[18]

The personified nature of political authority is apparent also in the words used to refer to entities such as 'the state' and 'government'. The Russian word for state, *gosudarstvo*, for instance, is simply a derivation from the word for lord or ruler, *gosudar'*. *Gosudar'* is in turn a word of ancient origin, the original meaning of which was that of a lord or master whose powers extended over both people and things (occasionally it meant 'slaveowner'). From the mid-fourteenth century it came to be used, in much the same sense, to connote political authority.[19] The closest English equivalent of the term *gosudarstvo*, the power exercised by such a ruler, might be 'dominion' or 'patrimony'; either term would better convey, at any rate, the notion that the state was not simply a legal expression, but essentially the private property of its ruler. The word for an administrative sub-unit of the state, *volost'*, similarly derives from the old Slavonic *vlast'*, connoting power or force rather than legally-defined and limited authority.[20] It is this wider conception of the nature of political authority which informs contemporary terms such as 'state power' (*gosudarstvennaya vlast'*) and 'the authorities' (*vlasti*).

Russia's lack of institutions capable of mediating the exercise of governmental authority was in turn related to the régime's *centralised and bureaucratic governing style*. The establishment of a quasi-Cabinet in 1905, in the form of a reconstituted Council of Ministers, appeared to presage a more limited and constitutional role for the monarch. The Council was empowered to oversee major decisions; it met regularly, with a formal agenda and prior circulation of ministerial memoranda; and a 'prime ministerial' figure, rather than the tsar himself, presided. The council, however, like the Duma, had no authority to consider the activities of the ministries of the army, the navy, the court or the department of the State Controller; and individual ministers remained responsible to the tsar rather than to the Council or, individually or collectively, to the Duma. The apparatus of state, moreover, was repeatedly changed, militating against the formation of established procedures or institutional *esprit de corps*; and the tsar's personal chancellery continued to perform governmental functions.[21] Indeed, given the absence of institutional checks upon the exercise of governmental authority, it might often seem that the only effective defence of local autonomy lay in the corruption of the bureaucracy and the absence of reliable communications with the centre. As late as the 1880s, it still took eight days for a letter to travel from St Petersburg to Moscow.[22]

Russians were accordingly inclined to regard government as something alien and external to the collectivity within which they themselves
lived, and they had little knowledge of or attachment to the political
institutions through which it was conducted. The Russian experience
of representative democracy, as we have noted, was a very limited one;
and the government took care to limit the diffusion of even this limited
experience among the population at large by restricting the reporting of
Duma meetings, impeding meetings between deputies and their constituents, and limiting the number and activities of political parties.[23]
Comprehension of party programmes and identities was extremely rudi-
mentary. Villages sometimes made their choice collectively, or demanded instructions from the authorities to this effect. 'Why weren't
we, dark and ignorant people, told for whom to vote?', ran one such
complaint; and even in the towns a reaction of this kind was not unknown.[24] Knowledge of democratic procedures was no more securely
founded; electors to the Third Duma thrust letters, petitions, passports,
insurance policies and even poetry into the ballot boxes, rather than the
voting slips which they were supposed to have brought with them.[25]

Levels of attachment to representative institutions were correspon-
dingly low. Voters often did not trouble to make use of the rights with
which they had been entrusted, and the proceedings of the Duma
appear to have been followed with no great attention (many were
simply unaware of its existence).[26] The dissolution of the First Duma
by the tsar met with little popular opposition; and when a number of
its members withdrew to Vyborg and issued a manifesto calling for the
nation to rally to its defence, the appeal, in the words of one its authors,
'fell flat' – its only consequence was the arrest and exclusion from future
sessions of some of the opposition's most effective debaters. Even by
1918, when Russia's 'constitutional experiment' came to an end, there
was no greater attempt to defend the Constituent Assembly, which the
Bolsheviks dissolved in that year as soon as it had met.[27]

## The scope of government

The major difference between states, Huntington has suggested, lies
rather in their degree than in their type of government.[28] In this respect
there is much which serves to distinguish Russia, both pre- and post-
revolutionary, from its major European partners. This is apparent, first
of all, in Russia's *lack of autonomous sub-group activity*. Trade unions
and strikes, for instance, were illegal until 1905. Strikes, for economic
purposes only, were legalised in December 1905, and the formation of
trade unions and other associations became possible in March 1906.
There were heavy penalties, however, for industrial action in government offices or state-owned enterprises or in the public services, and

regular attempts were made by the police to infiltrate the union leaderships (not to speak of the establishment of bogus 'trade unions' and the
employment of _agents provocateurs_).[29] Employers were subject to a
similar degree of government intervention in and detailed regulation
of their affairs. The factory inspectorate was regularly employed to
compel employers to withdraw concessions to their workforce, or to
dismiss individual employees;[30] and in general their presence made for
a highly controlled and bureaucratic, rather than autonomous and self-
regulating, economic sub-system.

The legislation of 1906 which legalised the existence of trade unions
also provided for the formation of associations of other kinds. Their
establishment, however, required the approval of the appropriate
minister or official, and their operation was subject to a large number
of restrictions. No society or body could be formed whose aims were
considered to represent a threat to public morals or social order, or
which had a political character and were directed by individuals or
bodies outside the country; and the Minister of Internal Affairs could
dissolve an association if he deemed its activities a threat to public
order. No meetings could be held in hotels, restaurants or inns, or in
educational institutions, or near public buildings; and any meetings of
any kind could be prohibited by the head of the local police. The police
attended all meetings, and had the authority to close them at any
point if they departed from their advertised subject or appeared
likely to 'incite hostility between one section of the population and
another'.[31]

It was difficult, moreover, to defend such civil liberties as did
exist through autonomous judicial institutions. The distinction between
_government and the courts_ was not one which was observed in the
political practice of medieval Russia, and as late as the nineteenth
century the courts were termed, with only slight exaggeration, 'exten-
sions of the administration and the police'.[32] The legal reforms of 1864
led to some changes (even the rich and powerful were dissatisfied with
the delays and complexity of the old system): court hearings became
open and public, judges were declared independent of the administration, and a system of advocates was introduced. The aim, in the words
of the statute, was to provide for a 'swift, just, merciful [and] equal'
legal system, to increase the authority of the courts, to give them a
greater degree of independence and 'generally to strengthen popular
respect for the law'.[33] A number of provisions were soon retracted,
however, and in 1881 a system of extraordinary courts was established
whose operation still further reduced the scope of the rule of law.
Originally intended to remain in force for three years but regularly
extended thereafter, the new legislation conferred virtually unlimited
powers upon the governors-general to arrest, fine or exile any citizen,
to ban any meeting, even of a private character, and to close any com-

mercial or educational institution or any newspaper or journal. Trial by jury in political cases had been suspended three years earlier.[34]

Of particular importance in Russian society was the absence of the familiar liberal *distinction between actions* (which must be subject to due process of law) *and beliefs* (which are a matter for the individual alone and can be no legitimate concern of the government). In Russia, on the contrary, it was considered entirely proper that the government should assume responsibility for all aspects of a citizen's welfare, moral as well as material, and that it should establish such rules as it saw fit for this purpose. One aspect of this 'paternal' conception of the nature of state authority was the censorship system. In Russia, under the legislation of 1882, any newspaper which had been three times 'warned' by the censor would thenceforth be obliged to submit the text of each succeeding issue to the censor in advance of publication. A Special Conference, composed of the ministers of education, justice and the interior, and the supreme procurator of the Holy Synod, was empowered to suppress any periodical and forbid its publisher or editor to edit or publish any other paper in future.[35] A number of liberalising changes were introduced in 1905–6; and it was true that censorship was never as severe or efficient as it has become in more recent times, nor did it always achieve its intended purpose – so far from hindering the circulation of advanced theories of politics and religion, it was noted at the time, the censorship was actually 'directly responsible for the circulation among the public of the strangest and most compromising reports as to the dealings and intentions of the court and the high governmental circles'.[36] It was nevertheless clearly the most illiberal system of any major European country at this time.

It was also of importance that the religious faith of the overwhelming majority of the population, Russian Orthodoxy, was never as independent of the state as was generally the case elsewhere in Europe. The Orthodox Church, on the contrary, had been so closely linked to the state since the time of Peter the Great (and even earlier) that it has often been termed a department of government. Church affairs were regulated by the Holy Synod, established in 1721, with a membership selected by the tsar and operating under the general supervision of one of his officers. The Orthodox Church was in turn represented upon the Council of Ministers and upon local councils in the provinces; it received financial support from the government; and it enjoyed a monopoly of religious propaganda, including religious education within the schools and the right to carry out missionary work. It was not actually a crime to leave the Orthodox faith; but the Criminal Code required that anyone who did so be sent to the clergy, who would advise him to return to his former belief, and that in the meantime measures should be taken to prevent him influencing his children. The Criminal Code also provided that those who had induced someone to give up his faith should be sent to Siberia or sentenced to hard labour; and it required that the children of marriages in which one partner was Orthodox should be brought up in that faith. There was clearly no suggestion, in any of this, that the religious faith or beliefs of its citizens was no proper concern of government. Indeed, it is precisely this equation between belief, nationality and citizenship – expressed in the celebrated formula *Samoderzhavie, Pravoslavie, Narodnost'* (Autocracy, Orthodoxy, Nationality) – which was in many ways the most distinctive contribution of the old régime to the political culture of the Soviet régime which succeeded it.

THE MAKING OF NEW SOVIET MAN

The new Soviet régime inherited a large, heterogeneous and backward empire from its tsarist predecessors. It also inherited a distinctive and deeply-rooted pattern of orientations to government. which we shall term the 'traditional Russian' political culture. It may be helpful at this point briefly to recall some of its essential features. Representative institutions, as we have noted, were weakly articulated and ineffective; levels of popular participation and representation were low; and governing style was centralised, bureaucratic and highly authoritarian. Popular political attachments, in consequence, were highly personalised; and political knowledge and experience, outside an extremely limited circle, was virtually non-existent. The scope of government was unusually broad: it extended not only to those spheres of life in which other governments of the time were active, but also into economic entrepreneurship and control, religion and morals, and the administration of justice. It was based, finally, upon a society of a highly 'traditional', *gemeinschaft*, type, in which there was a strong tradition of group solidarity, together with its converse, a suspicion of outsiders; a greater degree of reliance upon face-to-face relations than upon anonymous procedures; and in which it was accepted that every aspect of the life of the community, from taxation and agriculture to beliefs and behaviour, should be subject to the regulation of the community as a whole.[37]

Any account of the modern political culture of the USSR must largely rest upon an assessment of the extent to which distinctively 'Soviet' values and beliefs have absorbed and superseded these pre-existing traditional patterns. It is proposed in what follows to argue, first, that there is a large degree of congruence between this modern political culture and the political values and beliefs of the substantial majority of Soviet citizens: that there is, so to speak, a considerable degree of accord between the political culture of the USSR and its political system. It will be suggested, however, that this state of affairs is not necessarily to be explained by the comprehensive programme of political education which the Soviet authorities have sponsored since 1917. Many of the new régime's policies and institutions coincided closely with the welfare-oriented, collectivist nature of the 'traditional' political culture, and need no such programme to explain their popularity. The success which the régime has had in going beyond these traditional patterns and winning a degree of support for distinctively Soviet values, in fact, appears rather limited. Indeed there is some evidence, not simply that there is a limited degree of attachment to specifically Marxist-Leninist norms, but that the distribution of such attachments is stratified in a manner which has much in common with the distribution of political beliefs and behaviour in the non-Communist, but also industrialised, countries of the west. We shall return to this question in our final section. We must begin, however, with an account of the 'Soviet political culture' which the régime has sought to promote.

*The official political culture*

The most authoritative single statement of the régime's present objectives is the Programme of the CPSU, adopted by the 22nd Party Congress in 1961.[38] The Programme begins by outlining the contradictions of capitalist society, contradictions which cannot be overcome and which necessarily lead to the supersession of that society by a socialist one. Socialism leads in turn to the construction of a communist society, a 'classless social order with a single form of social ownership of the means of production [and] complete social equality of all members of society ... in which there will be realised the great principle – "from each according to his ability, to each according to his needs" '. Under communism, the Programme goes on, there will be no classes; the social and cultural differences between town and country will disappear; the division between mental and physical labour will be overcome; and nationalities will converge ever more closely. There will be complete equality in social life; all will have the same relationship to the means of production and the same conditions of work, and all will actively participate in the administration of public life. Every member of such a society will be characterised by a high communist consciousness, a love of labour and discipline, and dedication to the interests of society.

The qualities of the individual members of such a society are specified in more detail in the section entitled the 'Moral Code of the Builder of Communism'. These include dedication to the communist cause; love for the socialist motherland and other socialist countries; conscientious labour for the good of society; a high consciousness of social duty; collectivism and comradely mutual assistance and respect; moral integrity in public and private life; intolerance of injustice, dishonesty or careerism; friendship and brotherhood with the other peoples of the USSR, and solidarity with the workers and peoples of other countries; and firm opposition to the enemies of communism, peace and freedom. Analogous requirements are made of Party and Komsomol members in the statutes of their respective organisations; and the themes are repeated in a variety of popular and agitational literature.

The inculcation of values such as these has been the object of a lengthy process of *political socialisation*, extending back to the revolution and even (for members of the Bolshevik party at least) beyond it. The educational system has had a major part to play in this connection. Schooling, the new régime decided at an early stage, should aim not simply at the transmission of knowledge and the awarding of qualifications; it should also ensure that students were imbued with a Marxist-Leninist consciousness. Theatre, cinema and literature were similarly enjoined to concentrate their attention upon heroic moments in working-class life.[39] A party education system had already been established; it was developed further in 1924 in connection with the 'Lenin enrolment'. A system of Marxist-Leninist instruction for the population as a whole was established two years later. By 1965/66, when a new system of courses was introduced, more than eleven million students had been enrolled at three different levels. By 1972/73 this total had increased to almost sixteen million. Particularly noteworthy was the qualitative change concealed within these overall totals; for while students at the elementary level had declined in numbers almost by half, enrolment over this period at the intermediate and higher levels had doubled or almost doubled. By 1973/74, taking together the various levels of party, Komsomol, economic and other forms of instruction, it was reported that about sixty million people were engaged in some form of political education.[40]

Political socialisation, of course, is not only (or even mainly) carried on through a system of formal political instruction; and in the Soviet Union every appropriate agency, in home, work and school, is employed. In the Ukraine, for instance, there are about 50,000 'rooms of political education' or 'red corners' attached to institutions of various kinds, as well as 15,000 permanent agitational points (*agitpunkty*) and 750 agitational trains (*agitpoezdy*). An army of over a million and a half lecturers, propagandists and *politinformatory* is available to carry the Party's message to every corner of the land, not simply through lectures to a mass audience (about 50,000 of which are delivered every day), but also, and increasingly, on an individual basis at the place of residence.[41] Anniversaries of important events are utilised as occasions to mobilise large sections of the population (1 May and 7 November are probably the most important examples, but there are many others), and no effort is spared to ensure that the Party's assessment of the anniversary in question is widely diffused. The thirtieth anniversary of the victory over fascist Germany (9 May 1975), for instance, was an occasion not simply for celebrating the defeat of a formidable military opponent and the ending of the most terrible war of modern times: it was also a means of emphasising that the Party and the people were united during the period in question, that Communist Party leadership was crucial to the success of the Soviet forces, and that the only guarantee against the repetition of such catastrophes is the extension of socialism throughout the world. The point was reinforced through commemorative theatre, cinema and television programmes, the issuing of a jubilee medal, the unveiling of memorials, an amnesty, and in countless other ways.[42] Elections, the completion of annual and five-year plans, and the holding of Party congresses are the occasions for mass mobilisation campaigns of a similar character.

Particular importance is attached to the upbringing of youth in the revolutionary tradition. Schoolchildren are enrolled in the Octobrists, then in the Pioneers, and finally in the Komsomol, the 'active assistant and reserve of the CPSU', whose 'central task was and remains the upbringing of youth in the spirit of communist ideological commitment *(ideinost')*'.[43] Young people are engaged through these organisations in forms of political activity and instruction appropriate to their years. Regular meetings are arranged with veterans of the civil and second (Great Fatherland) wars, and with Old Bolsheviks. Schoolchildren are also encouraged to collect information about local historical figures and events. School and institution buildings generally contain a room of 'military' or 'Labour glory', and these are frequently used for meetings and lectures, the issuing of cards to new Komsomol members, and other occasions of note. Ceremonies are arranged when young people from the locality depart to serve in the armed forces; expeditions are organised to nearby places with military or revolutionary associations; and 'military-sporting' camps are arranged in which young people can spend their summer holidays. Figures or events of particular importance are commemorated by obelisks, memorials, plaques or street-names; and the places of birth and residence of major political leaders are often turned into 'house-museums'. Particular importance is attached to the personality of Lenin in this connection; his portrait adorns most public buildings, and his outstanding qualities are ceaselessly extolled.[44]

Finally, and perhaps most obviously, the mass media are not neglected. 'In the major and complicated task of the formation of the new man, in the ideological struggle with the capitalist world', the 24th Party Congress noted, 'the means of mass information and propaganda are a powerful instrument of the party – newspapers, journals, television, radio, the agencies of information'.[45] Their output, accordingly, has steadily increased. The daily print of all newspapers was seven million in 1925; by 1950, however, it had risen to thirty-six million, and by 1973 it had reached one hundred and fifty-seven million copies a day. *Pravda*, the organ of the Central Committee, is printed in an edition of nine million; its total readership is estimated to be as large as thirty million, since each copy will be read by three or four people (it is rumoured that some copies are disposed of in a less savoury manner). In all, more than fourteen thousand different papers and journals are published.[46] Some two hundred and twenty-six of them, with a daily print in excess of sixty-four million copies, are produced especially for young people, more than eight million of whom are estimated to read the Komsomol paper, *Komsomol'skaya Pravda*, every day. Books are not neglected: more than two million copies of the works of Marx and Engels, and over eighteen million copies of the works of Lenin, were printed in 1973.[47] Television is an institution of more recent origin; already, however, it is received by 70 per cent of the population, and it is intended that between 82 and 85 per cent of the population should be included within the national network in the near future. About three hundred radio and television services for young people have also been established.[48]

This, clearly, amounts to a political education programme of unusual scope and intensity; and it would be surprising if it failed to leave some impression upon the consciousness of the Soviet citizenry. Soviet scholars, at least, are in no doubt that it has done so. 'Over the years of Soviet rule', it has been asserted, 'a new, socialist type of personality has been brought up . . . a fighter, a revolutionary, a conscious toiler, characterised by such outstanding traits and qualities as unwavering faith in the communist cause, love of the Motherland and of labour, socialist internationalism, collectivism, a high level of civic and social activism and responsibility.' It is argued, similarly, that Marxist-Leninist ideology has 'conquered the consciousness of the absolute majority of the Soviet people [and] become the inspiration of their socio-political and labour activism'.[49] Western scholars, however, have generally remained sceptical. It is accordingly to this central question – to an assessment, that is to say, of the extent to which régime-sponsored values have gained the acceptance and support of the Soviet citizen – that we must now direct our attention.

VALUES AND POLITICAL BELIEFS

We might ordinarily expect to find at least part of the answer we require in *election results*. The greater the support for the principles for which the régime stands, ordinarily speaking, the greater the success which we should expect officially-sponsored candidates to enjoy at the polls, and the greater the level of turnout generally which might be expected.

Published returns do indeed indicate an increase in support of this kind (Table 2.1).

TABLE 2.1: Electoral participation (percentage poll)

|  | Town Soviets | Country Soviets |  | Town Soviets | Country Soviets |
|---|---|---|---|---|---|
| 1922 | 36.5 | 22.3 | 1928/29 | 70.8 | 68.8 |
| 1923 | 38.5 | 37.2 | 1931 | 79.6 | 70.4 |
| 1924/25 | 40.3 | 41.1 | 1934 | 91.6 | 83.3 |
| 1925/26 | 50.0 | 48.9 | 1939 | 99.31 | |
| 1926/27 | 58.4 | 48.4 | 1975 | 99.98 | |

Source: Belen'kii (n. 65); *Pravda*, 21 June 1975.

Given, however, that there have been no alternative candidates over this period and that negative voting – or even abstention – has been inhibited by a number of formal and informal circumstances, it would be unwise to argue that these results can necessarily be taken to indicate an increase in popular commitment to Marxist-Leninist values. This is not to say that they are of no interest to the social scientist; but it would perhaps be better to regard them as evidence of the régime's increasing ability to mobilise the population and integrate them into the political system – a development of by no means negligible importance – than as evidence of ideological commitment on the part of the citizen body.[50]

Another source of evidence might well be provided by data on the extent of *religious observance*. Formally, of course, the church is separate from the state, and the principle of freedom of conscience is enshrined in the constitution. In fact, however, atheistic propaganda has been an important part of the régime's programme of political socialisation from an early stage, and religion is certainly regarded at present as inimical to the 'scientific world outlook' which it seeks to promote. Here again there is no shortage of evidence indicating a decline in at least overt forms of religious belief.[51] But it would seem premature to conclude that a decline in levels of religious observance should necessarily be taken to indicate a corresponding increase in popular support for régime-sponsored values. It has, first of all, simply become more difficult to practice: the number of churches available for religious use has declined sharply, and opportunities for the production and distribution of religious literature have become considerably more limited. There is no reason to assume, moreover, that a decline in levels of religious observance is only and exclusively the result of internalisation of a 'scientific world outlook'. Other countries, at any rate, even those whose governments give organised religion their official or informal support, have also experienced a fall in levels of religious observance, and it may be that the urban, industrial way of life has more to do with this decline than atheistic propaganda. And finally, there is little evidence to suggest that the mass of non-believers have in fact become conscious and committed materialists, as officially-sponsored values would require. In general it appears that there is simply little interest in or knowledge of such matters, on the part of 'believer' and 'atheist' alike.[52]

We are on somewhat firmer ground in dealing with *surveys of political attitudes and beliefs*, an increasing number of which have been conducted in the Soviet Union itself, and for which corroborating evidence is in many cases available from studies conducted on Soviet citizens now resident elsewhere. Soviet opinion polls, it must immediately be conceded, do not bear directly upon popular attitudes to the government of the day (still less, upon its individual members). We do, however, now possess a substantial body of information relating to attitudes towards socio-political activity (*obshchestvenno-politicheskaya rabota* or *deyatel'nost'*). Given the central place which socio-political activism occupies in the official political culture and given that our concern is with basic political orientations rather than opinions about particular matters of policy, it seems not unreasonable to regard evidence of this kind as a useful indicator of the extent to which régime-sponsored values have found popular acceptance and support.

Such evidence is of broadly two kinds. In the first place, a considerable number of studies have been undertaken of the extent to which people express a willingness to take part in socio-political activity.[53] A recent examination of a series of such studies, covering a total of 10,000 respondents, found that between a third and a half of those polled took a generally favourable view of such activity, with a fairly even representation over different social groups. In comparative terms, these are fairly high proportions.[54] The second body of evidence relates to the expressed motives for participation in socio-political activity. Broadly ideological motives, it appears, are normally cited by a majority of those who are thus engaged, while 'negative' (careerist or egoistic) motives typically account for no more than 3 or 4 per cent of the total.[55] Again, on the face of it (we shall have occasion to examine these sources more critically at a later point), these are results which argue a considerable degree of at least passive support of officially-sponsored values.

We are fortunate in having at least one major study which complements and in part corroborates the account of Soviet political beliefs and values which we have derived from indigenous sources. This is the survey conducted upon the large number of people who either left or were displaced from Soviet Russia during the Second World War, the main product of which was published as *The Soviet Citizen*. Studies of emigrés, of course, are methodologically extremely problematic; but the authors made every effort to correct for conscious and unconscious bias, and their sample was a large and fairly representative one (membership of the Communist Party, for instance, was distributed in approximately the same proportion as among the Soviet population itself). Until such research becomes possible in the USSR itself, therefore, *The Soviet Citizen* must remain the most authoritative single source of information on Soviet political attitudes and beliefs.[56]

Respondents decisively rejected two familiar features of Stalinist Russia, the secret police and the collective farm. They were found, however, to favour many of the institutional features with which the régime was normally associated. Even among those who were substantially alienated from the system, some 86 per cent favoured state ownership of transport and communications; and there was a high level of attachment to 'collectivist' institutions of public welfare, especially in the fields of education and health. The achievements of the régime in eliminating illiteracy and developing education and developing education and health services were widely approved, even by those disposed in the most hostile manner towards the system as a whole. 'The desire to live in a welfare state', the authors concluded, 'is rooted in deep values of the Soviet citizen.' Respondents, moreover, were convinced that the welfare state which they desired could not be achieved under a free enterprise capitalist economy. Some two-thirds favoured state planning and ownership of the economy under 'ideal conditions' (only 14 per cent favoured a capitalist-type system), and there was 'virtual unanimity' with regard to state ownership of heavy industry, transport and communications. On the whole, it appeared, the system 'seemed to enjoy the support of popular consensus'.

There was general agreement also that the state should look after the spiritual, and not simply the material welfare of its citizens. The Soviet citizen's ideal, it appeared, was a 'paternalistic state, with extremely wide powers which it would vigorously exercise to control the nation's destiny, but which yet served the interests of the citizen benignly, which respected his personal dignity and left him with a certain amount of individual freedom of desire and a feeling of freedom from arbitrary interference and punishment'. A government, it was believed, should 'have the same relation to its citizens as a parent to its child – it should support, aid and nurture its people'. If a government were 'good' (friendly, helpful, solicitous), the majority of respondents considered, then political parties and factions had little special place or meaning. Less emphasis was placed upon the rule of law, and upon procedure in general, than upon moral justice and the public welfare. Only one-third of respondents felt that people should be allowed to criticise the government; and fewer than half felt that a government had no right to close an assembly, if it appeared that its purpose were 'to attack the government'. A government might do anything, in fact, and be approved for so doing, if it were believed to be furthering the public good; conversely, a government would not be regarded as legitimate, whatever its constitutional claim to power, if it were taking action which was not considered to be in the public interest.[57]

These findings are largely borne out in research which has been conducted into the political values and beliefs of former Soviet citizens in more recent years,[58] and with the impressions which a number of longer-term Western visitors to the USSR have recently obtained. Russians, one writer has noted, are simply incapable of grasping the Western liberal conception of freedom of speech. The state, they felt, had a right to control the activities of its citizens; and very few, with the exception of political dissidents, were disposed to question its right to censor and, if necessary, to suppress newspapers and journals. 'Ordinary people', in the words of one dissident, 'accept our system of government as the only possible way to live.' At least three-quarters of the country's population, another dissident conceded, given the hypothetical opportunity of doing otherwise, would vote for the existing system. The great mass of Russian people 'simply do not have the same liberal values and interests as the great mass of Western Europeans'.[59]

## Political beliefs and political behaviour

The expressed opinions of the Soviet citizen, then, appear to correspond reasonably closely with the contours of the official political culture. There is a strong degree of attachment to basic institutions of the Soviet system, such as public ownership of the economy, and there appears also to be a considerable measure of agreement upon the place of government in social life and upon the values which should inform its policies and decisions. Soviet data, moreover, suggest that at least one further value derived from the official political culture – socio-political activism – has secured a wide degree of acceptance. Soviet citizens, at least, are favourably disposed towards activities of this kind; and their expressed motives for engaging in it are generally (if not universally) principled and disinterested ones.

It would be unwise, however, to assume that expressed attitudes of this kind will necessarily correspond with actual behaviour. On the contrary, as Kharchev has pointed out, attitudes may well diverge from behaviour, and vice versa. As many approaches as possible, he has suggested, 'objective' as well as 'subjective', should be employed. Zdravomyslov and Borisov, addressing the question of socio-political activism more directly, have also pointed out that the formulation of the questions in many such investigations may leave much to be desired.

Questionnaires, for instance, are sometimes based upon the (plainly arbitrary) assumption that the motives for engaging in socio-political activity can vary only in their degree of disinterestedness; and they note that it may sometimes be difficult, given the nature of the question and the manner of the inquiry, to reply in any other than the 'expected' fashion.[60] It is necessary, therefore, to turn our attention to the extent to which the political values we have identified have found expression in actual political behaviour; a procedure which has the additional recommendation that it is precisely that which has been adopted by the Soviet authorities themselves in recent years.[61]

It is clear, first of all, that *overall levels of socio-political activism* have increased considerably over the period of Soviet rule. The earliest studies which lend themselves to a comparative analysis were conducted by S. G. Strumilin in the early 1920s. Strumilin found that the average worker spent about 2.9 hours a month engaged in socio-political activity, and that only about 3.3 per cent of workers regarded themselves as participating in such activity. By 1967 the average worker was estimated to spend an hour a week on organisational activity alone, and 45.3 per cent regarded themselves as participating in socio-political activity more generally. The average amount of time devoted to socio-political activity is estimated to have increased almost seven times over the period of Soviet rule, while the proportion of working people involved is estimated to have increased eighteen times over the same period.[62]

There have been important changes also in the *structure of socio-political activity*. In the 1920s, according to Strumilin's survey some nine-tenths of the time spent by the average worker on such activity was devoted to relatively 'passive' forms, such as attendance at meetings and demonstrations, and only about seven per cent of the total time was devoted to more 'active' forms of participation, such as work in social organisations. By 1966 these proportions had changed considerably: the amount of time devoted to attendance at meetings and demonstrations had dropped to three-tenths of the total, while more 'active' forms of socio-political activity, such as the carrying out of social commissions (*obshchestvennye porucheniya*), now accounted for seven-tenths of the total.[63] The change in the structure of socio-political activity may be expressed in the manner shown in Table 2.2. Clearly there has been a substantial change, not only in the time expended upon socio-political activity by the average worker, but also in the structure of his participation, from predominantly 'passive' to mainly 'active' forms of such activity.

*Levels of participation in socio-political activity* continue to vary considerably from place to place. At a collective farm in central Russia, for instance, only about one-quarter of the working population were involved; while at a Kishinev tractor factory, on the other hand, almost three-quarters (72.4 per cent) of the workforce were thus engaged.[64] Generally, however, overall levels of participation in socio-political activity tend to vary little from one-half of the group considered. The average level of participation among industrial workers in Kalinin and Kalinin oblast', for instance, was 53 per cent; at a factory in Krasnoyarsk it was 52.5 per cent; at two factories in Novosibirsk it was reported to be 47.8 and 56.0 per cent respectively; and among a stratified sample of some 17,000 workers in the Urals it was 58 per cent.[65] Analogous results were obtained at a factory in Perm' (58 per cent) and among industrial workers in three *oblasti* in the Urals area (45-52 per cent). Again, in comparative terms, these are relatively high figures.[66]

TABLE 2.2: Participation in socio-political activity of workers (percentage thus engaged)

|                                      | *1922–23* | *1966* |
| ------------------------------------ | --------- | ------ |
| Meetings and demonstrations          | 66.1      | 95.0   |
| Lectures, talks                      | 24.3      | 71.6   |
| Political study                      | 12.0      | 48.0   |
| Work in social organizations, etc.   | 3.3       | 51.0   |

Source: Kuznetsov (n. 74) p. 281.

The central values of the régime, then, would appear to enjoy a wide measure of popular acceptance and support. Basic régime institutions, such as a publicly-owned economy and state provision of welfare services, appear to be firmly rooted in popular expectations of government; and the régime appears to have had a considerable degree of success in mobilising support for at least one of the central tenets of the official value system, a high level of socio-political activism. The passage of time, moreover, is likely if anything to reinforce these predispositions. No régime, it has been posited, may be said to be moving away from repudiation unless it has survived long enough to have been the predominant influence upon the political memories of more than half of its present adult population from childhood onwards.[67] The present Soviet régime now abundantly satisfies this criterion: no fewer than 83 per cent of its population, at the beginning of 1973, had been born after the revolution, and more than half had been born after the Second World War. Studies have confirmed, moreover, that younger Soviet citizens are indeed likely to be less religious, and are likely to have specific rather than general complaints against the régime; while the major source of alienation of older Soviet citizens, arbitrary police terror, has now become an historical memory.[68] The régime, we may conclude, is now a substantially legitimate one; there is little evidence of dissonance between its political culture and its political system.

Need we necessarily conclude, however, that 'Soviet citizenship training has succeeded and the basic tenets of the ideology have been internalised'?[69] Our verdict on this point must be a more qualified one. In
the first place, the degree of support manifested for 'collectivist' institutions, such a publicly-owned economy, need not necessarily be explained by the régime's attempt to propagate support for institutions
of this kind. On the contrary, it is precisely the merit of a political
culture approach that it makes possible a broader historical perspective
upon matters such as this. In fact, as we have seen, the origin of many
institutions which are often taken to be characteristic of the Soviet
system – a centrally-directed economy, the absence of autonomous group
activity, a government concerned with the beliefs as well as the actions
of its citizens, the collective regulation of community affairs – lie deep
in Russian history, and their popularity in the present period may be
better explained in terms of the continued influence of the traditional
political culture than by agitation and propaganda. Values which are
unique to the post-revolutionary system and which appear to have
secured a wide degree of acceptance, such as socio-political activism,
clearly cannot be accounted for in this manner; but the evidence on
this point is more problematic than we have so far suggested. It remains to be demonstrated, that is to say, that distinctively *Soviet* political
values have secured that degree of acceptance and internalisation which
the régime has sought to achieve, and which would allow us to argue
that the 'Soviet' political culture has now superseded its traditional
predecessor.

Secondly, it is by no means obvious that such support as the régime
appears at present to enjoy is best explained in terms of its programme
of political socialisation. For too long political scientists have over-
looked an altogether more straightforward basis of régime support, the
performance of a given political system. In the Soviet case there is no
need to seek far to find the source of such 'rational legitimacy'.[70] Impressive progress has clearly been made in many fields; and there can
be little doubt that the Soviet citizen, conscious of the difficulties and
privations of the past, takes a real and understandable pride in such
achievements, as he does in the co-equal part which the Soviet Union
now plays in Great Power diplomacy, in the development of the
country's military might, and in the space programme.[71] It is true that
most Soviet citizens are denied a first-hand knowledge of developments
in other countries, and an informed discussion of political alternatives
is certainly not encouraged. The extent to which 'competing versions of
reality' are denied to the Soviet citizen, however, can easily be exaggerated;[72] and it would seem altogether arbitrary to suppose that the
régime's tenure of power is to a significant extent dependent upon its
control of the process of political communication (Russian dissidents,
at least, appear to harbour no such illusions).[73] We seem justified in

concluding that the régime's achievements provide a further, and perfectly rational, source of its support; and one which relates to perhaps
the most deep-seated attribute of the traditional political culture: a
strong and very Russian nationalism (or 'socialist patriotism', as the
régime presently prefers to describe it).

It remains, however, to consider more closely the impact of distinctively Soviet values upon the traditional political culture; and to this
our third section is devoted.

### THE DOMINANT CULTURE AND POLITICAL SUB-CULTURES

It has been apparent for some time (not least to party officials themselves) that a crudely quantitative approach to ideological work has
outlived its usefulness. Many party organisations, it has been noted,
continued for some time to see their task only as the maximisation of
the number of lectures held, the size of the audiences which they attracted, and so on, and failed to concern themselves with such matters
as the subjects to which the meetings were devoted, their ideological
level, and the extent to which the lecturer's message reached the 'hearts
and minds' of his audience.[74] The 23rd Party Congress accordingly
enjoined party organisations 'seriously to improve their mass-political
work'. In many enterprises and collective farms, it noted, agitational
work was not achieving its objectives and was not being conducted in a
satisfactory manner. At the following Party Congress, the 24th, in
1971, it was acknowledged that much had been accomplished in this
direction over the previous five years. 'It should be said', however,
the Central Committee's report made clear, 'that we are still not satisfied with the state of affairs in this area'.[75] Evidence which has appeared in recent years has established that these criticisms are not
without foundation.

Many of those who attend *political education classes*, in the first
place, evidently attend only because they are obliged to do so. In
Taganrog and Saransk, for instance, 20 per cent of those attending
party education classes and 35 per cent of those attending mass political
education classes made clear that the main reason for their attendance
was 'party discipline', 'administrative pressure' or a 'feeling of duty
or obligation'. At Kamensk, in Rostov *oblast'*, another poll found that
almost 39 per cent of those who attended political education classes
did so 'because they were obliged to do so'.[76] Even party members
(31.2 per cent in one investigation) often offered no more exalted
reason for their attendance; and those with higher education were more
than twice as likely to report that they had attended because they
were obliged to do so than those whose educational level was less

advanced. Lack of enthusiasm, however, is by no means a monopoly of the better educated. Out of a group polled at a Leningrad factory, for instance, no fewer than 75 per cent declared that they attended political education classes because they were obliged to do so by party or administrative discipline (a further 5 per cent attended simply because they 'did not wish to offend the lecturer').[77]

Students who attend classes of this kind, moreover, are by no means always distinguished by their readiness to consult the Marxist-Leninist classics, or even the party literature which is prescribed for them. More than two-thirds of those who attended party education classes in Rostov-on-Don, for instance, admitted that they rarely made use of the classics (a further 15 per cent frankly confessed that they made no use of them at all). Only a quarter of students polled in Khar'khov *oblast'* admitted to reading the primary sources regularly, and 12 per cent did not prepare for classes at all.[78] In Buryatia only about one-fifth of the students at the primary level of the political education system read any Marx, Engels or Lenin, despite the requirements of their programme; and investigations in a number of different urban locations revealed that about one-quarter of those enrolled in political education classes similarly made no effective preparation for their studies. In Uzbekistan as many as 61 per cent made minimal or no preparation at all.[79]

Not perhaps surprisingly, the level at which such political education classes are conducted is not always an exalted one. Students of a course in 'The Fundamentals of Marxism-Leninism', for instance, noted that about half of their time was devoted to the discussion of current political issues, and students of other classes frequently complained about the repetition of already familiar material. Despite an attempt to secure an increase in the amount of discussion at such classes, moreover, lively debate appears to remain the exception rather than the rule. In Krasnoyarsk *krai*, for instance, many students in the party education system made no contribution at all to discussion, or did so only once or twice a year. Only about half the students, in another investigation, took an active part in the proceedings.[80] About half of the students in one Moscow *raion* considered that their lecturer was not in effective command of his material, and almost as many complained that he was not generally able to connect the themes of discussion in class with practical everyday matters. Lecturers for their part (47 per cent in one investigation) were often of the opinion that their students had simply memorised the material which they were required to study, but had not absorbed it.[81]

The practical effect of such programmes of instruction is often distinctly modest. Only 31 per cent of those who attended party education classes in Saransk, for instance, were of the opinion that they were able to make use of their knowledge in everyday life, and in a Kishinev investigation only about half of those who were engaged in political study took part in practical political activity.[82] Workers at an aluminium factory in Novosibirsk, in one of the most detailed investigations of this kind, were asked to state what influence they felt their programme of political instruction had had upon them. Their answers were distributed as follows: 22.5 per cent reported that they listened to political broadcasts on radio and television more often; 21.8 per cent read more fiction; 17 per cent wished to know more and to be useful to society; 11.2 per cent wished to raise their educational and political level; 11.1 per cent took a more critical view of their colleagues' behaviour and of television and films (9.1 per cent); 8.6 per cent took a more active part in socio-political life; 5 per cent felt better equipped to take part in mass-political work; and 4.7 per cent read more socio-political literature. As many as 16.6 per cent replied that their political education had had no influence upon their behaviour of any kind; and 30 per cent refrained from answering the question altogether.[83] These are hardly the kind of results which a party propagandist could find gratifying.

The situation with regard to *other forms of ideological work* gives scarcely any greater grounds for satisfaction. Some lectures are simply too short; in the time available (typically a lunch break) there is simply no opportunity to deal adequately with subjects of any complexity.[84] It is more often objected, however, that lectures are too long and too repetitive. The reaction of audiences to lectures of this kind is manifest in questionnaire responses: lectures, it is overwhelmingly agreed, should not be routine and repetitive, they should preferably be less formal in character (for instance, 'question and answer' sessions or symposia), and the interests of the local audience should be more fully taken into account.[85] Some, indeed, go further and criticise the lecturer's 'lack of competence', lack of appropriate evidence, and failure to relate matters under discussion to events in the world, the country or the local collective.[86] Even in Leningrad, it emerged, some 90 per cent of ideological workers continued to employ the collective reading of newspaper extracts as their main form of political agitation – a method which may have had its uses when the majority of the population was illiterate, it has been pointed out, but which has now outlived its usefulness.[87] Other means of propaganda appear to have scarcely any greater effect. Only one-third of those who read *Izvestiya*, for instance, bothered to read the theoretical articles which it contained; and visual propaganda is rarely more successful. 'Abstract and banal' slogans are still put up, such as 'weeds are the enemy of the fields' and 'harvesting is a serious matter'; they are rarely changed; and they are often placed beside instructions on fire and first aid precautions.[88] An investigation among industrial workers in Minsk found that between 26 and 30 per cent were unable to call to mind any example of agitation of this kind; and another established that only 15–17 per cent of those who walked past a poster gave it any attention.[89]

*The propagandists themselves* have no less serious grounds for complaint. Most of them, to start with, have an excessive number of duties to perform. In Khar'khov, for instance, 32 per cent of propagandists polled had two or three other responsibilities; while in Tomsk some 62 per cent had one or two other duties, with a further 18 per cent having three or more additional duties to discharge. Analogous results have been obtained elsewhere.[90] Many propagandists, accordingly, feel dissatisfied with their work and have difficulty coping with their tasks as they would wish, particularly with regard to study and preparation. Some 40 per cent of propagandists at Rostov-on-Don, for instance, reported that they did not make use of the Marxist-Leninist classics in their work, and almost as many admitted to doing so only rarely. No more than 3 per cent regularly read theoretical and Party-educational journals such as *Problems of Economics, Problems of Philosophy* and *Problems of the History of the CPSU*.[91] Propagandists were generally anxious to specialise in a particular field, or at least to have a minimum of changes in their duties. Only 38 per cent in one investigation, however, knew on what subjects they would be speaking and before which audiences in the two or three months following, and only 18 per cent indicated that they received any assistance from their Party bureau in matters of this kind.[92] It is perhaps less surprising that they fail to cope with their duties as they would wish, but that they manage to do so at all.

We seem justified, then, in concluding that the degree of success which the régime has had in winning support for Marxist-Leninist values is a distinctly modest one. It should be emphasised that this is not a proposition which necessarily conflicts with our earlier conclusion that the régime is a substantially legitimate one. That conclusion was based upon the degree of accord which appears to exist between the political beliefs of the Soviet citizens and central elements in the pre-existing 'traditional' political culture, a coincidence which is the product of historical circumstances rather than of the régime's programme of political education. What we have suggested is simply that the régime does not appear to have a great degree of success in advancing beyond this point and gaining a comparable degree of acceptance and support for new, distinctively 'Soviet', political values and beliefs. 'New Soviet man', in short, does not yet exist; Soviet citizens remain overwhelmingly the product of their distinctive historical experience rather than of Marxist-Leninist ideological training. It would be wrong, however, to suggest that this is a proposition which can be applied without further modification to all the ethnic and other sub-cultures which the Soviet Union comprises. In the section which follows we propose to undertake a 'disaggregation' of this kind with respect to perhaps the most important of these sub-cultures, the non-Russian nationalities; and to examine the rather more general question of patterns of stratification in political values and behaviour based upon social and educational differences.

*Political sub-cultures and political stratification*

It is perhaps unnecessary to emphasise that the population of the USSR is composed of more than a hundred different *nationalities*, and that Russians, while the most numerous, account for no more than 52 per cent of the total.[93] Nationality differences have more than a purely ethnic, and in some cases administrative significance; in many instances the language, culture and stage of socio-economic development of the national group in question differ markedly from the Russian pattern. The historical experience of many national groups, moreover, has been a very different one. Russia proper has been under Soviet rule since 1917, but the Baltic republics for only about half that period; while some areas were under Nazi occupation, and thus effectively beyond the control of the Soviet government, for part of the Second World War. Generalisations about the Soviet population as a whole, therefore, cannot readily be extrapolated from findings which relate only to Russians (themselves, of course, no undifferentiated mass); each proposition advanced required detailed re-examination, and where necessary modification, in respect of the distinctive features of other national groups.[94]

With regard to religion, for instance, it is clear that levels of observance (if not necessarily of belief) are considerably higher among the Moslem population of the USSR than among Russians. Up to 34 per cent of senior school pupils in Uzbekistan and up to 40 per cent in Tadjikistan, for instance, thought it entirely proper to celebrate the Moslem religious feast of Kurban Bairam, and customs such as the payment of bride-money and childhood betrothals continue to be observed.[95] The role of women is also strongly influenced by national environment. Women, for instance, account for one-third of the membership of the Leningrad *oblast'* party organisation, but for only 18.2 per cent of party membership in Turkmenia, the efforts of the local party authorities notwithstanding.[96] The survival of what official ideologists call a 'private property mentality', moreover, seems more firmly rooted in some areas than others (individual farming, it should be borne in mind, was considerably more widespread in parts of the Ukraine and the Caucasus before the revolution than in Russia proper, and there was a greater degree of entrepreneurial development). Whereas the volume of private housing constructed on state credit in the USSR as a whole has declined since 1965, for instance, to take what would appear to be a reasonably 'objective' indicator, in Georgia,

Moldavia and a number of other republics it has registered a significant increase. The figure for Georgia, per head of population, is currently some three times greater than in the Russian Republic; and purges of the political leadership for alleged corruption have also been considerably more frequent in this part of the world.[97]

It was the contention of the most substantial investigation so far conducted into Soviet political values and beliefs, however, that national traditions of this kind notwithstanding, a person's occupation and education remained a much better predictor of his political orientation than his nationality.[98] The pattern of social change since that time may well have increased the force of this observation. The Soviet Union, for instance, has become a more urbanised society (some 60 per cent of the population now live in towns, compared with 33 per cent in 1940 and only 18 per cent in 1913); and it has become more industrialised (industrial production has increased some fourteen times by value since 1940 – in the Russian Republic and the Ukraine by rather less than this overall average, but among many national minorities by rather more: in the Armenian, Moldavian, Kazakh and Baltic republics in particular). Educational levels have also risen, and become more consistent throughout the USSR; and the Russian language, as a first or native language, is also more widely diffused.[99] It is ackowledged that the disappearance of national identities, especially of language, remains a matter of the far-off future; but it certainly appears that the nationalities of the USSR will differ far less in their socio-economic characteristics in the future than they have done in the recent past.

It is unlikely that changes of this kind will be without consequence for the national self-consciousness of ethnic minorities in the USSR. Attitudes towards marriage with a member of another nationality, for instance, are more favourable in towns than in the countryside, and among the educated than among the less educated. The higher a person's level of education and qualification, moreover, the more likely he is to know Russian and to have a wife and/or friends of a nationality other than his own.[100] A detailed investigation of matters of this kind was conducted in the Tatar ASSR. Russians and Tatars, it was found, were distributed in a broadly similar manner in the occupational hierarchy, received broadly similar remuneration, and were active in socio-political life in approximately the same proportions. Nationality as such appeared to have little bearing upon friendship circles, reading of newspapers, watching of television, or attendance at theatres and concerts. There were slight differences between Russians and Tatars in levels of religious observance and in size of family; but these were more or less accounted for by differences in the age structure of the two groups, and education was tending to reduce such differences as remained. The proportion of children receiving their education through Russian, moreover, was steadily increasing (although it continued to be exceeded by the demand for educational provision of this kind); while Russian-speaking Tatars were in turn less likely to prefer the absence of inter-nationality contact in their home or at work, and more likely to have friends of another nationality. In addition, they were likely to be better educated, and this was also likely to predispose towards more cordial inter-nationality relations.[101]

The Tatars, however, are an unusually well-assimilated group, and it would probably be unwise to base any general conclusions upon their experience. Marriages between partners from different classes, for instance, remain twice as common as those between partners from different nationalities; and in general the assimilation of the non-Slav population, particularly in Central Asia, appears to have made extremely limited progress.[102] Conflicts over the allocation of scarce resources between competing national-administrative areas, moreover, may well offset the reduction in national self-consciousness which urbanisation and industrialisation would appear to bring in their train. In sum, then, it seems safest to conclude that nationality is likely to remain an important base for the formation of political sub-cultures, at least for the foreseeable future.

Perhaps a more important lesson to be drawn from this examination of Soviet political values and their distribution is that political life in general, the régime's efforts notwithstanding, remains characterised by stable and reasonably predictable *patterns of political stratification*.[103] A greater degree of education and a non-manual occupation, in the first place, are closely associated with more favourable attitudes towards socio-political activity. Among highly qualified workers in the Urals, for instance, 87.6 per cent had a favourable attitude towards such activity, compared with 28.9 per cent among less qualified and unskilled workers. Those with complete or incomplete higher education, in another investigation, were twice as likely to take an interest in socio-political activity as those with primary education.[104] The relationship was expressed by a Sverdlovsk team of sociologists as follows (Table 2.3):

TABLE 2.3: Attitudes towards socio-political activity and education (percentages)

|  | To 4th class | 5–6 | 7–8 | 9–11 | Inter-mediate spec. | Complete and incomplete H.E. |
|---|---|---|---|---|---|---|
| Favourable | 77.4 | 79.3 | 88.0 | 86.1 | 87.6 | 96.0 |
| Indifferent | 18.7 | 19.2 | 11.8 | 12.8 | 12.4 | 4.0 |
| Hostile | 3.9 | 1.5 | 0.2 | 1.1 | 0 | 0 |

Source: Kogan *et al.* (n. 66) p. 180.

The average educational level of those favourably disposed towards socio-political activity was 8 classes; of those who were indifferent it was 6.5 classes; and of those who were unfavourably disposed it was about 6 classes. The better educated and qualified were also more likely to express a willingness to devote any additional free time at their disposal to such activity, and were more likely to have disinterested motives in doing so.[105]

Education and social position, moreover, appear to be closely related to different levels of political knowledge and political study. Grushin, for instance, found that 38 per cent of workers but about 70 per cent of white-collar staff attended political education classes. Qualified workers were also more likely than unqualified workers to engage in such activity.[106] Almost all white-collar workers, in another investigation, had a library of their own, and subscribed to two or three journals; among unskilled workers, however, only one in three had a library of his own, and even fewer (between a quarter and a fifth) subscribed to two or more journals. Political books, in particular, were 'almost never' encountered among them.[107] Fewer than a quarter of workers polled elsewhere had any works of Lenin in their possession; among white-collar staff, however, the corresponding proportion was one-third, and they were also more likely to read literature of a political character.[108] The better-educated took a greater interest in socio-political matters generally;[109] and they were likely to be better informed about them. A detailed investigation of the knowledge of the economic reforms in Taganrog, for instance, established that 20 per cent of workers were 'completely uninformed' on this subject, but only 3 per cent of white-collar workers; while 24 per cent of the latter, but only 2 per cent of the workers, had a 'very high' level of knowledge. Disparities related to educational differences were equally marked.[110]

Not simply are the better educated and qualified better informed and more favourably disposed towards socio-political activity; they also take a more active part in socio-political life, both in their immediate work environment and in the wider society. Those with higher education, in one investigation, devoted more than twice as much time to socio-political activity as those with complete or incomplete secondary education. Another study found that an average peasant spent about four hours a month engaged in socio-political activity; an average worker spent about six hours; technical and specialist staff, however, spent eight hours a month on such activity.[111] The relationship may be expressed as shown in Table 2.4 overleaf. Almost twice as many workers as technical staff, that is to say, spent less than half an hour a week engaged in socio-political activities; while one-third of the technical staff, but only a quarter of the workers, spent three or four hours a week thus engaged.

The proportion of those taking part in socio-political activity, in fact, tends to vary directly with level of education and social position (the two, as elsewhere, being closely related). Among young *kolkhozniki*, for instance, those with intermediate specialised education were three times as likely as those with education up to 4th class to be politically active. Among young people working in industry the respective proportions were 89 per cent (among those with intermediate specialised or higher education), as against 62 per cent (among those whose education did not exceed 4th class). Only a fifth (20.8 per cent) of those with education to 4th class, in another investigation, but some 83.3 per cent of those with higher education, took part in socio-political activity.[112] The average educational level of those who were involved in socio-political activity was 8.5 classes; of those who were not involved, however, it was less than 7 classes.[113] Skilled workers were similarly more likely than unskilled or semi-skilled workers to engage in such activity. An investigation conducted in the Urals, for instance, found that among those occupied in heavy manual or unskilled tasks 21.4 per cent had a high level of activism, but 60.4 per cent a low level; while among those engaged in highly qualified automated work the proportions were nearly reversed: 28.3 per cent had a low level, but 44.8 per cent a high level of socio-political activity. The proportion of such activity which was 'active' in character, moreover, tends steadily to increase with every increase in the level of education or qualification.[114]

TABLE 2.4: Expenditure of time on socio-political activity and occupation (per week, percentage of given category)

| | Workers | (of these, women) | Technical staff | (of these, women) |
|---|---|---|---|---|
| Up to 30 minutes | 21.1 | 27.6 | 11.6 | 12.1 |
| 1 hour | 25.1 | 23.0 | 26.7 | 31.8 |
| 2 hours | 28.1 | 28.9 | 27.7 | 30.7 |
| 3–4 hours | 25.6 | 20.4 | 33.8 | 25.3 |

Source: Zborovskii and Orlov (n. 63) p. 220.

A broadly similar relationship may be discerned between occupation and socio-political activism. Technical and white-collar staff, in almost every investigation, were found to be involved to a considerably greater extent than workers. One study, for instance, found that unqualified workers were only one-third as active as technical staff; another, that 64.4 per cent of technical and white-collar staff, but only 36.6 per cent of workers, were politically active; another, that levels of socio-political activity among unqualified workers might be as low as 7 per cent.[115] It may be convenient to summarise these findings in tabular form (Table 2.5):

TABLE 2.5: Occupation and socio-political activism (percentage involvement)

| | 1 | 2 | 3 | 4 | 5 | 6 | 7 | 8 | 9 | 10 |
|---|---|---|---|---|---|---|---|---|---|---|
| Workers | 45.8 | 36.2 | 47.1 | 24.7 | 25.5 | 55 | 30.4 | 37.5 | 31 | 20.5 |
| | | | | (*Average* 35.4) | | | | | | |
| Technical staff (ITR) | 66.3 | 64.4 | 79.9 | 65.7 | 57.7 | 70 | 57.3 | 84.1 | 65 | 67.2 |
| | | | | (*Average* 67.8) | | | | | | |

Sources: (1) *Sotsial'nye Problemy Truda i Proizvodstva* (Moscow–Warsaw 1969), p. 297; (2) *Voprosy Obshchestvennoi Aktivnosti Mass*, p. 110; (3) Ermuratsky, *Sotsial'naya Aktivnost'*, p. 94; (4) *Dukhovnoe Razvitie Lichnosti*, p. 181; (5) Pimenova, *Svobodnoe Vremya*, p. 198; (6) *Aktivnost' Lichnosti*, p. 255; (7) *Dukhovnyi Mir*, p. 222; (8) L. D. Terentii, *Vnutriklassovaya Struktura Kolkhoznogo Krest'yanstva i Problemy Trudovoi i Obshchestvenno-politicheskoi Aktivnosti Kolkhoznikov v Period Razvitogo Sotsializma* (avtoreferat kand. diss., Kishinev 1974); (9) *Trud i Lichnost' pri Sotsializme*, p. 37; (10) Chulanov, *Izmeneniya*, p. 66 (averaged).

A distribution of political activism of this kind has a number of consequences. One is simply practical: those who engage in such activity tend to be overburdened with duties, at the expense of family life, study and their main employment, and the general quality of their socio-political work inevitably suffers in consequence.[116] A more important consequence, however, may be ideological. Socialism, Lenin wrote, was possible only when all in turn took part in the running of the state, so it merged into the ordinary business of social life; it was possible, he wrote, only when ten, hundreds more workers than was then the case took part in the administration of state and economic life. Lenin established no precise criteria by which it might be established when such a stage had been reached. He did, however, indicate in notes prepared for a speech on the 'current tasks of Soviet power' that citizens of a socialist society might expect to spend four hours a day engaged in the business of state administration.[117] The available evidence, however, indicates not simply that this objective remains some distance from achievement (the average Soviet citizen, as we have noted, spends about 1.5 hours a week engaged in socio-political activity, rather than the 28 hours which Lenin specified). More seriously, it appears that even these levels of socio-political activism which have presently been reached are far from evenly distributed; in particular, they are far higher among technical and white-collar groups than among the mass of working people whom Lenin had particularly in mind. Soviet society, in fact, emerges as a society which is stratified politically in a manner very similar to that of other developed (but capitalist) societies, in which the middle class, typically, are more active, better informed, and more articulate than workers.[118]

The reconciliation of patterns such as these with the formal myths of what remains, at least officially, a 'workers' state' may be a matter of some delicacy.

### POLITICAL CULTURE AND POLITICAL CHANGE

We have argued above that the dominant political culture of the USSR has largely been shaped by the patterns of orientations to government which were inherited from the pre-revolutionary period; and that the official political culture, which the régime has promoted since 1917, has secured only a limited degree of acceptance. But the traditional political culture, we also argued, was strongly collectivist and welfarist in character, so that substantial prior support existed for many of the institutions and practices associated with the Soviet form of government. To that extent, we may suggest, the régime is a stable and substantially legitimate one; there is, that is to say, a substantial degree of congruence between the political culture and the political system (although important elements of dissonance, such as religion, have clearly continued to exist). Orientations to government in the pre-revolutionary period, however, were based upon a society of a highly traditional, *gemeinschaft*, type, within which there was a considerable degree of community self-regulation founded upon the collective owner-ship and control of the land in whose cultivation the majority of the population were then engaged. In this final section we propose to con-sider the extent to which socio-economic change since 1917 has under-mined these patterns, the extent to which it may be expected to do so in the future, and the consequences of these changes for the political culture.

Of the magnitude of socio-economic change in the post-revolutionary period there can be little doubt. As Table 2.6 makes clear, Soviet society has become a more highly urbanised, and also a more highly educated one:

TABLE 2.6: Some indices of modernisation

|  | *1913* | *c. 1940* | *c. 1956* | *1974* |
|---|---|---|---|---|
| Urban population as percentage of total | 18 | 33 | 45 | 60 |
| Industrial production (1913 = 1) | 1 | 7.7 | 29 | 113 |
| Industrial workers as percentage of population | 14.6 | 33.5 | 49.5 | 60.6 |
| Higher or secondary education per '000 aged ten or over | – | 108 | 361 | 537 |
| Motor cars (000) | – | 5.5 | 97.8 | 916.7 |
| Washing machines (000) | – | – | 182 | 2987 |
| Newspaper circulation (print per issue, millions) | 3.3 | 38.4 | 53.5 | 157.1 |

Sources: *Narodnoe Khozyaistvo SSSR v 1973g.*; *Pechat' SSSR v 1973g.*

Industrial output has increased enormously; and the production of consumer goods has also increased substantially, especially in the more
recent period. The circulation of newspapers and magazines, often
considered a particularly discriminating indicator of 'modernity',[119] has
registered a corresponding series of increases. The USSR, in sum, has
changed from a society predominantly agrarian in character (though
with a small, relatively 'modern' industrial sector) to one that may
reasonably be termed industrial (though with a larger proportion of
its population engaged in agriculture than in the major capitalist
countries).

It would be surprising if changes of this kind were without consequence for the country's political culture. For industrialism, it is widely
agreed, has a very considerable effect upon patterns of social and
political life. Ascriptive, diffuse and particularistic criteria, in Parsonian
language, tend to be replaced by achievement, specific and universalistic
criteria; and tradition and patrimonial forms of authority tend to give
way to impersonality, rationality and bureaucracy. In so far as the
Soviet Union becomes an advanced industrial society, Parsons has
argued, it must conform to these 'evolutionary universals', the operation
of which governs the development of all societies. Already, as we have
seen, there are marked differences in Soviet society in levels of political
knowledge, interest and activity, differences which run counter to the
official ideology but which find their analogy in industrialised societies
elsewhere. These and other similarities must become more notable in
future years, Parsonians would argue, as Soviet society comes to share
the 'bargaining' and 'secular' political culture by which a 'modern'
polity is characterised.[120]

I am not persuaded by the merits of such a thesis. In the first place,
it is simply premature: for more than 100 million Soviet citizens continue to live outside the urban areas (and in some cases outside 'modern'
society altogether), while many present urban residents are themselves
of fairly recent rural origin. Secondly, the theory carries strongly uni-
linear and determinist overtones. No doubt there is a great deal which
industrial societies have in common, and a great deal which serves to
differentiate them, as a group, from societies of a pre-industrial or traditional character. But 'modern' societies also differ from one another in
many important respects, among them their degree of traditionalism
and collectivism, and it is by no means clear that these differences need
necessarily be destined for historical obsolescence. We have properly
been reminded of the 'modernity of tradition'.[121] Many traditional and
customary usages, it appears, need not necessarily obstruct the process
of modernisation; they may be compatible with a developed as well as
a pre-industrial economy.

There would seem no reason to assume, therefore, that the traditional
features of Soviet political culture will shortly be replaced by those

supposedly more appropriate to a 'modern' polity. Many of the collectivist and welfarist institutions of the Soviet system, on the contrary,
seem firmly rooted in popular expectations of government, and are
likely to prove exceedingly resistant to change. They are supported, as
we have also noted, by two further factors: the slow but sustained
improvement in living standards which the régime has managed to
achieve; and the gradual increase within the society of the relative
proportion of those who have known only Soviet (or in many cases only
post-Stalin) rule. This is not of course to suggest that all elements of
dissonance between the political culture and the political system have
ceased to exist: the survival of religion is clearly inconsistent with official
values (although it should not necessarily be equated with opposition to
the régime as such); nationalist sub-cultures remain strong; and in recent
years it has become possible to speak of a dissident sub-culture or
counter-culture, composed of those who reject the values (or more often
the practices) with which the régime is associated.[122] The numerical
significance of anti-régime sentiment, however, should not be exaggerated; and one's overriding impression must be of the very considerable
degree of accord which appears to exist between the political system of
the USSR and its political culture. It would be surprising if future years
brought more than marginal changes in the distinctive blend of tradition
and modernity, 'autocracy' and 'industrialism', by which that political
culture may presently be characterised.

NOTES

The research upon which this chapter is based was greatly facilitated by an
exchange visit to the University of Leningrad in March–April 1975. I am
grateful to the British Council for making the appropriate arrangements, and
to I. N. Olegina and A. A. Fedoseev for their advice and assistance in Leningrad. Neither, however, should necessarily be identified with any of the text
which follows.

1   There are brief accounts of Soviet political culture in two recent texts,
F. Barghoorn's *Politics in the USSR* (2nd ed., Boston, 1972) and
J. Reshetar's *The Soviet Polity* (Toronto, 1971); and also in an older,
more impressionistic study, E. B. Lanin (pseud.), *Russian Characteristics*
(London, 1802). A fuller discussion of the relevant literature is available in A. H. Brown, *Soviet Politics and Political Science* (London, 1974).
The term 'political culture', it may be noted, was employed by Lenin
(*Polnoe Sobranie Sochinenii* (Moscow, 1958–65) vol. 41, p. 404), and it
has more recently been employed by Brezhnev (*Kommunist*, 1974, no. 9,
p. 10). Its use in Soviet social science is also registering a slow but per-
ceptible increase. F. M. Burlatsky, who appears to have been the first
to make academic use of the term in his *Lenin, Gosudarstvo, Revo-
lyutsiya* (Moscow, 1970) p. 327, notes in a more recent work that the
concept is 'winning an increasing degree of recognition' in Soviet

academic usage (*Sotsiologiya, Politika, Mezhdunarodnye Otnosheniya* (Moscow, 1974) p. 40).

2 H. Seton-Watson, *The Russian Empire* (Oxford, 1967) p. 10.

3 The *veche* concluded an agreement or *ryad*, with the prince, designed to limit his prerogatives, and it not infrequently expelled those who violated the terms of this contract.

4 The term *veche* did not itself immediately disappear from popular usage: Tikhomirov records that the term was still employed in Pskov as late as the early seventeenth century (*Goroda*, p. 231).

5 The discussion which follows, for reasons of space, is necessarily confined to the directly political aspects of the culture. It need hardly be said, however, that the distinctive character of the Russian absolutist state had much to do with the *social structure* of that society, in particular the relative weakness of the nobility *vis-à-vis* the monarch ('feudalism' is probably a misnomer here, although the question is a hotly contested one), and the weakness and political passivity of the bourgeoisie.

6 E. P. Eroshkin, *Istoriya Gosudarstvennykh Uchrezhdenii Dorevolyutsionoi Rossii* (2nd ed., Moscow, 1968) pp. 34, 64, and 79; D'yakonov, *Ocherki*, pp. 356–60.

7 Eroshkin, *Istoriya*, pp. 37, 53–4 and 104; Fedosov, *Voprosy Istorii*, 1971, no. 7, p. 54.

8 D'yakonov, *Ocherki*, p. 390; Pipes, *Russia*, p. 108.

9 Eroshkin, *Istoriya*, pp. 266–7; *Istoriya Gosudarstva i Prava SSSR* (Moscow, 1972) vol. 1, p. 587.

10 Ibid., pp. 588–9; Eroshkin, *Istoriya*, p. 267.

11 *Istoriya Gos. i Prava SSSR*, vol. 1, pp. 600–1, and 576–8 (between 1906 and 1917 almost four hundred laws were passed by this procedure).

12 M. Szeftel, 'The representatives and their powers in the Russian legislative chambers (1906–1917)', in *Studies presented to the International Commission for the History of Parliamentary and Representative Institutions*, vol. 27 (Louvain–Paris, 1965) pp. 219–67, makes this case strongly.

13 *Istoriya Gos. i Prava SSSR*, vol. 1, p. 583; S. M. Sidel'nikov, *Obrazovanie i Deyatel'nost' Pervoi Gosudarstvennoi Dumy* (Moscow, 1962) p. 73.

14 Sidel'nikov, *Obrazovanie*, p. 190; Milyukov, *Russia*, p. 5.

15 P. A. Berlin, *Russkaya Burzhuaziya v Staroe i Novoe Vremya* (Moscow, 1922) pp. 243–4 and 269.

16 M. Cherniavsky, *Tsar and People* (New York, 1969) p. 83.

17 P. Longworth, 'The pretender phenomenon in eighteenth-century Russia', *Past and Present* 66 (February 1975) pp. 61 and 70; P. Avrich, *Russian Rebels* (London 1973) pp. 257 and 269–70.

18 V. Dal', *Poslovitsy Russkogo Naroda* (Moscow, 1862) pp. 244–7; V. K. Sokolova, *Russkie Istoricheskie Predaniya* (Moscow, 1970) pp. 55–80.

19 *Etimologicheskii Slovar' Russkogo Yazyka*, ed. N. M. Shanskii (Moscow, 1972) tom 1, vyp. 4, p. 150; M. Fasmer, *Etimologicheskii Slovar' Russkogo Yazyka* (Moscow 1964) vol. 1, p. 448; D'yakonov, *Ocherki*, pp. 322–3.

20    As late as 1905 it was still possible for the term to be employed deliberately in this sense, (Cherniavsky, *Tsar and People*, p. 90); M. Fasmer, *Slovar'*, vol. 1, p. 344.

21    Eroshkin, *Istoriya*, pp. 278–9 and 206–9.

22    Ibid., pp. 230–1.

23    A. Levin, *The Second Duma* (2nd ed., Hamden, Conn., 1966) pp. 63 and 234.

24    O. Radkey, *The Elections to the Russian Constituent Assembly of 1917* (Cambridge, Mass., 1950) pp. 57–63; and A. Levin, *The Third Duma* (Hamden, Conn., 1973) p. 89.

25    Ibid., p. 90.

26    Chermensky, *Voprosy Istorii*, 1947, no. 4, p. 35.

27    Milyukov, *Russia*, p. 4; Radkey, *Elections*, p. 2.

28    S. Huntington, *Political Order in Changing Societies* (New Haven, 1968) p. 1.

29    J. Walkin, *American Slavonic and East European Review*, April 1954, pp. 174 and 183; Sidel'nikov, *Obrazovanie*, p. 62; *Istoriya Gos. i Prava SSSR*, vol. 1, p. 607.

30    Berlin, *Russkaya Burzhuaziya*, p. 205.

31    *Istoriya Gos. i Prava SSSR*, vol. 1, pp. 609–11; *Istoriya Sovyetskogo Gosudarstva i Prava* (Moscow, 1969) vol. 1, p. 53.

32    Eroshkin, *Istoriya*, p. 186.

33    Ibid., p. 241.

34    *Istoriya Gos. i Prava SSSR*, vol. 1, p. 514; Eroshkin, *Istoriya*, p. 212.

35    Seton-Watson, *Russian Empire*, p. 480.

36    M. Kovalevsky, *Russian Political Institutions* (Chicago, 1902) p. 257.

37    D. M. Wallace, *Russia* (London, 1912) pp. 120ff.; G. T. Robinson, *Rural Russia under the Old Régime* (London, 1932) pp. 117–28.

38    *Programma Kommunisticheskoi Partii Sovetskogo Soyuza* (Moscow, 1971 ed.) *passim*.

39    *KPSS v Rezolyutsiakh i Resheniakh S"ezdov, Konferentsii i Plenumov Ts. K.* (7th ed., Moscow, 1960) vol. 1, p. 733; G. I. Klyushin and S. N. Mostovoi, *KPSS – Vospitatel' Novogo Cheloveka* (Moscow, 1970) p. 25.

40    *Spravochnik Propagandista* (Moscow, 1973) p. 76; *Pravda*, 17 September 1974.

41    Yu. M. Khrustalev, *Lektsionnaya Rabota – Vazhnaya Forma Kommunisticheskogo Vospitaniya* (Moscow, 1973) p. 7; E. Shagalov, *Vospitatel'naya Rabota po Mestu Zhitel'stva* (Moscow, 1974) *passim*; Unger, *Totalitarian Party*, pp. 122ff.

42    'The oustanding achievement of the Soviet people in the years of the Great Fatherland war', as Brezhnev told a commemorative meeting in the Kremlin, 'is inseparable from the many-sided, purposive activity of the party of Communists . . . The war showed once again that the party and the people are united, that there is no force which can break their unshakeable unity' (*Pravda*, 9 May 1975).

43    *Materialy XXIV S"ezda KPSS* (Moscow, 1971) p. 79.

44    *Problemy Kommunisticheskogo Vospitaniya Trudyashchikhsya* (Kuibyshev, 1972) p. 96; O. E. Kutafin, *Postoyannye Kommissii Mestnykh Sovetov po Delam Molodezhi* (Moscow, 1974) pp. 4 and 14; *Internat-*

*sional'no patrioticheskoe Vospitanie i Formirovanie Lichnosti Sotsialisticheskogo Obshchestva* (Volgograd, 1973) pp. 264 and 320; *Formirovanie Novogo Cheloveka* (Moscow, 1974) p. 71; *Sotsial'nye Problemy Obrazovaniya i Vospitaniya* (Moscow, 1973) p. 167.

45 *Materialy XXIV S"ezda KPSS*, p. 89.

46 Klyushin and Mostovoi, *KPSS*, p. 41; *Pechat' SSSR v 1973 godu* (Moscow, 1974) p. 68; *Voprosy Teorii i Praktiki Partiinoi Propagandy* (Moscow, 1971) p. 298.

47 *Partiya i Gosudarstvo v Period Stroitel'stva Kommunizma* (Moscow, 1973) p. 403; *Pechat' SSSR*, p. 16.

48 *Materialy XXIV S"ezda KPSS*, p. 179.

49 K. F. Zugaparov, in *Partiya i Gosudarstvo*, p. 372.

50 See especially M. Weiner, 'Political participation: crisis of the political process', in L. Binder *et al.*, *Crises and Sequences in Political Development* (Princeton, 1971).

51 Two good general accounts are B. Bociurkiw and J. W. Strong, eds, *Religion and Atheism in the Soviet Union and Eastern Europe* (London, 1975) and M. Bordeaux, 'Religion', in Archie Brown and Michael Kaser (eds), *The Soviet Union since the Fall of Krushchev* (London, 1975).

52 *Lenin i Molodezh'* (Moscow, 1974) vyp. 2, p. 125; *Dukhovnoe Razvitie Lichnosti* (Sverdlovsk, 1967) p. 312.

53 V. N. Ermuratsky, *Sotsial'naya Aktivnost' Rabotnikov Promyshlennogo Predpriyatiya* (Kishinev, 1973), p. 105; *Molodezh' Sela Segodnya* (Moscow 1972) p. 117.

54 M. Matthews, *Class and Society in Soviet Russia* (London, 1972) pp. 232–3 and 240.

55 *Materialy Mezhvuzovskoi Konferentsii*, pp. 244–5; *Obshchestvennaya Aktivnost' Molodezhi* (Moscow, 1970) pp. 44–6; *Molodezh' Sela Segodnya*, pp. 111 and 121.

56 A. Inkeles and R. Bauer, *The Soviet Citizen* (Cambridge, Mass., 1959).

57 Ibid., pp. 233ff.

58 J. A. Ross, 'The composition and structure of the alienation of Jewish emigrants from the Soviet Union', *Studies in Comparative Communism* 7 (spring-summer, 1974) pp. 113 and 117.

59 S. Jacoby, *The Friendship Barrier* (London, 1972) pp. 42–3, 82, 196–7 and 212; 'An Observer', *Message from Moscow* (London, 1969) pp. 214 and 210.

60 A. G. Kharchev in *Voprosy Filosofii*, 1965, no. 1, pp. 49–50; *Nauchnye Osnovy Partiinoi Raboty* (Leningrad, 1972) pp. 55 and 84.

61 'Even the most advanced ideology', Brezhnev reminded the Twenty-Fourth Party Congress, 'became a real force only when, having been absorbed by the masses, it motivates them to action, defines the norms of their everyday behaviour' (*Otchetnyi Doklad k XXIV S"ezdu K.P.S.S.* (Moscow, 1971) p. 147).

62 S. G. Strumilin, *Byudzhet Vremeni Russkogo Rabochego i Krest'yanina* (Moscow-Leningrad, 1924) pp. 24–6.

63 Strumilin, *Byudzhet Vremeni*, p. 24; G. E. Zborovskii and G. P. Orlov, *Dosug: Deistvitel'nost' i Illyusii* (Sverdlovsk, 1970) p. 220.

64 *Gor'kaya Balka* p. 117; *Kommunist Moldavii*, no. 7, p. 35.

65    M. Sh. Tselishcheva, *Politicheskoo Vospitanie Trudyashchikhsya v period Stroitel'stva Kommunizma* (avtoreferat kand. diss., Leningrad, 1972) p. 17; V. Kh. Belen'kii, *Aktivnost' Narodnykh Mass* (Krasnoyarsk 1973) p. 202.

66    *Trud i Lichnost' pri Sotsializme* (Perm', 1972) p. 34; L. N. Kogan *et al.*, *Dukhovnyi Mir Sovetskogo Rabochego* (Moscow, 1972) p. 174.

67    R. Rose, *Governing without Consensus* (London, 1971) p. 35. Two interesting recent discussions of the theme of generational change in Soviet politics are P. Frank, 'The changing composition of the Communist Party', in Brown and Kaser, *Soviet Union*, pp. 96–120; and W. D. Connor, 'Generations and Politics in the USSR', *Problems of Communism* 24 (September–October 1975) pp. 20–31.

68    *Lenin i Molodezh'*, vyp. 10, p. 1; Inkeles and Bauer, *The Soviet Citizen*, pp. 254, 372.

69    Alfred Meyer, in D. Treadgold (ed.), *The Development of the USSR* (London, 1964) p. 24.

70    To borrow the title of Robert Rogowski's recent book (Princeton, 1974).

71    B. A. Grushin and V. Chikin, *Vo Imya Schast'ya Cheloveka* (Moscow, 1960) p. 66, found that only 98 of a total of 1399 whose opinions were polled thought that their standard of living had declined in previous years; see also the opinion of recent emigrés quoted in n. 58 above.

72    Jamming of Western-language broadcasts was ended some years ago, and British and American foreign services can now regularly be received (together with Finnish television, in some parts of the Baltic). All jamming of Western broadcasts in Russian – apart from those of Radio Liberty – was stopped in September 1973 (I am indebted for this and other information to Mr George Schöpflin). Postal, academic and touristic exchanges have also increased in volume. About one million Soviet tourists went abroad in 1965, but more than 2.2 million in 1974, 40 per cent of them to the non-socialist world (*Literaturnaya Gazeta* no. 26 (25 June, 1975) p. 14). Similarly about 1600 foreign academics visited the USSR in 1959 at the invitation of the Academy of Sciences, but more than 9000 in 1966; while more than 3500 Soviet scholars went abroad in the latter year, more than half of them to non-socialist countries (G. D. Komkov *et al.*, *Akademiya Nauk SSSR* (Moscow, 1968) pp. 210–14). One can only speculate upon the likely political impact of the 1980 Olympic Games, which are to be held in Moscow.

73    See, for instance, V. Chalidze, *To Defend These Rights* (London, 1975) p. 170; and N. Mandel'shtam, *Hope Abandoned* (London, 1973) pp. 94, 401 and *passim*.

74    E. M. Kuznetsov, *Politicheskaya Agitatsiya, Nauchnye Osnovy i Praktika* (Moscow, 1974) p. 9.

75    *XXIII S"ezd KPSS: stenograficheskii otchet* (Moscow, 1966) vol. 2, p. 316; *XXIV S"ezd KPSS: stenograficheskii otchet* (Moscow, 1971) vol. 1, p. 115.

76    N. S. Afonin, *Sotsial'no-politicheskie Aspekty Povysheniya Effektivnosti Partiinoi Propagandy* (avtoreferat kand. diss., Moscow, 1973) p. 19; *Usloviya Povysheniya Sotsial'noi Aktivnosti Rabochego Klassa v period Stroitel'stva Kommunizma* (Rostov on Don, 1974) p. 88.

77  I. S. Soltan, *Politicheskaya Ucheba i Razvitie Obshchestvenoi-politicheskoi Aktivnosti Rabotnikov Promyshlennogo Predpriyatiya* (avtoreferat kand. diss., Kishinev, 1973) pp. 18–19; Afonin, *Aspekty*, p. 20.

78  *Usloviya Povysheniya*, p. 101; *Voprosy Obshchestvennoi Aktivnosti Mass* (Khar'khov, 1968) p. 90.

79  G. I. Balkhanov, *Ustnaya Propaganda i ee Effektivnost'* (Ulan-Ude 1974) p. 66.

80  Ibid., p. 166; *Usloviya Povysheniya*, p. 101; *Problemy Kommunisticheskogo Vospitaniya*, p. 52.

81  *Deistvennost' Politicheskoi Ucheby* (Moscow, 1973) p. 41; *Sotsiologicheskie Issledovaniya v Ideologicheskoi Rabote* 1 (Moscow, 1974) p. 142.

82  N. S. Afonin, *Lektor i Auditoriya* (Saransk, 1973) p. 73; Soltan, *Politicheskaya Ucheba*, p. 15.

83  *Kollektiv i Lichnost'* (Irkutsk, 1973) pp. 133–4.

84  Ermuratsky, *Sotsial'naya Aktivnost'*, p. 152.

85  Balkhanov, *Ustnaya Propaganda*, p. 93; Afonin, *Lektor i Auditoriya*, p. 48; *Voprosy Teorii i Metodov Ideologischeskoi Raboty* 3 (Moscow, 1974) p. 189; P. V. Pozdnyakov (ed.), *Politicheskaya Informatsiya* (Moscow, 1974) pp. 87ff.

86  Ibid.

87  Kuznetsov, *Politicheskaya Agitatsiya*, p. 275.

88  *Voprosy Teorii i Praktiki Massovykh Sredstv Propagandy* 3 (Moscow, 1970) p. 38; I. P. Rudoi and A. M. Shumakov, *Naglyadnaya Agitatsiya – Sredstvo Vospitaniya* (Moscow, 1974) pp. 9–10.

89  *XXIV S"ezd KPSS i Problemy Povysheniya Proizvodstvennoi i Obshchestvennoi-politicheskoi Aktivnosti Trudovykh Kollektivov* (Minsk, 1972) p. 69; A. M. Shumakov, *Naglyadnana Agitatsiya* (2nd ed., Moscow, 1973) p.191.

90  *Voprosy Obshchestvennoi Aktivnosti Mass*, p. 90; *Sotsiologicheskie Issled. v Ideol. Rabote*, pp. 87–8.

91  *Voprosy Nauchnogo Kommunizma* 6 (Moscow, 1972) p. 232.

92  Balkhanov, *Ustnaya Propaganda*, p. 92; *Sots. Issled, v Ideol. Rab.*, p. 84. See also *Sotsiologicheskie Issledovaniya*, 1975, no. 2, p. 119.

93  *Itogy Vsesoyuznoi Perepisi Naseleniya 1970 goda* (Moscow, 1973) tom 4 *passim*.

94  No detailed examination of the nationalities question can possibly be attempted here. Two recent accounts may be referred to: Z. Katz (ed.), *Handbook of Major Soviet Nationalities* (New York, 1975); and J. A. Newth, 'Demographic Developments', in Brown and Kaser, *Soviet Union*, pp. 77–95.

95  *Lenin i Molodezh'* vyp. 10, p. 95; *Literaturnaya Gazeta*, no. 22 (28 May 1975) p. 13.

96  *Leningradskaya Organizatsiya KPSS v Tsifrakh* (Leningrad, 1974) p. 111; *Turkmenyskaya Iskra*, 21 February 1971, quoted in H. W. Morton and R. Tőkés (eds), *Soviet Politics and Society in the 1970s* (London, 1974) p. 125.

97  *Narodnoe Khozyaistvo SSSR v 1973 godu* (Moscow, 1974) pp. 613 and 9.

64     *Political Culture and Change in Communist States*

98   Inkeles and Bauer, *The Soviet Citizen*, pp. 351 and 372.
99   *Narodnoe Khozyaistvo SSSR v 1973 godu*, pp. 7 and 213; *Sovetskaya Etnografiya*, 1971, no. 4, pp. 20 and 28.
100  V. N. Pimenova, *Svobodnoe Vremya v Sotsialisticheskom Obshchestve* (Moscow, 1974) p. 298; Yu. V. Arutyunyan *et al.*, *Sotsial'noe i Natsional'noe* (Moscow, 1973) p. 280; *Sovetskaya Etnografiya*, 1974, no. 4, pp. 7–12; A. I. Kholmogorov, *Internatsional'nye Cherty Sovetskikh Natsii* (Moscow, 1970) *passim*.
101  *Sotsial'noe i Natsional'noe*, pp. 26–8, 52–3, 266–8, 280–9 and *passim*.
102  J. A. Newth, in Brown and Kaser, *Soviet Union*, pp. 86–7.
103  The concept of 'political stratification' is discussed in J. A. Brand *et al.*, *Political Stratification and Democracy* (London, 1972).
104  *Aktivnost' Lichnosti v Sotsialisticheskom Obshchestve*, p. 246; *Obshchestvennaya Aktivnost' Molodezhi* (Moscow, 1970) p. 54.
105  *Dukhovnyi Mir Sovetskogo Rabochego*, p. 181; *Problemy Sotsial'nykh Issledovanii* 1 (Tomsk, 1970) p. 136.
106  B. A. Grushin, *Svobodnoe Vremya* (Moscow, 1967) p. 78; Ermuratsky, *Sotsial'naya Aktivnost'*, p. 110; Belen'kii, *Aktivnost'*, p. 218.
107  N. M. Sapozhnikov, *Struktura Politicheskogo Soznaniya* (Minsk, 1969) p. 24.
108  *Voprosy Teorii i Metodov Partiinoi Propagandy* (Moscow, 1971) p. 333; B. A. Grushin, *Svobodnoe Vremya: Velichina, Struktura, Perspektivy* (Moscow, 1966) p. 24; Yu. V. Arutyunyan, *Sotsial'naya Struktura Sel'skogo Naseleniya SSSR* (Moscow, 1971) p. 179.
109  *Obshchestvenno-politicheskaya Zhizn' Sovetskoi Sibirskoi Derevni* (Novosibirsk, 1974) p. 153.
110  B. A. Grushin (ed.) *Gorodskoe Naselenie i Ekonomicheskaya Reforma* (mimeo., Moscow, 1973) pp. 67–8.
111  *Voprosy Effektivnosti Partiinoi Propagandy i Politicheskoi Informatsii* 1 (Moscow, 1973) p. 46; *Dukhovnoe Razvitie Lichnosti*, p. 174.
112  *Obshchestvennaya Aktivnost' Molodezhi*, pp. 88–9; Ermuratsky, *Sotsial'naya Aktivnost'*, p. 95.
113  *Dukhovnyi Mir*, pp. 117–8.
114  *Aktivnost' Lichnosti*, p. 249; Yu. G. Chulanov, *Izmeneniya v Sostave i v Urovne Tvorcheskoi Aktivnosti Rabochego Klassa SSSR 1959–1970gg.* (Leningrad, 1974) pp. 66–9.
115  *Chelovek i Obshchestvo* 3 (Leningrad, 1968) p. 40; *Voprosy Obshchestvennoi Aktivnosti Mass*, p. 110; Chulanov, *Izmemeniya*, p. 68.
116  One unfortunate activist, with ten commissions already to perform, found himself subject to party discipline when he objected to receiving an eleventh duty of this kind (*Pravda*, 11 May 1975).
117  Lenin, *Pol. Sob. Soch.*, vol. 37, pp. 425–6, and *Leninskii Sbornik* (Moscow, 1975) vol. 38, p. 338.
118  Evidence on this point is summarised in J. LaPalombara, *Politics within Nations* (Englewood Cliffs, N.J., 1974) pp. 457ff.; S. Verba and N. H. Nie, *Participation in America. Political Democracy and Social Equality* (New York, 1972); Dowse and Hughes, *Political Sociology*, ch. 9; and in M. Rush and P. Althoff, *An Introduction to Political Sociology* (London, 1971) ch. 3.

119  This point is strongly made by A. Inkeles and D. H. Smith, *Becoming Modern* (London, 1974) p. 144ff.

120  T. Parsons, 'Evolutionary universals in society', *American Sociological Review* 29 (June 1964) pp. 338–57, and *Societies* (Englewood Cliffs, N.J., 1966).

121  To borrow the title of L. I. and S. H. Rudolph's book (Chicago, 1967).

122  There is a good general discussion in R. L. Tőkés (ed.), *Dissent in the USSR* (Baltimore and London, 1975). On the notion of a 'counterculture' more specifically, see H. L. Biddulph, 'Soviet intellectual dissent as a political counter-culture', *Western Political Quarterly* 25 (September 1972) pp. 522–33.

# 3 Yugoslavia: Unity out of Diversity?

## DAVID A. DYKER

INTRODUCTION

The outstanding feature of the Yugoslav polity is *heterogeneity*. Whether at the level of governmental, social and business organisations, or in terms of the procedures established for negotiation between various forms of power centre, the sheer complexity of the Yugoslav system is such that the most experienced students of South Slav affairs are reluctant to claim complete comprehension, even at a given point in time. In our attempt to study Yugoslav political culture we come up against a similar heterogeneity, in terms of historical experience, historical rationalisation, levels of economic development, etc. The relationship between heterogeneity of different types and at different levels is a key issue around which much of the following discussion revolves. To provide a foundation for that discussion, let us look at the salient points of history, geography and economics characterising the Yugoslav areas.

Prior to the establishment of an autonomous Serbian state in the early nineteenth century, there had been no separate South Slav state since the Middle Ages, apart from the tiny mountain stronghold of Montenegro, which always resisted complete subjugation by the Turks, and the republic of Dubrovnik, which retained a precarious existence up to 1814. Prior to the formation of the Kingdom of Serbs, Croats and Slovenes in 1918 there had never been a unified South Slav state. From the fourteenth to the nineteenth century we find different parts of the Yugoslav area subject, at different times, to Austria, Hungary, Venice, Turkey and France. Much of the cultural heterogeneity of the area can be attributed to this pattern of history. The traditional Catholicism of the Slovenes and the Croats which remains, even among non-believers, an important badge of identity, reflects centuries of contact with Germans, Magyars and Italians, and has provided a powerful channel for orientation to the West in cultural matters. The existence

I wish to thank Richard Kindersley of St. Antony's College, Oxford, for help given in the preparation of this chapter.

of a large minority of Slavonic speech and Muslim religion in Bosnia and Hercegovina relates to specific characteristics of Turkish policy in this area, as well as to certain peculiar aspects of medieval Bosnian history.[1] On the other hand, foreign conquest or dominance destroyed or weakened indigenous aristocracies, so that the emergent South Slav nations of the nineteenth century did tend to exhibit a marked homogeneity in social terms, i.e. they were predominantly peasant. This was emphatically the case in the Serbian and Macedonian lands. In Bosnia and Hercegovina foreign conquest created a new Muslim aristocracy, or rather transformed the old Bogumil aristocracy. In Croatia the indigenous aristocracy survived in principle, but tended to be progressively diluted with foreign elements.

Perhaps the best way to sum up the picture that has emerged from these centuries is to tabulate the principal nations of Yugoslavia, with their linguistic, demographic and religious characteristics:

TABLE 3.1

| Nationality | Language | Traditional religion | Numbers ('000) in 1971 | Percentage of total |
|---|---|---|---|---|
| Slovene | Slovene | Roman Catholic | 1,700 | 8.3 |
| Croat | Serbo-Croat | Roman Catholic | 4,520 | 22.0 |
| Serb | Serbo-Croat | Serbian Orthodox | 8,140 | 39.7 |
| Ethnic Muslim | Serbo-Croat | Muslim | 1,730 | 8.4 |
| Montenegrin | Serbo-Croat | Serbian Orthodox | 508 | 2.5 |
| Macedonian | Macedonian | Serbian Orthodox* | 1,195 | 5.8 |
| Albanian | Albanian | Muslim | 1,310 | 6.4 |
| Hungarian | Hungarian | Roman Catholic, Protestant | 480 | 2.3 |

\* The Church in Macedonia attained autocephalous status in 1967.

It is, of course, an oversimplification to list Croats, Serbs, Ethnic Muslims and Montenegrins as linguistically identical. There are many variants of Serbo-Croat, and, though these do not always correspond to national groups, there has been sufficient correspondence to serve as a basis for nation-variant identification. The concern of the Croats to emphasise the distinctness of their language is well known, but it is worth noting that similar tendencies have emerged among Ethnic Muslims and Montenegrins.[2] Linguistic individuality, then, is an important symbol of identity among the Serbo-Croat-speaking nations. On the other hand, there is no question of variation in Serbo-Croat creating any barriers to the dissemination of information. The situation is rather different with the other groups, including the other Slavonic groups. In the survey on attitudes to the VIII Congress of the League of Communists, the figure obtained for Slovenia for percentage of total sample having followed the work of the Congress is below average, and this is attributed to the language barrier.[3] We have here, by the way, an example of interaction of political base and superstructure. The fairly loose federal structure adopted by the Yugoslavs, partly as a way of containing national aspirations, has maintained barriers to communication through hindering encroachment by Serbo-Croat.

A glance at the population figures in Table 3.1 will indicate another key feature of Yugoslavia. No single nationality has anything like an absolute majority of total population. The biggest group, the Serbs, cannot quite muster two-fifths. In this respect, then, Yugoslavia is much more similar to the countries of the Third World than to the nation-states of Europe.

We move now to another aspect of heterogeneity in the Yugoslav socio-political backdrop – extremely uneven levels of economic and social development. The basic facts speak for themselves (see Table 3.2).

TABLE 3.2  (All figures for 1971)

|  | Net material product per head in dinars at 1966 prices | Percentage illiterate over 10 years old | Number of hospital beds per '000 |
|---|---|---|---|
| Yugoslavia | 6,078 | 15.2 | 6.3 |
| Bosnia and Hercegovina | 3,856 | 22.5 | 3.8 |
| Croatia | 7,553 | 8.9 | 6.6 |
| Macedonia | 4,222 | 18.0 | 5.3 |
| Montenegro | 4,053 | 17.2 | 6.2 |
| Serbia proper | 5,979 | 17.7 | 5.4 |
| Slovenia | 11,395 | 2.6 | 8.5 |
| Vojvodina | 7,380 | 9.4 | 5.6 |
| Kosovo | 1,972 | 32.2 | 2.6 |

We are dealing with a country in which the most advanced areas have attained a level of development approaching Western European levels, while the most backward remain on a level which could be characterised as Middle Eastern, for all the advances made, e.g., in the development of medical services. Clearly if we expect cultural patterns to vary significantly with levels of socio-economic development we must be prepared for such variations to occur in Yugoslavia. The danger here is to seek to identify too closely the rich/poor division with nationality distinctions. We shall not go too far wrong in this with Slovenes, Macedonians, Montenegrins and Albanians. But with the two numerically most important nationalities we must be extremely careful. Although the average Croat has a higher standard of living than the average Serb, local variations are so great as to make meaningful generalisation difficult. The Serbs of Vojvodina are obviously among the 'haves', as are those living in the Belgrade conurbation. On the other hand, parts of southern Serbia proper are as underdeveloped as Kosovo, as indeed are a number of communes in the Dalmatian hinterland of Croatia. In addition, Serbs and Croats taken together form a majority of the population of Bosnia and Hercegovina.

EARLY POLITICAL EXPERIENCE

Occupation by imperial powers did not prevent peasant communities from going about their own affairs. In areas of Turkish rule, villages, particularly highland, often enjoyed virtual self-government. But statehood as such is a fairly recent phenomenon in the Yugoslav lands. Can we, then, speak of significant early political experience going beyond the parochial level? More specifically, can we speak of the development of any indigenous tradition of state administration, and of recognisable attitudes to this?

The South Serbian lands, Macedonia and Kosovo were emancipated from Turkish rule and serfdom only in 1913. 'Locals' were taken into the Imperial Ottoman service only to the extent of children being taken from their parents at a very early age, and comprehensively 'Turkified',[4] so that the answer here is a clear no. Bosnia was part of the Turkish Empire to 1878, when it was placed under Austro-Hungarian administration, being finally annexed to the Habsburg crown in 1908. There is no evidence, however, that the Christian population of Bosnia was introduced to any great extent into administrative positions before 1918. Indeed the conservative policy of the Habsburgs permitted the Ethnic Muslims, the traditional ruling class in the province, to retain their dominant position, not only in landholding, but also in state administration.[5] Thus there was some experience, however superficial, of modern administration by the Ethnic Muslims in this period. The very fact that Croatia always maintained some semblance of separate status within the Habsburg state limited Croat involvement in the bureaucracies of Vienna and Budapest, though the military traditions of the Croats, combined with the peculiar institution of the military frontier in the Croatian lands,[6] gave the nation a specific and unique role within the empire. To the extent that old-established rights of internal self-government were respected,[7] it was, up to the mid-nineteenth century, the nobles, frequently ethnically non-Croatian, who benefited. In the last half-century or so of the Habsburg state an emergent middle class, Croatian in language as well as sentiment, tended increasingly to dominate the public life of the kingdom. But frequently during this period, and increasingly towards 1914, Croatia was ruled directly by bureaucrats and soldiers imposed from outside.[8]

This leaves us with Serbia, the most important case. Although Serbia did not become a sovereign state until 1878, she succeeded in establishing autonomy from Constantinople as early as 1815. At an early stage state bureaucracy emerged as a major force in the new state. Svetozar Marković, the first outstanding Yugoslav socialist, was prepared, as early as the late 1860s, to characterise the bureaucracy as a fully-fledged separate social class.[9] P. A. Rovinsky, a Russian traveller in Serbia in the 1860s, remarks that the Serbian bureaucrat 'regards the people as something absolutely foreign to him, something to which he owes nothing, something with which he has nothing in common . . .'[10]

One interesting aspect of the development of bureaucracy in Serbia is that many of the individuals who joined the government service in the early days were in fact Serbs from the Habsburg lands – Vojvodina, especially Novi Sad, and even Vienna. Northward migration in the path of the advancing Turks had created many new Serbian communities, particularly in traditionally Hungarian and Croatian areas. These *prečani* appear again and again in key roles in the historical development of the Yugoslav lands, and it is worth emphasising their distinctive identity, *vis-à-vis* not only Croats and Hungarians, but also home Serbs.

Before jumping to conclusions about the emergence of a Petrine state in nineteenth-century Serbia, it is important to emphasise that the attitude of the peasants, the vast bulk of the population, was uniformly hostile to this 'new class'. Rovinsky noted that '. . . the people for their part regard the bureaucrat in a still worse light: they see in him their enemy, detest him, and do not allow him into their society';[11] and Tomasevich writes that 'there was little cause for the peasants to look at the newly emerging state of the 19th century either with confidence or benevolence'.[12] But it would be wrong to think in terms of a neatly divided Serbian society. Tomasevich continues: '. . . the peasant wanted nothing more than, himself, to become a servant of the state and thus a participant in the spoils of power.'[13] There is a paradox here, but it is a paradox which we can only explain after examining the myths and self-images which have prevailed in the South Slav lands.

VALUES AND FUNDAMENTAL POLITICAL BELIEFS

*The traditional ideal social and personal type.* First of all, we must describe a traditional institution common throughout the South Slav lands which has played a tremendously important role in the ideology of the Yugoslav nations, the *zadruga*. The traditional *zadruga* was a particular form of extended family agricultural unit, 'a household composed of two or more biological or small families closely related by blood or adoption, owning its means of production communally, producing and consuming its means of livelihood jointly, and regulating the control of its property, labour and livelihood communally'.[14] Argument has raged as to whether the *zadruga* was a form of backward but essentially transitional subsistence agricultural organisation, or a means of minimising the tax burden, or indeed the quintessence of the democratic spirit of the South Slavs. Certainly the more overtly political interpretation of the *zadruga* has played a tremendously important part in the Yugoslav peoples' view of their past. It is, in fact, no exaggeration to say that the *zadruga* has been a central theme, and a unifying factor, in the most diverse interpretations of South Slav development.

The idea of the *Dinaric patriarchal culture* was formulated by the Serbian geographer-sociologist Jovan Cvijić.[15] The Turkish conquests, Cvijić argued, had resulted in a reversion from feudal to tribal forms of organisation, and indeed to a 'heroic' culture. However primitive and patriarchal in character, the culture was given a 'progressive' complexion through emphasis on the *zadruga* as its basic organisational form. Cvijić insisted that the *zadruga* had been most prevalent in the Dinaric region. 'The Dinaric patriarchal culture and the Dinaric man were idealised to a large extent by Cvijić and his followers. To the Dinaric man were ascribed the attributes of a high sense of honour, mutual support for his fellow man, heroism, upholding of tradition, intensive national pride, and constructiveness in a political sense. Undoubtedly, the culture of the Dinaric man evolved through a process of continuous struggle against and adaptation to both hostile political conditions – that is, foreign rule – and scanty natural resources. It, therefore, commanded the admiration of many people. On the basis of such characterisation of the Dinaric man – and implicitly or explicitly that meant primarily the Serbs and Montenegrins and only parts of other South Slav nations – it was easy to claim for him the leading role in Balkan political life and to idealise his whole history. . . . Such thinking was almost tailored for the purposes of Serbian statesmen, educators, soldiers and administrators. In the Yugoslav state established in 1918 this reasoning was often used to defend and explain the hegemony of the Serbs and the crudely centralistic organisation of the new state.'[16]

It should be emphasised that Cvijić was nothing if not a scholar, and was in no way responsible for this vulgarisation of his ideas. But his attitude to the Croats of the Zagorje was rather negative, so it is hardly surprising that a Croatian writer should have come up with a completely different interpretation of the traditional cultures of the South Slavs. According to Dinko Tomašić, the Dinaric culture is essentially a power-seeking culture, and the Dinaric *zadruga* an authoritarian organisation. He contrasted this with the *zadruga* culture of the Croatian Zagorje, based on a settled rather than nomadic agriculture, with the *zadruga* as a key institution going beyond the limits of kinship bonds, organised on a collectivist-democratic basis, giving equal rights to women, etc.[17] So overtly political was the theorising of Tomašić that he ascribed authoritarian and extremist tendencies within the Croat nation, particularly the fascist *Ustaše*, to the prevalence of the Dinaric culture among certain sections of that nation.

The relationship between the Dinaric myth and the pan-Serbian form of the Yugoslav idea is obvious. But what about the *zadruga* myth and forms of the Yugoslav idea originating in Croatia? It was with the birth of the *Illyrian Movement* that the Croatian intelligentsia first became involved in the problem of Yugoslav identity. Following on the short life of the Illyrian province of the Napoleonic French Empire

> ... the reincorporation of the ex-French districts ... brought into Croatia a whole army of young men who, under the French *régime* and in the schools instituted by it, had imbibed a romantic nationalism of the most heady sort. . . . The new nationalism swept over Croatia like a heath fire in time of drought, setting students and young 'intellectuals' aflame, throwing out fiery streams of grammarians, lexicographers, poets and political journalists, and penetrating even the aristocracy.[18]

Even nationalist Croatian historiography recognises the strength of the Yugoslav ideal in the development of Croatian culture in the nineteenth century, while being careful to distinguish it from the Serbian-centralist conception of the ideal.[19] We can, then, postulate some relationship between the federalist ideas of Illyrian Yugoslavism and the collectivist-democratic conception of the *zadruga*. Now an interesting point emerges from all this. On the one hand South Slav myths tend to be universal, in the sense that they are about all the South Slavs. Different myths have, however, been associated with different South Slav groups. In other words, *there has been a tendency for myths to serve as a means of identifying, rationalising and legitimising the position of sections of the South Slav community vis-à-vis the community as a whole.*

*Other relevant aspects of traditional culture.* Ideal types, however, are not the only aspects of pre-modern ideas and attitudes with which we must concern ourselves. What kind of attitudes were bred and nurtured in a situation where political authority had been represented from time immemorial by a power totally alien, though not particularly oppressive, simply because not very interested in anything beyond the mundane matters of collecting taxes, etc., i.e. the situation prevalent in the southern parts of the Yugoslav area up to 1913, and over a much wider area up to the nineteenth century? We are fortunate in having at our disposal a study of the effectiveness of local democracy in Macedonia, whose author makes some very interesting remarks on the historical conditioning of attitudes in Macedonia:

> The Macedonian area is, from a research point of view, extremely

interesting, . . . a region which clearly traces its origin from traditional political characteristics. These peculiarities lie above all in the existence of a relatively distinct type of political culture formed on the basis of the age-old existence of a demotic and national organism without its own state-legal and political-institutional system, experience, or traditions. As far as the political culture of the masses is concerned, there was a long-established tradition of destructive reaction, scepticism, isolation, and perhaps to some extent adaptability towards state and political institutions which appeared to them as an alien government in the national as well as the class sense.[20]

*A propos* of adaptability, it was common among Albanians living in the Yugoslav lands on a *zadruga* basis to have part of the family cleave to the Christian faith, and part to the Muslim, with the head of the *zadruga* being chosen from one of the two halves depending on whether the régime of the time were Christian or Muslim.[21] In Bosnia and Hercegovina

> conversions to Islam were not always total . . ., so that by the middle of the sixteenth century there were a large number of 'Poturs' in Bosnia, that is, half-Turks, who would have their children both circumcised and baptized. . . . The apostolic delegate, Masarechi, in the year 1624, affirmed that the Bosnian Franciscan Fathers baptized the children of Muslims, and in 1625 the Franciscans went so far as to ask the Holy See for permission to continue this practice, and it was granted them.[22]

We must, then, be prepared for a degree, not only of negative reaction, but also of profound ambivalence towards state authority, particularly in the southern areas, but to some extent throughout the area of Turkish influence.[23] The Croats also, 'dominated by foreign powers for too many centuries . . . have developed a rather negative attitude toward any political authority'.[24] Putting the point more strongly, they have 'developed the habit of opposition for opposition's sake further than any [other nation] in Europe'.[25] Here, however, we are dealing with more straightforward 'agin the government' attitudes, rather than ambivalence and adaptability.

Having come down to brass tacks on the matter of traditional political culture, we can return to the paradox alluded to in the earlier discussion of the peasant and bureaucracy in Serbia. We can accept that in any impoverished society the more ambitious amongst the impoverished will take any opportunities for advancement that arise. As Tomasevich has said, in connection with the inter-war period:

> As the productive forces of the country were insufficiently developed, the state was not only the chief employer of all salaried people, but also the most important and quickest source of enrichment. . . .

Large-scale corruption was considered a natural concomitant of power. The service of the state, business with the state, and abuse of state power were the primary sources of wealth.[25]
But what relationship did this reality bear to the myth of Dinaric man, which we can take as the predominant myth in nineteenth-century Serbia and inter-war Yugoslavia? One inter-war author had a quite unequivocal and vivid answer:

> ... we will continue to sing about the 'violent type' and about the 'manliness and heroism' of our people because we have been taught so by our folk poetry. Meanwhile the 'violent type' ... will to-morrow, after having gone through a few grades of high school and acquired some position, be prepared to skin his brother ... he will understand nothing and will not want to understand anything of the dismal conditions of his native community. On the contrary, ... he will jump on the back of his hungry people and soil even the bloody spot which he hit with his forehead when his mother gave him birth in a field furrow.[27]

The stage may appear set for a grand generalisation involving Serbs, Croats, Dinaric men, *zadruga* men, bureaucrats, anti-bureaucrats, etc., with obvious implications for our interpretation of post-1945 Yugoslav man. We shall, however, do well to avoid the temptation to identify too many things with too many other things. What we have established is that:

1 Yugoslavia is the scene of enormous diversity in ethnic and linguistic terms, and also in terms of levels of economic and social development.
2 Involvement, positive or negative, in modern state administration has been uneven, but cannot be discounted.
3 There are at least two historical myths/rationalisations applied to the whole South Slav area, but associated with particular groups within that area, which we shall ignore at our peril.
4 We cannot discount the contemporary importance of traditions of alienation from, coupled with ambivalence towards, state authority.

POLITICAL EXPERIENCE IN THE MODERN PERIOD TO C.1953

The immediate *casus* of the First World War was an assassination committed by a Bosnian Serb, bringing to a head the Habsburg-Serbian tension that had been at an acute level since the annexation of Bosnia. Serbia was an Ally throughout the war, albeit most of the time an occupied one, while many Croats and Slovenes remained loyal to the Habsburgs until very late indeed.[28] It is hardly surprising, then, that the Kingdom of the Serbs, Croats and Slovenes that emerged in 1919 was dominated, and righteously dominated, by the Serbs. The Slovenes stayed quietly within the ample defences of their obscure language, but the Croats quickly became alienated from a régime that was crudely centralistic. The period of quasi-parliamentary rule was characterised by instability and violence – Stjepan Radić, the Croat Peasant Party leader, was murdered in the *Skupština* in 1927. The royal dictatorship established in 1929 was distinguished by the introduction of the name *Yugoslavia*, but by little else. A kind of rapprochement was engineered between Serbs and Croats in 1939, with the formation of an autonomous Croatian *banovina* (province), but Royal Yugoslavia was in any case destroyed by German invasion in 1941.

Almost immediately, old tensions began to take on a quite new form. In Croatia a puppet Fascist state was set up under the control of the *Ustaše*, who proceeded with policies tantamount to genocide against the Serb populations of Croatia and the areas of Bosnia and Hercegovina assigned to them. In Serbia the Germans set up a protectorate. Almost immediately a Serbian-Montenegrin resistance force using the name *Četnici* (singular *Četnik*) emerged under the leadership of Draža Mihailović The Mihailović *Četnici* rapidly received recognition from the Yugoslav government-in-exile. In the western mountainous regions *Četnik* bands owing little more than nominal allegiance to Mihailović soon found themselves engaged against the *Ustaše*. The defence of Serbian populations was undoubtedly the initial *casus* here, but the *Četnici* did go on the offensive and operate against civilian populations in much the same way as the *Ustaše*. In Bosnia and Hercegovina the *Četnici* behaved particularly brutally towards the Ethnic Muslims, who had allied themselves with the Croats.

The success of the other resistance movement, the Partisans, run by the Yugoslav Communist Party, which had been small and outlawed before the war, can be attributed to a number of reasons:

1 The organisational experience of men used to working underground and to the principles of Democratic Centralism.

2 The Pan-Yugoslav basis of the movement, which increasingly appealed to people horrified by the mutual genocide which seemed to be the only concrete achievement of the alternatives.

3 The aggressive stance taken *vis-à-vis* the German occupation. This contrasted with *Četnik* policy, which was to wait for the overall military position of the Germans to weaken.

4 The ability and personality of the Partisan leadership, particularly of the Secretary-General of the Communist Party, Josip Broz Tito.

Although Partisan operations against the occupying forces were successful in terms of tying down troops, rather than in inflicting heavy losses, the movement rapidly gained wide support, with 300,000 members by 1943.[29] After early attempts at co-operation the *Četnici* and Partisans ended up in open conflict. It must be emphasised, indeed, that what happened in Yugoslavia in 1941–5 was as much of the nature of civil war as of national liberation. The *Četnici* collaborated with the Axis against the Partisans. The Partisans at one point held discussions with the Germans on the possibility of a cease-fire, though nothing came of it.[30] In general, however, the Partisans maintained their anti-Axis momentum, while the *Četnici* did not. The Western Allies recognised the Partisans in 1943, the Soviet Union in 1944. The liberation of Yugoslavia was largely related to the turn of fortunes in the World War, specifically to the liberation of Belgrade by the Red Army in 1944. But Soviet troops did not stay on Yugoslav territory, so that in 1945 it was the Partisans who held the laurels of victory, and complete control over the Yugoslav lands. The Communists, then, emerged from World War II with an image that can be summed up in terms of Yugoslav internationalism, heroism and personality. It must, however, be stressed that the Partisans were dominated numerically by Serbs (though Tito is a Croat). In Bosnia, the heartland of the resistance, the overwhelming majority of Partisans were Serbs.[31] There were also many Serbs from Croatia in the movement. In Serbia proper, however, the *Četnici* retained a predominant position until very late indeed.[32] The *prečani* theme is thus again evident.

Knights in shining armour, then, the Partisans may have been in 1945, but they had plenty of ghosts to lay, and a few skeletons in the cupboard. Once it became clear that Partisan authority was to mean Communist Party control and government, it was necessary to draw up a 'canon' of 'official' nations, in the way the Soviet leadership had done in the 1920s. Serbs, Croats, Slovenes, Montenegrins, Hungarians, Macedonians (for the first time), and Albanians (under the pseudonym of *Šiptari*) were all given official recognition. An uneasy note was, however, struck by the relegation of the Ethnic Muslims to the limbo of 'undetermined Muslims', with the implication that the sooner they declare themselves Serbs or Croats the better.[33] In general terms the ethos of the new leadership was essentially anti-nationalist, not surprisingly, given their wartime policy and image, but also because the initial phase of Yugoslav Communism-in-power was heavily orientated towards a monolithic interpretation of the post-revolutionary situation.

The absence of a single history or tradition among the Yugoslav people, the strength of pre-war separatist tendencies, and the break-up of old Yugoslavia, sharpened to an exceptional degree the call for 'brotherhood and unity' within the framework of the new political system. The emphasis on unity was so marked that the expression of any kind of 'narrow' interests was immediately condemned as inadmissible, harmful, or even as enemy action. The danger of being dubbed a 'nationalist', 'local-patriot', or the like influenced people's conduct, so that they preferred to remain passive, giving hardly any expression to their particular concerns.[34]

But the most striking aspect of post-war Yugoslav government policy was the decision to go for a fully-fledged Stalinist-type centralised dictatorship. Post-war attitudes on nationalities was fully in accord with wartime policies. In the field of general social, political and economic policy there was a definite break with the wartime policy of soft pedalling all ideologically sensitive issues. Certainly the Yugoslav Communists did hold back on collectivisation of agriculture, as a concession to the biggest group amongst the population, which had given them such staunch support during the war. But in industrial and political fields the hard-boiled dictatorship was just that.[35] When the break with Stalin came in 1948 the crucial issue was not so much ideology as the independent stance taken by Yugoslav Communists on foreign policy matters[36] – a stance hardly to be wondered at in the case of a victorious régime with an indigenous power base. The Yugoslavs did, indeed, initially react to the Cominform excommunication, which was accompanied by accusations of ideological deviance, with a desperate attempt to be even more orthodox. A new and much more vigorous collectivisation campaign was launched in early 1949. It was not really until late 1949 that a serious trend towards rethinking the whole theoretical underpinning of Marxism and socialism started to emerge.

## *The reappraisal*

Workers' councils were initially set up by a law of 2 July 1950. By 1953 the new Yugoslav model was complete in its essentials, displaying the following outstanding features:

1 The market was re-established as the nexus of economic activity.
2 Sovereignty within the enterprise was to rest with a workers' council elected on the basis of manhood suffrage.
3 Mass collectivisation was abandoned, and the private farm reaffirmed as the predominant form in agriculture. Various forms of collectivism and co-operation continued to be encouraged.
4 The central government retained certain crucial elements of control over the economy, notably in the fields of investment and foreign trade.
5 A genuinely federal system was introduced, with republican and local governments having considerable power in all fields, including the economic.
6 Self-management (*samoupravljanje*) was to become the guiding principle of Yugoslav society, to be extended, in appropriate forms, throughout all spheres of social and economic activity.

POLITICAL CULTURE AND OFFICIAL POLITICAL CULTURE – A
PRELIMINARY EXAMINATION

Thus we come to the first major question that must be asked in connection with the political culture of modern Yugoslavia. How much
can we tie in the emergence of decentralised, self-managing market
socialism with the values and fundamental political beliefs and early
political experience discussed above? The actual conception of market
socialism was very much the brainchild of a handful of Party intellectuals.[37] A few short years witnessed the rejection of an old and the
emergence of a completely new approach:

> ... It was necessary for the Yugoslav leaders – given their Stalinist
> past and ideological commitment – to explain, not only to the Party
> they controlled and the non-Stalinist leftists they attempted to
> cultivate but also to *themselves*, where Stalin had gone wrong.[38]

To do this they had also to show how they were going to go right.

None of this, however, obviates the need to consider the extent to
which the reappraisal was in tune with the traditions and aspirations
of the Yugoslav population. After all, the system did survive and
prosper, and it could have collapsed – there were enough external
pressures. The important points that do emerge in this connection are:

1 The decision to reverse policy on collectivisation was obviously in
  tune with the aspirations of the great mass of the peasantry.
2 The movement away from bureaucratic methods in economic
  administration (*a*) may have been 'efficient' in that the bulk of the
  population had little experience, active or passive, of bureaucratic
  methods:[39] (*b*) may have corresponded to the preferences of the
  mass of the people.
3 The creation of a genuinely federal system was a first move
  away from the negative attitude to the nationalities of the war
  and immediately post-war years. At a more general level, it can
  be seen as a move away from the 'conflictless' model towards a
  model of 'institutionalised conflict'.[40] The reinstitution of the
  market in the economy has identical implications.

POLITICAL EXPERIENCE SINCE C.1953

Since the reappraisal the Yugoslav self-managing system has developed
and matured. Any discussion of political development in the fifties,
sixties and seventies must be set against the background of high, and
fairly sustained, rates of growth of national income, the transition from
a predominantly rural to a predominantly urban society, and the intro-

duction of a mass-consumption culture. To the movement of 'objective' variables has been juxtaposed movement in Government and Party policy (in 1953 the Communist Party became the League of Communists). It must be emphasised that, whatever the state of popularity of the authorities, and whatever pains they may have taken to consult the preferences of the people, the great changes of 1961–74 have, like the reappraisal itself, originated largely from the top.

The economic reforms of 1961 and 1965 moved in the direction of more autonomy for the enterprise, hence, *ceteris paribus*, more power to the workers' councils. The most important single aspect was divestment by government of much of its formal control over investment funds in favour of the banks. This has not precluded the continued existence of a degree of informal influence at Federal, republican and commune level, but it has represented a fundamental change. The constitution of 1963 re-emphasised the federal principle, extended the principle of self-management, and brought the structure of Federal and republican parliaments more into the line with general socio-economic structure.

One major problem which the economic reforms of the sixties raised was this: now that the banking system had been put on to a self-managing basis, how could social control over 'finance capital' be ensured? The fear of small coteries of bankers, effectively controlling the destinies of enterprises employing thousands of workers through loans, did seem to be becoming justified in the late sixties. The whole issue was tied in with the nationalities issue, but the authorities tackled the economic side of it through a number of constitutional amendments, now enshrined in the new constitution of 1974. In particular they tried to ensure that general credit policies of banks were decided by committees of bank users, rather than by professional bankers, and to establish the constitutional right of a working organisation to a share in the disposition of any funds accruing through its work.

Another problem which the authorities have grappled with in the constitutional amendments is that of making the self-management system more effective in the economy. By shifting legal 'sovereignty' from the enterprise to the 'basic unit of associated labour' (OOUR), constitutional reforms have tried to make self-management more meaningful in an environment of large industrial combines.

But constitutional developments in the early seventies were related also to a rising tide of centrifugal pressures. The most important of this was the trouble in Croatia, which started in 1967, and which will be discussed in detail later. In any case, a constitutional amendment of 1971 virtually converted Yugoslavia into a confederation. In addition, the autonomous regions of Kosovo and Vojvodina were granted what amounts to republican status. Now the amendment was followed in 1972 by a purge of alleged nationalists in Croatia. This in turn was followed by a purge of alleged liberals in Serbia. Purges occurred in other re-publics too, notably in Bosnia and Hercegovina, and there can be no doubt that the last few years have seen a tightening up of Party con-trol, as a counterweight to the dispersive characteristics of the amend-ments of 1971. Nevertheless these amendments stand out from all other major policy changes of the last twenty years in that they came essentially as a response to pressure from below. The same can be said, to some exent, about the moves to control finance capital, especially since this issue did tend to get mixed up with the nationalities issue.

### POLITICAL KNOWLEDGE AND EXPECTATIONS

A multiplicity of traditional cultures and a well-established penchant for periodic fundamental reform on the part of the authorities are, then, basic characteristics of the Yugoslav situation. To what extent have the authorities been prepared, or able, to use control over schools, press, TV, etc., to encourage homogenisation, and to 'take the people with them'? The following discussion looks at the general picture over the last couple of decades. In the last two or three years there have been some developments which may or may not have long-term signifi-cance, to which we shall return later.

On my first visit to Yugoslavia, in 1966, I shared a room with a young Norwegian socialist with sympathies towards market socialism, but few towards bourgeois liberalism. I recall that he pinpointed as a major weakness in the Yugoslav system neglect of youth organisations on the part of the League of Communists. Certainly youth and student organ-isations have been allotted few of the crucial roles which have fallen to the *Komsomol* in the Soviet Union. A major survey of student opinion done in 1960 came up with one interesting statistic which highlights this point: as many as 11.3 per cent of those among the sample who were members of the League of Communists itself were not prepared to call themselves Marxists.[41]

The evidence is particularly striking when we look at the general role of formal education as a force for homogenisation and socialisation. The 1960 survey found university and middle-school teachers very far down the list of opinion-forming factors.[42] Recent reports have varied in approach and point of view, but have arrived at the same conclusion. One writer argued, in 1970, that the trouble is that Yugoslav education still pushes the ideas of state socialism, the image of the 'conflictless society'.[43] A few months later the secretary of the Party Presidium commission for education spoke of the neglect of ideological education in schools, and argued that Party calls for a renewal of ideological teaching in educational institutions are based on changes in the world which call for a fresh evaluation of the achievements of the revolution and the self-management system, since world movements, contradictions and tendencies in our society can no longer be explained by the old ideological methods. . . . What we need is not a scholastic system that will indoctrinate people and feed them with illusions of happiness and goodness, but a system that will help them understand the laws, contradictions and paradoxes of contemporary social development.[44]

The report of the commission, which appeared in December 1970, had a dual emphasis. On the one hand, it criticised the education system for being outdated, not in a state socialist, but in a bourgeois sense, providing a purely passive interpretation of politics, economics and technical progress, of cramming children with facts, rather than preparing them to solve social problems. On the other hand, it talked of neo-Stalinist ideas being put across in the teaching of sociology, and of children being taught that there are just two enemies, capitalism and religion. It also complained of nationalist elements creeping into the educational system.[45]

A survey published in 1972 sheds interesting light on the question of the relative strength of Stalinist and bourgeois tendencies. The sample was taken from Belgrade secondary schools, and it was found that 67 per cent of the respondents did not know where and when the Communist Party of Yugoslavia was founded, and 70 per cent did not know who were the founders of Marxism.[46] (Would 'Marx' not have been a pretty good guess?) But the question is, for our purposes, secondary. What is important is that all the evidence suggests that neither secondary schools, higher educational institutions, nor youth organisations have played much of a role in socialising young people to the self-management system. Furthermore, to take up one of the points made in the Party commission report, 'alien' elements, in particular nationalistic elements, have found it easy to infiltrate. A quite extraordinary example of such infiltration is the primary school manual *Acquaint Yourself with your Country*, published in 1970 by the republican textbook publishing house of Serbia. The map on the title page shows, not Yugoslavia, but Serbia, and it is not the Serbia of contemporary Yugoslavia. Within its boundaries we find Montenegro, half of Macedonia, and parts of Bosnia and Hercegovina. In other words, this is the Serbia of Tsar Dušan, and of the Greater Serbian nationalists of the nineteenth and early twentieth centuries.[47] Now this is an extreme example, taken from an atypical period, when there was something of a nationalist hysteria, at least among certain groups of intellectuals. Nevertheless, it must lead us to draw certain conclusions about the Yugoslav educational system. Whether we use the word 'open' or the word 'vulnerable' makes little difference for our purposes.

What about the press and other media? There is very much more freedom of publication in Yugoslavia than in the Soviet Union. Newspapers are permitted to have their own editorial line, within broad limits. The Zagreb weekly *Privredni Vjesnik* was able in the late sixties and early seventies to take up a strongly anti-Belgrade stance, and to state, in November 1970, that in the event of the economic stabilisation programme failing, the government should fall – this in what is, after all, a one-party state![48] On the other hand, the editor of the paper was demoted and the editorial board reshuffled in January 1972, as part of the clampdown on alleged Croatian nationalism.[49] Publication of books has been fairly free, as we have seen in the case of the Serbian textbook. To the extent that there is censorship, it tends to be *ex-post* rather than *ex-ante*. The recent award-winning Yugoslav film *Mysteries of the Organism* has provoked something of a witch-hunt in the film industry. While the novel *When the Pumpkins Blossomed* does not seem to have run into any real trouble, sufficient pressure was applied to have the dramatised version taken off the stage.[50]

These judgements should not lead us to think that the Yugoslav authorities have no influence over people's minds. We are fortunate in having available a number of public opinion surveys on the crucial reforms of 1963–5, which give us a unique opportunity to study reactions to major policy departures. Let us look firstly at the one on the 1965 economic reform.[51] Of the sample, 75 per cent considered themselves well informed about the reform. There was a fairly general degree of optimism about the chances of its effective implementation, though with important regional variations. Perhaps more significant, 56 per cent thought that the responsibility for implementation of the reform should lie primarily with 'all working people'. Only 7 per cent thought that members of the League of Communists should bear primary responsibility, and only 6 per cent thought it should be borne by the Party leadership. There was also a widespread feeling that implementation by the working people should proceed on a participatory basis. As many as 67 per cent of the sample thought that implementation should be discussed at mass meetings of voters.

On the major political events of the same period – the introduction of the new constitution and the VIII Congress of the League of Communists the success of the 'selling' operation was more qualified. The 1964 *Current Problems* survey indicates that the new constitution certainly succeeded in raising the level of interest in the proceedings of the Federal *Skupština*.[52] On the other hand, 74.8 per cent did not know what the rotation principle was. Rotation, i.e. the compulsory retirement from political offices after one term, was one of the principal provisions of the new constitution. Of those who did understand the rotation principle, only 3.3 per cent thought that it would work.

We find the same sort of picture when we look at the survey on opinions about the VIII Congress.[53] Of the 90.7 per cent of the total number of respondents who said they had heard of the Congress, 79.5 per cent said they had followed the work of the Congress. On the other hand, the mass meetings organised for the discussion of the work of the Congress do not seem to have been a great success. Attendance was fairly good – 25.9 per cent said they had participated and 19.6 per cent that they had from time to time, but the meetings were dominated by Communists and other 'involved' people. Only 27.8 per cent of non-LCY people made any active contribution, only 31.6 per cent of the total thought that the meetings had any concrete results for them personally, and only 14.9 per cent of non-involved people thought they did any good at all.

The population, then, seems more interested in economic measures than in political measures – it is significant that 45.4 per cent of the VIII Congress sample thought that the most important problems discussed at the Congress were raising the standard of living and stabilising the economy. But the general impression is that the authorities have been fairly successful in publicising their policy departures, and in galvanising the populace into some kind of active involvement. This does not affect our conclusions on the extent to which the authorities have been able to homogenise Yugoslav culture. It simply emphasises that, quite apart from the issue of control over other inputs, the authorities themselves have provided important inputs into the politico-attitudinal situation.

We are thus brought back to the key issue of the relationship between 'old' and 'new' political cultures. We have already seen that there are a number of ways in which the main elements of the reappraisal may have suited important elements in traditional culture. There is, then, some *a priori* reason to expect that, side by side with traditional elements, a new but organically related element may have emerged. The litmus test for this must surely be an examination of how the self-management system has worked and been seen to work.

### 'NEW' POLITICAL CULTURE AND POLITICAL SOCIALISATION – THE DEVELOPMENT OF THE ETHOS OF SELF-MANAGEMENT

It is vital to distinguish between different levels and dimensions of the self-management system. It is well established that at commune level the system does not function particularly well on any dimension. The most detailed study of this area we have to hand is the 1970 Macedonian survey, which covered 912 individuals from six communes,[54] and produced the concept of a hard-core self-management establishment (*matična samoupravna struktura*), comprising 10–15 per cent of the total electorate, typically male, with higher education or highly skilled, member of the League of Communists, etc., dominating at the commune level. This is confirmed by a smaller study done on local communities (the sub-commune level) in Slovenia,[55] where a high degree of correlation was discovered, in most cases, between preparedness to participate in the work of the local communities and actual participation in the past. Another study at the commune level, based on a survey of sixteen communes, found that voters' mass meetings play a very minor role.[56]

Objectively, then, there seems to be little real participation by the mass of the public in local political affairs. How does the public itself view this state of affairs? Of the Macedonian sample 45 per cent thought that *samoupravljanje* works better at enterprise than at commune level. Private citizens rated themselves as having 'very little influence' in the communes, though the majority did not think that this ought to be changed. Most considered themselves motivated and capable of participation, but when faced with the direct question 'would you take on a socio-political function?' made excuses in terms of lack of experience and training. The conclusion was that 'in the political-cultural environment of the republic the physically dominant attitude towards the system on the part of citizens is co-operative and somewhat indifferent....'[57] Now there are other variables involved here, particularly the peculiar traditional elements in Macedonian political culture, which are conducive to indifference, ambivalence and adaptability. Certainly the Slovenian survey points to some degree of mass participation, particularly in economically more developed rural areas,[58] while the other commune study indicates domination by individuals with important functions in less developed communes, but with the local *skupština* increasing in importance with the degree of development of the commune. Nevertheless the general impression is that there is not a great deal of mass participation in local government, and that most people are not particularly concerned that there should be. In other words, we seem to have a fairly 'normal' local government situation, such as we might meet in the UK, and there is no question of *samoupravljanje* at this level having entered into mass consciousness to the extent that we could say that a qualitatively new element had been introduced into the political culture of Yugoslavia.[59]

The organs of self-management in business enterprises present a much more complex picture. It is, certainly, easy to make a case that workers' councils, management committees and mass meetings of workers function no more effectively than do the communes. One recent study states categorically that 'all the research that has been done on the self-management system tends to the conclusion that the working class participates very little in *samoupravljanje*'.[60] In this particular case the author argues that the prevalent culture continues to be autocratic. This does not mean that everyone wants to be an auto-crat, but it does mean that the majority are prepared to be subjects. Only through re-education of the workers can a genuinely democratic culture be created, as a basis for genuine *samoupravljanje*.

Other studies confirm the gist of this conclusion. A recent survey from Slovenia found that the majority of workers completing questionnaires believed that enterprise statutes and rules are commonly broken, if only for short periods, and that they have no way of effectively opposing this.[61] Another recent survey, covering 973 members of one particular collective, found that directors and professional management were be-lieved to have paramount influence in the organs of self-management, with technical specialists coming second, socio-political organisations (i.e. League of Communists, Socialist Union of Working People, Trade Unions) third, and workers last. Only 18 per cent of the workers interviewed believed that they really made the decisions, while 50 per cent of the management personnel interviewed believed that they really made the decisions.[62]

This essentially negative view of self-management in the enterprise is confirmed by various pieces of data available on people's views on the outstanding achievements of post-war Yugoslavia. In the 1964 *Current Problems* survey, in answer to the question 'What do you like best in Yugoslav society?', only 6.8 per cent said *samoupravljanje* – the com-monest responses were 'freedom and democracy' and equality.[63] An American survey conducted in 1970–71 rated *samoupravljanje* low as a 'formative experience'.[64] But the 1960 student opinion survey indi-cated an interesting ambivalence. On the one hand the introduction of workers' and social self-management came first as 'the most important event since the war'.[65] On the other hand, the students did not rate workers' participation in management as a 'matter of great importance in socio-political terms'.[66] Clearly attitudes among blue-collar workers differ somewhat from those of white-collar, or budding white-collar workers. Equally clearly, you can get a quite different answer on self-management depending on exactly what question you ask.

One of the oddest results of the surveys is the demonstration that enterprise organs of self-management appear to fulfil a very minor in-formational role. The 1965 *Economic Reform* survey found that only 7 per cent of the sample obtained information – on a measure primarily economic and very much affecting the enterprise – from work-place meetings. Certainly this may reflect the strength of the media and press, which were the primary sources for 74 per cent of the sample, rather than the weakness of the self-management organs. It remains a fairly startling statistic.[67]

But there is another side to the reality of workers' councils. There can be absolutely no doubt that the workers have been able, through the self-management organs, to exercise very considerable power on working conditions, welfare and wages, and that this has been a major contributory factor in the cost-inflationary pressures endemic in the Yugoslav economy.[68] A recent American survey, while confirming the absence of genuine participation, indicates that the power structure, in terms of individuals and their roles, may be very open indeed in the Yugoslav enterprise.[69] Lastly, and perhaps most important, there seems to be none of the complacency on workers' councils that there is in relation to the communes. The last-mentioned survey of opinions in the enterprise showed that, however pessimistic the view of the actual situation, it was in general thought that workers *ought* to have more power.[70]

At the risk of oversimplifying a complicated situation, we can sum up the position with regard to self-management in the enterprise in the following terms:

1 The system does not work effectively as a system of participatory management.
2 The system does work effectively as a means of ensuring 'trade-union' rights to workers.
3 The system is not an important element in the process of dissemination of information.
4 The mass of the people believe in the system, in the sense that they think it worth while to try to make the system work better.
5 The system does provide the basis for a very open influence structure within the enterprise, so that anyone who wants to 'get on', in a material, political or altruistic way, may find the system comfortable.
6 Producers' democracy as a precise concept does not score highly in popularity polls of important events. On the other hand, there seems to be virtually universal acceptance of the existing imperfect approximation as legitimate as well as stable.[71] We can, then, with some confidence say with Johnson that 'under the rubric of self-management, the doctrine of socialist democracy ... became so secularized that it lost most of its character as an ideological "action program" and was absorbed into a new Yugoslav political culture'.[72]

We conclude that self-management in the enterprise has introduced a new element into political culture in Yugoslavia, inasmuch as it has created a certain image of the millennium which has survived the imperfections of reality, and inasmuch as it has created, and has been seen to create, a kind of pluralism, at least at grass-roots level, which must have militated in favour of the 'institutionalised conflict' view of Yugoslav society, as well as providing an avenue for, and a rationalisation of, political activity.

NEW MYTHS AND TRADITIONS IN CONTEMPORARY YUGOSLAVIA

The advent of *samoupravljanje* is not the only substantial event in the past thirty years of Yugoslav history. It would, indeed, be surprising if wartime upheavals and the development of an original system of economic planning had not left some imprint on the consciousness of Yugoslavs.

### *'The market' as an element in contemporary Yugoslav mythology*

Objectively the Yugoslav economic system is, as we have seen, a fairly decentralised one, though with significant elements of direct government interference. What one might call the official ideology of the Yugoslav business management community is that the government interferes too much – that the market is not allowed sufficient free rein. In practice, however, attitudes to free competition and government interference are somewhat different. The operational culture of Yugoslav businessmen is, for example, strongly inimical to price competition, to the extent that price-cutting is actually considered to come into the category of *nelojalni*, i.e. unethical business practice.[73] In addition, attitudes on specific cases of government interference tend to vary a great deal depending on what the particular organisation stands to get out of it. An enterprise which complains loudly about the high percentage of its foreign exchange earnings taken compulsorily by the National Bank may complain equally loudly about a government decision to permit free import of goods which compete with 'own' products on the domestic market. A leader from a few years ago in *Ekonomska Politika* blamed inflation on the fact that 'it is always possible that the authorities may, by a special dispensation, waive the rule that anyone freely making a wrong decision will be punished. This can only result in a piling-up of accounts which no one ever pays'.[74] In other words, under the rubric of the ideological primacy of the market, we can expect to find businessmen jostling for favours from the political authorities. It is worth noting here that in a recent survey of 'opinion-makers' in Yugoslavia businessmen showed up as being fairly conservative/centralist on matters of economic policy – and very conservative/centralist on political matters.[75]

There is, of course, a danger of over-generalising about the business community. Businessmen from the wealthier areas may be quite genuinely anti-interventionist, if only because they tend to identify intervention with redistribution to their disadvantage. Croatian businessmen are almost by definition anti-Belgrade, which may mean they will not want to have much to do with the Federal government. The legitimate generalised conclusion we can draw is that the 'market' bit of market socialism has tended to operate, at the level of beliefs and values, more as a rationalisation for *mores* reminiscent of nineteenth-century Serbia and Royal Yugoslavia, than as a genuinely new ethos.

## The Partisan tradition

Any biographical snippet on a Yugoslav public figure will almost certainly include a reference to the year in which he 'became a participant in the National-Liberation Struggle'.[76] Shades of the wartime period do continue to play an important part in national life in a number of specific ways. Tito is still the great war hero, and as such remains an important focus of identification and loyalty. The continued dominance of managerial positions by old Partisans creates generational conflict and has been an obstacle to the introduction of modern management methods.[77] Anyone known to have been associated with the *Ustaše* or *Četnici* is excluded from public life. The numerical predominance of Serbs and Montenegrins in the Partisan movement has survived into the League of Communists and the armed and security forces. Serbs and Montenegrins made up over 58 per cent of the total membership of the LCY in 1966,[78] and just over 50 per cent of the delegates to the X Congress held in 1974.[79] Serbs and Montenegrins dominate the officer corps,[80] and a 1971 report suggests that the proportion of that corps made up by Slovenes, Croats, Hungarians and Albanians had been dropping steadily since the war.[81] One factor affecting Slovenes, Croats and Hungarians here may have been simply the financial unattractiveness, relative to other opportunities in their areas, of the career. Again, the old rule whereby officers must serve outside their native republic was at odds with the obvious preferences of the northern nationalities – we have here an instance of post-war 'negative' policy on nationalities contributing to the maintenance of a tradition which could only create problems in relations between nationalities. None of this, however, diminishes the importance of the original tradition. Recent measures aimed at increasing the attractiveness of the army career, coupled with the abolition of the rule on serving outside one's native republic, have, however, succeeded in raising the number of Croat applicants to military schools and academies by as much as five times.[82]

A particularly interesting set of statistics is available on national composition of 'leading personnel' in *Savezni* SUP (the Federal Ministry for Internal Affairs). The percentages are as follows:[83]

| | | | |
|---|---|---|---|
| Serbs | 61 | Yugoslavs | |
| Croats | 16 | (Ethnic Muslims) | 1 |
| Slovenes | 9 | Others (Albanians, | |
| Montenegrins | 9 | Macedonians, | |
| | | Hungarians etc.) | 4 |

Apart from the heavy over-representation of Serbs and Montenegrins, we note the under-representation of Ethnic Muslims and Albanians. It is, indeed, quite clear that the mountainous areas of the interior are of crucial importance here. If we look at the figures by republic we find that only 22.0 per cent actually come from Serbia, 42.2 per cent from Croatia, and 13.3 per cent from Bosnia. Taking account, then, of the almost negligible Ethnic Muslim representation, and the fairly small Croat population of Bosnia, a very large proportion of high-ranking SUP officials are Serbs from the 'heartland' area of Bosnia and Croatia. Once again we find Serbs from outside Serbia playing a crucial role, and it is not difficult to tie these figures in with the earlier discussion of the 'geography' of the War and Revolution.[84]

What are we to conclude from all this at the level of attitudes? We should not overstress imbalance in the national composition of the membership of the LCY. No major nationality is *grossly* under-represented. The Army and SUP figures are much more important. We can see a vicious circle of marginal involvement of, in particular, Slovenes, Croats and Ethnic Muslims. We can see how 'agin the government' attitudes may easily extend to including a strong feeling of alienation from the coercive forces of the state, and we can see how such attitudinal patterns could provide political rationalisation on a broad scale. An opinion poll conducted among officers in the forces in 1971 indicated 'nationalism and chauvinism' as the most popular response to the 'greatest danger to the community' question; as many as 72 per cent considered growing social differentiation and 'negative phenomena' in socio-economic life as the 'greatest weakness' in Yugoslav society.[85]

To a limited extent, then, the Partisan tradition may have provided a new symbol, personified in Tito himself. More substantially, however, it has been a vehicle for tendencies that fit only too well into the traditions of Dinaric man and of the Serbian state. Thus we are brought very firmly up against the general question of the importance of traditional values and key elements of early political experience *as such* in post-revolutionary Yugoslavia.

## TRADITIONAL ELEMENTS IN CONTEMPORARY POLITICAL CULTURE

Before going on to more general points, it is worth emphasising how important may be survivals of quite specific elements of traditional values and attitudes, economic progress notwithstanding. A report from 1970, for example, indicates that the incidence of crimes connected with blood feud had been increasing in recent years. Between 1966 and 1968 there were 141 victims of blood feud in Kosovo.[86] The survival of the idea of *sveta osveta* (sacred revenge) in Montenegro,

Kosovo, Macedonia and South Serbia confirms the continued importance of the traditional Dinaric culture, orientated towards crude
heroism and violence. Equally important, the persistence of blood feud
may reinforce feelings of ambivalence towards authority, and towards
socio-economic arrangements in general. An excellent illustration of
the importance, and the perception of the importance, of this kind of
atavism is the novel mentioned earlier, *When the Pumpkins Blossomed.*
Here a threefold correlation is suggested between teenage gangsterism
in Belgrade in the late forties and fifties, the traditional ethos of feud
and revenge, and the 'Old Stalinist' resistance to the reforms of the
early fifties. We should, then, be prepared for a certain amount of
direct continuity in attitudes and values. In most areas, however, the
very facts of a new régime and rapid socio-economic progress have
ensured that historically-conditioned elements have undergone some
transformation.

## Bureaucratic tradition and its absence

The importance of the Serbian bureaucratic tradition should not be
overstressed. The Serbian bureaucracy of the nineteenth century was
a petty, immature affair, enjoying little general acceptance. For all
that, it is easy enough to produce statistics from contemporary Yugoslavia which indicate its capacity for survival. In 1969 the national
composition of the staff of the organs of the Federation was as follows:[87]

| Serbs | 4335 | Montenegrins | 424 |
|---|---|---|---|
| Croats | 504 | Slovenes | 187 |
| Macedonians | 145 | | |

But this strongly marked disproportion is not simply a continuation of
a nineteenth-century tradition. What we are dealing with is a specific
dimension of the phenomenon of nationality and national sentiment.
The particular way in which the history of the inter-war period worked
out, with Serbian hegemony being answered by Slovenian and Croatian
isolationism, may be as important as the long-term historical factor.
Ambitious Slovenes and Croats just do not tend to gravitate to Belgrade
in the way that ambitious Scots and Yorkshiremen gravitate to London.
As with the army and SUP, so in the civil service the post-war tendency
to sweep the nationalities problem under the carpet may have helped
to perpetuate Serbian dominance. Given that Federal employment
is not normally a lifelong career, and given that, *ceteris paribus*, the
vast majority of Croats would rather live in Zagreb than in Belgrade,
how can the aspiring Croatian Federal civil servant ensure his future
and that of his family in terms of housing, education, employment, etc?[88]
The fact that Belgrade, the Federal capital, is in Serbia makes a big

difference, and the central Yugoslav authorities have never recognised and tried to make allowance for this.

The question of confidence in the Federal organs on the part of the northern nationalities receives interesting coverage in the 1960 student opinion survey, and in the VIII Congress and 1965 *Economic Reform* surveys. It emerged from these surveys that there was distinctly less confidence in their competence in Slovenia than in Yugoslavia as a whole. This may have been partly connected with attitudes to the central leadership itself – the VIII Congress survey confirms that the League of Communists had considerably less standing at that time in Slovenia than in the rest of Yugoslavia – but the emphasis on problems of *implementation* that emerges surely reflects attitudes to bureaucracy as well as to government. To put this in proportion, the 1964 *Current Problems* survey found Slovenes well above average in terms of feeling themselves adequate to participate actively in *samoupravljanje*. No doubt this has something to do with educational levels, but it emphasises that clearly delineated attitudes of Slovenes towards Belgrade should not be taken to signify any rejection of the official ideology of self-management.

As far as the Croats are concerned, these surveys do not show a strong divergence from the Yugoslav norm, though there is some tendency in the same direction as the Slovenes. We do not have comparable data for the late sixties and early seventies, but it is significant that in the early to middle sxties it was the Slovenes, not the Croats, who stood out in terms of lack of confidence in Belgrade.

The general issue of national feeling we shall come to in a moment. The point we are making here is that specific historical and attitudinal factors have created and preserved a situation where the civil service rests on a narrow base, and, in particular, receives hardly any life-blood from the two most advanced nationalities of the Federation. It is not surprising, then, that the bureaucracy in Yugoslavia enjoys less than universal respect, and that 'agin the government' attitudes are fairly strong, even among people who would never associate themselves with extreme nationalist positions.

*Traditional religion*

Yugoslavia is an atheist state, and no practising believer has attained high office since the war. But there is no policy of suppression and persecution of religious organisations and individuals such as prevails in the Soviet Union. Relations between government and the various churches have been fairly amicable. A survey from 1968 covering the whole of Yugoslavia came up with 39 per cent as the incidence of 'believer'.[89] A Slovenian survey from 1969 yields figures of 25–30 per cent among white-collar workers, 50–60 per cent among workers and 92 per cent among peasants as 'being religious', though this includes non-practising believers.[90]

It is clear that religious consciousness is strongly negatively correlated with involvement in organs of self-management, and with 'engagement' in general. This is confirmed by a 1965 Bosnian survey,[91] and the 1970 Macedonian commune survey. The 1960 student opinion survey and the 1973 Slovenian survey indicates a strong negative correlation between religiosity and educational level.

Religion, then, is, and is permitted to be, an important element in Yugoslav life. But is it an important element in *political* culture? Once again we become involved in the matter of nationalities. Traditional religion is to a great extent the badge of national identity in Yugoslavia. It is often quite impossible to distinguish a Serb from a Croat on any other basis.[92] What we are concerned with here, however, is the specifically religious element. Information is sparse, but the 1969 Slovenian survey does postulate, in attempting to explain the high incidence of religiosity among workers, and in view also of the correlation between religion and lack of education, that there may be some tendency for religion to become the ideology of the deprived, materially and culturally.[93] There may indeed, certainly in the case of the Catholic Church in Slovenia, be an element of church policy here. But there is little indication of any attempt by a religious body to adopt any kind of active policy *vis-à-vis* the government, in terms of representing their 'constituents'.[94] To the extent, then, that religion is an element in contemporary culture, it seems to take the form of a 'counter-culture', autonomous but essentially negative. What religiosity may do is to strengthen traditional tendencies to ambivalence in attitudes to authority.

### NATIONALISM

The phenomenon of nationality has entered into every one of the sections of this paper, and we have noted that there are major differences between the political cultures of the different nationalities. Croats and Slovenes are more likely to rationalise in terms of the virtues of free enterprise, Croats, Slovenes and Macedonians in anti-Belgrade, anti-bureaucracy terms, Serbs in terms of the need for unity, Montenegrins in terms of some kind of traditional heroic concept – and so on. Two crucial questions remain to be discussed. Firstly, to what extent do members of particular nationalities rationalise political standpoints in terms of animus against one or more of the other nationalities? Secondly, to the extent that they do, and given the general heterogeneity of political culture amongst the nationalities, has any kind of 'federal' political culture emerged as a way of dealing with this?

On the second point we shall overstep the boundaries of 'political culture' into the province of decision-making processes as such, so it is best left to our concluding section. Here we shall concentrate on the first.

Relations between nationalities were thought to be good by 73 per cent of the 1964 *Current Problems* survey sample. The interesting figures are those broken down by nationality. Of Croats, 69.4 per cent thought relations were good, slightly more than the corresponding figure for Serbs of 68.8 per cent. Of Macedonians 85.6 per cent thought relations were good, but only 58.7 per cent of Slovenes thought so. A similar picture emerges from a 1966 survey done on 'ethnic distance'.[95] Ethnic distance was defined in terms of attitudes to friendship, marriage etc. between members of different nationalities. Of Croats 85.3 per cent manifested very slight or negligible ethnic distance, of Serbs 81.7 per cent. The corresponding figure for Slovenes was 55.2 per cent. The only figure which suggests a slightly different picture from the 1964 data is that for Macedonians – 78.3 per cent. Other material tends to confirm this general picture. A 1967 survey found a fairly good general correlation between socio-cultural modernisation and cultural universalism, except amongst the Slovenes.[96] Material from a 1974 survey of Serbian schoolchildren indicates a fairly high degree of 'internationalism', and a low coefficient of 'social distance' with respect to Slovenes, Croats and Macedonians.[97] A survey of Ljubljana students done around the same time shows, predictably, a rather higher incidence of 'patriotism', i.e. moderate ethnocentrism.[98]

We are, then, going to have to be very careful about attributing specific political developments to feelings of national exclusiveness. The only Yugoslav nationality that manifests a strong tendency to exclusivism is the Slovene, but there is no case in post-war Yugoslav history of political change tying in with this. On the other hand the Croats, apparently the most nationalistic, certainly possessing a strongly nationalistic intelligentsia element, and with a strong tendency to become involved in political battles that look like national clashes with the Serbs, come out of all the surveys looking mild, tolerant and cosmopolitan. We must proceed, then, on the supposition that nationalistic feelings, in the sense of feeling directed against other nationalities, have been of relatively minor importance in the consciousness of the masses. This is not to deny that well-known historical events may retain considerable latent or intermittent force in people's minds. One of the interesting results of the 1974 Serbian schoolchildren survey is that individuals scoring very high on internationalism also scored quite high on 'patriotism', while there was a fairly high positive correlation between scores on 'patriotism' and ethnocentrism. So there is some empirical basis for suggesting that in times of crisis values might shift radically, and this may very well have happened, for example, in

Croatia in the period 1969–72. By definition, however, this cannot explain the *origin* of crises.

This discussion of nationalism may have left the reader confused rather than edified. In such a heterogeneous society, if nationalism does not give us something to hang on to, then what does? In fact, all we have shown is that most Yugoslavs are not ethnocentric. But by very virtue of the heterogeneity which has been the main theme of this essay, Yugoslavs have been concerned, even obsessed, with questions of *identity*. We have seen this in relation to myth-making, to language, to religion, to mention only the most obvious. *The common denominator which transmutes specific badges and symbols of identity into a more general focus is surely nationality.* This general focus has in turn served as a basis for rationalising attitudes to specific political and economic problems. In the majority of cases the position of an individual in relation to our main themes is likely to be determined, objectively and subjectively, by his nationality. This point will be further illustrated in our final section.

CONCLUSION: POLITICAL CULTURE AND POLITICAL CHANGE

There is no need to repeat our preliminary remarks on the reforms of 1950–3. We may simply add that even Dinaric man, while perhaps inclined to be unresponsive to the more high-level conceptions of self-management, would surely have found Stalinism just as uncongenial as his brother, *zadruga* man. It is worth noting that among the four major architects of the first reforms, Tito, Kardelj, Djilas and Kidrič, we find one Croat, two Slovenes and a Montenegrin – *zadruga* man obviously numerically ascendant, but with a powerful Dinaric minority!

Moving on to the reforms of 1961–5, the interesting point is that the only organised opposition to the reforms came from Aleksander Ranković, a Serb, very closely associated with the police, that stronghold of the *prečani*. There is nothing odd about this. We can expect policemen to be centralists, and we can expect Bosnian Serbs and *prečani* to dislike a reform likely to benefit the richer areas and, more particularly, the Croats. What is important is that the whole Ranković affair – Ranković was 'unmasked', deprived of all his posts, and expelled from the Party in 1966 – revived certain identifications in the public mind. That composite figure, the Serb hegemonist/centralist/bureaucrat/policeman, who after all really did exist in the inter-war period,[99] is never far from the Croat imagination, and is intensely disliked. Ranković and his clique seemed to fit only too well into the image, and though his ouster could only be interpreted as a victory for the anti-Belgrade forces – it was, of course, in the immediate sense, simply a victory for the Party line – a new consciousness of dangers present, or thought to be present, may have emerged and formed an important element in later developments.

We shall concentrate on two aspects of the events of 1967–71: firstly, the specific issue of Croatian nationalism (using the word without prejudice to any interpretation of the real content of what actually happened); secondly, the more general issue of the constitutional reforms and the movement towards a looser federal system.

Growing cultural nationalism, showing itself in the 'Declaration on the Croatian Literary Language' (1967) and the 'cultural separatist' policy of *Matica Hrvatska*, the Croatian cultural association, coincided with increasing discontent in Croatia with what was perceived as the exploitation of Croatia by Belgrade 'monopoly capital', particularly through investment in the Dalmatian tourist industry. The big Federal investment funds and import-export houses, which had been converted into autonomous corporations, 1963–5, were, it was argued, working with 'state capital', to which Croatia had contributed more than her share in the pre-1965 period. Now this state capital was being used to exploit Croatia in the interests of Serbia.

It is beyond doubt that explicitly nationalistic, anti-Serbian sentiments ran high at this time among a certain section of the Croatian intelligentsia, particularly among those associated with *Matica Hrvatska*. But we must repeat that as late as 1967 there is positive evidence of a lack of anti-Serbian animus in Croatia. What is equally clear is that the economic grouses which the Croats voiced were very clearly directed at Belgrade, and that, particularly with the memory of Ranković fresh, 'Serbia' was bound to be used as a shorthand for everything that the Croats felt themselves to be up against. In 1967–71 not only was 'Croatia' the positive symbol and focus for the great issues of the day, but 'Serbia' emerged as a kind of anti-symbol, but an equally strong, or even stronger, focus.

As we have seen, the constitutional amendments, culminating in the new constitution of 1974, have to a great extent converted Yugoslavia into a confederation. Republics delegate functions to the Federation rather than vice-versa, and representation at the Federal level and recruitment to the Federal civil service now proceeds on a parity/quota basis. It is plausible to interpret this as a response to Yugoslavia's general heterogeneity. A situation where different interest groups come together to negotiate on matters of common interest, and delegate authority to special executive bodies as they agree and see fit – and this is the theme of the new constitution in the fields of Federal social and economic management as well as in that of republican-Federation relations – is obviously well suited to such a heterogeneous society. It is also well suited to the real patterns of behaviour, as opposed to the self-images, of much of the Yugoslav business community. More generally, it fits in well with some aspects of the Dinaric tradition. But such a system can function only if participants are prepared to negotiate in terms of long-term as well as short-term, general as well as particular goals. In other words, the new constitution will only work if appropriate changes in the general climate of political culture can be achieved. It is for this reason, I believe, that there has been such an emphasis in the press and other media on the ideas of social compact and self-management agreement, and on the process of reaching them.

But the evidence does not suggest that it will be easy to establish firmly this new political culture at all levels. Tendencies to sectionalism and localism remain very strong, at the level of negotiation between republics and Federation and at the more specialised, functional level. The general political tightening up of the last two or three years, the reassertion of the role of the League of Communists, the deployment of that great focus of *Yugoslavian* identity, Tito, in the famous Letter of 1972 – all these may have something to do with a strongly-felt need to impose the new 'confederative' political culture. This is certainly the best explanation for the recent peculiar emphasis on regaining control in the media and in educational establishments. *Praxis* has been closed, the Philosophy Department of Belgrade University drastically purged.[100] There is a new emphasis on the need to revitalise youth movements and give them a clear socialist orientation,[101] while the outcome of the Party Commission on education has been a draft for a much more 'production-oriented' and much more positively Marxist curriculum.[102] The idea of more control in one dimension as a condition of more freedom, or at least more scope for heterogeneity, in another is a paradox. Whether that paradox can be resolved remains to be seen.

NOTES

1  See D. A. Dyker, 'The Ethnic Muslims of Bosnia – some basic socio-economic data', in *Slavonic and East European Review*, vol. L, no. 119, April 1972.

2  See A. Husarić, 'Bosna i Hercegovina nije ničija lingvistička kolonija', in *Borba*, 18 February 1971, p. 6; 'Kojim jezikom govore Crnogorci', in *Vjesnik u Srijedu*, 21 October 1970, p. 11.

3  F. Džinić, *Jugoslovensko Javno Mnenje i VIII Kongres SKJ*, Institut Društvenih Nauka, Centar za Istraživanje Javnog Mnenja, Belgrade, 1965, p. 13.

4  For a vivid description of these practices in Bosnia, see Ivo Andrić's novel *Na Drini Ćuprija*.

5  A. Purivatra, *Nacionalni i Politički Razvitak Muslimana*, Sarajevo, 1969, p. 151.

6  See S. Guldescu, 'Croatian political history 1526–1918', in F. H. Eterovich and C. Spalatin (eds.), *Croatia: Land, People, Culture*, vol. II, Toronto, 1970. Guldescu's emphasis on the Croatian military tradition is clearly coloured by his political position, but this serves only to underline the importance of that tradition in the belief structure of

militant Croatian nationalism. What Guldescu does not, understandably, lay emphasis on is the role played by the Serbian minority in the Military Frontier. Cf. discussion of *prečani* theme in text.

7 See ibid., p. 16, for a discussion of the *Statuta Valachorum* of 1630.
8 See C. A. Macartney, *Hungary. A Short History* (Edinburgh, 1962).
9 W. D. McClellan, *Svetozar Marković and the Origins of Balkan Socialism* (Princeton, 1964) p. 83.
10 P. A. Rovinsky, 'Belgrad, ego ustroistvo i obshchestvennaya zhizn'',' *Vestnik Evropy*, May 1870, Part II, p. 164, quoted in McClellan, op. cit.
11 Rovinsky, op. cit., p. 164.
12 J. Tomasevich, *Peasants, Politics and Economic Change in Yugoslavia* (Stanford and Oxford, 1955) p. 144.
13 Ibid.
14 P. E. Mosely, 'The Peasant Family: the *zadruga*, or communal joint-family in the Balkans, and its recent evolution', in C. F. Ware (ed.), *The Cultural Approach to History* (Port Washington, 1965) p. 95.
15 See J. Cvijić, *Iz Društvenih Nauka* (Belgrade, 1965).
16 Tomasevich, op. cit., pp. 194–5.
17 See D. Tomašić, *Društveni Razvitak Hrvata* (Zagreb, 1938), and D. Tomasic [sic], *Personality and Culture in Eastern European Politics* (New York, 1948).
18 Macartney, op. cit., pp. 141–2.
19 See, for example, F. H. Eterovich. 'Ethical heritage', in Eterovich and Spalatin, op. cit., vol. I, pp. 199–200.
20 D. Mirčev, 'Granice emancipacije samoupravne svesti', in *Sociologija*, no. 1, 1972, p. 92.
21 Tomasevich, op. cit., p. 182.
22 D. J. Mandić, 'The ethnic and religious history of Bosnia and Hercegovina', in Eterovich and Spalatin, op. cit., vol. II, p. 370.
23 Cvijić distinguished a 'central type' of character, found in Macedonia and South Serbia, conditioned by long subjection to Byzantines and Turks, and displaying many of the characteristics discussed by Mirčev. See I. Lučev, 'Socijalni karakter i politička kultura', in *Sociologija*, no. 1, 1974, p. 33.
24 Eterovich, 'Ethical heritage', in Eterovich and Spalatin, op. cit., vol. I, p. 203.
25 Macartney, op. cit., p. 189.
26 Tomasevich, op. cit., pp. 246–7.
27 B. Gusić, 'Today's Herzegovina', in *Nova Evropa*, July–August 1936, p. 207, quoted in Tomasevich, op. cit.
28 Guldescu, 'Croatian political history 1526–1918', in Eterovich and Spalatin, op. cit., vol. II, p. 91.
29 G. W. Hoffman and F. W. Neal, *Yugoslavia and the New Communism* (New York, 1962) p. 73.
30 W. R. Roberts, *Tito, Mihailović and the Allies 1941–45* (New Brunswick, 1973) pp. 106–12.
31 See Purivatra, op. cit.
32 See Roberts, op. cit.
33 See Dyker, op. cit., pp. 245–6.

34   Z. Mlinar, 'Društveni vrednosti, razvoj i konflikti', in *Sociologija*, no. 3, 1971, p. 380.
35   The term was originated by Hoffman and Neal. See op. cit.
36   See ibid., chapters 8 and 9.
37   See A. Ross Johnson, *The Transformation of Communist Ideology: the Yugoslav Case, 1945–1953* (Cambridge, Mass., and London, 1972).
38   Ibid., p. 231.
39   Central planning does not seem to have worked very efficiently in the short time during which it operated. See A. Waterston, *Planning in Yugoslavia* (Baltimore, 1962) chapter II.
40   See Mlinar, op. cit.
41   *Jugoslovenski Studenti i Socijalizam, Institut Društvenih Nauka, Centar za Istraživanje Društvenih Odnosa* (Belgrade, 1966) pp. 100–8.
42   *Ibid.*, p. 209. The 'top five' of opinion-forming factors were (1) experience in contact with people; (2) books; (3) the press; (4) father; (5) mother. Middle-school teachers and university teachers came respectively ninth and tenth out of 14.
43   R. Danilović, 'Odakle ideologija državnog socijalizma?', in *Komunist*, 12 March 1970, p. 9.
44   V. Lonchar, 'Obnova ideologije u školi', in *Borba*, 12 March 1970, p. 10.
45   M. Gligorijević, 'Pobuna protiv gradanske škole', in *Borba*, 24 December 1970, p. 4.
46   Statement by J. Kopčak, in *NIN*, 9 December 1972, p. 4.
47   D. Marković, 'Čas iz šovinizma', in *NIN*, 11 October 1970, p. 5.
48   'Kome i kako da služi ekonomska nauka?', in *Privredni Vjesnik*, 28 November 1970, p. 7.
49   'A. Gravranović – direktor "Privrednog vjesnika"', in *Privredni Vjesnik*, 13 January 1972, p. 2.
50   See discussion of the novel and play in *ABSEES*, January 1971, p. 252.
51   Firdus Džinić (ed.), *Jugoslovensko Javno Mnenje o Privrednoj Reformi 1965 (Institut Društvenih Nauka, Centar za Ispitivanje Javnog Mnenja*, Belgrade, 1965).
52   Lj. Baćević *et al.*, *Jugoslovensko Javno Mnenje o Aktuelnim Političkim i Društvenim Pitanjima (Institut Društvenih Nauka*, Belgrade, 1964).
53   See n. 3.
54   Mirčev, op. cit.
55   A. Barbić, 'Učestvovanje gradjana u seoskom i gradskim mesnim zajednicama', in *Sociologija*, no. 4, 1971.
56   A. Jerovšek, 'Struktura uticaja u opštini', in *Sociologija*, no. 2, 1969.
57   Mirčev, op. cit., p. 97.
58   Barbić, op. cit., p. 544.
59   I have not had access to a copy of R. Marinković, *Ko Odlučuje u Komuni?*, Belgrade, 1971, but this author's conclusions are apparently similar to my own.
60   V. Vujević, 'Utjecaj tradicionalnih društvenih odnosa na neka obelježa radničke klase', in *Sociologija*, no. 3, 1972.
61   P. Vindišar, 'Normativne mogućnosti samoupravljanja', in *Sociologija*, no. 3, 1972.

62  'Socijalna struktura i distribucija uticaja na nivou radne jedinice i preduzeća', in *Sociologija*, no. 4, 1972.
63  Baćević, op. cit., p. 64.
64  S. Zukin, *Beyond Marx and Tito* (London, 1975) chapter 3.
65  *Jugoslovenski Studenti i Socijalizam*, p. 22.
66  Ibid., p. 18.
67  *Jugoslovensko Javno Mnenje o Privrednoj Reformi 1965*, p. 15.
68  See S. Popov and M. Jovičić, *Uticaj Ličnih Dohodaka na Kretanja Cena* (*Institut Ekonomskih Nauka*, Belgrade, 1971).
69  I. Adizes, *Industrial Democracy: Yugoslav Style* (New York and London, 1971).
70  See article quoted under n. 62, p. 618.
71  For a similar statement see Zukin, op. cit., p. 98.
72  Johnson, op. cit., p. 249.
73  J. B. Dirlam and J. L. Plummer, *An Introduction to the Yugoslav Economy* (Columbus, Ohio, 1973) p. 94.
74  'Izmedu naredbe i igre', in *Ekonomska Politika*, 28 June 1971, p. 7.
75  M. V. Popović, 'Tvorci jugoslovenskog javnog mnenja i dilema liberalizam-centralizam', in *Sociologija*, no. 2, 1971.
76  See, for example, *Ko je Ko u Jugoslaviji* [*Who's Who in Yugoslavia*] (Belgrade, 1957).
77  See Dirlam and Plummer, op. cit., p. 33.
78  M. Nikolić (ed.), *Savez Komunista Jugoslavije u Uslovima Samoupravljanja* (Belgrade, 1967) p. 785.
79  'Zastupljenost', in *Privredni Vjesnik*, 31 May 1974, p. 2.
80  See 'National structure of the Yugoslav army leadership', *RFE research bulletin 1373*, 12 April 1972.
81  M. Paver, 'Hrvatska u JNA', in *Vjesnik u Srijedu*, 2 May 1973, p. 3.
82  Ibid., p. 4.
83  See feature on the police published in *NIN*, 3 May 1970, p. 30.
84  Note, however, that there seems some indication, though I have seen no documentary evidence, of a predominance of *prečani* in the police in the pre-war period.
85  V. Miletić, 'Šta misli vojska', in *NIN*, 20 June 1971.
86  B. Vojvodić, 'Protiv krvne osvete – preventivom ili oštrim sankcijama', in *Borba*, 7 October 1970, p. 4. On blood feud see also M. Karan, 'Krvna osveta: "patološko" ili "normalno" ponašanje?', in *Sociologija*, no. 1, 1973, and 'Sociološki i psihološkti aspekti etnološkog izučavanja krvne osvete', in *Sociologija*, no. 3/4, 1974.
87  'Poen za bolju upravu', in *Privredni Vjesnik*, 20 April 1969, p. 2.
88  See 'U federaciju s povratnom kartom', in *Privredni Vjesnik*, 22 April 1971, p. 6.
89  *Jugoslovensko Javno Mnenje 1968*, quoted in S. Vrcan, 'Religija kao oblik tradicionalne svesti', in *Sociologija*, no. 2, 1974, p. 227.
90  M. Kerševan, 'Industrijski radnici i religija u Sloveniji', in *Naše Teme*, no. 10, 1972, p. 1623, quoting N. Toš, *Slovensko Javno Mnenje 1968, 1960, Centar za Istraživanje Javnog Mnenja pri FSPN*.
91  E. Ćimić, 'Uticaj samoupravljanja na proces prevladavanja tradicionalne religije', in *Pregled*, Sarajevo, no. 7/8, 1968.

92  There is a group of traditionally Catholic Serbs in Dalmatia. See
    S. K. Pavlowitch, *Yugoslavia* (London, 1971) p. 46 n.
93  This idea does seem to receive some confirmation from M. Tomašević,
    'Kviz "Hristove nauke",' (quoting a *Centar za Istraživanje Javnog
    Mnenja* survey conducted in Belgrade) in *Borba*, 4 December 1973, p. 5.
94  But for a more serious view of the dangers of clericalism, see F. Šetinc,
    'Opasnost od oživljavanja klerikalizma', in *Borba*, 16 July 1973, p. 5.
95  D. Pantić, *Ethnic Distance in Yugoslavia* (*Institut Društvenih Nauka*,
    Belgrade, 1967), quoted in G. K. Bertsch, 'The Revival of Nationalism',
    in *Problems of Communism*, November–December 1973.
96  G. K. Bertsch, 'A cross-national analysis of the community-building pro-
    cess in Yugoslavia', in *Comparative Political Studies*, January 1972.
97  N. Rot, 'Nacionalizam i drugi oblici nacionalne vezanosti', in *Socio-
    logija*, no. 2, 1974.
98  Survey conducted by B. Peršič, quoted by Rot, op. cit., pp. 202–3.
99  Tomašič writes, *à propos* of Dinaric man, of the 'herdsman-brigand-
    warrior-police ideal'. See Tomasic, *Personality and Culture in Eastern
    European Politics*, p. 12.
100 V. Slijepčević, 'Nije spor oko marksističke kritike', in *Komunist*, 31
    December 1973; 'Belgrade dissident dons lose jobs', in *The Times*,
    29 January 1975, p. 6; 'Left journal closes in Yugoslavia', in *The Times*,
    22 February 1975, p. 4. On the tightening up of university appointments
    procedures see S. Stanojlović, 'Tko može opstati na univerzitetu', in
    *Vjesnik u Srijedu*, 19 December 1973, p. 4.
101 See 'Usporeno zapošljavanje mladih', in *Borba*, 24 July 1973, p. 5;
    R. Jovičić *et al.*, 'Nova jedinstvena organizacija mladih', in *Borba*,
    24 November 1974, pp. 1, 7.
102 R. Jovanović, 'Škola bliža životu', in *Borba*, 12 April 1974, p. 4.

# 4 Poland: Socialism for Everyman?

## GEORGE KOLANKIEWICZ AND RAY TARAS

More than most nations, Poland provides a most pertinent example of the role that historical consciousness may play in a nation's emergence from subservience. Partitioned for nearly 150 years, Poland came to depend heavily upon history and tradition as a means of maintaining its national integrity in the face of its official dismemberment. Its subsequent experience has done little to modify the intensity of 'living history', that continual appropriation of the past by the citizens of the present.[1] Historical controversies have sustained an immediacy not always intelligible to the members of the more historically phlegmatic nations.

### PERCEPTION OF HISTORY

Certain key periods which have implanted themselves in the Polish collective memory can be identified.

*Kingdom and 'great power' status* were associated with the birth of the Christian Polish State under Mieszko I. The Battle of Grunwald in 1410 and the glorious reign of Casimir the Great further went to complete this syndrome. *The period of partition and insurrection* is clearly a more masochistic element of the collective memory and concerns the controversy surrounding the causes of these partitions (enacted by Russia, Prussia and Austria), and the unsuccessful insurrections of 1830 and 1863.

Extraordinary sensitivity to democracy, bordering on anarchy, was encapsulated in the form of the *liberum veto*[2] which, along with the principle of elective kingship, made the emergence of an absolutist state impossible and the future survival of Poland improbable.

The by-products of this period were, however, impressive. The

George Kolankiewicz wishes to express his thanks for an Essex University Sociology Department Fuller Grant which made possible research visits to Poland.

romanticism of Mickiewicz, coupled with the contributions of Krasiński, Słowacki and Norwid, was to supply a patriotic diet for young generations in years to come. An ascendant intelligentsia came to fill the vacuum left by the abandonment of its leadership role by the nobility in the aftermath of 1830. At the same time the closure of the universities of Warsaw and Wilno forced intellectual activity underground, and thereby politicised it. A nation which had always prided itself upon its freedom of thought found a rigorous censorship imposed – so much so that any future censorship would inevitably be associated with alien domination.

The venues for intellectual gatherings became the French-style literary-artistic salons[3] attended by teachers, writers and professionals, though a feature of them was their democratic composition. Future patriots of both left and right frequented these gatherings, which apart from their role of maintaining cultural continuity emerged as admirable devices for enforcing political solidarity during a period of vicious repression. The face-to-face, word-of-mouth, informal nature of Polish politics was born. A whole spectrum of ideologies was articulated during this period – e.g. the doctrine of *organic work*[4] – and various forms of socialism, usually differentiated by their attitude to the peasantry and national liberation. The débâcle of the 1863 rising, with the subsequent intensified russification, served to clarify and polarise these incipient political tendencies. Needless to say the emancipation of the peasants in 1864 and the emergence of a working-class movement twenty years later put new actors on to the political stage, further complicating the question of nationalism versus socialism.

By the turn of the century Poland constituted a more politically heterogeneous entity than ever before, to the extent that during the 1905–6 revolution workers were known to have fought amongst themselves as well as against Russian troops.[5] On the eve of the First World War the main political alternatives to have emerged were the Anti-Russian Socialist (Piłsudski and the PPS), pro-Russian and anti-revolutionary (Dmowski and National Democracy) and the anti-nationalist revolutionary views of the SDKPiL (the forerunner of the Polish Communist Party).

The eighteenth and nineteenth centuries had provided the Polish intelligentsia with the major elements of its political memory, notably the 3 May constitution (1791), literary romanticism, exile and the independence struggle both cultural and military. Szacka[6] in her study of historical consciousness confirmed this, contrasting it with the more 'popular' interest in pre-partition and twentieth-century Poland. The dominant values she elicited referred to cultural achievements, the desire for a strong state and sound politics, all nourished by a deep-seated patriotism. Interestingly the evident popularity of the 3 May constitution, Poland's first real attempt at untrammelled parliamentary democracy, was not shared to the same degree by the youngest respondents in her survey (those born after 1931). They were also less moved by the values of tolerance and liberalism, than by the virtue of *struggle* against partition and occupation. The historical figures whom they honoured most were less political and more international, e.g. Copernicus, Marie Curie-Skłodowska, emphasising cultural-scientific achievements. It is striking that the younger generation were harsher in their assessment of the reasons for Poland's downfall focusing upon the demoralisation of the nation rather than the relative strength of the partitioning powers.

In Possart's study[7] the above general conclusions were restated except that she was able to show, not unexpectedly perhaps, that with increasing education there was a transition from a 'pride in Poland' complex of answers[8] (military might, examples of 'great power' status) to an analysis of the reasons for Poland's decline.

Poland rebuilt as an independent state in the aftermath of the First World War occupies a very special place in the national collective memory. Whilst supplying many examples of what were subsequently judged to be shameful political acts (e.g. the occupation of Zaolzie) it was nevertheless assessed by most respondents in Szacka's study as a positive episode characterised by genuine efforts of nation-building. Almost 25 per cent of Possart's sample, given the opportunity of choosing the historical period in which they would like to have lived, selected the inter-war period, this possibility being particularly attractive to the older respondents.[9] One has to conclude that despite the material and political shortcomings characteristic of the inter-war years, they are still viewed relatively favourably.

Little is written of the 'Forgotten War'[10] between Poland and Russia, settled after a fashion at Riga in 1921, although it considerably diminished the popularity of the Communists amongst both the radical intelligentsia and the working class of Łódź, Warsaw and the Dąbrowa Basin. Though various socialist measures were introduced in response to working-class militancy no coherent political system emerged and in 1925 the conglomeration of registered political parties (92 with 32 represented in the Sejm)[11] was making political life impossible. The May coup of 1926 and the introduction of Piłsudski's *sanacja* régime brought the short-lived parliamentary democracy to an end leaving, however, the March Constitution of 1921 as a residual memento for future generations to refer to, granting as it did basic civic freedoms. This interlude, however, did little to undermine the fundamental democratic ethos in Polish political culture, the best evidence of which was the participation in and the results of the municipal elections of 1938,[12] which signalled the emergence of more cohesive political groupings.

The year 1939 and the whole period of Nazi occupation, culminating in the tragic circumstances of the Warsaw uprising of 1944, is arguably

the most potent constituent of contemporary Polish historical consciousness. Included here are the role of the Home Army (AK), the
inactivity of Rokossowski's Red Army, the motives of the Provisional
Government in London in staging the Warsaw uprising, the Katyn
Wood murders, the Molotov-Ribbentrop pact. The list is endless and
its content explains the schizophrenic posture of the Poles not just towards the Soviet Union but towards 'Germany' as well. Data available
on evaluations of past military exploits reveal that glorious episodes of
the last war were cited by twice as many respondents as those of all
previous wars combined.[13] Significantly, but again not unexpectedly,
the Polish Army under Anders in the Western theatre was regarded as
more notable than the Polish army under Soviet general command,
and the battle at Monte Cassino was known to twice as many respondents as that at Lenino.

Post-war Poland emerged as ethnically more homogeneous, with
boundaries similar to those of a thousand years earlier. The Western
territories of Pomerania and Silesia, together with Mazuria and Warmia
in the east, became the symbol of a new national unity and consciousness. This unity withstood the Stalinist dark ages, the era of 'errors
and distortions' and 'intensification of the class struggle' culminating
in the Soviet-type constitution of 1952. Certain apparently irreversible
processes were, nevertheless, set in motion, notably the disenchantment
of the peasantry through the attempts at forced collectivisation and the
alienation of the intelligentsia through the latter's removal from active
and responsible participation in 'Socialist reconstruction'. The impact
of these years (1949–53) upon political culture is difficult to assess but
cannot be ignored. Several studies have indicated a severely estranged
minority in Polish society. Included amongst these would be the 19
per cent in Possart's study who anticipated a negative evaluation by
historians of the future of the first twenty years of post-war Polish
history.[14] Also we could look to the one-third of older respondents in
Nowak's[15] study in 1973 who believe that Poles possessed fewer valued
attributes than other nations. More concretely, Stalinism caused a
severe relapse in the delicate process of integration initiated in the Regained Territories.

(a) The attempts at forced collectivisation cut away a very powerful
    foundation for creating attachment to the region amongst the
    immigrants from beyond the Bug and reinforced the suspicions
    and experiences they had brought with them.
(b) Uneven industrialisation gave cause for searching questions about
    the 'unity' of Poland.
(c) But most important perhaps, the switch in official doctrine to
    'exaggerated internationalism' and the suppression of national-
    ism, allied with the emphasis upon the 'class struggle', did little

to nurture the embryonic bond of attachment to the newly settled lands in the West.[16]

The post-Stalin 'thaw' culminated in the 1956 disturbances centred in Poznań, the so-called 'Polish October'. Something of a repeat of this was enacted in Gdańsk and the northern seaboard in December 1970. Both events have acquired considerable significance since they represented *successful* demonstrations of working-class power. In each case the ruling group was at least reshuffled and during the following years care was taken to heed the demands articulated formally and informally by the 'leading class'. The further unrest in June 1976 in Radom, Płock and Warsaw served only to demonstrate publicly that party control at the shop-floor level has become a more complex and precarious activity than it was in the fifties and sixties. All this has given self-confidence to the Polish working class and, more important, has forced the 'intelligentsia' as well as the party to redefine its relationship to them.

### VALUES AND POLITICAL BELIEFS

From our examination of the imprint of history on contemporary Polish consciousness we have seen that values such as cultural and scientific achievements, military glory and self-criticism are widely found in Polish society. But a total belief system subsumes orientations to a wide range of issues apart from historical ones. For the past two decades Polish Social research has been highly advanced: for example, the Centre for Public Opinion Research (OBOP) has carried out an on-going evaluation of general political attitudes and expectations. We therefore have available a large body of data which reveal the Polish *Weltanschauung*. An outline of the principal findings will indicate the nature of current political beliefs.

### World outlook

Many surveys have been conducted of the Polish view of the world. Youth in particular has been a subject of extensive research, largely because it has been raised in a socialist society and should reflect quite distinct values of a political nature. Surveys carried out in 1958 and 1961 found that three-quarters of young respondents claimed they would risk their lives for the benefit of mankind, the family or the nation.[17] In 1960 young people were asked what matters they regarded as most important for the good of the world. By far the most common answer was the attainment of peace.[18] A survey taken in 1961 of interest in international affairs revealed that Polish-German relations and atomic disarmament were the two most common topics mentioned.[19] Both issues were related to the attainment of peace for Poland. A 1963 survey, carried out also in France and Norway, found the Poles to be most pessimistic about the chances of avoiding another war, of limiting the armaments race and of restricting destruction caused by another war.[20] The most commonly perceived threats to peace were the arms race, German remilitarisation and the Berlin impasse, and the statesmen most often considered to create world tension were Adenauer, Mao Tse-tung[21] and de Gaulle, while Khrushchev, Kennedy and U Thant were most frequently seen as reducing world tension.

Data collected in 1973 showed that in spite of increasing détente between East and West the concern over war had not diminished. School-children interviewed said that matters of most concern in the world today were wars, international conflicts and armaments.[22] From this wide range of data the conclusion we must draw is that the Poles, not surprisingly in view of their recent and not so distant past, continue to manifest a preoccupation with the problems of peace and security. In contrast, ideological issues such as class conflict, imperialism or economic exploitation do not enter into the discussion, particularly amongst the young.

Other surveys concerned with the Poles' world outlook have been reported by Siciński.[23] Two-thirds of respondents believed that only the great powers could influence world affairs. Although 42 per cent thought that Poland has greater influence on international matters now than before the war, 36 per cent said that she never has had any such influence. The survey also asked which nation had the friendliest relations with Poland. To those who visit both countries it comes as no surprise that 60 per cent of respondents mentioned Hungary and only 15 per cent cited the USSR.[24] That the United States was considered to be the wealthiest country and the one with greatest opportunities reflects the obsession that many Poles have with the United States, not unrelated, one would imagine, to the history of migration since the 1880s in search of work. The results taken together suggest a certain fatalism in the Polish belief system. The threat of war persists in the national consciousness. Germany is still regarded as a threat (media emphasis on the policies of the CDU, for example, reinforces this view).[25] Only a small proportion see Poland as carrying any weight in world affairs, hence perhaps the recourse to glorious moments in history as some kind of substitute. The findings imply a reluctant acceptance of *realpolitik* amongst Poles, especially of the younger generation.

## Political attitudes

Attitudinal surveys carried out between 1958 and 1973 have directly or indirectly examined the political orientation of respondents. The more specific manifestations of political attitudes, such as the disturbances in 1956, 1968 and 1970–71, are obviously not a subject broached in general questionnaires and we discuss these events separately in a later section. Here we look at the subjective political orientations of Polish citizens.

The first major study of political attitudes was carried out amongst Warsaw students in 1958.[26] The survey posed questions about fundamental political beliefs. Of students asked whether they considered themselves to be Marxists, approximately twice as many answered no as yes. Whilst 46 per cent of students from intelligentsia background said no (only 11 per cent said yes), the figure for students of working-class origin was 27 per cent (17 per cent said yes). These candid research findings cannot be attributed to dismay at the worst aspects of Stalinism, for at the time of the survey Gomułka was at the crest of his popularity. Rather, the results showed the general lack of popularity of Marxism as an imposed theoretical discourse.

That this is the case is shown by those results in the survey depicting widespread support for socialism, seen as an action-oriented programme. A majority or respondents agreed that the world ought to head in a socialist direction (53 per cent), and very few disagreed (7 per cent). A later survey found that nearly half of student respondents believed socialism would triumph throughout the world anyway.[27] Clearly students distinguished between Marxism and Socialism, regarding the former as abstract theory and the latter as a practical programme which ought to be applied universally. It would be interesting to know how these respondents felt ten years after the survey was taken.

In 1958 workers' councils were also viewed with much favour; an absolute majority of students replied that councils should manage the factories. But Nowak's research in 1973 found little support for developing various forms of self management.[28] Workers' councils appear to have been an integral aspect of the idealism generated by the Polish October, and in the more pragmatic climate of the 1970s they were easily dismissed, and as such only exist now in the rather artificial form of the Conference of Workers' Self-Management. To nearly half the 1958 student respondents socialism also signified greater egalitarianism: almost as many said that income differentials should be abolished as said they should remain. Nowak's 1973 research likewise found that nearly half of young respondents named *large* income differentials (even though based on qualifications obtained) as an undesirable feature of a good system, and very few considered it a desirable feature. If there is this marked egalitarian tendency amongst the young, it also must be pointed out that more meritocratic views are found amongst other social categories. Nowak showed that the best educated part of his sample stressed the retention of income differentials based on qualifications obtained. Koralewicz-Zebik's research in 1969 revealed that occupational categories affected respondents' views: engineers more than workers or craftsmen were concerned about high incomes (as well as professional qualifications).[29] Her conclusion was shared by Hoser, whose 1958 study of engineers found them to be very inegalitarian in their views.[30]

From this evidence we can conclude that there is a dominant egalitarian norm which has been internalised by a large part of society. But there is also a section of society which manifests inegalitarian views. The highly qualified, in particular the technical intelligentsia, are most likely to insist on income differentials. Such views are basically meritocratic: there is an acceptance that education and professional qualifications should be the criteria by which differentials are established. Moreover Nowak's research showed that there is a broad consensus, irrespective of social categories, that a good society should be characterised by equality of opportunity: three-quarters of respondents named equality of opportunity as the most desirable quality of a system, above freedom of speech. Egalitarianism, therefore, has been an important aspect of the Polish value structure, but whereas previously it was projected into the future, today it is rejected outright by those with higher education. Furthermore it could be argued that where egalitarian demands are voiced, particularly by the working class, it signifies a desire for *reduced* differentials, the elimination of wealth in the private sector, etc., rather than the discarding of differentials altogether.[31]

Results of Nowak's 1958 and 1973 surveys were similar in a further respect. In each case only about one-quarter of respondents thought that it was *im*permissible under any circumstances for the state to limit civil rights. Amongst Warsaw youth however this category represented 37 per cent of respondents. The father's level of education seemed to have a significant influence on how parents and youth replied to the question concerning suspension of citizens' rights.

The lower the educational level the more likely were respondents to see such suspension as permissible with the exception that the most *liberal*, i.e. those who could not permit such suspension under *any* circumstances, came from the families where father had *secondary* education only. Interestingly enough, this group were also most in favour of diminishing income differentials.

Nowak's 1973 research also provided evidence that there was also significant support amongst adult respondents for citizen obedience to government dictates and even great support, particularly amongst the young, for the state ownership of industry. Opposition to the view that a strong central power ought to decide all major issues was also not as great as one might expect (less than a third saw this as an undesirable feature of a political system). On the other hand, countering this statist orientation was a pronounced commitment to political freedom. *After* equality of opportunity and reasonable living standards came freedom of speech and a chance to influence government decisions, although these last two opinions were significantly less pronounced amongst parents than youth.

The data suggest a tendency to value strong government and obedience as well as individual freedom. The popular stereotype of the Pole, therefore, as a defender of individualism and liberty needs to be modified. He may well value liberty more than most other qualities, but he may also be attracted to strong government which he regards as security after Poland's experience under the partitions. Particularly amongst the still sizeable though decreasing peasantry, state direction is being regarded more favourably than previously. For example, the status of state farms has increased in the minds of the peasantry over the last decade. A larger number of peasants see the future of Polish agriculture in state farms and fewer see it in individual smallholdings (Table 4.1).

TABLE 4.1: The peasantry's view of the future of Polish agriculture

|  | *1959* | *1969* |
|---|---|---|
|  | % | % |
| (a)  in individual smallholdings | 49 | 18 |
| (b)  in individual smallholdings which co-operate closely with state institutions (such as agricultural circles) | 24 | 24 |
| (c)  in collective farms | 2 | 10 |
| (d)  in state farms (PGR) | 6 | 17 |
| (e)  no opinion | 19 | 22 |
| (f)  no response | 0 | 9 |

Source: W. Adamski, *Chłopi i przyszłość wsi* (Warsaw, 1974) pp. 141–54.

So far we have suggested that Polish political values are characterised by a certain fatalism towards world affairs, a general commitment to equality of opportunity and a combination of statism and individualism. Evidence on the self-perceived political efficacy of Polish citizens is disparate but it can help develop our composite of the existing political belief system. Surveys in 1961 and 1963 found equal support for the views that the economic and political élite alone determines foreign policy, and that society occasionally has influence where political democracy exists.[32] About one-third of respondents most often cited governments as the decisive agency influencing historical development but 20 per cent (even more amongst party members) mentioned societies. These results (apart from confirming that many Poles do not see historical development in Marxist terms) point out a relatively low sense of political efficacy in the foreign policy-making sphere. Nowak's research also revealed a sense of political inefficacy amongst older respondents but the pattern was reversed amongst the young: 60 per cent claimed it was possible to change the world. On the other hand an absolute majority of both generations said that individuals should intervene in societal affairs, even at personal risk. Different results were obtained, therefore, for normative and prescriptive evaluations of socio-political efficacy: possibilities for influencing events were considered limited but there was still an imperative to try.

## Social problems

Public perceptions of the problems encountered in contemporary Polish society can be a particularly revealing aspect of the analysis of political culture. It is a subject which comes as close as mass opinion surveys can come to identifying widespread discontent felt in society. The relevant Polish data focus once again on the opinions of youth and in some cases adults on perceived social ills.

A survey in 1963 asked its sample what it felt ought to be done with money saved if disarmament was brought about. By far the most common answer was that living standards should be raised.[33] Data obtained in 1971 also showed that an improvement in living standards was overwhelmingly considered by respondents to be the most important task facing the country.[34] Surveys taken in 1966 and 1971 revealed a similar concern with material questions: housing, education, employment and provision of consumer goods were items most frequently mentioned.[35] But nearly all respondents in the 1971 survey agreed that living conditions had improved markedly in post-war Poland, and most believed that opportunities for upward mobility and better education had increased. We can note, therefore, that a revolution in expectations (particularly amongst the young) has outpaced the material improvements achieved. Taken together with the fact that most of the employed population are at a stage in their lives when aspirations are being shaped, this could have severe consequences in the not too distant future.[36]

Research carried out in the 1970s by Gołembiowski, Jundziłł and Nowak produced similar results on the identification of negative aspects of Polish society.[37] Gołembiowski's findings are typical. Dysfunctional factors retarding the development of the country were thought to be lack of respect for public property (47 per cent of respondents), bureaucracy (36 per cent), favouritism and cliquism (31 per cent), alcoholism (26 per cent), suppression of criticism (23 per cent), apathy or indifference (22 per cent), poor quality of work (18 per cent), and uninformed people in top positions (17 per cent). These general themes centred on personal faults in administrative officials and in the public generally. Incorrect ideology or political direction was not given as a reason hindering Poland's development. The author concluded that the present generation of youth was the first in Poland to attribute problems of economic development and social achievement to shortcomings in people and society, and not to the system of government. Even so, systemic shortcomings such as bureaucratisation figured more highly in the assessments of youth than personal faults such as drunkenness, bribery, poor work discipline, most often referred to by adult respondents.[38]

The pattern of responses could reflect that of any industrial society and not necessarily a socialist one (although in the case of Poland the two are mutually reinforcing).[39]

*Religion and morality*

There can be no controversy over the statement that Poland remains in essence a Catholic nation, although 'laicisation' has been shown to have occurred since 1958. Data presented in Table 4.2 show only a minority of respondents claiming to be non-believers in the Nowak 1973 study, thus confirming the results of an earlier study in 1966 which examined 3167 urban *and* rural residents. Just as few atheists were reported in a study of socialist youth organisation members, and Fiszman found that in many cases the young appeared to be most religious.[40] But the fact that Poland is Catholic has been used to make many a claim which is a *non sequitur*, for example, that the Poles are thereby not committed to socialism. Catholicism and socialism are seen as irreconcilable principles, with an admission of being one acting as an automatic repudiation of the other.

TABLE 4.2

| How would you describe your attitude to religious beliefs? | Parents | Youth |
|---|---|---|
| 1. Ardent believers | 8 | 5 |
| 2. Believers | 55 | 43 |
| 3. Undecided | 10 | 19 |
| 4. Non-believers | 15 | 14 |
| 5. Decidedly non-believers | 10 | 17 |
| 6. Lack of response | 3 | 1 |

Source: S. Nowak *et al.*, 'Ciągłość i Zmiana . . .', p. 231, Table 16.1. These results refer to Warsaw, which is more secularised than other urban areas of Poland.

What this view ignores is the complexity of any belief system, whether religious or ideological. Thus many Catholics in Poland readily embrace the radical social and economic objectives of socialism, but disagree with its philosophic and theological foundations.[41] Since the first aspect is by far the more practical, the importance of the areas of disagreement in real life is minimal. The Church does provide an alternative focus of identification although the role of the Church establishment in political life is a separate question. It can and does act as an opposition party on various issues, but it does so less out of outright rejection of socialist policy (except in so far as the state attempts to carry out the philosophical tenet that religion will eventually disappear and ought to be helped on its way), as out of a consideration for practical politics: the Church wishes to extend its own power base in society.

The conflict between church and state in Poland, as in many European countries in the past, often has nothing to do with principles, only with *realpolitik*. The millennium celebrations of 1966 provided one of the keenest confrontations between the two sides. A more recent example occurred in May of 1976 with Cardinal Wyszyński's references to proposed constitutional amendments which he believed could have brought about certain disadvantages for religious believers. At about the same time he also espoused publicly the cause of the private landowning peasant, an obvious source of Church strength in Poland.

We can see three levels at which Catholicism functions in Poland. Firstly, there is the mass body of worshippers and believers who may also generally support socialist socio-economic objectives.[42] Secondly, there is the Catholic intelligentsia and political groups such as Znak and their Sejm representatives which try to bridge the gulf between Catholicism and socialism as action programmes. Thirdly there is the Church establishment, pursuing its own political as well as religious interests with all that that implies.

Related to religious and socialist practice is the question of social morality. Empirical evidence might indicate whether people's behaviour conformed to Christian or socialist ethics they claim to espouse. On the little reliable evidence available we can suggest that there was a tendency to attach greater value to behaviour which brought social rather than purely individual benefit.[43] But this proposition must await confirmation from future research into aspects of social morality.

## Political interest and participation

An examination of the political belief system of a nation would be incomplete without an assessment of general political interest displayed by citizens. But this is a subject difficult to analyse meaningfully in the Polish context. Much of the data relevant to political interest has limited value because it poses as many questions as it answers. For example, one

study found that between 30 and 40 per cent of manual workers read
Party newspapers and 46–53 per cent of non-manual employees read
Party papers.[44] But in both categories 85 per cent read non-Party
evening newspapers as well. Another example illustrates the problems
of interpretation. A 1970 survey of Kraków students found that, of their
declared outside interests, other forms of learning (13 per cent), sport
(13 per cent), music (12 per cent), literature (11 per cent) and travelling,
films and politics (each at 10 per cent) were the most common answers.[45]
One view of these results might be that interest in politics is very low.
On the other hand it could be argued that politics is a significant secondary activity after primary activities such as work, home, family and
recreation.

The most reliable research to date on political interest is an attitudinal survey administered in major industrial enterprises in the late
1960s. The findings showed that the more professional the socio-
occupational category of respondents the greater the likelihood of stating an interest in politics and ideology (Table 4.3). Likewise the more
educated the respondent the keener his political interest. In contrast
52 per cent of party members declared only a passing interest in politics
(8 per cent declared no interest at all).

TABLE 4.3: Declared interest in politics and ideology and socio-occupational
background (percentages)

| Degree of interest | Unskilled workers | Skilled workers | Clerical workers | Engineers and technicians | Total |
|---|---|---|---|---|---|
| Very interested | 18 | 25 | 27 | 48 | 29 |
| Slightly interested | 44 | 57 | 59 | 46 | 52 |
| Not interested at all | 37 | 18 | 14 | 7 | 19 |

Source: T. Gospodarek, 'Z badań nad kulturą polityczną w zakładach wielko-
przemystowych', in *Studia Socjologiczne*, no. 2 (1971).

One conclusion from the research is that the working class seems to
display least interest in state politics. Workers are generally not interested in broad questions of policy and ideology (such as this survey
involved). But they may be more enthusiastic about practical aspects
of politics, such as exerting their influence through workers' organisations in factories. Extensive research findings mostly published in the
early 1960s confirm this hypothesis, but the role of workers' self-
management institutions is too vast a subject to be examined here.[46]
Here we may suggest that politics, perceived as the activity of politicians and the national and local institutions of the government and
party, and ideology, seen as the principles of Marxism-Leninism, are

generally regarded with distinct lack of enthusiasm amongst the less educated sectors of society.[47] Even in such a stratum of the intelligentsia as teachers, however, politics may not be viewed with much interest.[48]

Political interest may be reflected in the extent of public participation in the political life of the country. Here too we require careful interpretation of data. Voting figures show a high turnout, but it is also thought that 80 per cent of people vote without marking the ballot.[49] Party membership is nearly two and a half million, youth organisations record a similar number and trade unions claim over eleven million members. But much of this membership is purely formal and the party has had to conduct verification campaigns (as in 1971 and 1975) in an attempt to eliminate apathetic members. Motives for joining have been suspect: 60 per cent of a sample in one survey gave careerist reasons as the motivating factor for *other* people becoming political activists,[50] although in the confusion of meanings hidden behind the label 'careerism' there is material for a whole book! Only 10 per cent named ideological considerations. It would be hazardous, therefore, to propose a participatory ethos in Polish society based on data on *formal* political involvement.

Wiatr's detailed study of local political culture found in fact that the public did not attach primary importance to participation in the political process.[51] A far more important consideration was the extent of autonomy enjoyed by local institutions. Factors which disinclined the public to value participation higher were the generally low level of conflict in the political process, the stable rotation of local leaders and the fact that these leaders were usually drawn from outside the state apparatus (that is, from the Party) in which participation would normally occur. This should not lead to what seems to be the inevitable conclusion, namely the lack of a participatory ethos in the Polish political belief system. Our knowledge of the 1938 municipal elections and the controversial referendum and elections of 1946 and 1947 indicate a profound respect for the ballot box.

POLITICAL KNOWLEDGE

The level of political knowledge of Polish citizens is also a subject fraught with methodological difficulties. It is not so much that research findings are prone to differing interpretations as that researchers have not asked illuminating questions.[52] Our assessment must perforce focus on the reliability of the channels of information rather than on attitudinal surveys.

In Poland nearly half of all newspapers sold are published by the Party but the evening non-Party press is the more popular and is often sold out. This is the first characteristic of the press, that limits are set on the number of copies published, and newspapers with a high readership are continually appealing to the authorities for an increased output.[53] This does not mean, of course, that the political information presented in non-Party newspapers is more candid than that in the Party press. It simply means that the public prefer newspapers with less political information altogether.

There have been no recent examples of bold radical newspapers such as *Po prostu, Nowa Kultura* and *Przegląd Kulturalny*, which flourished in the early years under Gomułka until the final one was banned in 1963. The weekly *Polityka* is officially not subject to control by the Chief Press Control Office, and its content contains a mixture of strong social criticism and political orthodoxy. In the Communist states self-censorship is as important a mechanism of control as individual censors attached to each publication. By all accounts the censors are young, well-educated and well-paid officials who do not conform to the popular stereotype of long-serving *apparatchiki* who are unable to read between the lines. Not all censors follow the same set of instructions and an article unacceptable in a popular publication may appear in a smaller-circulation journal.[54] Censors are willing to bargain with editors and contributors, and one social scientist describes how a censor once advised: 'Please submit this article in the summer. Comrades Kliszko, Werblan and Wróblewski will be on vacation.'[55]

Journals in the social sciences are always potential transmitters of information embarrassing to political authorities. Under Gomułka the social scientist was advised: 'Don't touch the government and the government won't touch you.'[56] Nevertheless the most enlightening of all sociological periodicals, *Studia Socjologiczno-Polityczne,* ceased publication after the 1968 intellectual disturbances. In 1975 an issue of *Problemy Rad Narodowych* (a journal containing empirical research with far wider implications than purely local government) was confiscated. All in all the fortunes of publishing freedom remain, as always, subject to startling vacillations.

The Poles, however, are not deprived of sources of political information independent of the official line. For the reader of a foreign language the press of other nations is available to him at branches of the International Press Club. Generally the much respected BBC broadcasts as well as the more propagandist Radio Free Europe may play a valuable role in providing essential information. More important is the existence of one of the largest emigré groups in the world. Estimates vary as to the size of *Polonia* (Poles resident outside the country) but ten million is a commonly ascribed figure (of which only one million live in other Communist-bloc countries, predominantly in the USSR). If, therefore, nearly one in every four Poles live in the West (over six million in the US alone, although how 'Polish' they are is an open question) then family contacts, whether by letters, newspaper cuttings or personal visits, are bound to divulge many facts about Western countries and about Poland herself. In any case most Poles know a lot about Western countries,[57] and the knowledge can only have been increased by the doubling of the number of Poles visiting the West between 1970 and 1974.

We must also not underestimate the valuable role in purveying frank political information played by rank-and-file Party members. Price increases, meat deliveries, even political manoeuvering within the top echelons are known in advance by many citizens with astonishing regularity. Ordinary Party members still display greater loyalty to family and friends than to top Party officials, and are willing to divulge confidential information where it is of some social value. This informal network has given Warsaw almost a 'small town' flavour, but it also makes the public susceptible to rumour and misinformation.

It is not possible to say whether official opportunities for political knowledge have increased within Poland since 1970, when genuine efforts to improve information and introduce meaningful discussion were made. In 1972 the Politburo passed a regulation encouraging greater press discussion of controversial issues, but in 1975 the same exhortation was still being made.[58] One could not detect any dramatic change in the content or style of press reporting compared to the 1960s. But generally the difficulty of acquiring political knowledge can be over-emphasised. Opportunities to become informed are officially regulated but if the public show little interest in formal politics then this must be regarded as the most important factor affecting political knowledge.

FOCI OF IDENTIFICATION

One of the running debates in intellectual circles in Poland since the war has been whether the extreme identification of citizens with the nation is desirable in a country constructing a socialist system. The controversy centred on the claim made in the immediate post-war period that the Poles had to disown their romantic tradition of heroism and become much more pragmatic in politics. Discussion was revived with publication of Załuski's *Siedem polskich grzechów głównych* in 1962, in which he contended that the traditions of heroism and military glory were valuable ones.[59] Bromke has given a detailed account of the debate based on Załuski's thesis and he concluded that currents of political realism and of political idealism (weaker since the war) continue to exist in Poland.[60] But the general consensus in Poland on Załuski's book (supported personally by Gomułka) was that for identification and loyalty to socialism to develop, the romantic model had to be replaced by the pragmatic one.[61]

But it could be argued that Poland's romantic tradition and her strong nationalist values actually helped promote the popularisation of socialist values.[62] Whereas in Western Europe nationalism was thought to have been a form of class domination, in Eastern Europe this was not true because of the part played by foreign political and economic domination. In Poland in particular the development of distinct élitist (whether aristocratic or bourgeois) and mass political cultures did not go as far as in Western Europe, largely because of the integrating function performed by nationalism (noted in our historical introduction). Consequently it was easier to reduce the gap between élitist and mass political values upon the Communist takeover.

Rawin has argued that there was a basic ideological compatibility of gentry and intelligentsia values on the one hand, and socialist doctrine on the other. Both were characterised by anti-capitalist, anti-bourgeois and egalitarian tendencies.[63] We can say, therefore, that dominant Polish nationalist values are at least not incompatible with socialist norms. But certain national traits do collide with those desirable under a socialist system. Phenomena such as political brinkmanship and a degree of anarchy continue to exist in post-war Poland. The 1970 riots showed that political action was still prone to take spontaneous and violent forms. Attitudes towards work (as the survey data revealed) still leave much to be desired.[64] Amongst bureaucrats of peasant origin, in particular, work attitudes are rather undisciplined. The peasant's lack of concern for time, his stress on hierarchy and his attachment to the autonomous smallholding have transplanted themselves into certain pathological activities amongst bureaucrats of peasant origin.[65] The tendency to retreat into conscious passivity at a time of crisis or opposition is another characteristic of these bureaucrats which results in further distortions.

Elsewhere we can see that the changes in Poland's geographical position were accompanied by a long process of transformation in the social consciousness of Poles. Territorial ambitions had always been directed towards the east and the Jagiellonian legacy. Little attention was paid to the legacy of Chrobry and the Piast dynasty in the west. Only after the acceptance (which may still not be total) after the war of the loss of the eastern territories (*kresy wschodnie*) was interest aroused in making up these losses in the west. The population which was re-settled from the east, however, was far less ready to adapt and identify with its new home than the re-immigrants from Western Europe or the settlers from crowded central Poland. The eastern settlers nourished hopes that the 'London government would appear and they would return beyond the Bug'.[66] There was controversy over the relative quality of the new land and its raw materials compared to the eastern land. Many felt it was not as rich. Most importantly the majority of these resettlers had had first-hand experience of Soviet collectivisation and were instrumental in nurturing the anti-collectivist attitudes which emerged during the late forties and early fifties.

The delicate process of historical re-education was hampered by the other vagaries of Stalinism. Much of the damage was repaired by the Polish October and the enormous amount of attention lavished on the western territories (with Gomułka leading the way). The continuing repatriation of remaining Germans has increased the immigrants' sense of security.[67] Autochthonisation was achieved in the end, however, through education.[68] The conviction was instilled that post-war territorial changes represented a return to historically Polish land and that in spite of germanisation and occupation there had been a continuity of Polish traditions in these lands.

An examination in detail of the development of Polish consciousness in the western territories would clearly portray the problems that lack of a sense of national identification and loyalty can pose for the Communist system. Society in other parts of Poland was willing in large part to tolerate mistakes committed under the new order and assist in post-war reconstruction that the transplanted population were less wont to. Only through a gradual process of education and political socialisation was the resistance overcome.

### POLITICAL CULTURE AND POLITICAL CHANGE

In our discussion so far we have tried to depict the important elements of Polish political culture since the war. But our analysis would be incomplete if we did not consider the ramifications of this political culture in political institutions, processes and policy and, in turn, their impact on the political culture. The period under Gierek is a particularly fruitful area of research into the interaction between political culture and institutional change.

The process of change in political attitudes between 1956 and 1970[69] from one of expectation and enthusiasm to one of disillusionment and revolt has been documented in several studies.[70] The political culture of the 1960s, which was characterised by an ever-greater alienation of individuals and groups within society from the institutions and processes of government, eventually catalysed in the 1970 disturbances in the seaports which had widespread support throughout Poland. The first year of the new leadership was concerned with political consolidation and soul-searching within society generally and within the Party in particular. Strikes continued after Gierek's accession to power and only his personal intervention in Szczecin and Gdańsk prevented a renewal of the troubles. An assurance that food prices would be frozen for two years partly appeased the workers, and promises of wage rises were also extracted. The power struggle in the Party had also to be resolved.

The slow process of eliminating opposition from Gomułka's followers and from the nationalist faction under General Moczar was initiated. This was not the time, in short, to attempt large-scale change in political institutions or in the political culture. An interim promise of a new style of political leadership was made and a substantive change in course was to be adopted at the next Party Congress.

The VI Congress, held in December 1971, planned the policies which the new leadership was to pursue for its first quinquennium. Much political change was recommended, not all of it was achieved. To a large extent the programme of reform was functional, aimed at applying Gierek's concept of a technocratic society. But the recommended policies were also designed to offset the hostile set of political beliefs and orientations that the public had developed towards the system in the 1960s. We saw the imposition of measures initiated as a result of pressure which were subsequently presented as policies – for example concern for the lower paid, and for some public debate on policy.

Perhaps the most ambitious measure of all was to draft a new constitution to replace the Soviet-style 1952 version. The constitutional draft was to reflect the changes in the social, economic and political order which had taken place in the last two decades. But the project ran into trouble almost immediately. Vested interests, especially the state bureaucracy, preferred the disadvantages of the existing constitution to the redistribution of power in a new one. More important was the opposition mounted to certain proposed sections of the constitution. An examination of the career of these key phrases in the new constitution is highly informative and the concern *publicly* voiced provides a picture in miniature of Polish political culture.[71]

Firstly there was concern as to who was involved in the discussion and drawing up of the draft constitution, since many Poles must have felt that they were presented with a *fait accompli*. Poland was designated as a Socialist state without any change in title from the original Polish Peoples' Republic. But rather than designating it as revolutionary in the 'October 1917' connotation it was explained that this referred to 'steps to be taken in the future', which had ominous implications for private agriculture since change had to be 'consonant with the socialist transformation for the countryside'. The PUWP was designated as 'the leading political force in society in the construction of socialism'. It was maintained that this was simply intended to underline the 'inspirational' role of the Party and was indeed a far less forceful formulation than that contained in the constitutions of other Communist states. Nevertheless the implication remained that anti-Party activity could now be construed as anti-constitutional and the formation of any otherwise legal opposition equally so.

The apology, that others had it worse, was also offered on possibly the most delicate of questions – the aim 'to strengthen friendship and co-operation with the Soviet Union and other socialist states'. Here the most timid objection made was, simply, need a country introduce principles of foreign policy into its constitution? Although the final format had diluted the original phrase referring to 'unshakeable fraternal bonds' with the Soviet Union, it was nevertheless felt that this was a one-sided alliance and could only be construed as a relinquishment of the prerogative of sovereignty regardless of any preamble which might make claims to the contrary.[72]

Although the press admitted that there was a lively discussion and recorded that 10 per cent of respondents in this debate were opposed to the changes, it is probable that the most vociferous objectors were the creative intellectuals, both Party and non-Party, and that the majority of the population was more concerned about the impending price rises in foodstuffs. What could cynically have been seen as simply introducing congruence between political reality and political statute obviously struck, however, at several neuralgic points in the traditional political culture and pointed to the precariousness of the overlap between the dominant and official political culture.

In one important respect the leadership could claim success. In 1973 the Party received for the first time legislative recognition of its directive programmatic role in society. This recognition was the logical outcome of Gierek's statement at the VI Congress that: 'We are the party of government and we must accept responsibility for all political life in the nation.' The Party would now publicly take responsibility for the economic management and political administration of the country and would not, as in the past, shift it to the governmental apparatus at a time of crisis. It was, however, something else to write it into the constitution.

In order for the Party to accept formal responsibility for policy, extensive reform had to take place within the Party structure so that it might become more responsive than previously. Two verification campaigns concerned with the exchange of Party cards took place after 1970, the first ones since 1958–59. They resulted in over 100,000 members being ousted from the Party, usually on grounds of political inactivity. The turnover of cadres after 1970 was great: nearly one-half of executive members of factory and base-level committees were elected for the first time in 1971. The number of manual workers on these committees was increased: for example, 37 per cent of provincial (*wojewódtwo*) executive committee members were manual workers in 1971 compared to 25 per cent in 1969.[73] Party members were also generally better qualified than previously: of the 49 new provincial party secretaries appointed in 1975 nearly all had higher education, predominantly as economists or engineers, and 36 of them were under 50 years old.[74] The social composition of the Party varied from place to place. In Warsaw in 1974, whereas only 10 per cent of manual workers belonged to the Party 22 per cent of non-manual workers were members. This included one-fifth of all engineers, one-quarter of teachers and one-third of the literary intelligentsia.[75]

The Party also gained much prestige from the personality of Gierek himself. Despite his attempts to suppress the development of a personality cult his direct contact with the strikers in 1971 and regular subsequent visits to major enterprises produced a popular image of an accessible, forthright and trustworthy leader. His managerial skills had already been proved as secretary of the Katowice industrial region. His successful visits to France and the US, where he was warmly received, were popularly interpreted with approval as confirmation that foreign contacts ought not to be confined to the Comecon bloc. Gierek's Silesian background symbolised to many the qualities of industriousness and technical advancement which he had campaigned so vigorously to implant in the whole of Polish society.

However, in June 1976 the Party was given a timely reminder that not even a popular leader providing increased standards of material well-being can permit himself the luxury of legislating by fiat on matters now considered to be central to the interests of the working class. Although the disturbances in Radom in 1976 were Szczecin 1970 in microcosm, they re-emphasised the increasing importance attached by all sections of Polish society to discussion and consultation with more access to information. That some real progress has been made in this direction was shown by the genuine demonstration of support for Gierek subsequent to the latest upheavals. Nevertheless, the adage, 'it's not what you do but the way you do it', seems singularly apt in this context.

Many institutional changes were made between 1971 and 1975. Local government was changed beyond recognition: the creation of 49 provincial authorities in place of seventeen in 1975 will have important implications for the distribution of power in both governmental and Party structures, for the control from above of 49 *quite* powerful Party secretaries is easier than that of seventeen *very* powerful secretaries. Certain new powers have been given to trade unions associated with a more vigorous labour code. In not all cases does the political culture appear to have been able to accept these drastic changes. For example, traditional attitudes of workers towards management persisted in spite of institutional reform: many trade unionists still expected to receive directives from management in matters for which factory councils were now responsible, and they considered the increase in the powers of these councils as a transitional post-1970 fad which would eventually disappear.[76]

This brief examination of change effected in political institutions has shown that since 1970 real reform has been carried out, in line with some of the values espoused by the leadership. In particular a threefold process of rationalisation, technocratisation (or polytechnisation, in Fiszman's terminology) and decentralisation (or increased local autonomy) has affected the various institutions. It is more difficult to say whether democratisation of decision-making has occurred.

At the same time, this institutional change was not easy to implement. It seems that entrenched interests have managed to hold up the process of reform. Possibly the bureaucrats in the central ministries, who have not seen the high turnover of cadres that took place in the Party apparatus, are responsible. On the other hand Hirszowicz has argued that lower levels of the state apparatus jealously guard their autonomy, and they are often responsible for sabotaging reform measures which would affect their position adversely.[77] There are signs that pressure for reform is subsiding. Already the resolutions prepared for the VII Congress indicate a less ambitious programme for 1976–80. For example, about one-third of investment is to complete projects already in progress, and the economy is to be geared more towards export than home production.[78] Material considerations, not least the large balance of payments deficit to the West, may well decelerate future moves in the direction of democratisation.

## Political socialisation and the socialist idea

The aim of creating a socialist man, the ideal member of a socialist society, is a very ambitious one. In theory the new man, brought up under socialised means of production, is attached to a materialist philosophy which excludes religious belief. His moral outlook is based on the need to subordinate his own interests to the general interest of society. In this respect participation in collective work can make the new man develop a proper moral relationship to other people. He is to be active, determining his own fate in life rather than having it determined for him as under capitalism. The new man is patriotic, working for the good of his own country, and he is internationalist, recognising that human values transcend nationalities. The socialist man is also characterised by discipline, a sense of responsibility, initiative and undogmatic thought.[79]

Under what conditions can socialist man develop? Obviously material conditions are primary: attitudes and values are a product of the objective conditions in which people live. According to Gramsci, however, a 'historical bloc', consisting both of material conditions and of social consciousness, can accelerate the process of transforming society into a socialist one.[80] The role of political institutions is also crucial. But their functioning is fraught with dangers that can retard the development of a socialist political culture. Thus according to Szczepański political institutions have also ideological and technical imperatives. Occasionally ideological goals (such as political socialisation) may be sacrificed in the interests of political necessity (for example, failure to collectivise agriculture) or efficiency (for example, a rational but not very democratic system of management). These decisions are based on the priorities of holders of political institutional power. The way in which various political institutions function is also likely to vary: post-1970 reform in the Party was governed by ideological and political considerations (the Party's directive role in society, regaining the confidence of the masses), but in the economic and administrative structures it was governed by criteria making for efficiency (one-man management). Political institutions also face dangers of goal displacement (as has happened in the state bureaucracy), or of lack of sufficient control over leaders (as occurred with Gomułka's inner cabinet of the Politburo).

Even a cursory appraisal of contemporary Polish society would reveal that the development of socialist man, socialist relationships in society and a socialist political culture – as set out in the foregoing account – are a long way off. The general lack of interest in politics and ideology expressed by survey respondents, their concern with non-ideological objectives in life, their indifference to productive work in the past all imply a lack of success in creating a political culture approximating the official one desired. To a great extent shortcomings in the functioning of the political institutions must be blamed for the lack of success.

Reaching a similar conclusion, Fiszman suggested that, since the socialist revolution in Poland had lost its momentum, 'the leadership may settle on mere "legal consciousness" [i.e. the acceptance of reality and acknowledgement of that reality's laws, however apathetically] rather than strive for the attainment of a "Marxist consciousness" among the masses (the internalisation of socialist values, norms, goals)'.[81]

We can agree with the second aspect of Fiszman's hypothesis that the institutional power structure is now less interested in infusing a socialist man ideal into the fabric of Polish society. But it does not follow that the authorities are willing to accept merely a legal consciousness amongst the masses.

Rather than the substitution of legal consciousness for Marxist consciousness, we see the development of a more popular kind of socialist consciousness which is not as over-arching and systematic as either philosophical Marxism or its official counterpart in Poland. Survey results showed that respondents desired socialist progress in the world, though they did not consider themselves Marxists, and were attached to equality (at least of opportunity) as a social value. Hirszowicz argued that there was a conflict between open Marxism (as she put it) and its official counterpart,[82] and Fiszman pointed out that malcontents in Polish society included those who took the socialist ideology seriously and were therefore inclined to judge harshly the reality which departed from the ideal.[83] Kołakowski succinctly summed up the issue: 'It is plain, if not notorious, that an ideology is always weaker than the social forces which happen to be its vehicle and try to carry its values.'[84]

What has happened in post-war Poland is that these social forces, having been mobilised to support the socialist idea (which has ranged from Stalinism and the Polish Road, to technocracy), have created a popular or everyday version of socialism. The events of 1968 and 1970 only strengthened the evolution of this popular socialism. The emergence of a more pragmatic leader obviously assisted the evolution. But the gap between the intelligentsia and the workers increased: the intelligentsia were in disarray after 1968, whilst the working class gained a greater sense of solidarity from the events of 1970–71, in which the intelligentsia were conspicuous by their absence. As a result of their earlier estrangement under Stalinism[85] the intelligentsia had come to exert very little influence on working-class thought. Hence the brand of socialist consciousness that emerged reflected most clearly the needs and aspirations of the socialist proletariat.

The idea of popular socialism subsumes the legal consciousness cited by Fiszman but it also signifies support for certain socialist principles popularised in the public mind. These include a commitment to egalitarianism on the part of the working class (and amongst the *technical* intelligentsia a commitment to meritocracy), as well as commitment to both state power and individual liberty, to patriotism and national self-determination, and to technical and economic progress. Popular socialism rejects capitalist means of production, international power politics and the suppression of information and debate. It is a pragmatic belief system rather than a total ideology, and although it cannot be elevated to scientific principles it is the way that Poles respond to political events.

NOTES

1   N. Assorodobraj, 'Żywa historia: świadomość historyczna, symptomy i propozycje badawcze', *Studia socjologiczne*, no. 2 (1963).
2   *Liberum veto* was the requirement of unanimity to permit the passage of laws through the Sejm. In practice it was used from 1652 and led to various ludicrous situations. Cf. J. Maciszewski, *Szlachta polska* (Warsaw, 1969).
3   H. Michałowska, *Salony artystyczno-literackie w Warszawie 1832–60* (Warsaw, 1974).
4   Organic work was the belief that economic strength was a prerequisite to national independence. As an ideology it was associated with Świętochowski and the Warsaw positivists in the post-1863 period. W. Modzelewski, 'Naród w teorii społecznej pozytywizmu warszawskiego', *Studia socjologiczne*, no. 4 (1973). Also W. Pobóg-Malinowski, *Najnowsza historia polityczna Polski*, vol. 1 (London, 1963) pp. 51–2.
5   A. Gieysztor *et al.*, *History of Poland* (Warsaw, 1968) p. 596.

6 B. Szacka, 'Zmiany w świadomości historycznej społeczeństwa polskiego', *Kwartalnik historyczny,* no. 2 (1973).

7 J. Possart, 'Niektóre elementy świadomości historycznej mieszkańców miast Polski współczesnej', *Studia socjologiczne,* no. 1 (1967). This was a questionnaire survey of 1811 adult urban inhabitants of varying social background.

8 A film version of the Battle of Grunwald has been showing *somewhere* in Poland, one suspects, almost continuously since its release in the mid-sixties.

9 There was also a very high correlation between those with the most negative attitude to the past and those expressing at the same time a desire to return to that past.

10 P. Wandycz, *Soviet–Polish Relations 1917–21* (Harvard, 1969) and Pobóg-Malinowski, op. cit., vol. 11. A 'forgotten war' in both East and West, although for different reasons.

11 A. Polonsky, *Politics in Independent Poland 1921–39* (Oxford, 1972) p. 52. See also J. Holzer, *Mozaika polityczna drugiej rzeczypospolitej* (Warsaw, 1974).

12 E. D. Wynot, Jr., *Polish Politics in Transition* (Athens, Georgia, 1974) pp. 234–235.

13 Battles regarded by respondents as the most glorious in Polish history were: those before partition (22 per cent), during partition (16 per cent), 1920 (1 per cent), 1939 (14 per cent), underground resistance (4 per cent), Warsaw uprising (8 per cent), battles of the People's Army (21 per cent), battles of the Western Army (25 per cent), battles of other nations (5 per cent). J Gesek, S. Szostkiewicz, J. Wiatr, 'Z badań opinii społeczeństwa o wojsku', *Studia socjologiczno-polityczne,* no. 13 (1962) p. 121.

14 In a survey of political attitudes amongst 'post-war' Poles carried out by Radio Free Europe, 17 per cent of persons with higher education would have voted conservative (as opposed to Social Democrat, Christian Democrat, etc.) in hypothetical elections in 1975. Although the percentage in general had dropped since 1968, this was a clear indication of an anti-government attitude on the part of an alienated minority. APOR Radio Free Europe, *Party Preferences in Poland 1968–75: A Trend study of hypothetical elections.*

15 S. Nowak *et al.,* 'Ciągłość i zmiana tradycji kulturowej', unpublished manuscript (University of Warsaw, 1974). A summary of the results has been published in *Polityka,* 10 April 1976.

16 M. Orzechowski, W. Wrzesiński, 'Przemiany terytorialne Polski po II wojnie światowej w świadomości społecznej', W. Markiewicz *et al., Przemiany w świadomości społecznej mieszkańców województw zachodnich i północnych w latach 1945–1970* (Warsaw, 1974) p. 25. 'In addition we concluded that the political pressures accompanying collectivization in the early 1950s were by far the most destructive force that adversely affected all components of the population in the Western areas. These political pressures disrupted the newly established social ties and considerably slowed down or reversed the stabilization process.' Z. A. Kruszewski, *The Oder–Neisse Boundary and Poland's Modernization* New York, 1972).

126    *Political Culture and Change in Communist States*

17  J. Wiatr, *Czy zmierzch ery ideologii?* (Warsaw, 1968) p. 208.
18  M. Szaniawska, 'Światopogląd młodzieży', OBOP, *Społeczeństwo polskie w badaniach ankietowych* (Warsaw, 1966) p. 58.
19  A. Siciński, 'Opinie o problemach międzynarodowych jako element współczesnej ideologii społeczeństwa polskiego', *Studia socjologiczne*, no. 2 (1966) p. 146.
20  A. Siciński, 'Peace and War in Polish Public Opinion', *Polish Sociological Bulletin*, no. 2 (1967) p. 32.
21  The Chinese fear (Sinophobia) is very marked in the average Pole – contrary to what might be expected – and together with the perceived German threat it has promoted dependence for security on the Soviet Union.
22  I. Jundziłł, *Aktywizacja wychowawcza młodzieży* (Warsaw, 1974) p. 236.
23  A. Siciński, 'Stereotypy krajów, narodów, mężów stanu', *Kultura i społeczenstwo*, no. 2 (1967) pp. 196–7.
24  Poles' sympathy for the Hungarians is founded on certain shared insurrectionary movements, for example in 1848 and 1956. The fact that the nations have no common border also contributes to harmony.
25  Thus in the 1970 disturbances use was made by Gierek and Jaroszewicz of the German threat (e.g. by referring to the views of Barzel); *Rewolta szczecińska i jej znaczenie* (Paris, 1971) p. 55.
26  S. Nowak, 'Środowiskowe determinanty ideologii społecznej studentów Warszawy', *Studia socjologiczne*, no. 5 (1962) pp. 143–79.
27  No respondent could foresee the triumph of capitalism. J. Jerschina, *Osobowość spoteczna studentów Uniwersytetu Jagiellońskiego chłopskiego pochodzenia* (Wrocław, 1972).
28  Nowak, 'Ciągłość i zmiana tradycji kulturowej'.
29  J. Koralewicz-Zębik, *System wartości a struktura społeczna* (Warsaw 1974).
30  J. Hoser, *Zawód i praca inżyniera* (Wrocław, 1970) chapters III and IV.
31  Although 'urawniłówki [levelling]' demands appear among workers at critical moments such as 1956 and 1970.
32  Siciński, 'Opinie o problemach międzynarodowych', pp. 154–5.
33  Ibid., p. 164. Allied to this attitude is the belief that fewer resources should be allocated to foreign aid, at least by Poland.
34  B. Gołembiowski, 'Młode pokolenie o sobie i swoich dążeniach', *Nowe Drogi*, no. 10 (1972) p. 149.
35  Gołembiowski, 'Młode pokolenie . . .', pp. 146–7; M. Kęsy, J. Wiatr, 'Wiedza obywatelska mieszkanców małych miast', B. Suchodolski, *Upowszechnianie nauki* (Warsaw, 1971) p. 105.
36  The average age of those employed full-time in the socialised economy was 35 years in 1973. *Rocznik Statystyczny 1975*, p. 56.
37  Golembiowski, 'Młode pokolenie . . .', pp. 149–51; Jundziłł, *Aktywizacja wychowawcza młodzieży*, p. 310; Nowak, 'Ciągłość i zmiana tradycji kulturowej'. That separate surveys should agree so strongly on youth's dislike of bureaucracy and passivity reveals the extent to which antibureaucratic values have been internalised.
38  Nowak, op. cit., p. 165.

39  Which, given Poland's agricultural-country status, is still some achievement.

40  W. Bieńkowski, 'Nieporozumienie pokoleń', *Kultura i społeczeństwo*, no. 4 (1961) p. 20; J. Fiszman, *Revolution and Tradition in People's Poland* (Princeton, 1972) pp. 196, 210. Nowak found that the family unit was the most important factor reinforcing religious views in the young. In these circumstances it is not surprising that the political authorities have made little headway in creating a materialist society. 'Ciągłość i zmiana tradycji kulturowej', pp. 231–8.

41  See T. Mazowiecki, *Rozdroża i wartości* (Warsaw, 1970); J. Zabłocki, *Na polskim skrzyżowaniu dróg* (Warsaw, 1972).

42  How deeply this mass body is committed to either religious or social objectives is debatable. In the survey of issues which were thought worth risking one's life for, both religion (given by 31 per cent of respondents in 1961) and a social ideal (30 per cent) came close to the bottom of the list. Wiatr, *Czy zmierzch ery ideologii?*, p. 208.

43  One study found that an absolute majority of respondents said they would obey work regulations because it would result in better-organised work, regarded as a concern for the collective good. Only one-tenth said that an incorrect regulation should not be obeyed, suggesting a high level of legalist attitudes. Violations of personal and state property were regarded as equally reprehensible, indicating that collective property was not valued in a different, 'socialist', light. M. Borucka-Arctowa, *Świadomość prawna robotników* (Warsaw, 1974) pp. 87–9. Siciński's findings in 1961 showed even greater respect for personal rather than public property. 'Postawy wobec pracy i własności oraz ich społeczne unwarunkowania', *Studia socjologiczne*, no. 2 (1961) p. 190. Another study found, however, that the importance attached to the collective good was greater in economic than in political matters. A. Podgórecki *et al.*, *Poglądy społeczeństwa polskiego na moralność i prawo* (Warsaw, 1971) pp. 89–90.

44  W. Bielicki, 'Niektóre elementy kultury robotniczej w świetle badań w wybranych środowiskach przemysłowych', *Socjologiczne problemy przemysłu i klasy robotniczej*, no. 2 (1967).

45  K. Gonet-Jasińska, 'Udział studentów w odbiorze kultury', *Studia socjologiczne*, no. 4 (1971) p. 103.

46  For an account of the political orientations of the working class in Poland see G. Kolankiewicz's chapter in D. Lane and G. Kolankiewicz (eds), *Social Groups in Polish Society* (London, 1973). Selected Polish sources are: S. Widerszpil, *Skład polskiej klasy robotniczej* (Warsaw, 1965); M. Hirszowicz, W. Morawski, *Z badań nad społecznym uczestnictwem w organizacji przemysłowej* (Warsaw, 1967); K. Ostrowski, *Rola związków zawodowych w polskim systemie politycznym* (Warsaw, 1970); W. Morawski, *Samorząd robotniczy w gospodarce socjalistycznej* (Warsaw, 1973); A. Matejko, *Socjologia Zakładu Pracy* (Warsaw, 1970).

47  Even general surveys indicate lack of interest in these areas of politics. For example, 40 per cent of respondents in a 1961 survey said they were not interested in information about the Sejm and local government (20 per cent said they were interested). Siciński, 'Opinie a problemach międzynarodowych', p. 143. In a 1969 survey 28 per cent of respondents

thought there was an excess of political reports in the daily newspapers (only 2 per cent thought there were not enough political reports). Z. Gostkowski, 'The Range and Direction of Bias in a Press Questionnaire', *Polish Sociological Bulletin*, no. 2 (1969) p. 120.

48   Fiszman found that only 9 per cent of teachers rated a citizen-related role as of primary importance. *Revolution and Tradition in People's Poland*, p. 220.

49   Z. Jarosz, 'Zmiana prawa wyborczego do rad narodowych', *Państwo i prawo*, no. 11 (1973) p. 29. Changing the order of candidates on the ballot paper, deleting names, etc., implies dissent, cf. n. 57.

50   J. Kulpińska, *Społeczna aktywność pracowników przedsiębiorstwa przemysłowego* (Wrocław, 1969) pp. 80–3.

51   International Studies of Values in Politics, *Values and the active Community* (New York, 1971) p. 282.

52   A current study, based on a national public opinion survey, by J. Wiatr and R. Siemieńska may provide a more illuminating picture of present-day Polish political culture. It is as yet unpublished.

53   Thus Bromke notes how *Tygodnik Powszechny*, the Catholic weekly, has been trying to have its edition increased from 40,000 to 50,000 copies. A. Bromke, 'Catholic Social Thought in Communist Poland', *Problems of Communism* (July–August 1975) p. 72.

54   J. Fiszman, 'Political Socialisation in People's Poland', *International Journal of Contemporary Sociology*, x, no. 1 (1973) p. 35. Generally self-censorship in popular publications leads to narrower limits being set than if an external censor had imposed his limits, and is therefore a more effective device.

55   S. Chodak, 'How was Political Sociology Possible in Poland?', *International Journal of Contemporary Sociology*, x, no. 1 (1973) p. 59. Two general accounts of the kind of controls imposed on the press are: A. Buzek, *How the Communist Press Works* (London, 1964); B. Michalski, *Prawo dziennikarza do informacji* (Kraków, 1974).

56   M. Hirszowicz, 'Marxism, Revisionism and Academic Sociology in Poland', *International Journal of Contemporary Sociology*, x, no. 1 (1973) pp. 40–52.

57   Thus Siciński reported a remarkably high level of political knowledge about international affairs. 'Opinie o problemach międzynarodowych', pp. 148–9. In contrast Gostkowski found nearly as many respondents did not know (39 per cent) as did know (44 per cent) what a basic voting device such as casting an unmarked ballot paper signified. 'Zainteresowanie wyborami do rad narodowych wśród ludności w Łodzi roku, 1958', *Studia Socjologiczne*, no. 2 (1961) p. 149.

58   Z. Andruszkiewicz, 'Kilka uwag o krytyce prasowej', *Nowe Drogi*, no. 4 (1975) pp. 87–91. One survey published in 1969 revealed that only 3 per cent of respondents praised one Party newspaper for its objectivity. Gostkowski, 'The Range and Direction of Bias . . .', p. 121.

59   Research carried out in 1966–67 at Kraków University confirmed the continued attachment to the heroic tradition: 72 per cent of respondents believed that there was a Polish national character. Positive elements of the heroic type were identified as bravery, perseverance and passion,

national pride, attachment to tradition, love of freedom, solidarity in crisis periods and idealism. Jerschina, *Osobowość społeczna* ...

60 A. Bromke, *Poland's Politics: Idealism vs Realism* (Harvard, 1967).
61 See F. Znaniecki, *Ludzie teraźniejsi a cywilizacja przyszłości* (Warsaw, 1974).
62 Lenin argued that the integration of nations (like the abolition of classes) would follow a transitional period of complete emancipation of individual nations. The ripening of nationalism would eventually allow nations to perceive not only their own identity but that of other nations, and it would encourage the development of an international community. V. I. Lenin, *Collected Works*, XXII (London, 1969) p. 147. Brzezinski has noted, however, that the nationalism found in Communist states has led to sectarian Communism rather than internationalism. Z. Brzezinski, *Between Two Ages* (New York, 1971) pp. 176–93. Nowak's research in Poland found that three-quarters of respondents still thought *patriotism* to be an important value ('Ciągłość i zmiana tradycji kulturowej').
63 S. Rawin, 'The Polish Intelligentsia and the Socialist Order', *Political Science Quarterly*, no. 3 (1968). Wiatr goes much further and argues that there is considerable overlap between the values rated highly by Poles and the values of a socialist culture, such as attachment to freedom, justice, autonomy and the readiness to defend these values courageously. See his various works: *Społeczeństwo, Polityka, Nauka* (Warsaw, 1973) p. 155; *Naród i Państwo* (Warsaw, 1973) pp. 382–4; *Polska – Nowy Naród* (Warsaw, 1971) pp. 114–36.
64 In the survey of Kraków students negative features identified in the patriotic type were laziness, egoism and excessive faith in other nations. Jerschina, *Osobowość społeczna* ...
65 W. Kiezun, *Autonomizacja jednostek organizacyjnych* (Warsaw, 1971).
66 See n. 16.
67 It must be remembered that German emigration from these territories began long before 1945. Between 1843 and 1944 over five million Germans left this area to increase their social status in central Germany. J. Kokut, *Logika Poczdamu* (Katowice, 1961) p. 139.
68 See M. Kutym *et al., Funkcja świadomości historycznej i efekty polityki oświatowej w procesach integracji* (Opole, 1974); W. Markiewicz, *Socjologia a służba społeczna* (Poznań, 1972).
69 We have ignored the period 1946–55 since understandably there was little reliable sociological research carried out in that time.
70 See N. Bethell, *Gomułka* (London, 1972); T. Cieplak, *Poland since 1956* (New York, 1972); A. Bromke, J. Strong (eds), *Gierek's Poland* (New York, 1973). For a case study of one alienated group, the *Ruch* movement, see *Sąd orzekł* (Paris, 1972).
71 For an indication of the problems involved see *Trybuna Ludu*, 23 January 1976, *Życie Warszawy*, 9 February 1976, and *Kultura* (Paris) no. 1–2, 3, 1976.
72 Unpublished open letter by W. Bieńkowski, March 1976.
73 *VI Zjazd Polskiej Zjednoczonej Partii Robotniczej* (Warsaw, 1972) p. 73. There had been an extensive purge of manual workers in the Party under Gomułka: of over 900,000 recruited between 1960 and 1970, 247,000

were removed in the same period. E. Babiuch, 'O niektórych problemach rozwoju i umacniania partii', *Nowe Drogi*, no. 9 (1971) p. 9.

74   'Kto jest kto w 49 województwach', *Polityka*, no. 25 (21 June 1975).

75   B. Porowski, 'Metody pracy nad rozwojem szeregów partyjnych', *Nowe Drogi*, no. 12 (1974) p. 129.

76   W. Adamski, 'Związki zawodowe – twórczym czynnikiem rozwoju budownictwa socjalistycznego', *Nowe Drogi*, no. 9 (1971) pp. 23–4.

77   In Hirszowicz's mixed organisational model she identifies a fundamental contradiction between political power monopolised by the leadership and a certain degree of autonomy of local organisational units. This leads to chaos and paralysis in the overall structure. M. Hirszowicz, *Komunistyczny Lewiatan* (Paris, 1973) ch. iv.

78   Z. Szeliga, 'Zmiana warunków', *Polityka*, no. 38 (20 September 1975).

79   J. Szczepański, *Odmiany czasu teraźniejszego* (Warsaw, 1973) pp. 313–15.

80   A. Gramsci, 'Wstęp do studiów nad filozofią i materializmem', *Prisma wybrane*, 1 (Warsaw, 1961) p. 48.

81   Fiszman, 'Political Socialisation in People's Poland', p. 27.

82   Hirszowicz, 'Marxism, Revisionism and Academic Sociology in Poland'.

83   Fiszman, 'Political Socialisation in People's Poland', p. 33.

84   Kolakowski continues: 'There is no reason to believe that the restoration of the perfect unity of the personal and communal life of every individual . . . is possible and, least of all, that it could be secured by institutional means.' L. Kolakowski, 'The Myth of Human Self Identity', L. Kolakowski, S. Hampshire (eds), *The Socialist Idea* (London, 1974) pp. 26, 32.

85   A. Borucki, *Kariery zawodowe i postawy społeczne inteligencji PRL 1945–1959* (Wrocław, 1967).

# 5 Hungary: An Uneasy Stability

## GEORGE SCHÖPFLIN

The modern history of Hungary can be said to have begun with the 1867 *Ausgleich* (compromise) between the Hungarian gentry and Vienna, whereby the Hungarians were granted complete self-government. It was during the k.u.k. period – the abbreviation for *königlich und kaiserlich* (Royal and Imperial) used to denote the Austro-Hungarian system – that the beginnings of a modern economy were laid down and that the political system began to emerge from late feudalism. With the defeat of Austria-Hungary in 1918, the Hungarian state was stripped of three-fifths of its territory and over half its population, a sizeable portion of which was ethnically Hungarian.

Defeat was followed by the collapse of the social order, first with the creation of a radical democratic and then a Communist government, to be followed by a neo-feudalist restoration under Admiral Horthy. The Horthy government joined the Axis powers to regain some or all of the territories lost in 1918 and Hungary was again on the side of the defeated in 1945, this time with the difference of having suffered almost total disruption through the Hungarian Nazi Arrow Cross coup of 1944 and the Soviet conquest that followed. Free elections were held in 1945 and the centre and centre-right Smallholders won an absolute majority, but ruled in coalition with other more left-wing parties including the Communists. The last gradually forced all the other parties out of power and established a political monopoly by 1948–9. The Stalinist terror under Mátyás Rákosi was followed by the failed revolution of 1956 and the gradualist consolidation supervised by János Kádár who has successfully stabilised the country and promoted a fair measure of prosperity.

### PERCEPTION OF HISTORY

The factors that dominate the Hungarians' view of their history are the continuity of the Hungarian state, the dominant role of the Hungarian 'nation' (however defined) within that state and the repeated attempts by external and internal enemies to destroy the state and subjugate it. Although the nineteenth-century nation was quite different from the medieval *natio* that had formed the ruling élite before the

Ottoman conquest in the sixteenth century, Hungarians of the modern period automatically identified the one with the other and thereby created the integral nationalism of the 1848 revolution and after.[1] In essence, this was a claim that all the inhabitants of the Crownlands of St Stephen were members of the Hungarian nation and must, therefore, be ethnically Hungarian. If they were not, then they would have to be assimilated.

The struggle to maintain the continuity of the state left behind another legacy, the inclination towards legalism and legal fictions that has to some extent persisted. This can sometimes be seen as expressed in a preference for form over substance and, equally, in the adherence to outdated forms – the inter-war period of the 'Kingdom without a King' was only the most striking of these. At a lower level, the persistence of a great deal of litigation until the present day has been remarked on by several observers.[2]

The legacy of struggle against perceived external encroachments has affected the Hungarian political tradition by making it to some extent acceptable that Hungary should be within the ambit of a great power, whilst simultaneously generating resentment at the fact. National independence has been an idealised goal, but *de facto* subordination – whether to Vienna after 1867 or Moscow after 1948 – is tacitly tolerated.

On the other hand, regardless of this tacit acceptance of subordination, Hungarians retain a strong sense of their national or ethnic uniqueness – felt most obviously in the isolation of their Finno-Ugrian language – and in parallel with that an insecurity about their survival as a nation. This insecurity, fear of extinction, is particularly noticeable among the intelligentsia and the sense of isolation can be found among broader strata as well.[3] It has been intensified by the circumstances of the dissolution of the historic Kingdom of Hungary in 1918–20 and the anxiety about the existence of national-Hungarians on the borders of Hungary but outside the Hungarian state. This insecurity, in turn, has enabled political leaders to mobilise opinion on the national issue through slogans both of 'national regeneration' and of 'threats to the nation'. Insecurity of this kind has permitted political leaders to pursue policies on an 'emergency' basis, to maintain mobilisation in the face of perceived threats.

*Previous political experience*

The pre-Communist attitude towards the state and the ambit of state power was generally to accept them as far broader than their equivalents in Western Europe. The proper role of the state was seen as having a wide function in society as supervisor, arbiter, entrepreneur and initiator. This was particularly striking in the economic field, in that virtually all large-scale investment, like the railways, was at all times carried out by the state or occasionally by individuals in collaboration with the state.[4] Large-scale social engineering and modernisation, as under Joseph II, were initiated by the state, usually against local resistance. In the political sphere, the discretionary power of the state was never challenged by any group in society and it was noteworthy that governments were never overthrown through a vote in parliament. The state created a bureaucracy to maintain and extend its power and succeeded in co-opting a substantial section of the gentry and neo-gentry into its service.[5] In essence, both the k.u.k. and neo-k.u.k. systems in Hungary were étatist authoritarian régimes with a constitutional façade. The constitutional controls that may have existed in theory were never exercised, given that no social group had the power or even necessarily the aspirations to do so. This system and the values generated by it were readily carried over into the post-war Communist system, which benefited particularly from the tradition that modernisation was a prerogative of the state.

In parallel with this, Hungarian society, especially in the neo-k.u.k. period, was characterised by a good deal of violence and arbitrary action. The revolution and counter-revolution of 1918–20 were both marked by the use of terror, and during the inter-war period the agents of the state (like the gendarmerie) ensured that no 'dangerous' opponents of the state were elected to parliament. Rural violence, both ritual and casual, was extensively chronicled by the 'Village Explorers' group of the 1930s. The wartime dispossession of the Jews and their partial annihilation served to habituate large sections of society to violence against a particular segment of itself.[6]

State procedures were complex and bureaucratic, making it relatively straightforward to manipulate them in the personal interest of office-holders. Regulations were seldom adhered to, whether by the bureaucracy or those otherwise affected. Nepotism, influence, 'protection' were all characteristic of the operation of the system, as was peculation. The degree of political literacy was necessarily low, given that large sections of society, like the peasantry and much of the urban proletariat, were disenfranchised. The practice of discretionary power was inherently hostile to the emergence of an informed public opinion.

The neo-k.u.k. tradition was thus created and preserved by the ruling élite in the inter-war period, despite efforts by both the left and the right to effect fundamental changes. The dominant features of this tradition, which survived largely intact until 1944, did, therefore, include a certain respect for legality and institutional politics, even if the procedures appropriate to both were frequently dishonoured.[7] The Hungarian parliament continued to be the focus of formal and to some extent substantive political activity, even while politicians secured their control by 'making' elections in the interests of the single, dominant 'government' party on the basis of a completely unrepresentative electorate and open balloting in the countryside. The 'government' party of the neo-k.u.k. period went through several changes of name, but essentially it remained the same all-encompassing political organisation dominated in the 1920s by István Bethlen and in the 1930s by Gyula Gömbös. Both the Smallholders' Party that emerged as the majority party in the 1945 elections and the Communists who remained the sole political party after 1949 had a resemblance to the neo-k.u.k. 'government' party. Trade union activity was legal in the inter-war period, but only in urban areas and even there it was regularly exposed to police supervision and harassment. The courts and the administration operated on the whole without departing excessively from their ostensible remit, but they were open to political influence.[8] The press too was relatively free and the strong tradition of political debate was never totally suppressed, even if limits to oppositional activities were recognised. This system of managed semi-democracy or diluted dictatorship survived in virtually the same form until Admiral Horthy was removed by the Arrow Cross coup in October 1944. This was followed by the collapse and when the reconstruction began in early 1945, a wide range of hitherto suppressed social interests had the strength to influence the direction of the reconstruction. While the events of 1944–45 marked one of the numerous caesuras in Hungarian history, it was clear that there was a good deal of agreement on the need for a thorough transformation on the basis of what was worth keeping in the old system.

There was no rejection, for instance, of parliamentary democracy. On the contrary, the elections of 4 November 1945 demonstrated both a readiness to accept major changes and the desire to keep them within the familiar framework. Freedom of the press was immediately re-established and while the old administrative apparatus had disintegrated during the collapse, a new one, building on the personnel and traditions of the old, was rapidly created. The physical rebuilding of the war-shattered country was obviously seen by all sections as the first priority, but there was wide consensus over the other objectives as well, notably land reform, stabilisation of the currency and the nationalisation of large-scale industry. In this sense, there was broad agreement over creating a more equitable society. By and large, there was no dissent from the need to implement this transformation, from the methods to be used, from the institutional framework and from the procedures to be followed by those institutions.[9] These factors in the neo-k.u.k. tradition made for a certain stability in Hungarian political culture, inasmuch as there were recognised procedures and institutions; but there were serious factors of instability likewise in existence.

The limping nature of the institutional framework under the old order to some extent discredited the institutions themselves and some groups, like the newly legalised Communist Party, were prepared to act outside the framework or to pervert it for their own ends. Two features of the political experience contributed to this. One was the insurrectionary tradition found in some form in virtually every East European nation, namely the belief that revolution was desirable as the sole means of effecting changes and guaranteeing freedom. (The distinction between national and individual freedom has been hazy, indeed the two are frequently seen as different facets of the same phenomenon.) This faith in revolutions is all the more paradoxical in the light of the uniformly bad experience that Hungary has had from them – they have all failed and resulted in a massive reaction. The other destabilising experience was that of the collapse itself, which imprinted itself on the consciousness of the middle classes and to a lesser extent on that of the urban proletariat (the peasantry was mostly outside the political system in the inter-war period, although the upper and middle peasants did achieve some representation) and left behind a legacy of distrust of all established order. These two strands coexisted with the belief in institutional order outlined above, but the former could seriously hamper the latter in a crisis.

Another factor in the Hungarian political experience was the personal nature of politics itself. Political parties in the inter-war period tended to be groups united around a political leader rather than by a cohesive ideology. This phenomenon re-emerged after 1945 and contributed to the destabilisation promoted by the Communists, both because it meant that the organisation of most parties was weak and because it enabled the Communist leader, Mátyás Rákosi, to exercise a personal domination. Against this background, Rákosi's later personality cult was to some extent only an extension of an existing political tradition and Kádár's low-key pre-eminence also rests in part on the acceptance of personality.

The experience of the Stalinist period, during which a conscious effort was made to destroy every trace not only of the values of the pre-1944 system, but also of what had begun to emerge after 1945, can be seen as a second caesura. The extraordinary attempt by the Communists, a small minority,[10] to force their system of values on a hostile population has been extensively described elsewhere, whether in the Hungarian context or that of other East European countries. The failure of the attempt was shown in the total rejection of the Soviet model of Marxism-Leninism in 1956.[11] But the impact of the Rákosi period on Hungarian society and its attitudes to politics was far-reaching and thorough, affecting every part of the population.

This period was generally seen as one where all the legitimate aspirations of society were perverted and ignored and replaced by a set of values acceptable only to a small minority of self-seeking bureaucrats.[12]

The constantly proclaimed high ideals of Communism had become empty phrases and were rapidly perceived to be so. The all-pervasive deployment of terror or the threat of it to enforce these policies resulted initially in fear and apathy; and subsequently, after the gradual improvements of Imre Nagy's Prime Ministership (1953–5), in demands for a total transformation of the then existing Communist system of government, including its values, to conform with its proclaimed ideals. Thus the explosion of 1956 provided several clues as to the mood and attitudes of the Hungarian population, and although it is impossible to be precise about the aims of the revolution in detail, a reasonable idea can be gained from the numerous proclamations and manifestos issued during the events.[13]

## VALUES AND POLITICAL BELIEFS

These demands can be summed up as being directed towards individual and national freedom, the traditional aims of political change in Eastern Europe for a century. In particular, various proclamations called for the re-establishment of parliamentary democracy and the multi-party system, for an end to police terror, for the restoration of sanity in the economic sphere (i.e. reducing the breakneck speed of forced industrialisation and improving the position of the consumer), the ending of collectivisation in agriculture, the restoration of the right to revive small-scale private trade while large-scale industry remained nationalised.

The striking feature of 1956 was that the newly recruited urban proletariat, which had swollen during Rákosi's forced industrialisation and was entering the political system fully for the first time, generally associated itself with some or all of these demands, so that it had evidently assimilated a fair part of the traditional political culture. In addition, the workers rapidly organised workers' councils. They also put forward the standard demands for the right to strike, free trade unions and rejected any idea of a return to capitalism.[14] At least as important as the demands for changes at home were those concerned with the country's international position, above all, for the end of Soviet tutelage and Soviet economic exploitation.

### Changes after 1956

The failure of the revolution represented a third caesura in the political experience of Hungarian society, one which deeply marked both the government and public opinion. The failed revolution led directly to a decline in political expectations on the part of the latter, to an acceptance of the *status quo* as far as the leading role of the party and Hungary's relations with the Soviet Union were concerned. But the change in attitude, accompanied by a widespread disillusionment about the country's perspectives, did not extend as far as active support of either of the two principal interlocking constraints on the fundamental aspiration to be free to choose a preferred social order and international status. The choice was limited and this had come to be seen as an inescapable political factor, something which had not been the case before the revolution. In this situation, the consolidation offered by Kádár in the 1960s[15] was taken up by Hungarian society, but without any enthusiasm and without any substantial support for the proclaimed goals of the Party. The overall aim of the Party, that of constructing socialism, was probably seen as a necessary evil which had to be tolerated, together with all the other constraints, but as far as possible individual – not collective – material advancement, particularly conspicuous consumption, had become the main goals. The acceptance of these constraints did not, however, lead to a total abandonment of the traditional aspirations of Hungarian society, but – as a Hungarian writer remarked in 1966, 'We had the Turks here for 150 years and who speaks Turkish here now?' – it suggested that they had been shelved for the time being.[16]

As far as the government was concerned, certainly Kádár himself, it had no illusions about the degree and intensity of support for its aims. The lessons of 1956 were perfectly clear on this. However, Kádár offered a kind of tacit compact to Hungarian society, namely that as long as a reasonable standard of living was guaranteed by the system, secret police terror and arbitrary government behaviour were largely eliminated, and the individual was permitted to opt out, the Party would expect the population to subscribe broadly to its goals. The essence of this tacit compact – symbolised by Kádár's slogan of the early 1960s, 'He who is not against us is with us', the explicit reverse of Rákosi's philosophy – was probably to be seen in its breadth. Neither side would pursue its aims to the limit and would thus permit a limited area of free choice. Inevitably, this has not precluded an element of mutual distrust, but aspirations for leading what is regarded as a 'normal' existence appear to have acted as a partially stabilising factor, inasmuch as 'normal' is interpreted in material and not in political terms.

Extensive and thoroughgoing efforts have continued to be made by the government to impose its own set of values on society and to have these values dominate it through genuine conviction, as distinct from lip-service. The success of these efforts cannot be assessed with any claim to accuracy, but it has probably been limited. The results of a survey among young people taken in 1967 indicated that traditional values and attitudes, as transmitted by family influence, continued to hold a strong place in young people's outlook on life.[17] The distrust for authority, the refusal to take anything at face value, the feeling that all statements emanating from the system, the schools included, had to be proved before they were accepted have in no way been eradicated.

The nature and degree of identification by Hungarian society with the Hungarian government is intimately linked with the absence of trust between rulers and ruled. The Hungarian people identify with the Hungarian state and to that extent they automatically identify with the Communist system of government as well, but there is considerable evidence of the comparative weakness of this identification. This is shown by the indifference exhibited by many people towards the system and its institutions, the widespread and frequently criticised apathy,[18] and the preference for the pursuit of material welfare regardless of official exhortations. These attitudes stand far from any kind of overt or covert opposition and need not be expressed as hostility, but in view of the divergence between the aspirations of society and the aims of the system, a measure of tension and uncertainty is inevitable.

Under Kádár efforts have been made to adapt the Communist system to some extent in the direction of popular expectations, both through changes in the institutional structure and by upgrading existing institutions in the life of the country. These moves, intended to introduce a greater element of consent into the political system and thus help to underpin the legitimacy of the Party, were taken as a conscious extension of the New Economic Mechanism (NEM) of 1968 into other spheres and form the kernel of the model associated with Kádár's name. They are characterised by a considerable regard for the observance of legal forms and processes and by the fostering of several pre-Communist institutions, of which the parliament is most important.[19] These steps include a new electoral law which provides for multiple candidacies and the expansion of the role of the legislature, notably through the (re-)introduction of interpellations. The Ministry of Interior has been enjoined to maintain the crucial distinction between political crime and political error. The trade unions were given a genuine role in the protection of the interests of the workers – the Hungarian trade union movement has a respectable and largely Social Democratic tradition – and this clearly went beyond the transmission-belt concept.[20]

The press too has been encouraged to play an appropriate part in the political process in a way that differs from other Communist states and it has done so with some success. In particular, newspapers are quite openly urged to fulfil a kind of Ombudsman role and, on occasion, government ministers have been taken to task for bureaucratic arrogance or a failure to give a convincing account of doubtful decisions. The tradition of relatively free press debates can be traced back to the last century.

The hallmark of the operation of the Kádár model has been caution. Changes have been gradual and frequently imbued with a legalism that, at first sight, might seem to sit oddly with the theoretical commitment to revolutionary action. In practice, of course, none of the institutions operates without some degree of party supervision and this is felt to circumscribe their effective limits. Many Hungarians feel that the Kádár model is not and cannot be entrenched and there is anxiety beneath the surface that it could be 'switched off' at a word from the Kremlin. This anxiety, which is derived ultimately from the perceived dependence of Hungarian affairs on the Soviet Union, has been a potent source of the lability of Hungarian opinion in its attitudes, reactions and expectations. Public response to political change tends to be unfavourable – the Politburo changes of March 1974, for example, were regarded as bordering on the catastrophic and many people feared that the entire Kádár system faced imminent collapse. It took the authorities weeks to reassure public opinion that nothing had changed fundamentally. Yet at the same time, the very fact that the present system has survived without any serious backtracking for well over a decade has to some extent been seen as the guarantee of its strength.

## OFFICIAL VALUES AND DOMINANT POLITICAL CULTURE

Many of the methods and a fair proportion of Communist objectives have failed to generate much enthusiasm within Hungarian society. Yet, to judge by popular demands in 1945 and in 1956, it would be misleading to claim that all the overt objectives of Communism are rejected summarily. The aspiration for social justice has been part of the Hungarian political tradition since 1848 at least, however fitfully at times, and in this sense the 'Liberation' of 1945 was widely seen at the time as a genuine Liberation from the injustices of the old system.[21] Egalitarianism has arisen regularly in political demands, pardoxically going hand-in-hand with personal ambition and social deference, and has, for instance, emerged over income differentials resulting from the NEM.[22] The evidence suggests that whilst industrial workers may grumble about the substantial salaries of the managerial élite and the technical intelligentsia generally, their strongest resentment is reserved for the private craftsmen, people whom they regard as having much the same social status as themselves and whose incomes can be very much higher.[23] The current of egalitarianism was, of course, reinforced by Party ideology in the 1950s and it is striking that a decade later the Party was forced to argue against its own earlier theses in an area close to the central ideas of Marxism-Leninism. Social deference – very evident in the survival of the intricate forms of address inherited from the pre-Communist system – exists *vis-à-vis* representatives of authority, the intelligentsia and anyone else perceived to be of a higher social status.

The major concern on the part of the authorities in the early 1970s was to combat what was officially termed 'petit-bourgeois attitudes'. This has generally been described as behaviour by 'people who turn their backs on obligations towards the community and live only for themselves'. The role accorded to individual initiative under the NEM has been used by many people as an opportunity for personal enrichment. The resurgence of these attitudes has clearly shaken some sections of Hungarian society and it has been argued officially that for the time being, the two mentalities – petit-bourgeois and collectivist – will continue to exist side by side.[24] But what has been a source of extra concern is that these petit-bourgeois attitudes have made major inroads into the working class, the semi-mystical repository of collectivist values, and also into the Party and the youth movement.[25]

Hungarian opinion undoubtedly supports the official goal of transforming Hungary into an industrially strong country – this has been a basic demand since the middle of the last century – and in this context, the state ownership and control of large-scale industry probably has the approval of the majority.[26] Here the official line, which has consciously or unconsciously written its own mythicised version of Hungary's economic and labour history, has become largely assimilated into popular conceptions. Agriculture is a more difficult problem. Recollectivisation was completed in the early 1960s, but the traditional agrarian aspiration of a society of smallholders continues to have its adherents. The survival and prosperity of the private plot play an important role in sustaining this.[27] This attitude is to some extent a generational one, however, and the drift off the land, as well as local surveys, suggests that the younger generation is less interested in agricultural labour as such. Those families which do remain partially or entirely in agriculture – only 17 per cent of rural families were in the second category in 1973 – have tended to focus their attention on the private plot as their primary economic activity. Peasant objectives, now that the acquisition of more land has become impossible, have been transmuted into a quest for material improvement of the family home and the acquisition of consumer durables. Thus urban attitudes have been extensively replicated in the countryside.

Despite the resentment felt at the higher earnings in the private crafts sector, the official policy of permitting and even encouraging such small-scale private enterprise has extensive approval. The ethos of individual initiative, which has been traditionally strong both on the land and off it, has probably survived with greater tenacity than the government would welcome. The lengthy discussions in the press in the 1970s on the survival of petit-bourgeois attitudes were a good indication of this. On the other hand, an important distinction must be made between government rhetoric and government practice. Whereas publicists may fulminate freely against petit-bourgeois morality, official action tends to be cautious and gradual. Public opinion perceives this dichotomy and responds accordingly.

### The Soviet constraint

If in these areas the political system and popular values are by and large in harmony, there are a number of fields where dissonance is potentially or actually serious. Arguably the most significant of these is Hungary's relationship with the Soviet Union. As noted, the constraints inherent in this relationship have been generally accepted, although there is evidence that the youngest generation, the under-25s, is less circumspect in voicing its objections. However, Soviet influence on Hungarian affairs, whether direct or indirect, is seen as a substantial burden. There are some indications that the crisis in the West of the last few years has led to a certain decline in its attractiveness and a corresponding improvement in the image of the Soviet Union. There is some predisposition towards accepting the benefits of association with the Soviet Union's economic stability. With this proviso, the Soviet Union's control of Hungarian affairs is felt to be frustrating and Hungarian helplessness in this only exacerbates the situation.

At the centre is the recognition, stemming from the failure of the revolution, that Hungarians are not masters in their own house. At the popular level, the reactions that this brings forth are not much more than unfocused resentment at (vaguely defined) Soviet interference, together with an awareness of the military presence maintained by the Soviet Union on Hungarian territory. Certainly, in 1968 popular reactions to the invasion of Czechoslovakia were a mixture of *Schadenfreude* – 'now the Czechs will learn what we learned in 1956' – and a certain uneasiness that Hungary had been forced into participating in a morally dubious enterprise from which it had little or nothing to gain. This did not exclude acceptance of the fact that Soviet pressure would have made it virtually impossible for Hungary to opt out, but Hungarians realised that they had no interest in helping the Soviet Union to normalise the Czechs.

The tripartite relationship, involving Hungarian opinion, the Hungarian political leadership and the Soviet Union, has produced one important development in Hungarian attitudes. Even if there is no great enthusiasm for the construction of socialism as embodied in the Kádár model, Hungarian opinion does recognise that its introduction has brought about a substantial and sensible improvement in both the standard of living and the political atmosphere. Hence Hungarian opinion now feels that it has quite a lot to lose from any threats to that model and to that extent identifies with it. Inasmuch as a large body of opinion accepts this, it can be said that the moderated authoritarianism of the Kádár model has been assimilated into Hungarian political culture.

Although detailed knowledge of how Soviet institutions and practice differ from Hungarian is restricted to a few intellectuals, there is a general awareness that the situation is much better in Hungary. But the possibility that these advantages could disappear through decisions in which Hungarian society had no say whatever acts as a factor to reinforce anti-Soviet attitudes.

One of the most painful restrictions that follows from the Soviet-Hungarian relationship is what Hungarians see as their isolation from the West. In common with other East European nations, the Hungarians regard themselves as members of a semi-mythical community of European peoples. 'Europe' in this case also embraces the United States, but it has traditionally meant the principal cultural centres of Western Europe – France, Germany, Italy and to a lesser extent England. Hungarians argue that Hungary has always been a part of the West politically and a member of the Western cultural community, so that the isolation that was imposed on the country after 1949 was bitterly resented. The denial of the right of freedom to travel – it is still a privilege, albeit fairly freely dispensed – remains an irritant for many Hungarians. Whilst for the intelligentsia access to the West has been prized broadly on cultural grounds, for many of the new bourgeoisie (the managerial élite) a trip to France or Italy has become a status symbol on a par with the country cottage or the car. At that level, there is envy of the higher standard of living, though without any automatic acceptance of Western political values. A similar approach may be found with the youngest generation's adulation of pop music.

Most of this affects the intelligentsia or largely so. Among other strata, the subordination of Hungarian policies has resulted in not much more than a general unfocused resentment which has merged with the traditional dislike of Russia (associated with the suppression of the War of Independence of 1849 and with Panslavism) and with a dislike of Communism (which is seen as a Soviet device). Evidence of this has emerged from time to time in the form of prison sentences on individuals for 'incitement', which almost invariably means abuse of the Soviet Union in a public place. The dominant features of Hungarian opinion are not merely the resentment and frustration over the Soviet Union's power over Hungary, but also passivity and reluctance to articulate that resentment.

### 'Collectivist' and 'bourgeois' values

There is considerable anxiety within the Party at how little headway a Communist culture has made; and conversely at the tenacity of pre-Communist attitudes, including those of the youngest generation. Those who were in the grip of such petit-bourgeois ideas 'either demand that socialism should provide for the entrepreneurial spirit of capitalism or for the egalitarian ideals of communism or frequently for the two together'.[28] This mentality is said to be widespread. It affects those who have only recently moved into the consumer market, as well as those with a genuine bourgeois background. The influence of the family has been thought to have been chiefly responsible – the same article refers explicitly to 'dual education' – but there are other factors, notably the lack of social experience of revolutionary situations and 'petit-bourgeois extremism'. Overt conformism, which masks indifference, is seen as equally undesirable for 'it can emerge that those who are indifferent are indifferent only towards progressive ideas and can join forces with nationalist cosmopolitanism, West-worship and left extremist ideologies'.[29]

This concentration on consumption and its attendant values, the tacit acceptance of them by the Party and the unstable equilibrium of the social order have been compared by at least one writer with the k.u.k. and neo-k.u.k. periods, when a bureaucratised élite, in alliance with the neo-feudal gentry, ruled over a largely passive population. The whole system was made tolerable by a measure of individual and entrepreneurial freedom and genteel corruption.[30] This analysis, which also has some currency among intellectuals in Hungary, is made more plausible by the argument that the various groups that function in society today show a similarity to the roles and mores of their equivalents of the pre-Communist period. Thus the Party and state machine, *mutatis mutandis*, play the role of the gentry; the new bourgeoisie, which overlaps with the remnants of the old bourgeoisie, has to some extent had its post-war dream of being able to carry on where it left off in 1939 fulfilled; and the industrial proletariat, now much more numerous, is as low on the social scale as before. The only marked difference is that the peasantry in contemporary Hungary has been brought into the ambit of the political system – the achievement of the 1945–56 period – and has prospered in the 1960s and 1970s, thanks to the economic reform.

### National identity and national ideology

Hungary, like Poland and East Germany, is almost entirely homogeneous nationally, so that the national question does not arise in the form that it does in multi-national states (Czechoslovakia, Yugoslavia or Roumania). On the other hand, Hungary was precisely such a multi-national state until 1918 (and from 1938 to 1944) and its transformation from the one into the other has been a central part of the country's political experience. In a phrase, the Hungarian nation has yet to come to terms with the loss of empire. The territory of the Crownlands of St Stephen had been perceived as 'God-given' in exactly the same way as the French perceive the 'Hexagon', and the loss of two-thirds of this territory to various successor states has still to be finally assimilated. Had it merely been a question of loss of territory alone, this might perhaps have been digested, especially after 1945 when the old neo-feudal élite which had made integral revisionism the keystone of its state ideology had been shattered.[31] But the loss of territory was accompanied by a loss of a considerable portion of the substance of the nation, as perceived in Hungary, namely the forced cession of over three million Hungarians to other national states.

Consequently, Hungarian politics, at least as far as the national question is concerned, has been dominated by the fate of the national-Hungarians (Hungarians outside the Hungarian nation state) and this has complicated Hungary's relations with all its neighbours to a greater or lesser extent. The national question has also had its impact on the state-Hungarians (the Hungarians of the Hungarian state), in so far as it has helped to intensify the occasional outbursts of helplessness, the sense of isolation and the rejection of responsibility.[32] Although the nexus is very difficult to demonstrate, it can be argued that a substantial proportion of Hungarian opinion feels that a third of the body of the nation, the national-Hungarians, has been cut off from it, that there is nothing that Hungary can do about this the overriding problem of the Hungarian nation, and, therefore, that little can be done about Hungarian society itself. This pattern of thought may lack logic, but it is not inherently implausible. It has been aggravated by a further factor, the idiosyncratic information policy of the Hungarian authorities regarding the national-Hungarians.

The result was not only a widespread semi-ignorance, but also a feeling that the entire question of the national-Hungarians was best left alone. At a provincial university in Hungary, first-year undergraduates were asked what language was spoken by the Szeklers of Transylvania. The response to this, as Gyula Illyés pointed out at the centenary celebrations of the Magyar Nyelvőr Society, should have been automatic. In fact, 23 per cent of the respondents were uncertain and, indeed, some stated that the Szeklers spoke a language of their own or Roumanian.[33] Contracts with the national-Hungarians have only recently become possible. Mass tourism to Czechoslovakia was permitted from the mid-1960s onwards and to Transylvania from about 1970. Of course, the fact that at different times these minorities were actually exposed to assimilatory pressure only helped to confirm the state-Hungarians in their distorted views of the national-Hungarians.

A significant change in the national ideology in this sphere must be mentioned in this context. Whereas before 1945 both official and popular nationalism demanded that the entire area of the Crownlands be restored, today concern exists mainly for the national-Hungarians themselves and the territories they inhabit, and not all of them at that. There is a curious parallel here with the inter-war period, when the national-Hungarians of Yugoslavia were largely ignored in Hungary and interest focused on Slovakia and Transylvania. The preponderant feeling in Hungary today is that the national-Hungarians of the Vojvodina are well treated and that there is no cause for Hungarian concern about them. This might partly be explained by the fact that the Serbs have a better image in Hungary than either the Slovaks or the Roumanians. In any case, the events of 1968 in Slovakia, when there was serious tension between Slovaks and national-Hungarians, were followed very closely in Hungary. Indeed, the entire Dubček programme was judged by what the national-Hungarians would gain from the reforms.[34] This is partly explained by distrust of Slovak intentions and by memories of the 1945–8 period, when the Hungarians of Slovakia were exposed to extremely severe pressures. Transylvania is an even more emotionally-loaded case, partly because this is the numerically largest Hungarian minority (1.7 million), partly because it has been exposed most recently to assimilatory pressure and partly because Transylvania is a crucial factor in the Hungarian national ideology, since it is perceived as the area which ensured the survival of the Hungarian nation during the Turkish occupation.

This concern for the national-Hungarians should not be equated automatically with irredentism. In fact, there appears to be an odd split in attitudes, which are not irreconcilable. On the one hand, the loss of the relevant territories to the successor states seems now to be grudgingly accepted, inasmuch as very few people in Hungary would approve of a campaign to regain them (though on this issue, opinion could be very easily manipulated). There is criticism of the authorities that they appear to be doing so little to articulate public concern on this score – the remarks made by Zoltán Komócsin in the Hungarian parliament in the summer of 1971, that the Hungarian party had a right to comment about the Hungarians of Transylvania on a Marxist basis,[35] were well received in Hungary – but this is not the same as irredentism. At the same time, the overwhelming majority of state-Hungarians find it extremely difficult to recognise that the national-Hungarians are developing an autonomous nationality-consciousness of their own – that they may insist on being Hungarian culturally, but that this is not the same as loyalty to the Hungarian state. The hostility expressed by the national-Hungarians of Slovakia to the state-Hungarian military units stationed there after the invasion was only the most striking instance of this.[36] For obvious reasons, the Hungarians of the Soviet Union – some 170,000 in Subcarpathian Ruthenia – remain a taboo subject, but it is noteworthy that this minority was by and large ignored in pre-war Hungary too.

Over the last few years much more has been published in the Hungarian press about the national-Hungarian question and official and unofficial contacts have multiplied. None the less, it will take years before the accumulated effects of the period of silence are dispelled. For the moment, Hungarian opinion remains credulous about horror stories of oppression of the national-Hungarians and has yet to assimilate the different political consciousness of the national-Hungarians.

The nature of Jewish assimilation or non-assimilation is, on the other hand, a central problem of Hungarian national identity within the Hungarian state. Whilst Hungarian society has traditionally enjoyed the reputation of having successfully assimilated a large body of Jewish incomers before 1914, the official and popular anti-semitism of the inter-war period demonstrated how superficial that assimilation had been, above all from the point of view of the assimilators. The distinction between Jewish Hungarian and Hungarian Jew was never seriously made and the destruction of the bulk of Hungarian Jewry in 1944–5 was tacitly abetted by most social strata. The post-war period added a further complication, inasmuch as the top leadership of the Communist Party was Jewish, but before and during 1956 Jews were active both as anti-Stalinists and as Stalinists. There are conflicting reports as to whether there were any instances of popular anti-semitism during the 1956 explosion, but there appears to have been little or none among intellectuals at this time. By the early 1970s, however, the problem had been reopened, albeit in a highly allusive and tangential fashion, indicating the degree of sensitivity over the entire issue.[37]

The authorities have generally attempted to make a clear distinction between anti-semitism and anti-Zionism. The question has emerged, indirectly and covertly, to colour the revived populist-urbanist debates among the intelligentsia concerning the nature of Hungarian national identity. These debates evidently aroused official concern, for a warning was formally issued condemning anti-semitism as a criminal offence.[38] The evidence on the nature and the extent of anti-semitism is fragmentary and impressionistic, so that conclusions are bound to be tentative, but the distinction between Jew and non-Jew has re-emerged in Hungarian society as a source of division.

In general, it might be said that among intellectuals, there is a certain tendency to identify Jews with the Party and its objectives to a greater degree than non-Jews. This in turn predisposes certain intellectuals – especially among the nationalist populists – to revive the argument that Jews are an alien element in Hungarian society. Within the new bourgeoisie and at the popular level, 'traditional' anti-semitism seems to have lost little of its strength.[39] Surveys on attitudes towards 'outsiders' have avoided the question of anti-semitism, but its existence can be inferred from indications of popular prejudice towards all sectors of society perceived to be 'alien'.[40] Evidence of rural anti-semitism was brought back by Western visitors from the early 1960s, who reported that synagogues had been attacked by hooligans in several provincial centres and also in the capital.

### POLITICAL KNOWLEDGE AND EXPECTATIONS

In line with the general political apathy, Hungarian opinion has shown little interest in the most recent period in alternative models of social order. The new bourgeoisie, which, as noted, to some extent overlaps with the old bourgeoisie and has adopted many of its values, appears to have a certain sense of security about its place in the system and is not looking for basic changes.[41] But as long as the system functions to the satisfaction of the new bourgeoisie, which means in practice a fair amount of latitude to pursue consumerism and officially condemned 'petit-bourgeois' objectives, interest in alternative political models tends to remain inchoate. The attractiveness of the West has in any case declined somewhat, perhaps temporarily, as a result of the political and economic failures of the early 1970s. The practice, as distinct from the rhetoric, of the Kádár system has made it relatively attractive.

In general, inasmuch as alternatives are offered, these tend to be improvements on the existing system or at most complaints about its failures. The workers, who probably have most cause to feel dissatisfied, may argue in favour of greater egalitarianism and equal distribution of benefits, but whenever the opportunity presents itself, they tend to try and satisfy their personal ambitions. A good many of the workers who regularly changed their jobs did so because they were able to increase their wages by each change and were indifferent to arguments about the dislocation of the labour market to which this high turnover led.[42] Nor does there seem to be any strong interest among workers in politics as such. A survey of workers with some involvement in Party educa-tion – thus with a degree of political commitment – showed that 52.9 per cent of workers under 25 took only an occasional interest and 8.4 per cent took no interest at all. The survey showed serious gaps in the knowledge of workers about politics, especially in international affairs, and for those over 50 fear of war was the dominant stimulus in main-taining their interest.[43]

As far the Soviet model of Communism itself is concerned, Com-munists in Hungary immediately after the war showed the same un-critical enthusiasm for it as their comrades anywhere else. The impact of the Rákosi era left many of them disillusioned, but not all of them abandoned their faith in Communism as such.[44] This group provided the backbone for the 'opposition' that grew up around Imre Nagy in the mid-1950s and then supported him in 1956. Some members of this group subsequently rallied to Kádár. They saw the Soviet model as inefficient and inappropriate to Hungarian conditions, particularly as regards the over-rapid drive for industrialisation; among economists the search for permissible alternatives began soon after the revolution. The debate on the system of economic management resulted in the introduction of the NEM in 1968 and discussions have continued since on the most effective implementation of the system.[45] The debate has been carried out at a highly sophisticated level, so much so that few non-specialists have been able to follow it.[46]

This has had a serious impact on the cultural intelligentsia, which feels excluded from what has probably been the most significant political debate in Hungary in the last decade and, as a result, has been unable to play its traditional role of articulating popular demands. Indeed, one of the more striking features of Hungarian society in the Kádár era has been that the cultural intelligentsia, with literature as its medium of communication, has been mostly supplanted by economists, sociologists, historians and jurists. Individuals working in these fields have come to constitute a kind of licensed para-opposition, in that they feel free to offer criticism of aspects of the system, often producing trenchant comment on its shortcomings, but do not become involved in questioning the fundamentals of the Kádár system. Only a small and uninfluential current of opinion, the new left, does so and its hostility to the NEM may on some issues overlap with the more traditional Stalinist opposition of the old left.

The old left is composed of middle-level functionaries, notably strong in provincial Party organisations like Csongrád county, who have viewed the expression of various phenomena under the Kádár system with considerable distaste, although they have never been strong enough to challenge Kádár's leadership directly. They dislike the relatively relaxed cultural atmosphere, in which a wide range of un-committed material has been published, and they appear to be par-ticularly incensed by the 'modern' trends adopted by some film-makers, including Miklós Jancsó, whose work, they argue, cannot be under-stood by the workers and should have no place in a workers' state. They retain a traditional, rather Stalinist, approach to inner-Party democracy and resent Kádár's attempts to democratise Party pro-cedures. Equally, they feel themselves to be threatened by the power of the managerial élite and they profess themselves markedly hostile to the 'petit-bourgeois' life-style adopted by the latter. To this extent, these functionaries are finding it difficult to come to terms with the shifting complexities of contemporary Hungarian society – as distinct from the certainties of the 1950s – and they have been successful in part in articulating their opposition to the Kádár model by building on the very genuine frustrations of the industrial workers at growing income differentials. This group then may be defined as strictly neo-Stalinist, possibly with contacts in other Communist states, but without any intellectual underpinning to its position.

By contrast, the new left is strong on theoretical argument, but weak on political muscle. The proponents of the new left accept the arguments of the old on income differentials and the resurgence of bourgeois attitudes, but then go on to draw radically different conclusions. They argue that the true aim of communism should not be to maximise economic growth through the profit motive, but rather that it should introduce a genuine workers' democracy by destroying bureaucratisation and thus humanise social relations, which the Kádár model has manifestly failed to do. The new left in Hungary is very small. Apart from a few students at Budapest university, its views are restricted to the neo-Lukácsists around András Hegedüs. In the summer of 1973, the best-known exponents of these views were banned from public life, after having been accused by the Party of having propagated a mixture of new left and right revisionist ideas.

While the new left in Hungary has certain affinities with other similar groups in Eastern Europe, notably the Praxis group in Yugoslavia, there is little evidence of broader interest in other political models. During the Rákosi period, there was a measure of interest in Yugoslavia but more as an indicator that alternative models of Communism were possible than in the actual content of Titoism.

The significance of the Dubček reforms was appreciated only by the intelligentsia (apart from its impact on the Hungarian minority, as noted) and even at that, the primary factor was a certain concern that matters would go too far and too fast and, in consequence, the Hungarian reforms could be jeopardised. Similarly, interest in Polish affairs has been muted in recent years – there were next to no reactions to the events of December 1970 – the only exception being a certain awareness of the continued existence of a private agricultural sector. In 1956, of course, Polish developments were followed closely and one of the earliest moves in the Hungarian revolution was the gesture of laying a wreath at the statue of General Bem, the Polish revolutionary general who commanded an army in Hungary in 1849.

Attitudes to the West, although no longer quite as uncritical as before, are still in some ways close to adulation. A rather limited and admittedly unscientific poll among 14–18-year-olds suggested that respondents were impressed by the high level of economic development and modernity of the West and that they were attracted to it by what they regarded as the greater freedom of the individual in politics and economics.[47]

## POLITICAL KNOWLEDGE AND OFFICIAL INFORMATION POLICY

Political knowledge and political sophistication have undoubtedly spread under the present system. Illiteracy was low even before the war, mobilisation after 1945 has brought virtually the whole of Hungarian society into the ambit of the political system, and the mass media have had the predictable impact. Within this general framework, the Party's information policy can be described as unsatisfactory, despite an ostensible commitment to full information. Two problems have arisen in this area: the emergence and identification of a widening gap between 'élite' and 'mass' culture and dissatisfaction with officially released information. Several commentators have noted that high (or élite) cultural output has failed to penetrate beyond the cultural and to some extent the technical intelligentsia. Although official policy is based on the need to narrow the gap, the intelligentsia has largely failed to meet this challenge.[48] The output of the cultural intelligentsia has remained well beyond the comprehension of a mass audience and readership, with the result that the latter ignores it and turns to what it can understand instead. What the majority likes is easily accessible adventure stories with a well-defined plot without moralising or agonising; crime thrillers are especially popular, and so are historical adventures and romances.[49] (*Love Story* was a smash hit in Hungary, and Western thrillers are guaranteed a good audience both in the cinema and on television.) The existence of this gap is perhaps a further explanation for the demoralisation and stagnation that have been observed among Hungarian intellectuals.[50]

The second aspect of the government's information policy tends to be especially pronounced among intellectuals, namely dissatisfaction with political information. The residual tradition of a free press has already been mentioned in this connection, but the desire for information is borne out by a survey carried out in the summer of 1969. In this inquiry 1223 intellectuals (defined as those whose work required a higher educational qualification) were surveyed in three counties and it revealed a very marked feeling that the existing information pattern was inadequate. Of those questioned, 33 per cent failed to give any answer at all to the question, 'Are you satisfied with existing information?'; only 20.6 per cent were satisfied; 32.1 per cent thought the level of information insufficient and 14.4 per cent doubted its reliability. Television was given as the primary source of information by 81.2 per cent of respondents; the national press by 42.4 per cent and radio by 42 per cent; party organs and the local press were far less important.[51]

The anxiety of the authorities regarding information policy has been frequently observed. It derives partly from lack of trust, partly from recognising that the Soviet Union is unusually sensitive on this score and partly from a fear of misinterpretation.[52] When in March 1972, the Hungarian press revealed the existence of disagreement with the Soviet Union over long-term raw material deliveries, public opinion instantly concluded that if that much could be admitted openly the situation must have been far worse. In vain did the authorities protest that such disagreements were perfectly normal in inter-state relations, even among Communist states.

Some improvements in the mass media have been put into effect. The most recently established Budapest daily, *Magyar Hírlap*, has proved to be fairly lively and informative. The introduction of the occasional television 'phone-in' programme 'Forum', where questions on domestic and foreign affairs are answered live by journalists, has been successful and popular. A radio magazine called '168 Hours' has maintained a reasonable standard. None the less, the authorities are aware that anyone interested in politics will supplement his information by listening to foreign broadcasts, principally Radio Free Europe. Hungarian sources tend to be distrusted simply because they are Hungarian.

POLITICAL SYMBOLS AND NATIONAL LITURGY

Symbols and rituals associated with the state and the nation have continued to play an important function in the liturgy of politics in Hungary, just as they have done in other East European countries. In this connection, the present rulers of Hungary have adopted many of the practices of their predecessors and, at times, have even gone as far as taking over particular rituals virtually unchanged. However, several of the symbols directly associated with Communism are rejected by public opinion, or evoke limited identification and in 1956, at least, there were numerous demands for a return to pre-Communist practice.

The Communists have retained the traditional red-white-green tricolour as the state flag, but have added their own coat-of-arms to it. As a result, during the revolution this coat-of-arms was excised and one of the symbols of the revolution was the tricolour with a hole in its middle. The new coat-of-arms bears a predictable panoply of objects associated with Communism – hammer, sickle, wheatsheaf – and was regarded as wholly alien. The national coat-of-arms had been the one linked with the Hungarian monarchy and the 1848 revolution, known as the Kossuth címer (coat-of-arms), and this reappeared in 1956. Interestingly, until after the war the Kossuth címer had been displayed surmounted by the Apostolic Crown of Hungary, but there were no demands for the reinstitution of the crown, presumably indicating that monarchist sentiment was largely dead.

The crown itself has been an object of mystical veneration for centuries and actually conferred legitimacy by possession. This is certainly part of the explanation for the extraordinary perseverance with which the present government of Hungary has sought to recover the crown from the United States (to whose safe-keeping it had been entrusted in 1945). In 1970, when the millennium of St Stephen, Hungary's first Christian king, was commemorated with the traditional procession in Buda castle, the Hungarian press commented with some bitterness that the crown had not been returned and that a substitute had to be used.[53] St Stephen's day itself is 20 August; and the Communists consciously proclaimed this to be constitution day in an attempt to supplant the historic anniversary with associations of its own by a ritual more appropriate to a socialist republic. This device readily recalls the practice of the early Christian church which took over pagan festivals and converted them to its own use.

Two other anniversaries are of importance. One is 4 April, the day on which the last German units in Hungary in 1945 surrendered and on which the country was deemed 'liberated'. This is probably the most important festival celebrated under the existing system, although it does not appear to attract substantial popular identification. The other is 15 March, Hungary's national day for a century, which is the anniversary of the outbreak of the 1848 revolution. This event, with its aim of national independence and social reform, could be readily taken over. In the early 1970s, left-radical students have, in turn, tried to appropriate it and organise counter-demonstrations in competition with the official celebrations.

One of the more bizarre demands put forward in 1956 was to replace the Soviet-style uniforms of the Hungarian army and return to the traditional neo-k.u.k. style. Evidently, the new uniforms carried unacceptable associations. The red stars that feature so prominently on public buildings also attracted unfavourable attention in 1956, especially the largest one at the top of the façade of the parliament building, as the most potent symbol of Communist rule. One of the least welcome tokens of the Soviet presence in Hungary are the innumerable war memorials to the Red Army. By contrast, there is apparently not one memorial to the Hungarian army that was defeated at Voronezh in 1943 with enormous losses – not surprisingly, given that this army had fought against the Red Army with the Wehrmacht. The toppling of the statue of Stalin in 1956 was one of the earliest events in the revolution and its ritual quality recalled the earlier toppling of the statue of Péter Pázmány, the seventeenth-century Jesuit, after the war on the grounds that he had been a reactionary. Other moves under the present order aimed at removing obvious signs of the previous one include the renaming of streets and occasionally of places. The boulevard that currently bears the name 'Népköztársaság útja' ('Avenue of the People's Republic') has had about six different names since it was first built around the turn of the century and it is generally known today as

'Andrássy út', after the Austro-Hungarian politician, the name it had borne the longest.

By and large these Communist-inspired symbols and rituals fail to attract the identification that is their objective, for the meanings of the traditional rituals are evidently passed on through the family. However, in line with the current political climate, even if these symbols are generally rejected, no active efforts are made to have them replaced.

POLITICAL CULTURE AND POLITICAL CHANGE

There is something of a paradox in the relationship between political culture and political change in Hungary. On the one hand, the official Marxist-Leninist set of values is overtly – or at least ostensibly – committed to producing a revolutionary transformation of society along highly egalitarian lines, whilst on the other the existing government has succeeded in creating a relatively stable, rather cautious system that bears an uncanny resemblance to the pre-war, neo-k.u.k. order. The paradox may be explained by the failure of the Communists to effect fundamental changes in the dominant political culture of Hungary, so that, once the revolutionary breakthrough period came to an end and policies of partial reconciliation were adopted, traditional values resurfaced. The caesuras of 1944–8 and 1956 and the changes they produced have, in effect, cancelled one another out. Under Rákosi, a total mobilisation backed up by terror forced Hungarian society into acquiescing superficially in a Stalinist ideology as the ruling value system. This system was dismantled in and after 1956 as unworkable and under Kádár a new and at the same time familiar political system was built up along lines rather more congenial to Hungarian society. The result has been a period of consolidation, with attendant stability and a measure of economic achievement.

The caesuras have, however, had their legacy in reinforcing an already strong sense of insecurity about political change. In a society where emphasis is placed on the survival and continuity of the state and the nation, events that have shaken that society and over which it appeared to have little control, have tended to perpetuate resistance to change and fear of instability. The reverse of this is that consolidation carried out by Kádár has been welcomed in so far as his policies did not diverge substantially from dominant values.

The evidence indicates that there is considerable surface acquiescence in the values of the existing system in Hungary and that some of the aims of the Communist Party receive support. But this surface acquiescence seems to be accompanied by no deeper identification with Communist ideology, and the acquiescence is largely the consequence of a recognition of the foreign constraints on Hungarian society. In this sense the Kádár leadership has achieved a partial legitimacy – a major success given its origins – but it has failed to entrench either itself or its values in Hungarian society. In the circumstances, this *modus vivendi*, which has lasted for over a decade, has paradoxically created a fair measure of stability, which is in itself welcome to Hungarian society. The unwillingness of either party to the tacit compact to jeopardise this provides a firm foundation for its continuation.

NOTES

1 Jenő Szűcs, 'A nemzet historikuma és a történetszemélet nemzeti látószöge', *in Nemzet és Történelem* (Budapest, 1974) pp. 13–183. (All books in Hungarian cited here were published in Budapest, unless noted otherwise.)

2 Gyula Szekfű, 'A magyar jellem történetünkben', in *Mi a Magyar?* (1939) pp. 489–556; Mihály Gulyás, 'Birtokháborítás', *Valóság*, vol. 19, no. 2 (February 1976) pp. 95–103; György Hámos, 'Ha per, úgymond...', *Élet és Irodalom*, 9 October 1971, noted 'the flood of litigation has inundated the legal departments of local councils and also the lower and appeal courts'.

3 Szekfü, op. cit.; Gyula Illyés, 'Szakvizsgán – nacionalizmusból', in *Hajszálgyökerek* (1971) pp. 440–59 and the interview with Illyés in *Jelenkor*, vol. 14, no. 12 (December 1971).

4 The tradition that large-scale economic investment is primarily the prerogative of the ruler emerges from the argument in Péter Gunst, 'Kelet-Európa gazdasági-társadalmi fejlödésének néhány kérdése', *Valóság*, vol. 17, no. 3 (March 1974) pp. 16–34.

5 Péter Hanák, 'Vázlatok a századelő magyar társadalmáról', in *Magyarország a Monarchiában* (1975) pp. 343–404; Ferenc Erdei, 'A magyar társadalom a két háború között', *Valóság*, vol. 19, no. 4 (April 1976) pp. 25–53.

6 Mária Ember, *Hajtűkanyar* (1973) provides a chilling account of this process.

7 Erdei, op. cit.

8 Erdei, ibid., notes that where the power-interests of the gentry were in conflict with the demands of professionalism, the latter suffered, but where there was no such conflict – as with communications – standards in inter-war Hungary were high.

9 István Bibó, 'A magyar demokrácia válsága', *Harmadik Út* (London, 1960) pp. 32–79; István Vida, 'A felszabadulás utáni átrétegeződés kérdéséhez', *Tiszatáj*, vol. 28, no. 6 (June 1974) pp. 66–76.

10 In the 1945 elections the Communist Party of Hungary received 16.9 per cent of the vote. The number of Communists who returned with the Red Army was no more than a few dozen and the number who survived in Hungary probably did not exceed 2000.

11 Charles Gati argues that the extent of support for revolutionary change in 1945 was greater than generally accepted – about half of Hungarian society. Even the other half favoured evolutionary change, so that a certain level of commitment to transformation was not in doubt. But those

supporting radical change – the Communists, some Social Democrats and some peasants – were themselves divided about the shape and direction of the change. On the basis of Gati's figures, the Communist-industrial model of change had the support of about a quarter of the electorate in 1945 at most and the rest of Hungarian opinion found it unpalatable. See Charles Gati, 'Hungary: the Dynamics of Revolutionary Transformation' in Charles Gati (ed.), *The Politics of Modernization in Eastern Europe* (New York, 1974) pp. 78–84.

12  Described by Julius Hay as 'the Kucseras'. See *Geboren 1900: Erinnerungen* (Hamburg, 1971) pp. 320–2. The Czech name is a reference to the Habsburg bureaucrats imported into Hungary in the Bach era in the 1850s.

13  Vilmos Juhász, 'A forradalom követelései', in Gyula Borbándi and József Molnár (eds), *Tanulmányok a magyar forradalomról* (Munich, 1966) p. 459.

14  Ferenc A. Váli, *Rift and Revolt in Hungary* (Cambridge, Mass., 1961) p. 334 gives the details of the memorandum of the Csepel Metallurgical Works workers' council, which called for the release of political prisoners, the withdrawal of Soviet forces, free elections, a multi-party system and national independence. Miklós Molnár, *Budapest 1956* (London, 1971) pp. 175–9, describes similar demands put forward by workers' councils in the provinces.

15  Paul Ignotus, *Hungary* (London, 1972) ch. 14; William F. Robinson, *The Pattern of Reform in Hungary: a Political, Economic and Cultural Analysis* (New York, 1973) pt I.

16  In conversation with the author.

17  *Élet és Irodalom*, 7 January 1967. Katalin Kékesi, 'A tizenévesek kispolgárisága', *Ifjúkommunista*, November 1973, noted that it was an illusion to think that the youngest generation was immune to petit-bourgeois ideas and attributed this to the 'dual education' that children received.

18  A survey taken in Szolnok county of nearly 4000 people produced some interesting data on this. In answer to the question 'What does the word "homeland" conjure up for you?', 62 per cent of respondents included 'our socialist system'; and 64.3 per cent regarded the 'liberation' as the most significant event in history. Intellectuals showed a stronger attachment to the bourgeois democratic past than workers and a minority of respondents would have preferred to strengthen links with the West and sought neutrality. Jenő Faragó. 'A politikai munka része' *Népszabadság*, 19 November 1973.

19  It is worth noting that this regard for form and procedure was nothing new in the history of Hungarian communism. During the inter-war period, the Hungarian Communist Party (KMP) was repeatedly criticised by the Comintern for 'harbouring legalistic delusions'.

20  Details of these changes are set out in William F. Robinson, *The Pattern of Reform in Hungary: a Political, Economic and Cultural Analysis* (New York, 1973) pp. 196–230.

21  See n. 18.

22  A clear admission of this came from Sándor Gáspár, Secretary-General of the Trade Unions, at the 10th Party Congress: 'The workers have yet to

identify themselves completely with the principle of wage and income differentiation based on performance. To the majority, egalitarianism is more attractive ...' *Népszabadság*, 27 November 1970.

23 *Pártélet*, November 1973, advanced the following thesis, if only to rebut it: '[People say] there is a high and meritorious élite that has grown up under socialism, which is doing more for society in general than others. It deserves, therefore, to enjoy a special position financially. This stratum is allowed to live in the style ... of the former ruling class.' This attitude, although rejected by the journal, is probably not uncommon.

24 Jenő Faragó, 'Magasabbrendű kollektivizmus', *Népszabadság*, 11 February 1973.

25 Lajos Mesterházi, 'Az új ember jegyében', *Új Irás*, vol. 13, no. 2 (February 1973) pp. 78–93.

26 Gunst, op. cit.; however, György Ránki, 'Has Modernization made a Difference?' in Gáti (ed.), op. cit., argues that a section of the intelligentsia and the new bourgeoisie, the lineal descendants of the gentroid middle class of the neo-k.u.k. period and the populists, retain their traditional suspicion of industrial growth in general and of 'the city', i.e. Budapest, in particular.

27 István Márkus in *Társadalomtudományi Közlemények*, 1972, no. 2.

28 Katalin Kékesi, op. cit.

29 Ibid.

30 Ignotus, op. cit., pp. 287–90. The same author argues in his essay 'Hungary 1966' in Tamás Aczél (ed.), *Ten Years After* (London, 1966) pp. 95–7, that the authoritarian methods used by the Communists after 1948 were deployed in a society that had already learned to accept them after 1918; that there was a widespread faith in authority, in bureaucratic and militaristic superiority and a tradition of oppressing national and social minorities.

31 The loss of territories without Hungarian inhabitants, e.g. the Burgenland, has been fully assimilated. Cf. Roumania and the southern Dobruja.

32 This line of response has been particularly strong in the writings of Gyula Illyés, one of Hungary's most talented literary figures.

33 Gyula Illyés, 'A Magyar Nyelvőr ünnepére', *Népszabadság*, 16 January 1972. For a severe critique of official information policy on Transylvania, which takes up the point made by Gyula Illyés, see Lajos Für, 'Milyen nyelven beszélnek a székelyek?', *Tiszatáj*, vol. 26, no. 8 (August 1972) pp. 57–66.

34 Rudolf Tőkés, 'Hungarian Intellectuals' reaction to the invasion of Czechoslovakia', in E. J. Czerwinski and Jaroslaw Piekalkiewicz (eds), *The Soviet Invasion of Czechoslovakia: Its Effects on Eastern Europe* (New York, 1972) p. 148.

35 *Népszabadság*, 25 June 1971.

36 I heard very similar comments from a young Hungarian journalist and convinced Party member just before the invasion, who complained that 'suddenly all these Hungarians have become Czechoslovaks'. Equally Transylvanian Hungarians often resent interventions on their behalf from Hungary because, they argue, these only make their relations with the Roumanians worse.

37 A serious contribution to the debate, with a long analysis of the history of Hungarian Jewry, is in György Száraz, 'Egy előítélet nyomán', *Vaslóság*, vol. 18, no. 8 (August 1975) pp. 60–82. A subsequent interview with the same author was significantly published under the title 'Why rock the boat with this question?' ('Minek bolygatni ezt a kérdést?', *Élet és Irodalom*, 11 October 1975). A useful summary of the articles that appeared in Hungary on the subject in 1975 is in D. Silagi, 'Zum Thema "Judenfeindschaft" in Ungarn – Drei Budapester Publikationen erregten 1975 Aufmerksamkeit', *Wissenschaftlicher Dienst Südosteuropa*, vol. 24, nos. 11–12 (November–December 1975) pp. 237–42.

38 *Magyar Hírlap*, 26 October 1974.

39 The case of a party official called Sütő is instructive in this context. Sütő delivered a strongly anti-semitic speech to a closed Party meeting and evidently met with some favourable response, but the Party itself was highly embarrassed by the affair and Sütő was sent abroad in a diplomatic capacity. *Financial Times*, 23 January 1973.

40 Vilmos Faragó, 'Kicsi ország', *Élet és Irodalom*, 7 January 1967. Several of the letters received by the journal after the publication of Faragó's inquiry among secondary school children were clearly anti-semitic. Ágnes Havas, a school teacher, reported that anti-semitic comments were not infrequent among the 7–10-year-olds that she taught and that often these children had no idea of why they were using the word 'Jew' (*zsidó*) as an expression of abuse. 'Nacionalista hatások gyermekeinkre', *Társadalmi Szemle*, vol. 22, no. 3 (March 1967) pp. 97–111. The survival of popular anti-semitism is hinted at by Oszkár Zsedényi, *Új Élet*, 15 July 1975, and István Nemeskürty, *Élet és Irodalom*, 23 August 1975.

41 The ideology of the new bourgeoisie is vividly described in these terms in the short story by Ferenc Karinthy, 'Házszentelő', *Kortárs*, vol. 20, nos. 1 and 2 (January and February 1976) pp. 41–61, 203–36, especially at p. 230.

42 *Népszabadság*, 6 December 1972, reported that 35–50 per cent of young workers had changed their employment for this reason over 'the previous three years'. Cases are recounted in Budapest about enterprise managers being forced to turn a blind eye to workers using factory equipment for moonlighting.

43 Mihály Tamási, 'A munkások politikai műveltsége', *Pártélet*, vol. 17, no. 4 (April 1972).

44 See Tamás Aczél and Tibor Méray, *Tisztító Vihar* (London, 1961). This is the Hungarian-language edition of *The Revolt of the Mind* (New York, 1959).

45 Robinson, op. cit., chs 2, 5 and 6.

46 Gyula Somogyi, *Társadalmi Szemle*, October 1971, called for more information to be made available on economics, because the public was being misled by propaganda from the West and as a result, people were distorting reality by comparing Hungarian levels with those of the West. He also argued that Hungarian opinion was badly informed about trade relations with the Soviet Union, particularly as far as bauxite and uranium were concerned.

47 Ervin Bán, ' "Túl Napnyugat, innen Kelet . . ." ', *Középfokú Szakoktatás*,

October 1972. Some 80 pupils were involved in this poll in Budapest and its results are clearly impressionistic.

48  Vilmos Faragó, 'Az izlésolló két szárnya', *Élet és Irodalom*, 7 August 1971.

49  *Északmagyarország*, 7 November 1969.

50  Tibor Gyurkovics, 'Ami az íróknak hiányzik', *Élet és Irodalom*, 1 January 1972.

51  Details in *Társadalomtudományi Közlemények*, no. 4, 1972.

52  I was told by an authoritative source in Budapest in 1968, just before the invasion, that the Hungarian press had failed to publish an adequate account of the Czechoslovak '2000 Words' manifesto because of anxiety of this kind. The manipulation of information by the authorities has been vigorously attacked by the veteran writer Tibor Déry, in his regular column 'Egy nap hordaléka', *Élet és Irodalom*, 22 November 1975.

53  *The Times*, 1 May 1971.

# 6 Czechoslovakia: Revival and Retreat

## ARCHIE BROWN and GORDON WIGHTMAN

Any comprehensive attempt to understand political change within Czechoslovakia in the Communist period, and, in particular, the reformist trends of the nineteen-sixties, which culminated in the events of 1968, would involve a study of developments within Czechoslovak society and a detailed examination of the tendencies and conflicts within the Communist Party of Czechoslovakia.[1] To appreciate the preconditions of these changes, however, we must delve deeper into Czechoslovak history and culture than that. The two major contexts in which changing attitudes and practices within the Czechoslovak Communist Party, and the constraints upon them, have to be understood are, on the one hand, the political cultures of Czechs and Slovaks and, on the other, the geopolitical environment in which Czechoslovakia is situated. While it is thus clear at the outset that we are not suggesting that political change in Czechoslovakia can be explained *entirely* in terms of political culture, we shall argue that analysis of the political culture is an essential *part* of an adequate explanation of change in Czechoslovakia after 1956 and especially in the period from 1963 until the late summer of 1968 when the trends were arrested by outside intervention.[2]

Before going on to consider the subjective orientation of Czechs and Slovaks to their history and politics, a brief introduction to the historical experience of the peoples of Czechoslovakia is necessary. The 'objective' outsider, in common with (as will later be shown) the 'subjective' Czech and Slovak, cannot do other than attach enormous importance to the period of the First Republic. The Czechoslovak Republic was one of the new states which arose from the ruins of the Austro-Hungarian Empire in 1918. Although it was conceived as a state of the Czechs and Slovaks, two small Slav nations, a substantial proportion of the population consisted of other nationalities. There were more Germans than there were Slovaks and there were large Ukrainian and Hungarian minorities. These other nationalities had their own political parties, and until the foundation of the Communist Party there was no one party uniting all the national groups. Parties representing Czechs and Slovaks were formed mostly as unitary Czechoslovak organisations, in harmony with the official view that the Czechoslovaks were a single nation.

Even prior to the creation of the republic, the Czechs had some experience of political pluralism, though the same could not be said for the Slovaks, for whom Magyar domination was much greater than that of Vienna over the Czechs. Though there were periods when Czechs refused to participate in the Bohemian and Moravian Diets and in the Parliament in Vienna, from the 1870s they began to participate more actively in the political process. All the Czech deputies entered the Bohemian Diet in 1878, and in 1879 they resumed participation in the Parliament of the Austrian Empire, while at the same time attempting to assert the historic rights of the Kingdom of Bohemia. In the words of Robert J. Kerner, 'they were there to get what they could and prevent others from injuring them' until better times should arrive.[3] In the experience of any nation there is a variety of divergent traditions. This particular strategy (making use of alien and unpopular political structures for the sake of ameliorating existing conditions) is one which Czechs have had recourse to in more recent times.

Czech experience of universal adult suffrage dates from 1907 when the concession of this right in the Austrian Empire facilitated the growth of social democratic and agrarian parties. The nationalities under Hungarian rule were accorded different treatment. A few years after universal suffrage had been granted in the Austrian Empire, the Magyar government of Dr Ladislas Lukacs promised electoral reform 'in the spirit of liberty and democratic progress, on the basis of the principle of Universal Suffrage, but in such a way as to preserve the due influence of the developed and riper strata of society and also the unitary national character of the Magyar state'.[4] When an electoral reform was introduced in 1913 it amounted to much less than universal suffrage, and an increase in the number of voters was counteracted by raising the voting age from twenty to thirty, by introducing minimum educational qualifications, and by gerrymandering the constituencies. On the eve of the birth of the Czechoslovak Republic, pressures to Magyarise the Slovaks remained intense.

Following the foundation of Czechoslovakia as an independent state, both Czechs and Slovaks, and the Germans and the minority nationalities too, enjoyed full freedom of political organisation and free elections on the basis of universal suffrage. These conditions resulted in a multiplicity of parties and interest groups. In 1925, for example, Czechoslovakia had twenty-nine political parties.[5] A very important characteristic of Czech social life even in the nineteenth century and, still more, during the First Republic, was the existence of numerous voluntary associations which gave large numbers of people experience of self-government and group interaction, as well as a practical understanding of political pluralism. Of particular importance in these respects (as well as to the national movement of the nineteenth century) was the cultural and gymnastic association, the Sokol, which was founded in 1862 and 'rested on essentially democratic principles, without any distinctions of rank or class'.[6] It is vital also not to overlook religious groups. Both before and after 1918 Protestants were disproportionately significant in Czech society – though the Czech Lands were not so overwhelmingly Catholic as Slovakia, Catholics were numerically the largest religious group – in terms of the prominent political personalities they produced, the experience of self-government they provided, and the tradition of dissent (political as well as religious, dating back to Jan Hus) which they embodied.

The Slovaks were much less satisfied with the political arrangements which emerged during the First Republic than were the Czechs, for the numerical superiority of the latter, together with their greater political experience and higher level of education, meant that a dominant role in the political system was played by Czechs. This was a logical outcome of the attempt to create a unitary Czechoslovak state based upon the assumption that there existed a single Czechoslovak nation. Many Slovaks had, however, expected a considerable degree of autonomy within the republic, and the Pittsburg Declaration of 30 June 1918, which was signed by Thomas Masaryk, among other representatives of the Czech and Slovak peoples, expressed itself in favour of this policy. In spite of the fact that the representatives of the Czechs and Slovaks who signed the agreement had explicitly stated that actual decisions on such matters would have to await the judgement of constitutionally elected representatives in the new state, there was subsequently some feeling on the part of the Slovaks that they had been let down.[7]

Czechoslovakia had strong claims to be regarded as by far the most democratic, libertarian and tolerant country within Central or East Europe between the wars. Its bicameral National Assembly acted as a critic of the succession of coalition governments which ruled Czechoslovakia and as a forum for the airing of grievances. The nationalities problem was both a major pluralistic element in the state and a severe strain on its cohesion, this despite the fact that official Czech nationalities policy was incomparably more enlightened than that of most of her neighbours. The rise of fascism in Germany and the degree of support which this brand of National Socialism won among the large German minority within Czechoslovakia became a major threat to the internal unity of the state, while from without Hitler's Germany threatened the sovereignty and very existence of Czechoslovakia.[8] Despite the enormous strains which were placed upon constitutional government in Czechoslovakia, liberty and the rule of law prevailed for twenty years following the foundation of the republic at the end of the First World War. The independence of the judiciary was preserved and justice was administered humanely. During the First Republic, in sharp contrast not only with the mass executions which took place when the Czech Lands were a German Protectorate from 1939 to 1945 but with the early years of Communist rule, capital punishment was carried out on only eight occasions.[9]

Czechoslovakia, however, suffered like other countries from the Great Depression, and for the victims of unemployment the First Republic was no golden age. In 1933 industrial output was only 60 per cent of the 1929 figure, agriculture declined, and approximately a million people were out of work.[10] Notwithstanding this, in 1968 the positive rather than the negative aspects of life in Czechoslovakia between the wars were increasingly stressed by Czech Communist intellectuals. The extent to which the political system of the First Republic rested upon consent was admitted even by its more hostile critics. Karel Bartošek, for example, a Czech Communist historian sympathetic to the European New Left, wrote that 'bourgeois hegemony in Czech society was based not only upon a coercive apparatus [*mocenský aparát*] but was also "a spiritual hegemony", founded on the "agreement" of the majority of the population; nationalism and nationalistic reformism played a role of the first order in its defence'.[11]

Throughout their history, neither the Czechs nor the Slovaks have been able to take their national existence for granted. For long periods they have come close to being submerged by stronger neighbours. In many respects other than this one, the experience of the two nations has been notably different. Even within the period of less than six decades since the Czechoslovak Republic was founded, great events and crises have affected Czechs and Slovaks quite differently. This is true both in the sense that their actual historical experience has often been different and in the sense that at times the same political framework has affected Czech and Slovak consciousness differently. The most important example of a quite distinct historical experience well within living memory is that of the Second World War when the Czech Lands constituted a German Protectorate and the Slovaks had their own clerico-fascist state which was wholly independent of Czech influence and was granted partial autonomy by the Germans. In Czechoslovakia, unlike Yugoslavia, there was no widespread resistance or partisan movement during the war. Any possibility of an uprising in the Czech Lands following the assassination of Reinhard Heydrich was eliminated by the destruction of the village and villagers of Lidice. In Slovakia an abortive uprising was organised in August 1944 by members of the Slovak Communist Party and the Slovak Democratic Party. After the war its significance was underplayed until the mid-sixties and its Communist leaders, including Gustáv Husák, were imprisoned as 'bourgeois nationalists' in the nineteen-fifties.

Government in Czechoslovakia between 1945 and February 1948 was by a coalition of Communist and non-Communist parties in the National

Front. It has been argued by at least one Communist historian that there was no continuity between the political systems of pre-war Czechoslovakia and the immediate post-war period.[12] It is true that in comparison with Britain, Holland or Denmark, there were vast changes in Czechoslovakia, including the emergence of the Communist Party as the largest single party in free elections in 1946, but continuity was to be found not only in the person of Edvard Beneš, who remained President, but in the parliamentary institutions which continued to function in much the same way as before. The National Front was not a complete novelty, although the absence of opposition outside it was. In the pre-war years the leaders of the political parties which made up the government coalition met to discuss and decide government policy in a body known as the 'Pětka' ('The Five'). All this was to change in 1948 when the Communists seized full power and the Czechoslovak political and economic structure was fully assimilated to the Soviet model. Nationalisation, which already in the period of coalition government had embraced banking, insurance, and key industries, was extended throughout industry to include even small shops and the businesses of craftsmen. From February 1949 the collectivisation of agriculture got under way. In November of that year a wave of arrests began. The political trials in Czechoslovakia from 1950 until Stalin's death and after (Husák received his sentence as late as 1954) were on a larger scale than in any other East European country, partly as an antidote to the very strength of Czech social democratic traditions. Only in 1956 did the first signs of a 'thaw' appear and not until the early sixties did anything like a serious political movement for reform, albeit one which had to act circumspectly, begin to emerge.

PERCEPTION OF HISTORY

As a result of an extremely significant investigation of 'the relationship of Czechs and Slovaks to their history' which was carried out by the Institute of Public Opinion of the Czechoslovak Academy of Sciences in the autumn of 1968,[13] we are fortunately able to compare the two nations' perception of their history. Among the most important of the questions were those which elicited the beliefs of Czechs and Slovaks on the most and least glorious periods in the history of their own nation. The first of these and certain other questions substantially and deliberately replicated ones which had been asked in a survey of public opinion in Czechoslovakia in late 1946. We are thus in a position (and this is probably unique in the study of Communist states) of being able to compare the beliefs of the public about their political history after twenty years of Communist rule with those which they held a little over a year prior to the Communist seizure of power. The comparisons over time (which we shall consider first) cannot unfortunately be made for the Slovaks: the 1946 survey was conducted only in the Czech Lands.

TABLE 6.1: Czechs' perception of their history (October 1968)

(a) The most glorious periods

*Question: When you contemplate the history of the Czech nation, which period do you consider to be the most glorious, a time of advance and development?*

|  | % |
|---|---|
| The First Republic [1918–1938] | 39 |
| The age of Hus [1369–1415] | 36 |
| The reign of King Charles IV [1346–1378] | 31 |
| The period after January 1968 | 21 |
| The National Revival [of the 19th century, including 1848] | 15 |
| 1945–1948 | 9 |
| The reign of King George of Poděbrady [1458–1471] | 5 |
| The reign of King Přemysl Otakar II [1253–1278] | 5 |
| Great Moravia [9th century] | 3 |
| The period after February 1948 | 3 |
| The age of St Wenceslas [10th century] | 1 |
| Other periods | 7 |

(b) The least glorious periods

*Question: And which period do you consider to be the least glorious, the most unfortunate time for the Czech nation?*

|  | % |
|---|---|
| The German Protectorate of Bohemia and Moravia [1939–1945] | 59 |
| The Age of Darkness [the period of approximately two centuries following the Battle of the White Mountain, 1620] | 51 |
| August 1968 | 31 |
| The 1950s | 20 |
| Munich and the Second Republic [1938–1939] | 11 |
| The Battle of Lipany [1434] | 3 |
| The Hussite wars | 1 |
| Foreign invasions (other than those already mentioned) | 1 |
| Other periods | 4 |

Source: *Vztah Čechů a Slováků k dějinám* (Prague, 1968) pp. 7 and 10. Respondents were permitted to name up to two periods, which is why the percentages total more than one hundred.

TABLE 6.2: Czechs' perception of their history (December 1946)

*Question: Which period of Czech history do you consider to be the most glorious?*

|  | % |
|---|---|
| The Hussite wars | 19 |
| The reign of King Charles IV | 17 |
| The present time (1945–46) | 16 |
| The age of St Wenceslas | 8 |
| The First Republic | 8 |
| The reign of King George of Poděbrady | 7 |
| The National Revival | 3 |
| The Baroque period | 0 |
| Don't know | 22 |

Source: *Vztah Čechů a Slováků k dějinám*, pp. 8–9. The respondents were allowed to name one period only and – as the registered negative response to the Baroque period indicates – they were presented with a list to choose from.

Note: The December 1946 survey was based on a quota sample of one thousand respondents. The Czechoslovak Institute of Public Opinion was founded early in 1946 and it quickly achieved high professional standards. In order to judge the reliability of their methods, the Institute carried out a pre-election survey prior to the General Election to the Czechoslovak National Assembly of 26 May 1946. The results of this were not published before the election (and so – unlike post-war British and American electoral surveys – had no possibility of actually affecting the outcome, and thus rendering less accurate the prediction), but they were deposited under seal with a notary prior to the election. The following is the comparison between the results of the inquiry and the actual results:

| Political party | Inquiry % | Election results % | Difference % |
|---|---|---|---|
| Communist Party | 39.6 | 40.2* | 0.6 |
| People's Party | 19.2 | 20.2 | 1.0 |
| Social Democratic Party | 16.0 | 15.6 | 0.4 |
| National Socialist Party | 22.5 | 23.7† | 1.2 |
| Blank voting slips | 2.7 | 0.4 | 2.3 |

Source: *What's Your Opinion? A Year's Survey of Public Opinion in Czechoslovakia* (Prague, 1947) p.13.

* This figure (and the others) applies, of course, to the Czech Lands only. In Slovakia the Communists received only 30 per cent support in the 1946 elections.

† It should be noted that the National Socialist Party, the second most successful after the Communists, was a democratic socialist party. It must not be confused with the National Socialists of pre-war Germany.

Both the elements of continuity in the assessments and the differences are revealing. Two of the periods placed among the first three 'most glorious periods' in Czech history in 1946 appear again in the first three in 1968 (Tables 6.1a and 6.2). In 1946 the period of the Hussite wars was regarded as the most glorious in the history of the Czech nation (19 per cent of respondents) with the reign of King Charles IV coming second (17 per cent). In 1968 the Hussite period occupied second place (with 36 per cent) and the time of Charles IV third place (31 per cent). (The higher range of figures in the 1968 survey is to be explained by the fact that whereas each respondent in 1946 was allowed to name only one period, respondents in the 1968 survey were permitted to mention two periods.) The great and significant difference concerns Czech attitudes to the First Republic. In December 1946, when the first survey was carried out, only 8 per cent of the Czech respondents thought that the First Republic was the most glorious period in the history of the nation. In 1968 it occupied first place in the affections of the Czech people, pushing even the Hussite period into second place.

In 1946 dissatisfaction with the First Republic (partly because of all too vivid memories of its failure, and the failure of its British and French allies, at the time of Munich) led twice as many people to favour 'the present period (1945–46)' as favoured the First Republic. (See Table 6.2.) The dissatisfaction with the pre-war republic existed among many Social Democrats as well as Communists and there was great enthusiasm for 'building socialism' in those years. While the timing of the 1968 survey (two months after the armed intervention in Czechoslovakia by Soviet, East German, Hungarian, Polish and Bulgarian troops) doubtless added to the emotional appeal of the First Republic, it is remarkable that following twenty years of denigration of 'bourgeois democracy' in general and the institutions and achievements of the Masaryk republic in particular, the esteem in which that same republic was held should have increased enormously.[14]

Though the published material of the Institute of Public Opinion of the Czechoslovak Academy of Sciences does not provide a full statistical breakdown of differences in perception of history according to age, social class, education, and sex, it indicates that differences along these lines existed. The report of the survey states that the youngest respondents more often put in the first place the post-January 1968 and the Hussite periods and less often the time of King George of Poděbrady. Women more often mentioned the First Republic and 1968, and men more often named the Hussite period. There was a positive correlation between higher education and a more frequent choice of the reign of Charles IV, the Hussite period and the National Revival, and those with higher education less frequently mentioned the 1945–8 period and 1968. The First Republic was named most often by people of middle-level education.[15]

While we may infer, therefore, that the First Republic received disproportionately strong support from women and white-collar workers and that it was held in less high esteem by male industrial workers, the growth in enthusiasm for the 1918–38 republic between 1946 and 1968 is nevertheless remarkable. Part of the explanation of this phenomenon is to be found in the fact that even many Czech Communist voters in 1946 accepted values and norms of political behaviour which were part of Czechoslovakia's cultural heritage. While the policies they supported differed (in many cases, sharply) from those of their opponents in other parties, at a deeper level of political culture they had much in common.[16] Others who consciously rejected not only capitalism but the political institutions and procedures of 'bourgeois democracy' gradually changed their beliefs under the influence of actual experience of a political system which followed the model of Stalin's Russia. In many cases enthusiastic Communists of the late nineteen-forties who had nothing but contempt for 'bourgeois democracy' became the reformers of the nineteen-sixties who had decided that competition for political office, freedom of political organisation, of the press, of speech, and of assembly, independence of the judiciary and curtailment of the power of the police were characteristic of democracy as such and were no less essential in a socialist than in a bourgeois democracy. The fact that Czech Communist intellectuals who had already reached adulthood by the end of the Second World War had experience of such institutional arrangements is of crucial importance. It is partly in terms of the different funds of political experience which they had to draw upon that we must explain the great differences in the strength and goals of political reformism in Czechoslovakia and in the Soviet Union in the period of 'de-Stalinisation'.

Some Czech writers have argued that as a result of their distinctive experience their nation acquired a greater political knowledge than most others.[17] Jiří Hochman, making essentially that point, also set the changes of the recent past in the context of an historically conditioned political culture (though without using the actual terminology, 'political culture'): 'The tempo of development of democratic forms is influenced by historical tradition, national mentality and by previous political experience. In contrast to Czechoslovakia where for more than a hundred years a bourgeois parliamentarianism gradually evolved, the rest of Eastern Europe has had a minimal experience, or no experience at all, of bourgeois democracy.'[18]

One comparison seldom explicitly made by Czech writers, however, was that between Czechs and Slovaks, though such comparisons were made in Slovakia. It seems likely that in the autumn of 1968, as a result of the dramatic experiences of that year, Czechs and Slovaks had come closer together than ever before in their basic political beliefs and nearer to a sympathetic appreciation of their distinctive national identities and problems. In the mid-seventies they are once again on terms of distrust, though with an important difference from the period before 1968. Whereas then it was the Slovaks who envied the greater economic prosperity of the Czechs and what they perceived as Czech political hegemony, it is now the turn of the Czechs to resent what they see as privileged treatment for Slovakia since Husák became First Secretary of the Party as well as the very fact that this unpopular Slovak holds the key Party post – and in 1975 even added the Presidency of the Republic to it. The fact that the popular Dubček was also a Slovak appears already to be a much less salient factor in the minds of Czechs. Anti-Slovak jokes – e.g. 'Did you hear that Bohemia is to be dug up? The Slovaks need a lake' – abound in contemporary Prague.

If it be true that the period of several months immediately after the Soviet armed intervention in Czechoslovakia in 1968 was the time of greatest mutual sympathy between Czechs and Slovaks thus far achieved, it is noteworthy that even in October 1968 the perceptions of Czechs and Slovaks of their historical experience and their evaluations of the most and least glorious periods in their nations' history diverged markedly. Less than half as many Slovaks as Czechs named the First Republic as one of the two most glorious periods in their history. (See Tables 6.1a and 6.3.) Approximately one Slovak in six, compared with an astonishingly meagre 3 per cent in the Czech Lands, regarded the 'period after February 1948' as the most glorious. Yet if this suggests greater militancy and more strongly-held 'hard-line' Communist attitudes among a significant minority of Slovaks, there is, surprisingly, a group of almost comparable size (13 per cent) who declared their support for the wartime Slovak state. It would be over-simple to regard all of them as fascists, for many are doubtless nationalists attracted by the element of autonomy which Slovaks then enjoyed. Perhaps this figure can be taken, rather, to reflect the extent of separatism among the Slovaks, a desire on the part of over one-eighth of the population for a complete break with the Czechs.[19]

TABLE 6.3: Slovaks' perception of their history (October 1968)

(a) The most glorious periods

*Question: When you contemplate the history of the Slovak nation, which periods do you consider to be the most glorious, a time of advance and development?*

|  | % |
|---|---|
| The Age of Štúr [in particular, the 1840s] | 36 |
| The period after January 1968 | 36 |
| The Slovak National Uprising [1944] | 26 |
| The First Republic [1918–1938] | 17 |
| The period after February 1948 | 16 |
| 1945–1948 | 13 |
| The Slovak State [1939–1945] | 13 |
| Great Moravia [9th century] | 3 |
| Other periods | 3 |

## (b) The least glorious periods

*Question: And which period do you consider to be the least glorious, the most unfortunate time for the Slovak nation?*

|  | % |
|---|---|
| The Slovak State [1939–1945] | 44 |
| Austro-Hungarian Empire | 38 |
| The 1950s | 31 |
| August 1968 | 25 |
| The First Republic [1918–1938] | 5 |
| The collapse of Great Moravia | 2 |
| Foreign invasions | 1 |

Source: *Vztah Čechů a Slováků k dějinám*, pp. 9 and 11. Respondents were permitted to mention a maximum of two periods.

To put the separatist orientation into perspective, however, it must be noted that a very much larger percentage of Slovaks named the Slovak state as one of the *least* glorious periods in their nation's history, and indeed this turned out to be the most unpopular of all in the eyes of Slovaks questioned in the 1968 survey. The years of the Second World War are seen by both Czechs and Slovaks as the most unfortunate in the history of the two nations, though the proportion in Slovakia who view the Slovak state in this light is admittedly appreciably lower than the proportion of Czechs who regard the protectorate as the most unhappy period in Czech history. (See Tables 6.1b and 6.3b.) The period of Magyar domination in the Austro-Hungarian Empire was the second most unpopular historical era in the eyes of Slovaks, whereas for Czechs the 'Age of Darkness', the period of approximately two hundred years following the Battle of the White Mountain in 1620 (which saw the destruction of the Czech kingdom and of the native Czech nobility and the incorporation of the nation in the Habsburg empire) followed close behind the German Protectorate in the references to the most unfortunate time for the Czech people.

In their reflections on more recent history, an interesting degree of convergence occurred between Czechs and Slovaks, both sharing a strong hostility to the Soviet-style political order of the 1950s and the Soviet armed intervention in Czechoslovakia of August 1968 (Tables 6.1b and 6.3b). There are, then, some areas of significant agreement between Czechs and Slovaks in their understanding of their nations' historical experience as well as divergent perceptions. The differences are most apparent in their respective attitudes to the First Republic and in their identification with, and loyalty to, different historical personalities. Whereas the First Republic was regarded by Czechs in 1968 as the greatest era of Czech history, it is the 'age of Štúr' (the period of Slovak national awakening' in the nineteenth century, in which the leading figure was L'udovít Štúr) and the post-January period of 1968 which share top place in the affection of Slovaks. The 'age of Štúr' did not, naturally enough, figure as such in Czech replies to the survey (though 15 per cent mentioned the Czech 'national revival' which was broadly contemporaneous with it) and the period after January 1968 was placed in fourth place by Czech respondents, more of whom apparently applied a longer-range historical perspective.

### VALUES AND FUNDAMENTAL POLITICAL BELIEFS

A belief in the virtues of political pluralism has almost certainly been a dominant one throughout the existence of the Czechoslovak republic. Even in 1946, a time when enthusiastic support for the Communist Party reached probably its highest point, and eight political parties competed for electoral support (four in the Czech Lands and four in Slovakia), only 34.2 per cent of Czechs regarded this as too many parties, while 5.6 per cent thought there were too few parties and 57.5 per cent were satisfied with the existing number.[20] In a pre-August 1968 survey, citizens' response to political pluralism was explored in a question which asked them whether they thought that there should be 'one political line valid for all' or whether there should 'exist' side by side, many concepts and proposals of different parties and groups'. In favour of many concepts were 81 per cent of respondents, including even 68 per cent of the respondents who were members of the Communist Party and 79 per cent of those with only lower education. Among non-Party members, the support for such a political pluralism was 86 per cent and among respondents with higher education 94 per cent.[21]

Values which may conveniently be termed 'social democratic' are deeply entrenched in Czechoslovak society. This has been recognised both by reformist and conservative members of the Czechoslovak Communist Party. In a paragraph which was censored from an article which he wrote in October for the journal, *My 1967* (No. 10), and which could be published in full only in 1968, Jan Procházka (a prominent writer and at the time a candidate member of the Central Committee of the Party) argued:

> In our tradition we have something which socialism in the other fraternal states did not have the opportunity to encounter: democracy. I am not thinking only of those twenty years of the pre-Munich republic, where it was this very condition which granted the Communist Party of Czechoslovakia itself its unprecedented advance. I am thinking also of the whole period since the Revival: the struggle for the language, for the nation, was realised hand in hand with the fight for social progress and civil liberty.[22]

The widespread support for social democratic values has frequently been accorded a substantial measure of recognition by the present political leadership in Czechoslovakia and its supporters, though they have naturally found a number of other less complimentary names for it. Thus the prevalent value orientations within Czechoslovakia were summed up by a document drawing 'lessons from the crisis in the party and society', which was presented to a plenary session of the Central Committee in December 1970, in the following terms:

> The faults and shortcomings in this country after the 13th Party Congress of 1966 were all the more serious in that great weight in the social structure of our society was wielded by numerous petty-bourgeois strata in the villages and among the town population. These strata represented a significant political current with great tradition, strong organisation and a clear-cut petty-bourgeois ideology of nationalism, Masarykism and social-democratism which was deeply rooted and also penetrated certain parts of the working class. In Slovakia, a considerable role was played by religious survivals which were misused by Ludakist fascism. These strata were for scores of years politically and culturally oriented upon the West. All this created in this country fertile ground for the infiltration and application of opportunist and revisionist tendencies.[23]

Which were the petty-bourgeois strata in a society in which all agriculture had been collectivised and all industry state-owned for almost twenty years is not immediately clear, but it is interesting to find *de facto* recognition of the significance of political culture in the Czechoslovak context in such a source. Writing in 1971, a Party High School teacher and strong ideological opponent of the reform movement within the Czechoslovak Communist Party, Miroslav Šolc, was even more forthright in his acknowledgement of the strength and widespread nature of social-democratic beliefs within Czechoslovak society. Šolc argued that Czechoslovak 'right-wing opportunism' had three specific characteristics which were not to be found in other countries: firstly, that 'for many years strong social democratic traditions have existed – and continue to exist – in this country and in the entire Czechoslovak workers' movement'; secondly, the fact that 'Masarykism, which adopted the main features of social democracy and Bernsteinism, has exerted and continues to exert a strong influence in this country'; and, thirdly, 'the so-called "cult of western educational background" in our nations, which has led to the rejection of Leninism in the ČSSR, over-emphasis on national specifics, repudiation of the general laws governing the construction of Socialism, and refusal to accept international experience, particularly that of the Soviet Union and the CPSU – which reached its climax in overt anti-Sovietism.'[24]

Both of the spokesmen for the official political culture quoted above refer to 'Masarykism', and it is indeed the case that the values of Thomas Masaryk are widely respected among Czechs and, to a somewhat lesser extent, Slovaks. Between the end of the war and February 1948, no other party enjoyed as much support for its policies as did the Communist Party for theirs. Yet in 1946, the only year in which the Communists emerged as the largest single party in genuinely competitive elections, the Czechs attached greater positive significance to Masaryk (whose values were scarcely compatible with those of Klement Gottwald and Rudolf Slánský) than to any other personality in their history. (See Figure 6.4, p. 180.)

Even at that time it is probable that most of the basic beliefs which Masaryk represented, such as his attachment to pluralism and libertarianism, his view of democracy as 'a conversation among equals, the thinking of a free people open to complete publicity',[25] his wholehearted support of political, religious and ethnic toleration,[26] and his devotion to a 'cultural internationalism' which does not exclude the intimate love of one's own nation, nor the desire to preserve its cultural autonomy'[27] were shared by a majority of Czechs, including many thousands of Czech Communists. It also seems likely, however, that this was a time of acute cognitive dissonance within the Czechoslovak political culture as well as a period of severe tension in the arena of political action. Political crises can be particularly important influences in the formation and re-formation of a political culture.[28] The Munich betrayal of Czechoslovak interests, the subsequent dismemberment of Czechoslovakia, and the horrors of German occupation during the Second World War were traumatic experiences and immense national crises in the recent past which strengthened some elements in the Czech political culture and weakened others or, as it may perhaps be better expressed, gave added force to certain significant sub-cultures at the expense of the dominant political culture. Pan-Slavism, and Russophilism (a tendency to look to Russia as a friendly Slav 'big brother' – in a pre-Orwellian sense of that term), together with the traditional Czech fear of being politically and culturally submerged by the Germanic peoples, had been enormously strengthened by the war experience. Not surprisingly, anti-Germanism reached its greatest heights during and immediately after the war and, as a corollary, gratitude to the Soviet Union for the major part which it was perceived to have played in the liberation of Czechoslovakia was much in evidence and contributed materially to the success of the Czechoslovak Communist Party.

Between 1945 and 1948 it was far from evident to many Czechs that there was a tension between the political culture of which Masaryk was a symbol and the basic political beliefs and orientations of the Communist Party leadership. (Indeed, it was not until their monopoly of power had been safely secured after February 1948 that Communist leaders openly attacked Thomas Masaryk.) It subsequently became clearer that though the official Communist political culture – in its ideal form – overlapped with the 'traditional' Czech political culture, at many points the values they embodied and orientations to the political process which they embraced were incompatible. The contrast between the expectations of a majority even of Czech Communists and what actually followed February 1948 was within a few years to strengthen attachment to those values and political beliefs on which the Party leadership and the mass media poured scorn.

In the course of his recent interesting analysis of the reform movement in Czechoslovakia, the political theorist and former Secretary of the central Committee of the Party, Zdeněk Mlynář, has noted that 'Masarykism', even 'in the primitive and ill-thought-out form of a simple belief in the renewal of democratic principles "which after all used to exist in Czechoslovakia before the war" ' was influential '*in this form* on a mass scale'.[29] But in contradistinction to the ideological spokesmen of the present Party leadership, Mlynář argues that the important place given to 'pre-revolutionary beliefs' in the consciousness of society cannot simply be explained away as ' "survivals and traditions" of so-called Masarykism' or by blaming the strength of petty-bourgeois strata when the petty-bourgeoisie had died out as a class and when all means had been used to propagate the officially approved ideology over a period of twenty years.[30] On the contrary, Mlynář argues, these values had come to fill a void created when the expectations of the majority of society who had supported the ideology of 'the first phase of the revolution' were not met. Disillusionment set in first among the working masses 'because it is their concrete, everyday life which first teaches them not only what the revolution has changed, but also all that has remained unchanged by revolutionary actions'.[31] For Mlynář, therefore, it is wholly understandable that 'the void in societal consciousness' came to be filled with 'those ideas, political attitudes and values (*hodnotová měřítka*)' which had in the past seemed to offer the strongest guarantee against the recurrence of the type of phenomenon which appeared in 'the second phase of the revolution' and which 'societal consciousness . . . refused on a mass scale to accept'.[32]

Among the few points at which the post-1948 political reality corresponded with what we feel justified in calling the dominant political culture were its promotion of a relative egalitarianism in the field of income distribution and provision of socio-economic security. The latter is a general feature of Communist societies (with the exception of some political deviants and their families), but income equalisation went further in Czechoslovakia than in any other country in the world for which data are available.[33] Those on the highest echelons of the political élite were exceptions to the egalitarian rule, but the Czechoslovak intelligentsia enjoyed what was in their view the dubious privilege of being the most levelled-down intelligentsia in East Europe. One of the aims of the Czechoslovak economic reform, officially adopted in 1966 but never completely implemented, was to allow income differentials to increase by providing greater material rewards for the acquisition of skills and qualifications. This evoked a good deal of distrust on the part of unskilled workers, though it was widely supported by the professionally qualified and a majority of skilled workers, especially after the case for the economic reform as a whole had been stated by Ota Šik, the leading spokesman of the economic reformers and by 1968 a Deputy Prime Minister, in a series of influential television broadcasts.[34] While a relative egalitarianism met with popular support, a majority of the population seemed to believe that this policy had been taken too far.

The Action Programme of the Czechoslovak Communist Party (published in April 1968) which set out the Party's provisional agreement on political and economic reform (including proposals for the institutionalisation of political pluralism) was supported by the overwhelming majority of the population of Czechoslovakia. In a September 1968 opinion poll, 94.6 per cent of respondents expressed their support for it and the level of support was the same among both Communist Party members and those outside the Party.[35] Though the Action Programme was a compromise document which did not go as far as many of the reformers wanted, no ruling Communist Party has ever produced a programme containing more fundamental self-criticism or more radical proposals for reform of the political system. This Programme, for which there was such a broad basis of support, outlined plans for building what it called 'a new model of socialist society, one which is profoundly democratic and conforms to Czechoslovak conditions'.[36] The reformers within the leadership of the Communist Party found, indeed, that pressure from society for reform was both more urgent and more far-reaching than many of them had anticipated. They were faced with the impossible task of attempting to satisfy two different publics whose demands conflicted fundamentally – those of the vast majority of the citizens of Czechoslovakia and those of the Soviet leadership and of Communist leaders in the other Warsaw Pact countries (with the exception of Roumania). As Alex Pravda has put it: 'Popular support, the real mainstay against conservative domestic opposition and Soviet pressure, ebbed with every sign of back-sliding on reform, while socialist allies [i.e. foreign Communist opponents!] were not satisfied with any concession short of effective abnegation of the whole programme of reforms designed to create a socialist democratic political system.'[37]

Hard evidence that the programme and policies of the Czechoslovak reformers of 1968 were in line with popular beliefs and values is to be found in the opinion poll support for those politicians who symbolised reform and the rejection of those who had supported the pre-1968 political system. This can be seen clearly in Figure 6.1 which charts

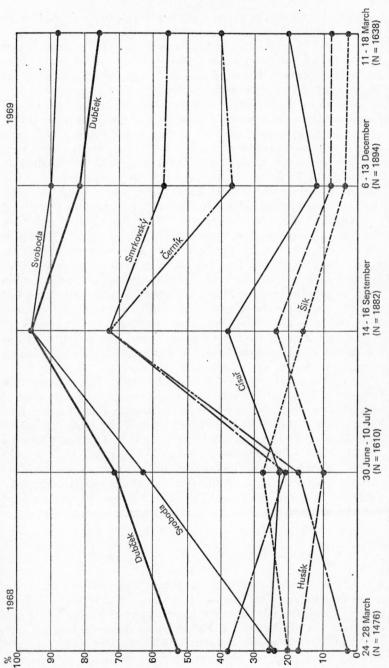

Fig. 6.1 Levels of trust of Czechoslovak citizens in their politicians

Note: The question was: 'Name the personalities of contemporary public life in whom you have the most trust.' Only those public figures who, at some time in the period, were named by at least 20 per cent of respondents are included. We have thus excluded Rázl, Colotka and Sádovský, who in March 1969 received stronger support than Šik (but still less than 10 per cent).

the support of Czechoslovak politicians between March 1968 and March 1969. Alexander Dubček, not himself so much a pioneer reformer as a symbol of the process of democratisation, was rivalled in popular support only by Ludvík Svoboda (at that time also a symbol of reform). Dubček lost some support in late 1968 and early 1969 as concessions to the Soviet point of view were increasingly made, but on the eve of his removal from the Party First Secretaryship he still retained the trust of more than three-quarters of the population of Czechoslovakia. Husák, who at no time received as much as 25 per cent support, had much more rapidly accommodated himself to Soviet wishes after August 1968 and, as a consequence, his support at the time when he was about to take over the leadership of the Czechoslovak Communist Party had dropped to below 10 per cent. More conservative Communists than Husák – such as Bil'ak, Indra or Kolder – did not come near to attaining even Husák's modest level of support. Of the more radical reformers, Ota Šik's support was close to 30 per cent when he was in the public eye in early July, but fell rapidly after the invasion when he was, for most of the time, abroad. Josef Smrkovský, who was regarded as one of the most stalwart reformers within the Party Praesidium, came third in order of popularity to Svoboda and Dubček. If any further proof of popular support for the reformist leadership is required, we need look no further than the remarkable degree of national unity shown on 21 August 1968 and the days that followed when demonstrative support for Dubček and his colleagues was so great that the Soviet leadership found themselves unable to achieve one of their minimum immediate objectives – the replacement of the First Secretary of the Czechoslovak Communist Party by someone more reliable from the Soviet point of view. They were forced to restore recognition to Dubček whom they had publicly described as the leader of a minority group within the Praesidium of the Czechoslovak Communist Party who had adopted a 'frankly right wing opportunist position'.[38] Another eight months elapsed before the goal of Dubček's removal was attained, though in the meantime the gradual dismantling of the reform programme by the politicians in whom Czechs and Slovaks had placed their trust worked to Soviet advantage.

FOCI OF IDENTIFICATION AND LOYALTY

It is noteworthy that none of the personalities of 1968 succeeded even at the time in removing Thomas Masaryk, the founder and first President of Czechoslovakia, from the highest place of honour in the eyes of Czechs. As can be seen in Figure 6.2 (p. 179), the October 1968 survey of 'the relationship of Czechs and Slovaks to their history' fully supports the significance which has been attached to Czech loyalty to

Masaryk. This loyalty has posed great problems for the Communist Party leadership in Czechoslovakia since 1948, for Masaryk, a Christian humanist who was deeply devoted to social democratic values, is a symbol for Czechs both of national independence and of decency and libertarianism in political life. It has made the task of remoulding the political culture especially difficult, even in comparison with the problems of political socialisation in the Soviet Union and possibly the other East European states. As Gordon Skilling has put it:

> In most cases, as, for instance, Soviet Russia, the past . . . rejected was autocratic and reactionary, and only selected radical traditions were regarded as forerunners of communism. In Czechoslovakia, however, the dominant tradition was itself democratic, deeply rooted in the feelings of the people, and regarded positively by most Czechs. The communists, therefore, had to renounce the advanced and progressive features of their nations' past, such as the legacy of Masaryk, since these were integral elements of the dominant tradition.[39]

Thus throughout almost the entire Communist period – especially from the early fifties until the middle sixties and from 1970 onwards – Masaryk has been a frequent object of attack in books and in newspaper articles. Many members of the Communist Party were embarrassed by this approach, for not infrequently they shared a number of Masaryk's values and venerated his historic achievements. Their attitude to Masaryk is represented by the position of Jan Procházka who, discussing education and the school curriculum (from which, he suggested, truthfulness had been eliminated in Czechoslovakia), wrote:

> To the more intelligent boys and girls, it was hard to understand that, in the history of other nations, it was possible and permitted to pay homage even to tsars and tyrants, while in our own country, there was no place in history for a man who was the founder of our democracy, who was neither a usurper nor the murderer of his own children but an educated, democratic and highly moral man.[40]

The thinly veiled reference to Russian history and to Ivan the Terrible and Peter the Great draws attention to an additional point to that brought out by Skilling. Not *all* Russian autocrats have fared badly in the hands of Soviet historians. Ivan the Terrible and, to a much greater extent, Peter the Great regained under Stalin an official favour (which they continue to enjoy) as 'progressive for their time' and as symbols of Russian national strength. Their popular standing (especially high in the case of Peter I) has been supported by the socialising process under the ultimate control of the Party leadership.

The continuing popularity of Thomas Masaryk is, in a sense, the more significant in that the high esteem in which he is held is in spite of the hostile propaganda directed against him by all the agencies of political socialisation with the exception of that of the family. Family ties in Czechoslovakia remain strong, however, and it would appear that Czech and Slovak families have played crucially important roles as instruments of socialisation.[41] Children received at home a different account of Masaryk – and (in the Czech Lands) of the First Republic – from that which they were given at school, and it was the former which proved to be the more influential. Yet at an official level Thomas Masaryk was fully rehabilitated only during the months of radical political change of 1968. On 13 April of that year, in an unprecedented step for a Communist President, Ludvík Svoboda laid a wreath of flowers on Masaryk's grave at Lány. In 1968 Masaryk's values were once again publicly asserted, his books were published, and thousands of photographs of him were sold on the streets. Since April of 1969, when Gustáv Husák succeeded Alexander Dubček in the First Secretaryship of the Czechoslovak Communist Party, all this has changed. References in the press to Masaryk and 'Masarykism' have become uniformly unfavourable.

It is of interest that Thomas Masaryk was even more popular in 1968 than he was two years before the Communists came to power. In 1946 he was named by 74 per cent of Czechs as the most significant personality in Czech history, but by 1968 the number who esteemed him so highly had risen to 81 per cent (Figures 6.2 and 6.4). The gap between Masaryk and his nearest rivals had also risen enormously. The standing of Edvard Beneš, in contrast, was drastically lower in 1968 than it had been twenty-two years earlier. In the later survey he was mentioned by only 7 per cent of Czechs compared with the 62 per cent who had ranked him second only to Masaryk in 1946. Even this however was stronger support than that accorded by the Czechs to any Communist politicians other than Ludvík Svoboda and Alexander Dubček, as can be seen from Figure 6.2. That Svoboda was a Czech and Dubček a Slovak may have had something to do with the fact that the former received greater support than the latter, though more important is the point that Svoboda's popularity reached its peak in the autumn of 1968 when the public memory of his role in the events of August 1968 was still fresh. At that time he won great popular credit for his resistance to those who tried in vain to secure his presidential blessing for a new government of 'workers and peasants' led by Alois Indra at a moment in history when Czechoslovakia had just been occupied by over half a million foreign troops. (Subsequently, Svoboda was persuaded to accommodate himself almost totally to the new political situation, whereas Dubček continued to defend the course he had followed in 1968. Though Dubček was expelled from the Communist Party in the summer of 1970, Svoboda remained President of the republic until 1975.)

Fig. 6.2 Czech evaluations of historic personalities (October 1968) *Question: Which personalities in our history do you esteem most? (Czech respondents)*

Fig. 6.3 Slovak evaluations of historic personalities (October 1968) *Question: Which personalities in our history do you esteem most? (Slovak respondents)*

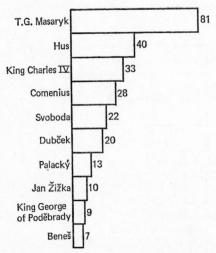

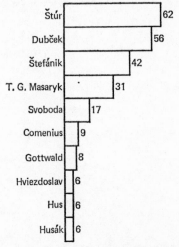

Source: *Vztah Čechů a Slováků k dějinám*, pp. 15–18. Respondents were allowed to mention up to three people. In addition to those named above, St Wenceslas was mentioned by 6 per cent of Czech respondents, Karel Havlíček Borovský by 4 per cent, and Jan Masaryk, Štefánik and Gottwald by 2 per cent.

Source: *Vztah Čechů a Slováků k dějinám*, pp. 15–18. Respondents were allowed to mention up to three people. The only other person to be mentioned by a significant number of Slovaks was Clementis (4 per cent).

Significant differences between the foci of loyalty of Czechs and Slovaks emerge clearly from a comparison of Figures 6.2 and 6.3. In Slovakia Dubček was held by more than half of the population to be the greatest personality in Slovak history, coming second only to the nineteenth century hero, Štúr (see Figure 6.3). Masaryk (who was half Slovak by descent) also retains a substantial measure of loyalty in Slovakia in addition to his unrivalled popularity with the Czechs, though both he and Hus are much less important as political symbols in Slovakia than in Bohemia and Moravia. Rather interestingly, Communists figure more prominently in the Slovak list of 'great men' than they do in the Czech Lands. In Slovakia, in addition to Dubček (56 per cent) and Svoboda (17 per cent), honourable mention is made of

Gottwald, Husák and Clementis by 8, 6 and 4 per cent respectively of respondents.

Fig. 6.4 Czech evaluations of historic persona-
ities (December 1946)
*Question: Name the three men in Czech
history whom you consider to be the most
significant?*

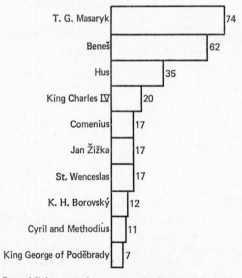

In addition to those named above, the only
men mentioned by 1 per cent or more of
respondents were King Přemysl Otakar II
(3 per cent) and Josef Dobrovský (1 per cent).

In the immediate post-war years the Communist Party was an unambiguous focus of loyalty for almost half the population in the Czech
Lands and a smaller proportion of citizens in Slovakia. By the 1960s
the extent of the support was much reduced, though surveys which
attempted to discover the extent of popular support for the Party during
the relatively short period in 1968 and early 1969 when citizens were
prepared to answer such a sensitive question frankly could not provide
clear-cut answers. This is because to speak of 'the Party' is in itself an
oversimplification at a time when there were quite clearly different
groupings and tendencies within the Party. The support for the reformist tendency was *unambiguous* (see Figure 6.1), but support for the
Party as a whole was much more qualified. A survey attempt to find

out what would have happened in a hypothetical election in the summer of 1968 indicated that the Communist Party would have polled between 39 and 43 per cent of the votes.[42] In early January 1969 (i.e. when Dubček was still First Secretary) an Institute of Public Opinion survey showed that 50 per cent of respondents had 'complete trust' (11 per cent) or 'trust' (39 per cent) in the Party. A third of the respondents hedged (the 33 per cent who expressed 'neither trust nor distrust'), and 17 per cent expressed varying degrees of distrust.[43] In contrast, only 17 per cent of these respondents claimed to have had any degree of trust in the Party in the pre-January 1968 period (26 per cent showed 'neither trust nor distrust', and 57 per cent varying degrees of distrust).[44] In July 1968, 8 per cent of survey respondents had recalled that they had 'complete trust' in the Party prior to January of that year and 17 per cent 'trust'.[45] Even if we take this earlier and higher figure as the more reliable one, it would appear that support for the Party as a whole doubled under Dubček's leadership.

Lack of identification with the Communist Party (1968 partially excepted) on the part of a majority of the population has been paralleled by the lack of success of the official political culture in altering fundamentally evaluations of particular occupations and social groups. The large-scale sociological survey of the Machonin team showed that in the mid-sixties a majority of skilled workers, as well as a majority of professional specialists and clerks, considered that they would have been better off if they had lived 30–40 years ago. Semi-skilled workers rated 'the old days' and the present period as equal and only agricultural workers and unskilled workers evaluated the present-day situation more highly.[46] In a study of Party members at that time, Lubomír Brokl found that higher status characteristics were determined by occupational group, degree of authority, size of income, and style of life, and that old Communists (i.e. pre-1945 members) had the lowest status in all analysed indices of social status. Generally, workers' occupations and working-class origins were of less consequence in relation to social status than qualifications and education.[47] The essence of the matter has been expressed by Jaroslav Krejčí: 'Despite the official claim that the workers are the ruling class, to cease to be a worker is generally accepted as a promotion and to become a worker . . . a demotion.'[48]

The identification of Czechs and Slovaks with nationalities other than their own is also a question of considerable interest. Crises, as we have noted, can strengthen or weaken certain elements in a political culture, and just as the Munich betrayal of 1938 weakened Czechoslovak faith in Western governments and strengthened the sub-culture within Czechoslovak society which was oriented towards the Soviet Union and Slavophilism, so the armed intervention of August 1968 almost destroyed the sympathy for the Soviet system which a significant minority had harboured and the warm feelings towards Russians which had been shared by a probable majority of the Czechoslovak population.

Unlike the Poles, who have a history of suffering at the hands of both Russians and Germans, the oppressors of the Czechs had been Austrians and Germans. When Palacký was invited to attend a pan-German Congress in Frankfurt in 1848, he refused to do so on the grounds that the Czechs were Slavs. Long before the Communists came to power in 1948 the Russian influence on Czech literary culture, though sometimes exaggerated,[49] had been an important one. Pan-Slavism in practical terms meant looking to the Russians for salvation from Austrian oppression. In the 1930s, and more especially during the Second World War, the Czechs looked to the Soviet Union as a benevolent and powerful ally. While the events of 1948 and the next few years did much to destroy the credit of the Soviet Union in the eyes of many non-Communist Czechs, there was no overt Russian intervention. The seizure of power by Czechoslovak Communists in February 1948 was carried through without Soviet military help and the role of the Soviet 'advisers' in the investigations which preceded the political trials was not publicised. Thus, even while an increasing number of Czechs and Slovaks were becoming critical of the extent to which their political and economic system had been modelled closely on the Soviet one, they did not, on the whole, harbour feelings of animosity towards the people of the Soviet Union. Non-Communist Czechs frequently adopted a patronising attitude towards Russians whom they regarded as being on a lower cultural level, but their view of them was benign in comparison with the anti-Russian feelings of Hungarians and Poles. As for the reformist Communists in Czechoslovakia, before 1968 they were in general well-disposed towards the Soviet Union and when they criticised what they saw as slavish adherence on the part of the Czechoslovak Communist Party to the Soviet model they tended to blame their own leadership, rather than the CPSU, for disregarding Czechoslovakia's distinctive cultural heritage and social and economic conditions.

The impact of the entry of Soviet troops into Czechoslovakia in August 1968 on the deep-rooted cultural sympathies and historic fund of goodwill of both Czechs and Slovaks for Russia was devastating. When in October 1968 Czechs were asked which nation was closest to them in character and culture, more named Austrians and Germans than mentioned 'the peoples of the USSR'. Only 10 per cent of Czechs named the latter, which was a very much lower level of identification with Russians than might have been expected at any time within the previous hundred years.[50] That Czechs should say they felt closer to Austrians and Germans may be regarded as rather remarkable in the light of past relations between the latter two nations and the Czechs. The Russophile strand within Czechoslovak political culture has, then, been seriously weakened and though this very fact illustrates the possibility of great change within a political culture, it is not clear how this particular trend will be reversed so long as the events of 1968 remain within the national consciousness. Even though it is the case now that all the formal institutional agencies of political socialisation are applying themselves to the task of reinterpreting the events of 1968 along approved Soviet lines, we have already seen that, starting from a much more auspicious base, the political socialisation programme introduced after 1948 was surprisingly ineffective.

Almost twice as many Slovaks as Czechs named the peoples of the Soviet Union as those to whom they felt closest in character and culture, but even in Slovakia the Soviet people came a poor third to Yugoslavs and Poles. For both Czechs and Slovaks the Yugoslavs were the people to whom, by an overwhelming margin, they felt closest. When they were asked which foreign countries had had the greatest influence on the culture of the two peoples, both Czechs and Slovaks placed France and Germany in the first two places. In the Czech Lands, 42 per cent mentioned France and 38 per cent Germany, whereas 24 per cent of Slovaks named Germany and 32 per cent referred to France. Having in mind, evidently, the influence of their classical civilisation and culture, 21 per cent of Czechs put Italy and Greece in third place, while Austria and Russia were both mentioned by 11 per cent. Further indication, perhaps, that more Slovaks than Czechs feel affinity to Russia was provided by the fact that Slovaks put Russia in third place in the list of countries which had most influenced their cultural development.[51]

### POLITICAL KNOWLEDGE AND EXPECTATIONS

For nations with experience of free elections, a parliament in which debate on basic issues took place, a political environment in which parties had to compete for office and in which citizens could give vent to their varied and conflicting views on political and social issues, the attempt to give a Stalinist meaning to such familiar concepts as elections, parliament, democracy and freedom could not be wholly successful. A number of Czechs and Slovaks recognised the problem of the language of political discourse to be a substantive, not pedantic, one and devoted considerable attention to it. Thus, in the period after the Soviet intervention, a Czech political scientist wrote: 'It is our duty radically to reject discredited ideological jargon which would ultimately drag us to its own level, which would, quite simply, deceive us. We could never completely succeed in outwitting this jargon, either by sly, hidden textual equivocations or by suggestive hints. Neither can it be silenced by courageous civil actions.'[52] The same author, Petr Pithart, pointed out how scrupulously attentive to accuracy and nuance within the narrow limits open to them were many Czechoslovak intellectuals at an earlier stage. He observes:

> At the end of the Fifties and at the beginning of the Sixties, when the real substance of what Stalinism had meant was only beginning to be understood in our latitudes, our social scientists and journalists adopted a special code: the more enlightened authors did not write about the personality cult as such, but rather about the 'personality cult' or about the so-called personality cult... Since more accurate terms were missing or 'forbidden', they chose at least these agreed signs, because quite rightly they thought that they would not be able to get at the truth if they used ideologically ordained terms which entailed the risk of new untruths, new lies being created.[53]

Pithart's observation is apposite when he implies that an understanding of what Stalinism had involved came only gradually. Political knowledge in Czechoslovakia was, of course, sharply reduced in the years after 1948 by strict censorship of the domestic news media and the cutting off of foreign contacts other than those with Communist countries. The extent of the 're-education' and the blocking of inexpedient information should not be underestimated. It is sufficient to note that for many rank and file Communists and for a not inconsiderable section of the Czechoslovak people, the revelations of Khrushchev at the Twentieth Congress of the Soviet Communist Party came as a great shock. Many who had accepted the Czechoslovak show trials at their face value realised only in the late fifties the extent to which they had allowed their critical faculties to become dulled in the atmosphere of the early Cold War.[54]

Yet in a country so close to the West geographically and culturally as Czechoslovakia the process of isolation and re-education was necessarily far from complete. There was a widespread awareness of the nature of Western political institutions and of the economic progress of Western Europe in the post-war period. By the early 1960s, economic expectations in Czechoslovakia were high, partly because Czechoslovakia had already obtained solid experience as an industrial country between the wars, partly because the economy had done well in quantitative terms throughout the 1950s, and also in view of the knowledge that a higher standard of living was being enjoyed in some West European countries which had started the post-war period from no more developed an economic base than Czechoslovakia herself. Expectations of political change were also given an important external stimulus by Khrushchev's attack on Stalin at the Twentieth Congress of the CPSU in 1956 and, more openly, at the Twenty-second Party Congress in 1961.

Even in the nineteen-fifties the Party leadership did not have a monopoly control over information because of the existence of foreign broadcasting stations. What proportion of Czechoslovak citizens listened to such broadcasts in the fifties is not known, but interesting survey data on the late sixties were provided by a Czech Party journal in 1970. When censorship within Czechoslovakia itself withered away in 1968, only 16.98 per cent of Czechoslovak respondents listened to foreign broadcasts. This contrasts with 47.16 per cent in June 1967 and 56.50 per cent in March 1969.[55] Since a wider range of political information and of political views could still be found in the mass media of March 1969 than were to be permitted subsequently, it may be possible to infer that an even higher percentage than 56.50 per cent of Czechs and Slovaks are listening to foreign broadcasts at the present time, for there appears to be an awkward correlation from the point of view of the present Party leadership between unfreedom of the domestic mass media and propensity to listen to foreign radio stations. Young people and those with higher education listen to foreign broadcasts to a disproportionate extent, with a majority of the young listening to Radio Free Europe or West German broadcasts.[56] Older citizens prefer the BBC and the Voice of America; in the case of the former network this is a habit acquired during the German occupation when the BBC gained a reputation for reliability.[57]

Throughout the 1960s an increasing number of Western tourists visited Czechoslovakia and from the mid-sixties (until the end of the decade) study and business trips, as well as tourist travel, became much easier for Czechs and Slovaks. In 1967 one in six Czechoslovaks travelled abroad, compared with about one in a hundred and eighty citizens of the Soviet Union.[58] Since late 1969 the outward movement of Czechs and Slovaks has been greatly curtailed, but in the mid-seventies the extent of tourism and of contact between Czechoslovak citizens and foreigners is substantially in excess of that in the 1950s, even if much reduced in comparison with the second half of the sixties.

In addition to all this, the year 1968 saw the dissemination of so much information about current politics[59] and the preceding twenty years that the information at the disposal of Czechoslovak citizens today is by no means as one-sided as it was in the 1950s, and many of the disclosures of 1968 were to the disadvantage of those at present in positions of institutional power at various levels of the Party and state hierarchy. The prospects for the official political culture becoming the dominant political culture in respect of political knowledge and expectations can scarcely provide its proponents with much joy.

POLITICAL CULTURE AND POLITICAL CHANGE

The stimulus to political change provided by Khrushchev's attack on Stalin and his style of rule at the Twentieth and Twenty-second

Congresses of the Soviet Communist Party has already been noted in passing. By shedding light on the crimes of Stalin and upon the extent to which Communists had been at worst destroyed and at best duped,[60] there is no doubt that Khrushchev played a crucial role in stimulating a fundamental reappraisal of previously held political beliefs on the part of Czech Communists. Though the growing strength of the reform movement within the Czechoslovak Communist Party was a complex phenomenon influenced by many factors – among the most important of which was the economic crisis of 1963 when Czechoslovakia registered a negative growth rate[61] – Khrushchev's exposure of Stalin's arbitrariness and contempt for legality raised more questions for many Czech and Slovak Communists than such deeds did for Khrushchev himself. It is fair to say, in the words of Jiří Pelikán, that 'the contrast between the ideals of socialism and the reality, disfigured as it was by the show trials, was among the mainsprings of the political crisis that had been maturing for years until it erupted with volcanic force in January 1968'.[62] Participation in the movement for change which began with the intelligentsia but which later became a more widespread social phenomenon and received mass support in 1968 was seen by many Communist reformers as 'the last chance of rehabilitating their own past errors, a compensation for the long, excruciating doubts and final despair of the value and usefulness of their own life-long work'.[63]

If there was within this reform movement even before 1968 an element also of Czech nationalism, it was not generally a spirit of aggressive nationalism towards the Slovaks or towards the smaller nationalities. It was rather a desire for greater independence from Soviet influence in so far as Czechoslovakia's internal political structure and domestic policies were concerned. Slovak nationalism, a powerful element in the political crises in Czechoslovakia of the nineteen-sixties, was of a different sort. Slovak grievances, as a result of repeated failures to fulfil their national aspirations, became harder to contain in the early sixties. The new Constitution which Czechoslovakia adopted in 1960 provided authoritative confirmation that the Slovaks no longer had independent political institutions. The following year Khrushchev's public exposure of the show trials intensified demands within Slovakia for the rehabilitation of Slovak Communists such as Husák, Novomeský and Clementis who had been attacked as 'bourgeois nationalists' and tried on trumped-up charges. On the whole, the problems in the relations between Czechs and Slovaks in the nineteen-sixties were more in the realm of subjective perception than a matter of objective exploitation of the latter by the former. Many Slovaks felt that they were, in the words of the Slovak writer Laco Novomeský, 'a tolerated race of vice-chairmen and deputy-ministers, a second-class minority generously accorded a one-third quota in everything. . . .'[64]

The Slovak sense of national identity, their insistence upon making a distinction between a Czechoslovak state to which a majority of them were prepared to give their allegiance as citizens and a 'Czechoslovak' nationality which they overwhelmingly rejected, must be seen as part of the cultural background to the overt political changes of the late sixties. Indeed, one of the major reasons why Dubček was chosen as Novotný's successor in the most powerful political office in the land was precisely the fact that he was a Slovak, since it was felt that this could hardly fail to go a long way towards assuaging Slovak nationalism.

At the beginning of the chapter we noted that the question of political culture in Czechoslovakia could not be considered in total isolation from the problem of Czechoslovakia's place in the world, and the latter point requires some brief elaboration. Czechoslovakia has since 1945 been within the Soviet 'sphere of influence', and since 1948 part of the Soviet 'power bloc'. The fact that in 1952 or 1972, for example, there were few outward manifestations of a distinctive Czech and Slovak political culture need not surprise us. Since the present leadership of the Czechoslovak Communist Party is as oriented towards the Soviet Union as was the leadership in the early fifties (perhaps more so), and since the Soviet leadership has given them full political and military backing, it is not difficult for them to prevent the free expression of the dominant Czechoslovak political culture, though it is exceedingly difficult for them to change it. The fact that Czechoslovak political culture became a matter of immediate political significance in the 1960s can only be understood if it is appreciated that Soviet influence over Czechoslovakia has been of a far from uniform kind and that the degree of Soviet surveillance of, and encroachment upon, the Czechoslovak political scene has varied over time. Soviet influence was crucial in the late forties and early fifties, in 1956, in 1961, and it has again been decisive from August 1968 onwards. The mere mention of these dates, however, underlines the changing directions of Soviet guidance. At the end of the forties and the beginning of the fifties there was pressure on the Czechoslovak Party leadership from the Soviet Union (and from the Hungarian and Polish Party leaders also) to hold Party purges and political trials.[65] Such a process, once begun, acquired its own momentum, and it required events in the Soviet Union to provoke a reassessment of these actions. The death of Stalin helped to bring about a change of course, but a much more radical influence was the Twentieth Congress of the Soviet Communist Party and Khrushchev's secret speech. The bubble of infallibility which surrounded the Party had been pricked and it was only with difficulty that Novotný resisted demands for an extraordinary Congress of the Czechoslovak Party in that year and settled for a conference at which the necessary minimum concessions to the Soviet exposure and reassessment of the period of the trials were made. When Khrushchev renewed his attack on Stalin at the Twenty-second Party Congress in 1961, and this time publicly, fresh demands for a review of the political trials which had taken place in Czechoslovakia sprang up from within the ranks of the Czechoslovak Party. The Soviet leadership and Khrushchev personally were putting their weight behind a policy of 'de-Stalinisation' and Novotný was forced to announce at the Twelfth Congress of the Czechoslovak Party in December 1962 that a new commission to review the trials had been set up.

In 1956 and 1961, then, Soviet influence over Czechoslovakia was of a 'liberalising' kind. Between 1962 and the beginning of 1968 Soviet influence on Czechoslovakia was less crucial than it had previously been. The leadership of the CPSU had its own problems to contend with and the events leading up to the fall of Khrushchev in October 1964 and the consolidation of the new leadership thereafter meant that the Soviet leaders had little inclination to intervene drastically in the affairs of a country such as Czechoslovakia which had much of the outward appearance of a model (Soviet-style) socialist state. Relations with China and with the United States doubtless preoccupied them to a much greater extent than those with Czechoslovakia until the dramatic events of 1968 forced Czechoslovakia to the top of the agenda. In that year political, economic and finally military pressures were brought to bear in order to bend Czechoslovakia to the Soviet will and by the end of 1969 the Soviet leaders had succeeded in removing all reformists from the leadership of the Czechoslovak Party and in 1970 this was followed by the expulsion of the most active supporters of reform in a purge of the Party ranks.

It would be foolish to suppose, then, at the moment in time when the Soviet Union has the desire, as it most certainly has the power, to impose its will on the Czechoslovak Communist Party (which, in turn, controls all the key institutions within Czechoslovakia), that an indigenous Czech and Slovak political culture could clearly manifest itself, still less become a significant determinant of public political behaviour. To alter the values and orientations of Czechs and Slovaks in the particular direction desired by the present Soviet and Czechoslovak leaderships has, however, become more difficult than ever before. There is little doubt that the Soviet armed intervention, so successful in the realm of political action, was counter-productive in terms of its effect on political culture.

In 1968 the overwhelming majority of the Czechoslovak population gave their support to the new Party leadership under Alexander Dubček, to a pluralistic version of socialism, and to further democratisation. There was disagreement on the best means of institutionalising political pluralism – whether within the context of the 'leading role' of the Communist Party (by amending its rules to permit individual or even group dissent and through legitimising the pressures of organised interests) or through the introduction of a competitive Party system, including possibly the revival of the Social Democratic Party. But on the broad values represented by the reformist leadership and their Action Programme, there was perhaps a larger measure of agreement than had ever previously been reached in Czechoslovak politics.

It cannot be denied by any objective observer that the political trends of 1968 – which could only be reversed with the help of armies from five Warsaw Pact countries – were supported by the overwhelming mass of the Czech and Slovak peoples.[66] Even the limited selection of survey data presented here amply illustrates the point.[67]

The political system constructed by the Czechoslovak Communist Party after February 1948 did not accord with the values and fundamental political beliefs of the great majority of Czechs and Slovaks, though many of the actual policies (especially economic and social) of the Communist Party received substantial popular support. Neither the new economic base nor the new institutional structures succeeded in changing the political cultures of Czechs and Slovaks in the direction which the holders of institutional power desired. If anything, the opposite happened. The old values and beliefs were reinforced. Masaryk became more highly esteemed than ever and by 1968 the First Republic was perceived both far more positively than was the post-1948 political system and far more than it had been in the immediate post-war period when Czechoslovak citizens were not yet in a position to compare it with a system modelled on that of the Soviet Union. If a Czech 'new man' had been created by 1968, he was, ironically, one more firmly devoted to social democratic and libertarian values than the Czech of 1946. In the interaction between structures and cultures, it would appear that the dominant Czech political culture came much closer to changing Czechoslovak Communism than Czechoslovak Communism came to procuring acceptance of its official political culture.

We headed this chapter, 'Revival and Retreat'. In the spring and summer of 1968 the word most often used to describe the process which was under way within Czechoslovakia was 'revival' (*obroda*), with its connotation of spiritual renaissance as much as political change, and evocation of the 'national revival' of the nineteenth century. Enthusiasm and political participation reached their highest levels for two decades. In 1968 there is no doubt that a greater degree of congruence was achieved between the evolving political system and political conduct of Czechoslovak leaders, on the one hand, and the dominant political cultures of Czechs and Slovaks, on the other, than at any time since the Communists came to power.

The 1970s, in contrast, have so far been a decade of retreat – a retreat (in the face of overwhelming odds) from the attempt to put into political action the ideals and values so clearly expressed in 1968. The predominant behavioural response of Czechs (in particular) and Slovaks has been to retreat into their private lives and do their best to ignore a political system which they feel they cannot change. Up to a point the conservative Communists who now rule Czechoslovakia have secured the conformity in political behaviour which they desire and their institutional power is, for the time being, secure. But they are faced by apathy and alienation. For the corollary of the success of the Soviet intervention in reintroducing orthodox Communist norms into the political system is that the dissonance between the system and the political culture has become greater than at any time since the end of the Second World War. In short, the tasks which face Czechoslovakia's present leaders in the realms of political socialisation and political culture have become gargantuan.

NOTES

1   There is already a considerable scholarly literature on Czechoslovakia in the 1960s (as well as a great many more ephemeral works). Among the most important of the interpretative books published thus far are: Otto Ulč, *Politics in Czechoslovakia* (San Francisco, 1974); V. V. Kusin, *The Intellectual Origins of the Prague Spring* (Cambridge, 1971); V. V. Kusin, *Political Grouping in the Czechoslovak Reform Movement* (London, 1972); V. V. Kusin (ed.), *The Czechoslovak Reform Movement 1968* (London, 1973); Galia Golan, *The Czechoslovak Reform Movement* (Cambridge, 1971); Galia Golan, *Reform Rule in Czechoslovakia: The Dubček Era, 1968–1969* (Cambridge, 1973); Jaroslav Krejčí, *Social Change and Stratification in Post-War Czechoslovakia* (London, 1973); and Alex Pravda, *Reform and Change in the Czechoslovak Political System: January–August 1968* (Sage Research Paper, London, 1975). The most comprehensive discussion of political change in Czechoslovakia will almost certainly be that provided by H. Gordon Skilling in his forthcoming major book, *Czechoslovakia's Interrupted Revolution* (Princeton, 1976). A book on which the authors of the present chapter are collaborating will concentrate specifically on the role of, and changes within, the Communist Party. See Brown and Wightman, *The Communist Party of Czechoslovakia* (Macmillan, London, forthcoming). Two Czechoslovak works of very different type, but of outstanding importance, are: Pavel Machonin (ed.), *Československá společnost* (Bratislava, 1969); and Zdeněk Mlynář, *Československý pokus o reformu 1968: analýza jeho teorie a praxe* (Cologne, 1975).

2   The writings of Professor Gordon Skilling include several valuable contributions to an understanding of Czechoslovak political culture – most notably (though he does not here use the terminology, 'political culture') his article, 'Communism and Czechoslovak Traditions', *Journal of International Affairs*, vol. xx, no. 1, 1966, pp. 118–36. More recently, in an as yet unpublished article, 'Stalinism and Czechoslovak Political Culture', he has employed the concept along the lines suggested by Robert C. Tucker (in his 'Culture, Political Culture and Communist Society', *Political Science Quarterly*, vol. 88, no. 2, June 1973, pp. 173–90) to analyse political developments in Czechoslovakia during the 1950s. The

first explicit use of political culture in analysis of Czech politics was by one of the present authors in 'Political Change in Czechoslovakia', *Government and Opposition*, vol. 4, no. 2, spring 1969 pp. 169–94, esp. 189–94. The most extensive application of the concept to the study of Czechoslovakia is to be found in David W. Paul, 'Nationalism, Pluralism and Schweikism in Czechoslovakia's Political Culture' (unpublished Ph.D. dissertation, Princeton, 1973). Paul (ibid., p. 7) defines political culture as 'a system (or systems) of values, orientations, and behavior patterns relating to the politics of a society'. His main emphasis throughout his interesting thesis is on *political behaviour* and on *objective* rather than *subjective* history, and his approach is thus substantially different from that adopted here. A part of Paul's analysis has been published in an article, 'The Repluralization of Czechoslovak Politics in the 1960s', *Slavic Review*, vol. 33, no. 4, December 1974.

3   Robert J. Kerner, 'The Czechoslovaks from the Battle of the White Mountain to the World War', in Kerner (ed.), *Czechoslovakia* (Berkeley and Los Angeles, 1940) p. 45.

4   R. W. Seton-Watson, *A History of the Czechs and Slovaks* (London, 1943) p. 281.

5   Petr Pithart, 'Politické strany a svoboda slova' in *Literární listy*, no. 17, 20 June 1968.

6   R. W. Seton-Watson, op. cit., p. 213. See also Václav Beneš, 'Background of Czechoslovak Democracy' in Miloslav Rechcigl, Jr. (ed.), *The Czechoslovak Contribution to World Culture* (The Hague, 1964) pp. 267–76; Edward Táborský, 'The Roots of Czechoslovak Democracy' in Miloslav Rechcigl, Jr. (ed.), *Czechoslovakia Past and Present* (The Hague, 1968), vol. 1, pp. 117–23; and Václav Beneš, 'Czechoslovak Democracy and its Problems, 1918–1920' in Victor S. Mamatey and Radomír Luža (eds), *A History of the Czechoslovak Republic, 1918–1948* (Princeton, 1973) pp. 39–98.

7   See Seton-Watson, op. cit., p. 306; and Eugen Steiner, *The Slovak Dilemma* (Cambridge 1973) p. 18.

8   The most balanced account of the German minority problem in pre-war Czechoslovakia is by J. W. Bruegel in his *Czechoslovakia before Munich: The German Minority Problem and British Appeasement Policy* (Cambridge, 1973).

9   Petr Pithart, 'Politické strany a svoboda slova', op. cit.

10   Věra Olivová, *The Doomed Democracy: Czechoslovakia in a Disrupted Europe, 1914–1938* (London, 1972) p. 175.

11   K. Bartošek, 'Československá společnost a revoluce' in *Československá revoluce v letech 1944–1948* (Prague, 1966) p. 17.

12   Vojtěch Mencl, 'K některým zkušenostem z období buržoazní předmnichovské republiky' in *Československá revoluce v letech 1944–1948* (Prague, 1966) pp. 73–6.

13   *Vztah Čechů a Slováků k dějinám*, Ústav pro výzkum veřejného mínění ČSAV (Prague, 1968). The investigation (using a quota sample of 1088 respondents) was carried out in October 1968 to mark the fiftieth anniversary of the foundation of Czechoslovakia, which fell on the 28th of that month.

14  The advantages of the timing of the survey in early October 1968 out-
    weigh the disadvantages. In the view of senior members of the Institute
    of Public Opinion expressed later in 1969, it was only in the period be-
    tween March 1968 and March 1969 that political conditions in Commun-
    ist Czechoslovakia were such that people could be relied upon to answer
    honestly the most sensitive political questions. It can also be argued that
    it is only at a time of crisis in the life of a nation that people reflect
    deeply upon their history. If the survey had been conducted not in
    October 1968 but a year earlier, the responses would have been not only
    less frank but more superficial and offhand.

15  *Vztah Čechů a Slováků k dějinám,* p. 8.

16  As Vladimir Kusin has put it: 'To say that these voters and supporters
    of the "Czechoslovak road to socialism" were privy to Gottwald's and
    Stalin's long-term plans is ridiculous. After all they voted in 1946 to make
    the Communist Party the strongest in the country but not to endorse its
    monopoly of power for all times to come. If such monopoly had been at
    issue in a democratic election, the result would certainly have been differ-
    ent. The Communist voters were victims just as much as the more provi-
    dent, who saw the danger clearly.' Kusin, *The Intellectual Origins of the
    Prague Spring,* p. 7.

17  See, for example, the speech of Milan Kundera to the Fourth Congress
    of Czechoslovak Writers: *IV sjezd svazu československých spisovatelů –
    Protokol: Praha 27–29 června 1967* (Prague, 1968) p. 27.

18  Jiří Hochman, 'Jaká východiska' in *Reportér,* no. 38, 1968.

19  For an uninhibited émigré expression of Slovak separatist views, see Štefan
    Polakovič, 'Evolution of the Slovak National Philosophy' in Joseph M.
    Kirschbaum (ed.), *Slovakia in the 19th and 20th centuries* (Toronto,
    1973), esp. pp. 36–7.

20  There were 2.7 'don't knows'. See *What's Your Opinion?* (Prague, 1947)
    p. 13.

21  See Jaroslaw Piekalkiewicz, 'Public Political Opinion in Czechoslovakia
    during the Dubcek Era' in E. J. Czerwinski and Jaroslaw Piekalkiewicz
    (eds), *The Soviet Invasion of Czechoslovakia: Its Effects on Eastern
    Europe* (New York and London, 1972) p. 15. Two other readily accessible
    sources of public opinion poll data from Czechoslovakia are: Ithiel de
    Sola Pool, 'Public Opinion in Czechoslovakia' in the *Public Opinion
    Quarterly,* vol. XXIV, spring, 1970, pp. 10–25; and Jaroslaw A.
    Piekalkiewicz, *Public Opinion Polling in Czechoslovakia, 1968–69: Re-
    sults and Analysis of Surveys Conducted during the Dubcek Era* (New
    York and London, 1972). Whereas de Sola Pool makes clear that all of
    the data which he publishes are those of the Czechoslovak Institute of
    Public Opinion, Piekalkiewicz unfortunately does not give his sources,
    and so there is no way in which the majority of his readers can know
    whether the surveys he cites were conducted by the Institute or by a
    less professional body. The great majority of survey data used in this
    chapter are taken directly from the primary sources: the small-circula-
    tion booklets and cyclostyled sheets produced by the first Czechoslovak
    Institute of Public Opinion in 1947 and by the revived Institute of Public
    Opinion of the Czechoslovak Academy of Sciences in 1968–69.

22 Jan Procházka, *Politika pro každého* (Prague, 1968) p. 190. This book provides unique insights into the nature of the constraints imposed by the Czech censorship. It consists of a collection of Procházka's articles written between 1962 and 1968 with especially heavy type used to delineate those articles and passages in articles which were rejected at the time by the censor.

23 *Documents of the December 1970 Plenary Meeting of the Central Committee, Communist Party of Czechoslovakia: Lessons drawn from the Crisis Development in the Party and Society after the 13th Congress of the Communist Party of Czechoslovakia* (Information Bulletin, No. 2, Peace and Socialism Publishers, Prague, 1971) p. 9.

24 Miroslav Šolc, *Pravda* (Bratislava), 25 August 1971.

25 *Masaryk on Thought and Life: Conversations with Karel Čapek* (London, 1938) p. 191.

26 The expulsion of the great majority of the German population from Czechoslovakia after the end of the Second World War, though entirely understandable in the light of what had gone before, may, however, be regarded as an act of ethnic intolerance contrary to the spirit of Masaryk.

27 *Masaryk on Thought and Life*, p. 175.

28 Cf. Sidney Verba, 'Comparative Political Culture' in Pye and Verba, *Political Culture and Political Development* (Princeton, 1965) p. 555.

29 Zdeněk Mlynář, *Československý pokus o reformu 1968*, op. cit., p. 159.

30 Ibid., p. 157.

31 Ibid., pp. 154–5.

32 Ibid., p. 157.

33 See Jan Adam, *Wage, Price and Taxation Policy in Czechoslovakia 1948–1970* (Berlin, 1974) pp. 167–81; Otto Ulč, *Politics in Czechoslovakia*, pp. 51–4; Jaroslav Krejčí, *Social Change and Stratification in Postwar Czechoslovakia*, p. 130; and Radoslav Selucký, *Czechoslovakia: The Plan that Failed* (London, 1970) p. 62.

34 The text of these television talks has been published in several languages with new introductions by the author. For the English edition, see Ota Šik, *Czechoslovakia: The Bureaucratic Economy* (New York, 1972).

35 *Některé otázky současné politické situace, Výzkum 68–15* (Institute of Public Opinion of the Czechoslovak Academy of Sciences, Prague, 1968) p. 17.

36 *Akční program Komunistické strany Československa* (Prague, 1968) p. 62. Full, though stilted, translations of the Action Programme appear in Hugh Lunghi and Paul Ello (eds), *Dubcek's Blueprint for Freedom* (London, 1968); and Robin Remington (ed.), *Winter in Prague: Documents on Czechoslovak Communism in Crisis* (Cambridge, Mass., 1969).

37 Alex Pravda, *Reform and Change in the Czechoslovak Political System: January–August 1968*, op. cit., p. 7.

38 *Pravda* (Moscow), 22 August 1968.

39 H. Gordon Skilling, 'Communism and Czechoslovak Traditions', op. cit., p. 118.

40 Jan Procházka, *Učitelské noviny*, 7 March 1968.

41 See David Rodnick, *The Strangled Democracy: Czechoslovakia, 1948–1969* (Lubbock, Texas, 1970), esp. pp. 70 and 77. Cf. Zdeněk Salzmann,

*A Contribution to the Study of Value Orientations among the Czechs and Slovaks* (Research Report No. 4 of the Department of Anthropology, University of Massachusetts, Amherst, 1970). The works by Rodnick and Salzmann are both based upon interviews conducted by the authors in Czechoslovakia. Though Rodnick's book in particular contains some interesting observations, neither work can be accorded anything like the same status as the surveys conducted by the Institute of Public Opinion of the Czechoslovak Academy of Sciences. Whereas the Institute applied the most professional sampling techniques, the two American studies lack a similar degree of rigour.

42    Jaroslaw A. Piekalkiewicz, *Public Opinion Polling in Czechoslovakia, 1968–69*, op. cit., pp. 247–9.

43    *Veřejné mínění o některých politických problémech, Výzkum 68–17* (Institute of Public Opinion of the Czechoslovak Academy of Sciences, Prague, 1969) p. 19.

44    Ibid., p. 20.

45    Ibid.

46    Věra Rollová, 'Sociální diferenciace podle ekonomického postavení a problém společenských tříd' in Pavel Machonin, *Ceskoslovenská společnost*, op. cit., p. 339.

47    Lubomír Brokl, 'Moc a sociální rozvrstvení' in Machonin, ibid., pp. 263–4.

48    Krejčí, *Social Change and Stratification in Postwar Czechoslovakia*, op. cit., p. 153.

49    The title, for example, of Milada Součková's book, *A Literary Satellite: Czechoslovak-Russian Literary Relations* (Chicago and London, 1970) is very misleading, bearing in mind that it deals with Czechoslovak-Russian literary links in both the nineteenth and twentieth centuries, and not merely with their relations in the nineteen-fifties.

50    *Vztah Čechů a Slováků k dějinám*, p. 24.

51    Ibid., p. 22.

52    Petr Pithart, *Listy*, no. 3, 21 November 1968.

53    Ibid. See also Archie Brown, 'Pluralistic Trends in Czechoslovakia', *Soviet Studies*, vol. XVII, no. 4, April 1966, p. 471.

54    How widespread was the acceptance of authoritarian values in Czechoslovakia in the early 1950s is difficult to assess. Certainly 'hard-line' and illiberal attitudes were held by a larger and more vociferous minority in that period than earlier or later. Yet, there is little reason to believe that the dominant political culture – even at the time, say, of the Slánský trial of 1952 – corresponded with the official political culture being promoted from above, though there was, of course, a high level of conformity in political behaviour. (Cf. H. Gordon Skilling, 'Stalinism and Communist Political Culture', op. cit. For an account of the limited amount of doubt expressed at the time within the party concerning the authenticity of the trials of the early fifties, see Václav Brabec, 'Vztah KSČ a veřejnosti k politickým procesům na počátku padesátých let' in *Revue dějin socialismu*, vol. IX, no. 3, 1969, pp. 363–87.)

55    Jan Kašpar, *Nová mysl*, no. 5, May 1970 (cited by Ulč, *Politics in Czechoslovakia*, p. 122).

56 Ibid.
57 *What's Your Opinion?* pp. 19–20.
58 Ulč, *Politics in Czechoslovakia*, p. 122.
59 In mid-February 1968 the Institute of Public Opinion conducted an investigation into popular information about, and attitudes to, the December 1967 and January 1968 plenary sessions of the Party Central Committee. The publication of their results includes a valuable breakdown of answers in terms of nationality, social group, Party membership, sex, age and education. There was still some doubt so early in the year about how substantial the changes inaugurated would be, but only 1.5 per cent of the total sample thought they would influence society unfavourably. 19.5 per cent thought nothing would change, 20.6 per cent were 'don't knows', and 55.3 per cent thought the results would be favourable. The optimistic view was taken by 64.3 per cent of Slovaks compared with 51.7 per cent of Czechs, no doubt reflecting Slovak pleasure at the fact that the sessions had resulted in the accession of a Slovak (Dubček) to the Party First Secretaryship. Scepticism was greater among younger people than older, and scepticism or professed lack of knowledge greater among women than men. A higher proportion of non-manual than manual workers said the outcome would be favourable, but the differences along class lines were less than those between men and women or between the youngest and oldest age groups. In terms of social group, the answers to the question, 'What do you think of these meetings [the December and January Central Committee plenums]? Will they influence our society favourably, unfavourably, or will nothing change?', were as follows:

|  | Favour- ably | Unfavour- ably | Nothing will change | Don't know | Other answer | No answer |
|---|---|---|---|---|---|---|
| Unskilled workers | 48.7 | 0.4 | 20.3 | 27.6 | 1.7 | 1.3 |
| Skilled workers | 54.1 | 1.6 | 22.5 | 18.1 | 3.0 | 0.7 |
| Farmers | 55.3 | 1.8 | 12.4 | 28.2 | 2.4 | 0.0 |
| Non-manual employees | 59.2 | 1.7 | 20.9 | 14.7 | 3.1 | 0.5 |

(Source: *Veřejné mínění o zasedání ÚV KSČ v prosinci 1967 a lednu 1968*, *Výzkum 68–2*, Institute of Public Opinion of the Czechoslovak Academy of Sciences, Prague 1968, esp. pp. 11–12 and Appendix 3.)

60 This is to say nothing of the fate of non-Communists, with whom Khrushchev was not greatly concerned.
61 While economic difficulties gave impetus to the political reform movement around 1963, by 1968 the economy had picked up and in 1967–68 there was neither an economic crisis nor outstanding economic success. The general picture throughout the sixties was one of unspectacular economic growth and of intensified industrialisation. National income per head (in constant prices) increased by almost 50 per cent between 1960 and 1970 and between 1961 and 1970 the agricultural population as a proportion of total population dropped from 14.1 per cent to 10.3

per cent. (*Czechoslovakia: Statistical Abstract 1963: Statistická ročenka ČSSR*, 1972, 1974.)

62  Jiří Pelikán (ed.), *The Czechoslovak Political Trials, 1950–1954* (London, 1971) p. 9.

63  Kamil Winter, in his Introduction to Radoslav Selucký, *Czechoslovakia: The Plan that Failed*, p. xv. Cf. Pelikán, *The Czechoslovak Political Trials*, p. 13.

64  *IV sjezd svazu československých spisovatelů*, op. cit., p. 55.

65  See the report of the Commission headed by Jan Piller which was set up by the Central Committee of the Czechoslovak Communist Party in 1968. It appears in full in Jiří Pelikán (ed.), *The Czechoslovak Political Trials, 1950–1954*, op. cit.

66  For the position of the ethnic minorities in Slovakia, see E. J. Czerwinski and Jaroslaw Piekalkiewicz (eds), *The Soviet Invasion of Czechoslovakia* (esp. p. 109); Vladimir V. Kusin, *Political Grouping in the Czechoslovak Reform Movement*, ch. 5; and Grey Hodnett and Peter J. Potichnyj, *The Ukraine and the Czechoslovak Crisis* (Canberra, 1970).

67  Note, for example, Figure 6.1 and 94.6 per cent support for the Action Programme. See also *Některé otázky současné politické situace, Výzkum 68–15*, p. 3.

# 7 China: Communism and Confucianism

## JACK GRAY

China[1] alone among the Communist countries studied in this volume
lies outside our own Western Graeco-Christian tradition. Communism
in China is Communism in the context of Confucian civilisation. It
should be of particular interest in comparative Communist studies to
see how far China's divergence from the orthodox Soviet norms has
been the consequence of this different historical background. Ideally,
the study of Communism in the Confucian context should include comparisons with China's Confucian neighbours which are now also Communist, North Korea and Vietnam. It should also include comparisons
with the non-Communist Chinese communities abroad, in Hong Kong
and Singapore. It is not, however, possible to develop such comparisons
here.

The Chinese situation has the further special interest that China is
the only Communist country in which not only has a new Communist
political culture been created explicitly in opposition to the Soviet
model, but in which the inculcation of this new political culture has
been regarded as the most important area of change – so much so that
the Maoist leadership embraced three years of chaos and the threat
of civil war to make it good.

It is too soon to attempt to measure how far this new official political
culture has been accepted and 'internalised' by the Chinese people.
Mao Tse-tung himself does not expect quick results; he hopes to change
the political culture by a novel, comprehensive and long-term process
of social change and economic growth. This indicates the third point of
special interest in the Chinese situation: Mao's creation of a specific
social process towards ends which include the transformation of Chinese
political culture. He does not use the phrase 'political culture'; but the
problem of political attitudes, habits and expectations is one of his great
themes.

### THE CHINESE PERCEPTION OF HISTORY

The intense Chinese consciousness of the past is itself a factor in the
political culture. Confucius claimed to be first and foremost a historian,

and he urged his students to look at history 'without prejudice, without anger, without fear and without favour'. He thus laid the basis of China's long tradition of the objective study of the past, both as a necessary part of intelligent policy-making, and as one means (among others) of control of the autocratic emperors. Appeals to the lessons of history are listened to with attention in China. The historical parable, in the form of an academic history or of a play with a historical theme, is a traditional means of criticism of rulers. Wu Han's 1960 play *The Dismissal of Hai Jui* was in the grand tradition of the dramatic political parable, which went back to the very birth of the Chinese theatre under the oppression of the Mongols.

The Chinese idea of historical causation is important in the political culture. At first sight, it was naïvely moralistic, and ascribed to the dominance of virtue or of vice the prosperity or the ruin of the country. This moralism, however, was not unrealistic. China was committed to the idea of rule by a moral élite. The examinations through which the mandarins were chosen were essentially examinations in the Confucian moral system. Moreover, Chinese governments never possessed sufficient force to cope with widespread disaffection; in a very real sense, in the last analysis the official ruled by moral authority.

Moreover, the corruption of the magistrate was ascribed to predictable social pressures. Society was regarded as being in a precarious balance of classes. The prosperity of the peasant-proprietor majority depended on maintaining this balance, and the revenues of the government depended on the prosperity of the peasant proprietor. With only a small margin over subsistence he was prone to fall into debt, foreclosure and permanent tenancy. He was then lost as a taxpayer, and his landlord would evade taxation by corrupting the mandarins (themselves usually landlords). As tenancy and landlordism grew, government revenues sank. The tax collector pressed the remaining taxpayers harder, until some of them were faced with the choice 'either to starve or manfully to play the thief' and took to the hills. Many oppressed tenants were forced to do the same. Growing disorder meant an increased demand for revenues from fewer and fewer taxpayers. This form of social decay could accelerate until a bankrupt government was faced with uncontrollable rebellion, and the dynasty fell. Historians saw a regular cycle of this kind in Chinese history.

Whether this is a true picture or not is irrelevant for our purpose. The point is that such a picture was basic to Chinese expectations about politics. The lessons of history in this respect were: only continuous positive action by government can maintain social harmony; the government must stand above class in order to do this; if the government permits one class to tyrannise over another, the government itself will sooner or later suffer the consequences; if the ordinary people are pressed too hard they will rebel; if they ever do rebel, they are probably justified; and even if repression is necessary it should be accompanied by the redress of grievances and by redoubled education.

The second major historical myth of the Chinese political culture is the idea of China as the moral and political centre of the world. Confucianism as a means of political control and socialisation drew much of its strength from the idea that it was the only philosophy which could 'civilise', which could allow men to rise to their full moral potential. When, in the late nineteenth century, the Chinese were forced to accept that some of the outer barbarians had at least equal claims to high morality, the rationale of Chinese nationalism received a severe blow. The Chinese suffered an 'identity crisis' which has created a need to identify with some philosophy which offers a transcendent morality, as Confucianism did. One way out is to accept Marxism as a surrogate for the moral and intellectual certainties of Confucianism; if this is a Chinese form of Marxism with claims to a special moral superiority, so much the more satisfying. The Chinese are a highly moral people who are unlikely to accept identification with any system of morality which they regard as second-rate. What is regarded as second-rate differs from individual to individual; it may be capitalism based on the pursuit of self-interest, liberal politics with their expedient bargaining, or 'goulash communism'; and some may be dismayed and alienated by the gap between aspiration and reality in the Maoist system itself. As we have seen, in Chinese tradition history and politics are *about morality*; there is little sign that this has changed.

### TRADITIONAL CHINESE POLITICAL VALUES

The chief function of government, in Chinese tradition, is the preservation of social harmony. As to the means to maintain it, the two poles of Chinese thought were represented by Legalism and Taoism. The Legalists believed that human beings were motivated only by self-interest. Harmony could be maintained only by a government with unlimited power to prescribe the rules and inflict punishment. At the other pole, the Taoists believed that men were essentially sociable. Harmony would be best maintained if governments intervened as little as possible in the natural social relationships of men.

Confucianism represented a compromise view, one might say a common-sense view. To the Confucian, human nature included social instincts, but these instincts had to be cultivated by education and the inculcation of good habits. The primary means of government were therefore education and the control of ceremonial in which good habits were imposed by the ritualisation of social relationships. The Confucian also conceded, however, that individual moral development was incomplete and uneven: we are all liable to go off the rails now and again, some of us oftener than others. Force was necessary therefore as a stand-by, to deal with situations in which education had failed; but the use of force was always a confession of failure.

It is impossible to discuss Confucian values separately from the Confucian process of socialisation. Confucian philosophy, having made its assumptions about human nature, passed straight to prescriptions for socialisation.

In the socialisation process, the supreme virtue was filial piety. The inculcation of parental authority in the home was the psychological basis of social solidarity and political obedience. The absolute authority of the father was repeated in the teacher, the mandarin and the Emperor. The whole of society was seen in family terms.

Harmony in the family was maintained by two means. The first method was the creation of an elaborate hierarchy according to generation, age and sex. By the time a Chinese child left the family he sought, and society provided, a hierarchical organisation into which he could fit.

The second method for the maintenance of harmony was the systematic suppression of any display of aggression on the part of the child. He was not permitted to show anger, disappointment or jealousy. At the same time, Chinese children were in other ways treated with an indulgence which would astonish Western parents; but only in ways which increased rather than diminished dependence on their elders. The fear of conflict thus engendered was carried outside the family into wider social relationships.

The implications of this Confucian system for the political culture concern on the one hand the role of government, and on the other the role of citizens. Given the Confucian view of human nature, government was in the first place a moral force, the supreme representative of moral absolutes. Political authority was morally legitimated. The moral legitimation of government always has totalitarian implications, and this was so in China.

It also followed from the Confucian view of human nature that the main means of government should be education. Even when the Confucian scholar-counsellor had become a bureaucrat, this function remained his most important in theory and was by no means negligible in practice.

Within the family, harmony was maintained not by the free interplay of rival interests but by the suppression of competition. This also was carried into government. The maintenance of social harmony was not conceived in terms of the interaction of legitimate interest groups, but in terms of authoritarian control of them. Where possible they were assimilated into the system by being treated as mutual surety groups. This was applied to local communities in the form of the *bao-jia* (hundred and tithing) system, to clans and to guilds. Interest groups existed only on sufferance; neither groups nor individuals had legally defined rights, except the graduates, and their rights were more ritual than real. Existing rights were prescriptive and conventional only. When Mao states, as a Marxist, that 'there are no natural rights; the only rights of the individual are those which society gives him', he is still in the tradition. The idea of individual rights (and consequently of limited government) is a feudal idea, and China has never been feudal at any time relevant to the formation of her traditions.

In 255 BC the kingdoms of China were united by the First Emperor of Ch'in, using Legalist methods proposed by Legalist scholars. His ruthless bureaucratic system led to the downfall of his dynasty in a generation in the face of a rebellion, part aristocratic backlash and part popular revolt, under the banner of Confucianism. But the succeeding dynasty, the Han, were conscious of the advantages of Ch'in centralisation and preserved the system, employing the Confucians as bureaucrats. This was later and gradually made systematic by choosing officials through examinations in the Confucian classics.

Thus Confucianism in practice was strongly influenced by Legalism. Much of its ambiguity springs from this association. It has been said that there was a Confucianism of the state and a Confucianism of society, one leaning to Legalism and the other to Taoism. Not only in society but within the mind of every Confucian scholar-official this ambiguity existed.

## POLITICAL EXPECTATIONS

The implications of the traditional political culture for the political expectations of citizens emerged through the nature of the socialisation process. Authority was accepted in personal life, in intellectual life and in politics; to resist authority, to fail to conform, was to feel guilty. Hierarchy was accepted; the Chinese performed well in a hierarchical situation but badly in groups of peers. Conflict was feared and avoided; the idea, so important for pluralist democracy, that controlled and legitimised conflict can be creative was missing in China.

It is clear that such a political psychology could promote stability – *in theory* at least. It is equally clear that the same psychological characteristics will militate against the creation of democratic politics aimed at radical change. As will be seen, the political culture which Mao seeks to create is concerned very largely with overcoming these psychological obstacles to effective mass organisation for change.

The Chinese citizen expected to put himself under ideological leadership, expected government to be at least potentially totalitarian in its scope, expected government to be conducted by a moral-intellectual élite in which he could play no part unless he passed the examinations, and expected that his relations with government would be via a recognised group who came before the official authorities only as petitioners.

If we turn to the scholar-official himself, in spite of the ambiguity of his position his basic role was clear. As a graduate he was a member of an exclusive moral élite, whether in or out of office; and indeed the question of whether or not to hold office would ideally depend upon where he could best serve in maintaining Confucianism. He might do so best by serving the Emperor. In other circumstances he might do so best by retiring to the position of the *ming-i dai-fang* – 'the enlightened who awaits the call' – in the confidence that when a bad situation became worse, his Confucian wisdom would again be in demand. His duty was to educate; to educate the population under his charge, and to educate the Emperor, in Confucian ideals and prescriptions. This latter task could be dangerous; but the ideal Confucian counsellor would remonstrate with the autocrat at the risk of his life, as his Confucian loyalty to the Son of Heaven demanded. Such courageous counsellors were the great heroes of Chinese history. One example was Hai Jui of the Ming dynasty, the subject of Wu Han's play already mentioned, a play in which the Ming official represented P'eng Teh-huai, purged in 1959 for his stubborn and outspoken criticism of the Great Leap and the Communes. And P'eng himself accepted the analogy: 'I will be Hai Jui!', he declared when warned of the consequences of opposition. Identification with the heroic Confucian 'remonstrators' thus still exists, and within the Communist Party itself. After his dismissal, too, P'eng Teh-huai played the *ming-i dai-fang*, quietly moving about the countryside preparing his 'Eighty-thousand Word Letter' for the day when events would prove him right.

### CONTRADICTIONS WITHIN THE CONFUCIAN TRADITION

Confucianism was born in compromise. It was made ambiguous by its association with the semi-legalist state. And in any case, in a civilisation as long-standing and as rich as the Chinese, in which the orthodoxy was only gradually defined in opposition to rivals (just as the sacraments of the Christian church were gradually defined in response to heresy), contradictions and alternatives are to be expected. Imperial China handed down to modern times not one consistent set of ideas and attitudes, but a range of choice. Let us look at the main types of conflicting ideas.

First of all, although the theory of government was totalitarian in its implications, in practice Chinese local communities, clans, guilds and other groups enjoyed very considerable independence. In a real sense they governed themselves. The Chinese local magistrate was more like a district officer of the British Empire than a French prefect. He presided over informal consultations among the gentry. He took local custom into consideration in his court, though accepting the obligation to reform 'bad customs' where necessary, especially those which were repugnant to national law. As for the Chinese citizen, he combined readiness to appeal to the government to intervene in any aspect of life in order to protect his interests or opinions, with a fierce resentment of government interference when applied to himself, and infinite resource in evading his obligations.

The second contradiction was that represented by the idea of the 'mandate of Heaven', according to which the winning of the throne itself indicated that Heaven had blessed the endeavour, and justified a change of allegiance to the winner. Thus the moral legitimation of government was combined with the most pragmatic possible test of which party held the moral mandate. Yet as has been shown earlier, the theory of the dynastic cycle implied that widespread rebellion indicated that the government had failed in its moral responsibilities. When such rebellion became irresistible, the Emperor lost by the same token both his throne and his right to it.

The third contradiction was that while Chinese society was elaborately hierarchical, egalitarian voluntary associations of all kinds flourished in China in great strength and numbers. Whether the prevalence of voluntary associations might have provided the basis for a pluralistic alternative to the orthodox political system is one of the most interesting questions in Chinese history.

The fourth contradiction was between the theoretical dominance of the civil government and the practical fact that the military leaders have played as large a part in Chinese history as the Confucian official. Perhaps the very contempt of the Confucians for the soldier was a factor in producing this situation. The military official was excluded from the benefits of a normal Confucian education. The consequence of this failure to socialise the soldier was the existence of a body of men who were despised, irresponsible and dependent entirely on their military resources, who in times of division in the civil government were very ready and able to deal with Confucian Tweedledum and Tweedledee. Modern China inherited this unresolved dilemma.

The fifth contradiction was that while the Chinese had a powerful sense of cultural identity, and that sense may be said to have been strongly nationalist, nationalism in the sense which includes a strong consciousness of one's moral responsibilities to others as fellow-nationals was little developed. The moral community in China was the clan or the village and dimly beyond it the province. It did not extend to the nation; it still does so only imperfectly. It is a paradox that the oldest nation in the world is now engaged in nation-building. Only the mandarins were conscious of a wider moral community; indeed that is what their education was about. With their fall, such consciousness was badly prejudiced.

The sixth contradiction was the conflict between the scholar as mentor and the scholar as bureaucrat, which has already been touched upon. The public examinations represented almost the only route to social advancement. Consequently, the Chinese population, while on the one hand revering the idea of the Confucian moral élite, on the other usually regarded the actual members of the élite as corrupt place-hunters. Like the Mexicans studied by Almond and Verba, the Chinese combined intense devotion to their political system with the lowest possible expectations that it would do anything for them. Distrust of government of any kind proved a major obstacle to political innovation in the twentieth century, as Chinese leaders of all parties agreed.

This contradiction affected the official himself as well as the population. Never sure of his own motives, he was inclined to suffer an anxiety which has been inherited by both intellectuals and political leaders in the twentieth century, who while embracing Western liberalism in theory, often could not bring themselves to sully their hands in the struggle for power, even if this power was constitutionally bestowed by the electors. Many preferred to confine themselves to an educational role. These attitudes are still influential.

The seventh contradiction was that while the normal way of dealing with potential conflict was to use authority to suppress it, at the same time there was a strong belief in the virtues of moderation, a keenly felt obligation to avoid humiliating the victims of authority, and a widespread belief that the best solution to any problem was a bargain which gave something to both sides. These related attitudes were expressed in the ideas of 'face' and of the 'golden mean'. At the level of government the imperial authority was not in practice generally exercised in a despotic or legalistic way. On the contrary, the authorities maintained their rule largely through an informal system of consultation and compromise. Even the land tax, for example, although in theory it was based on the most elaborate rules and regulations, was in practice determined by what was essentially a *bargaining* process. In so far as such consultation and bargaining dealt with conflicts of interest among groups, it represented a kind of politics.

#### FOCI OF IDENTIFICATION

Traditional political identification in China was with the Confucian classics and their authors.

After the authors of Confucianism came its exemplars. Two types predominated: the founders of dynasties (who had restored harmony), and the model officials, who were usually impartial magistrates or courageous 'remonstrators', or both.

These foci of identification were shared by officials and common people. Their stories formed part of a common realm of discourse, linking the 'great tradition' of the scholar-élite with the 'little tradition' conveyed in plays and in novels and by itinerant story-tellers.

Not all popular literature was concerned with such political stories. Most of it was about romantic love, loyal friendship, bloodthirsty revenge and other predictable themes. Among this literature, however, other stereotypes can be found which may have some relevance to the political culture. One was the social bandit, the outright rebel. The greatest story in this genre is *The Water Margin*, China's Robin Hood legend; but unlike Robin Hood's adventures, which have little direct relevance to present-day political activity of any sort, the heroes of *The Water Margin* were part of a history of social banditry and lower-class guerrilla resistance which continued into the history of the Communist Party and which could still occur again.

Another type of hero is the strategist, the intriguer, shading off into the fairy-tale figure possessed of magic powers. Such stories are typical of the weak and the oppressed – Anansi in the West Indies, Brer Rabbit in the American slave states, figures who defeat their powerful enemies by deception or by pretending to yield. The Chinese example is *Monkey*.

Finally, expressed in China's most beloved novel, *A Dream of Red Pavilions*,[2] is the figure who finds the brutal realities of power in Chinese society too much to accept. The hero is Bao Yu, born into a rich and powerful family of favoured imperial slaves, whose power is, however, for that reason fragile. He is born with a magic jade stone around his neck. He rejects male authority personified in his austere and domineering father, and seeks the company of the young girls of the clan; at one point he hurls his jade stone away, saying that he does not want it, none of the girls have one – the stone having at this point become a phallic symbol of male power and male responsibilities. The framework of the book is supernatural, derived from Buddhism. The message (the Red Pavilions are only a Dream) is that the world is an illusion; what world? – the world of politics, power, public service. Power is precarious, eventually destroyed by its own inevitable corruption. The only reality is one's personal relations; but power brutally destroys even these. The nihilistic streak is a significant one in the Chinese tradition, and the negative attitude to politics which it expresses is an important factor in the political culture.

The Emperor as a focus of identification has not yet been discussed. He was generally accepted as the supreme exemplar of Confucianism, the patron of men of talent (a necessary attribute in any account of a great Emperor), and even as the mediator between heaven and earth. He was the sole, final focus of political loyalty. Sun Yat-sen was disturbed to find that in some of the ancestral temples of Kwangtung, after the fall of the Empire in 1912, the character for 'loyalty' had been scratched out of the ancestral tablets, an act which one can perhaps link with the warlord chaos which soon followed, and which suggests that the Chinese were not ready to accept the idea of allegiance to an abstract republic.

Justice cannot be done to the whole rich Confucian tradition in a few pages, but perhaps enough has been said to demonstrate that, when China entered the crisis which succeeded her defeats in the nineteenth century and was reluctantly forced to accept the necessity for modernisation, the tradition provided within it a range of choice. The image of a rigid orthodoxy which would break but not bend, eventually broken by Communism, is too simple.

Most of the ideas imported from the West could be rationalised in terms of some part of the tradition. Different possibilities, however, appealed to different social groups. The decision as to which strain of the traditional political culture would dominate in the new conditions depended less on the relevant strength of these strains, and more on the relative strength of the groups who employed them.

Perhaps the best approach to this problem is to pose the question: what possibilities were there for the creation, out of Chinese materials, of a pluralistic alternative to traditional totalitarian autocracy?

One can conceive the possibility of the following line of political development: the elements of a pluralistic polity might have been created out of existing local groups of gentry, clans, guilds, voluntary associations of all kinds, and the new business groups which were growing up. These groups might have developed the existing processes of informal consultation, and the 'bargaining' relationship with local officials, into a more formalised system, especially as the power of the central government diminished. The ethic of the 'golden mean' might conceivably have provided a rationale for limited and legitimised competition and political conflict.

For a few years at the turn of the century, such a line of development seemed possible. In some of China's great treaty-port cities, where Chinese and foreigners were closely associated in business and administration, notably in Shanghai, and where some of the old gentry had entered into association with new Chinese business firms, the familiar processes of informal consultation were partly formalised into representative government – oligarchic, corrupt, but (as was once said in another context) not wholly fraudulent.[3]

In the end, however, the passing of imperial government in 1912 brought about the collapse of national unity. The new city governments either disintegrated or fell under warlord domination. In these new circumstances, it was other and more obvious elements of the political culture which asserted themselves. Warlordism was a familiar problem, and produced familiar reactions; reunification of the country was accepted as the need which overwhelmed all others.

The new proto-pluralist politics, however, were distinctly local. The economic interests which supported such politics were provincial rather than national. They were urban rather than rural, at a time when the age-old hostility of town and country was being sharpened by economic changes. They were associated (often falsely) with dependence upon privileged foreign trade. Although from 1920 to 1921 a federalist move-ment grew up in China, it was significantly short-lived.[4]

Western liberal ideas were interpreted by many influential leaders in the light of these conditions. Sun Yat-sen, in analysing democratic gov-ernment, made his famous distinction between authority and power; authority (the legitimation of government) was in the hands of the sovereign people, but power was in the hands of the government once elected. Sun realised that in existing Chinese conditions the first necessity of democratic government was that the government should be strong, that its writ should run everywhere. He realised just as clearly that no government was likely to enjoy such unprecedented strength in China unless it was in some sense representative, but his proposals on this aspect of government were vague.

In these conditions of national division, Sun argued that in China as opposed to the West, the problem was not one of too little freedom but of too much, and he contradicted his own sincere belief in the value of individual freedom by asserting that 'freedom for the nation' must take precedence over freedom for the individual, thus providing an argument for the Chinese fascism created by the right wing among his successors. He himself was later to accept, through Comintern advisers, a democratic-centralist organisation for his Nationalist Party, which has retained this ever since.

Sun's insistence that China had too much freedom was a denial of the value of pluralism, an insistence that sectional interests were inimical to national unity. In China's 'soft-state' situation this was natural, but even during the honeymoon years of the Republic, when it was hopefully expected that the newly created parliamentary system would provide a sufficient framework for Chinese political life, Sun showed the traditional distaste for competition among sectional inter-ests by preventing the members of his party from seeking to build a majority and impose a government on the new president. He was never certain if his proper role as leader was to take power or simply to educate. Thus even this Western-educated doctor of peasant stock in-herited the ambiguity and the anxiety of the Confucian mandarin.

In a word, Sun and his associates could not accept that conflict could be anything but destructive. This was why Sun, in spite of his origins and education, was always strongly drawn to the older Chinese political values, in contradiction to his professed acceptance of Western liberal politics. Filial piety was still to Sun the greatest of human virtues; loyalty, not competition, the basis of politics. Yet at the same time he showed himself to be perfectly well aware that the older values, centred on social harmony maintained by filial piety, were patently the major psychological obstacles to political modernisation. Sun's confusion was not personal, it was cultural and national.

By 1927 when the united front of the Nationalist and Communist Parties ended in a blood-letting that polarised Chinese politics into two armed extremes, the hopes of development in the direction of liberal pluralism were destroyed. By that year, peasant rebellion of the traditional kind was spreading throughout China. We must now ask if it is possible to find in China a distinct lower-class alternative to the Confucian orthodoxy, a peasant sub-culture.

Of the continuity and prevalence of peasant revolt in Chinese history there is no doubt. The much-emphasised stability of pre-modern China is largely a myth, part of the mythology of the political culture.

It is also true that some parts of the popular literature glorified rebellion. We have referred to the novel, *The Water Margin* and its continued relevance to guerrilla resistance, and it is interesting that the Taiping Rebellion of the mid-nineteenth century gave rise not only to legends glorifying its leader Hung Hsiu-ch'uan which circulated among the peasants (Sun Yat-sen heard them in the fields as he worked with his peasant uncles and cousins), but also inspired a powerfully written and entirely traditional novel, *Hung Hsiu-ch'uan Yen-I*. In this, Hung appears as a hero of gigantic frame, immense physical prowess, and all-seeing wisdom. He is a perfect Emperor, but of the greenwood, not the court. The episodic form of the book strongly suggests that it was based on many stories then current among the people.

The various forms of voluntary association which, as we have pointed out, were extraordinarily prevalent in China, provided potential organisation for lower-class protest (and for upper-class resistance also). Among these were the secret societies. Some were religious congregations, some were mutual benefit societies. Many served as mutual protection for those whose occupations took them away from the normal family and village relationships – traders, mountain miners, migrant farm workers, and sailors, trackers and dockers on China's long inland waterways. Some societies were explicitly political, the most notable and powerful being the Triads, a southern society formed after the Manchu conquest as an underground resistance to the alien dynasty – which indeed in the end provided the rank and file of more than one of the revolutionary armies which destroyed Manchu rule. Mostly lower-class, usually egalitarian, and sworn (with elaborate ceremonial) to a mutual loyalty stronger than any other, their political potentialities were great, and not merely for armed rebellion. So pervasive were they, and so secret, that it is still a question if we can ever explain the events of Chinese history satisfactorily without much greater knowledge of their penetration. Even Communist efforts to suppress 'superstitious societies' have not yet been completely successful.

Often, part of their power came from the fact that a protective society easily turns into a protection racket, and this evolution might be said to represent the normal history of a Chinese secret society.

All the main peasant risings of Chinese history were associated with one or more such associations. In the nineteenth century the Taiping rebels were in origin a religious sect which flourished first among the immigrant Hakka in Northern Kwangtung and Kwangsi, where they maintained simple armed forces for defence against the hostile native Cantonese.

Chinese peasant movements varied widely in their political aims, from simple social banditry to millenialism. In the nineteenth century the Nien rebels, who held part of north China throughout the first half of the nineteenth century and then burst forth in great strength after the devastating change of course of the Yellow River, seem to have had no clear political aims. At the other end of the spectrum, the Taipings attempted to create a new quasi-Communist society.

It is true that the Taipings' philosophy had foreign origins, and this would suggest that it was atypical. Their leader, Hung Hsiu-ch'uan, had failed the imperial examinations three times. During a consequent mental breakdown he recalled a Christian pamphlet which he had once casually read, and saw a vision in which the Christian God called upon him to cast out the Manchus and cleanse China. He founded the Society of God-Worshippers among his fellow Hakkas. He received instruction from an American Southern Baptist missionary, Issachar Roberts. It is curious, however, that what Hung took from his contact with this missionary, whose ideas seem to have been the nineteenth-century middle-class ideas one would expect, were the elements of a sort of anabaptism which Roberts must have communicated to Hung from his own buried denominational memory. At any rate, Hung sought to create a new society, based on self-governing religious congregations with elected leaders, holding land and property in common, practising a Puritanical control of morals, millenial in spirit ('Taiping' is equivalent to 'millennium)', and ruled by a theocracy interpreting the divine revelation which had been made directly to Hung. This Chinese rebellion therefore in one sense must take its place as one of the millenial, collectivist, and Puritanical movements which Protestant Christianity has so constantly thrown up since the days of Zwingli and Münzer. Yet it was no less Chinese. Roberts' foreign ideas seem to have served as a catalyst in producing a form of Chinese peasant ideology which differed only in its greater systematisation of prevailing peasant aspirations. Egalitarianism, Puritanism, primitive direct democracy, an armed people; these had occurred before and were to recur in the twentieth century in the Hailufeng peasant movement, and in the Hunan movement of 1927 which Mao witnessed and which was probably the most influential experience of his youth.

The Taiping Rebellion, although it was perhaps the high point of peasant millenialism, was equally significant for its failure ever to implement its ideology. The grandiose new society remained largely theoretical. The main social effect of the rebellion was the restoration of peasant proprietorship in the areas where the rebels were most powerful; and this fact may indicate the extent of the ambitions of most Chinese peasant rebels. The Taiping court became a parody of the imperial court at its worst. In so far, in fact, as the Taipings succeeded in creating a settled political system, this was drawn back into the orbit of familiar, traditional political behaviour.

The Taipings showed all the predictable weaknesses of peasant political organisation. Constantly on the move, they had very little settled territory and they made no attempt to co-ordinate the nation-wide wave of revolt which was then taking place.

In sum, on present information (and one must stress that little research has been done) Chinese peasant political values and behaviour suffered from the usual peasant weaknesses; aiming more at justice within the system than at social change, but open – in contradiction to this – to millenial appeals; and lacking the capacity for sustained action above the local level.

The millenial, egalitarian collectivist streak was persistent, and still persists; P'eng Teh-huai, criticising the Communes in 1959, remarked that the Chinese Communist Party has always had more difficulty in dealing with the Left than with the Right, and he equated the Left in this context wtih peasant Utopianism. He also, implicitly, equated peasant Utopianism with the policies of Mao Tse-tung.

The ambiguity of Chinese peasant political values reflected the state of Chinese rural society. There was a gradation from the land-hungry semi-proletarian labourer to the shrewd and prosperous little commercial farmer. The vagaries of the monsoon could reverse their positions very easily; in any case they were probably cousins.

### MAO TSE-TUNG AND THE TRADITIONAL POLITICAL CULTURE

It was in the context of peasant revolt that the development of Mao's own distinctive view of politics originated. Before looking at this situation, however, it must be emphasised that the background to Mao's thought was not only the Hunan Peasant Movement and Marxism, but the whole debate on the transformation of politics which was then going on in China.

The demoralising failure of the first republican experiment after 1912 led Chinese radical leaders to accept that no form of democracy in

China could work, and that no effective national solidarity could be created without profound psychological changes in China. 'Cultural revolution' must have priority; and this meant primarily a revolution in political culture.

The main problem was the narrowness of Chinese loyalties, the narrowness of the moral community, which scarcely extended beyond the clan and the village. 'The clansman who will fight to the death for the continuity of the blood and food of the clan', wrote Sun Yat-sen, 'will look on unmoved at the destruction of the nation. We must make him see that with the destruction of the nation is involved the destruction of his clan.'

Liang Ch'i-ch'ao, the most devoted of China's parliamentarians, agreed. The result of narrow loyalties was that China lacked 'public spirit'; so much so, wrote Liang,[5] that the government could not even acquire the information necessary to run a modern state, so determined were the people to withhold any information which might be used to their disadvantage. Liang proposed to start at the grass roots, by creating representative village governments, and giving them powers and encouragement to undertake for themselves developments which were in their own immediate interests. They were to create their own militia to maintain public order; to found, support and run their own schools; and to take the first step to local economic development in the form of roadbuilding programmes. Liang believed that the intense local loyalties which were *an obstacle* to nation-building could, if thus harnessed, become the *foundation* of nation-building. This idea complemented Sun's programme for the creation of democracy gradually from the village up. But far more striking are the parallels between Liang's proposals of 1919 and Mao's policies after 1957.

The writings of Hu Han-min[6] are especially interesting in this context because although he was on the right wing of nationalist politics, his ideas were still similar to those we have discussed. In his *Revolutionary Theory and Revolutionary Work*, written just after the foundation of the Nationalist Republic when the first attempts to create a new political system began, he takes it for granted that the centre of gravity of policy must be the creation of democracy at the local level. He then discusses the nature of the necessary leadership. He was alarmed by the already obvious signs that the cadres of the Nationalist Party had rapidly changed from political leaders to state administrators, and were already reverting to the habits and attitudes of the mandarins. The graft had failed; the ancient stock was taking over from the modern scion. Hu condemned the Nationalist cadres for having adopted the traditional style of autocratic behaviour and of aloofness from those they governed, and the élitist pretensions of their predecessors. He insisted that they must 'go deep among the people' and 'share weal and woe with them' – phrases which we wrongly associate with Mao

Tse-tung personally, but which even in the late twenties and early thirties came readily to the writing brush of every Chinese political commentator.

Hu also condemned the Nationalist cadres for their inability to criticise or to accept criticism, an inability which reflected traditional characteristics to which we have already alluded – fear of authority, acceptance of hierarchy and avoidance of conflict.

Liang Ch'i-ch'ao was even more eloquent than Hu Han-min on this. In his last political essay – a sort of political testament – Liang appealed to the Chinese to break out of the 'slavery of the mind' which inhibited democratic politics. They were, wrote Liang, the slaves of tradition, authority and conformity. They would not think against tradition, speak out against authority, or act against customary behaviour. There is an obvious verbal parallel with Mao's 'Dare to think, dare to speak, dare to act'. In the overlapping writings of Sun, Liang and Hu we can thus find a general critique of Chinese political culture, and the adumbration of a substitute.

In 1923, Nationalists and Communists formed an alliance, and Mao's first recorded speech in the councils of the allied parties criticised the leadership for concentrating its resources too much in a few cities, and recommended their dispersal throughout the countryside. His subsequent experience was to turn the theme of this speech into a life-long concern.

The peasant rebellion in Hunan in late 1926 led Mao to believe not only that peasant discontent could provide the main motive force for revolution, but that the peasants when they had seized power – and only when they had seized power – soon articulated their own aspirations, and that these aspirations could and should be the basis of policy. The role of leadership was simply to rationalise these popular aspirations. In this way the Maoist 'mass line' was born. Experience in the Kiangsi Soviet, 1927–33, strengthened Mao's conviction in this respect; dependent for survival on majority support, Mao's guerrillas had to take account of the complexities of the rural social structure in China and had therefore to relinquish the doctrinaire and egalitarian policies of the Central Committee and adopt a mass-line approach to land reform. In Yenan, Mao, forced by defeats at the hands of the Japanese to maximise the resources of the shrinking Border Regions, dismantled the state apparatus of the Communist areas and dispersed a large proportion of its personnel to lead a rural-based drive for increased production in co-operative forms; the young intellectual patriots from Yenan were thus thrust directly into contact with peasant guerrilla leaders. It was in this context that Mao finally elaborated his ideas of mass-line leadership.

It was in this context also that experience of the non-Communist Chinese Industrial Co-operative movement,[7] with its intermediate-technology operations and its thoroughly democratic organisation, brought home to Mao the tremendous possibilities of local economic development on the basis of popular self-help.

All the seeds of the Great Leap Forward and the Communes were already present in the Indusco movement. The hopes and perspectives of the co-operative workers anticipated those of the Great Leap. The motives of the young technicians and intellectuals who founded them, created their improvised technologies, and shared all the poverty and hardships of their fellow co-operative members, served as a model to their successors in 1958. They provided precisely the kind of leadership which Mao was himself seeking to create.[8]

This was a decisive experience which changed the mass line from a matter of political style into a whole novel strategy of community-based economic growth, social change and political development.

During the Five Year Plan 1953–7, Border Region ideas and policies were replaced by those of the Russian planners, and almost every aspect of Chinese life was remade on Russian lines. By 1956, however, Mao was in full rebellion against this Russian model.

We have seen that every twentieth-century Chinese radical acknowledged that developments in China must start at the grass-roots. The attempt by the Party in 1955 to increase the amount of grain procured produced immediate disincentive effects, and showed that there was a very sharp limit indeed to the central mobilisation of resources for investment by taxation or by controlled prices for agricultural produce. At the same time, the flood of criticism of the Party and its policies in 1957 had shown that both the right and the left of the Communist Party were violently opposed to the centralised bureaucratic system created in the course of the First Five Year Plan. The left were not content merely to criticise bureaucracy, but set about the creation of a non-bureaucratic alternative, based on Border Region precedents. This was the beginning of the Great Leap Forward.

The Great Leap sought to reduce centralised bureaucracy and replace it with a system of autonomous local communities, which in the democratic pursuit of collective self-improvement would form new relationships with the state. Hierarchy was short-circuited, state authority minimised. All China's public institutions pledged themselves to accept the criticism of the masses, to encourage debate and to replace administrative fiat with democratic conflict.[9] The modern state sector of the economy was to serve the needs of local, self-help economic growth, based on the investment of the local community's savings and surplus labour in labour-intensive construction and intermediate-technology industry to serve, in the first place, the local communitiy's own needs.

Collective economic growth, organised through democratic decision-making, was expected to be the centre of a process by which successful increase in incomes would encourage further investment by the community, would lead to the acceptance of new forms of social organisation (higher levels of collectivism), would raise new cultural needs in direct relation to the development of the economy, would create a new sense of national interdependence as new economic relationships ramified, and would produce citizens with a new political outlook. Economic growth, new social organisation, new culture and new political consciousness would feed each other in a single process that would lead both to abundance and to communism, and in the course of this would transform the political culture.

One can see in this strategy Mao's reaction to the traditional political culture. Narrow local loyalties were (as Liang Ch'i-ch'ao had proposed) to be exploited in nation-building: collective local self-help would generate widening economic relationships, which would eventually make 'the whole nation a single chessboard'. Democracy was to be built up from the grass roots. Politics – persuasion, debate, organisation – were to replace administrative *fiat*. Hierarchical government was to be replaced by self-government in communities of peers. Authority was to be subject to criticism, and conflict – limited, legitimised conflict – was to be part of the normal process of decision-making. The poor majority were to seize power again and their aspirations would determine the shape of local development, while their leaders, working with them in the fields, would respond to rationalise these aspirations. The Great Leap and the Communes summed up China's twentieth-century radical criticism of the old political culture.

We have so far discussed Mao's new ideas and policies almost as if Marxism were irrelevant to them. It is certainly true that every one of these ideas and policies, taken individually, can be paralleled in other and non-Communist developing countries. To Mao Tse-tung himself, however, his proceedings were wholly Marxist. If they were produced by the conditions of China itself, where absolute standards of life were lower than in the Soviet Union, where there was far less capital and a far greater labour surplus, and where there were stubborn political traditions rooted deeply in the whole Chinese socialisation process, yet at the same time these very problems, and the solutions to them which had been applied in the Border Regions, seemed to offer the possibility of creating a new society on the basis not of Stalinist bureaucracy but of the alternative socialist tradition of Marx and Engels' *Civil War in France* and Lenin's *State and Revolution*. The starting point of this tradition was of course the Paris Commune. The word used in China for the Chinese commune – *gong-she* – was not an old Chinese word; it had been invented in modern times as a translation of 'Paris Commune'.

The repudiation of Soviet orthodoxy, both in its Stalinist form and in its subsequent 'revisionist' development, was conscious and deliber-

ate. So was the return to Lenin's *State and Revolution*, which became
the key pre-Maoist text in Chinese political education. Mao's criticisms
of Stalin have been kept from the Chinese public, but they were published by a group of Red Guards and proved to be devastating. They
are very close to the criticisms of Stalin made in the liberal West:

> In thirty years Stalin did not succeed in creating a truly collective
> system; all he did was to perpetuate the counter-productive exploita-
> tion of the landlords . . .[10]

> Stalin set the rate of accumulation too high; this rate of accumulation
> adversely affected industry . . . he drained the pond to catch the
> fish . . .

> Stalin's fundamental failure was that he did not trust the peasants . . .
> as a result, the state hamstrung the peasants, and the peasants ham-
> strung the state . . .[11]

> If disagreements arose Stalin dealt with them by suppression; he
> knew no other way to deal with dissent . . . when this failed . . . he had
> no other resource . . . and politics in the Soviet Union ceased to have
> any foundation . . .

> Stalin was a bit of a *lao-yeh* (paternalistic, authoritarian). Educated
> as a priest, he understood neither materialism nor dialectics. He was
> out of touch with reality and had no idea how to handle relation-
> ships . . .[12]

From the point of view of Mao's attitude to Soviet political culture, the
last phrase can provide a starting point: 'he had no idea how to handle
relationships . . .' Elsewhere, Mao brings this idea into sharper focus,
in words which give the key to his own very different view of economics
and politics:

> There have been [in the USSR] no *dynamic and proliferating re-
> lationships* between short-term and long-term interests . . .[13]

Mao then goes on to define the conditions in which 'dynamic and pro-
liferating relationships' can be created:

> There were many problems for which Stalin had no solution: simul-
> taneous development of heavy and light industry, of industry and
> agriculture, of local and central industry, etc.; all the people and all
> the party create industry; mass movements; rectification; politics in
> command . . .

To sum this up, Mao seeks to create these dynamic relationships by a
high level of popular participation, made possible by concentration on
local development, based on the investment of surplus labour in agricultural construction and in small simple industries. This will bring
short-term gains which will both inspire and provide the means for

long-term effort. The modern sector is reorientated to serve these local developments. The political implications of such an economic strategy are obvious. It both requires and stimulates a kind of democratic politics. Centralised, dictatorial direction from above would be at best irrelevant.

The first attempt at this process in 1958 failed. In the West it is widely believed that the Great Leap Forward was a disaster because its economic basis was irrational. Analysis of its economic theory,[14] however, does not suggest that this was true, while on the other hand analysis of the course of the Great Leap Forward as it developed in practice strongly suggests that the problems which caused its failure were problems partly of the Chinese political culture which would be recognisable from our discussion of Chinese traditions. It was already clear in 1959 that the main reason for the breakdown of the commune system was that the commune embraced not one village but several, which traditionally had no sense of mutual obligation. Mao's own private comments, since revealed, have confirmed this view. Far more important, however, was the fact that the cadres of the Chinese Communist Party, when driven to take vigorous action, were quite incapable of performing the role which was given to them of acting as *political* leaders, quite incapable of performing the task of creating the greatest possible measure of agreement on policies which would reconcile local aspirations with national aims. They acted as bureaucrats. They showed themselves incapable of making the distinction, which is as clear in Mao's thought as it is in our own thought in the West – a distinction unknown in pre-modern China – between politics and administration.

There was another factor in the behaviour of local cadres during the Great Leap. Drawn primarily from the former poor peasants, and chosen for their commitment to socialism, the rural cadres probably concentrated in their ranks much of the traditional poor peasant millenialism. Under the stimulus of the visionary propaganda of 1958 (it is difficult to know whether this propaganda was cause or effect) they took off into flights of egalitarianism and collectivism. For a few weeks even the Central Committee was caught up in this euphoria. The exhausted and disillusioned peasant majority were now dragooned into action, stripped of their remaining property and plundered of their savings, to feed an attempt to transform agriculture and to industrialise the countryside overnight.

Mao reacted sharply, insisting that to take the peasant's property away by force was 'banditry', and that peasant resistance was 'right and proper'. The worst excesses were abruptly stopped.

However, the ideas of the Great Leap and the Communes were discredited. It was not until 1969, after the completion of the Cultural Revolution, that Mao was in a position to reimpose the policies which he favoured. Since then the Great Leap policies have been reimposed, though without haste, and accompanied by the creation of a new institution, the Revolutionary Committee, which is supposed to ensure that the Party cadres can act only as leaders of a mass-line process.

## A NEW POLITICAL CULTURE?

The relationship between Mao's ideas and the Chinese political culture is very close. Mao's Marxism is an almost symmetrical antithesis of the main psychological characteristics of traditional Chinese political attitudes. In this paradoxical sense, his 'sinification' of Marxism may have gone a great deal further than is generally appreciated.

The main theme of Mao's writings and speeches, both in his author-ised *Selected Works* and other publications, and in the Red Guard collections, is conflict. At the level of philosophy, Mao insists that con-flict is the permanent human condition. It will not end even with the achievement of Communism and the elimination of class conflict; there will continue to be struggles among interest groups and opinion groups, 'contradictions among the people'. Such conflict will then carry human progress on to levels higher than Communism and as yet undreamed of. Without it politics will become unhealthy and society will decay; Mao is as apprehensive of consensus politics as any Western liberal. It is not the duty of the statesman to fudge over difficulties by unprincipled compromise, but to force them into the open in order to ensure their proper definition through public debate, to resolve the contradiction in a unity at a higher level, and then to prepare for the new conflicts which will grow out of this new unity. Mao criticises Stalin and his successors for their constant stress on unity and for their refusal to recognise the existence of the contradictions which should be the driving force of the system.

Fruitful conflict, however, can be inhibited not only by false unanimity and unprincipled compromise. It can also be repressed by force, and this is equally unacceptable. 'Stalin', said Mao, 'killed a great many people in 1936 and 1937 and quite a few in 1938; in 1939 he killed hardly anybody. It is not possible to deal with dissent by killing all your opponents.'[15] When that method failed, however, Stalin knew no other: 'After that, class conflict ceased in the Soviet Union and Soviet politics had no foundation.'

These criticisms of consensus politics on the one hand, and the re-placement of politics by force on the other, are directed formally at the Soviet Union, but they are equally relevant to the Chinese political culture, in which conflict was either evaded or suppressed.

Several of Mao's writings are concerned with laying down rules for legitimised conflict. These rules are summed up in the slogan 'unity–

criticism–unity'. It has usually been interpreted in the West as a demand for rigid uniformity, but there has always been ample evidence that it was nothing of the kind; and we now have, in the Red Guard collections, Mao's own explicit formulation: fruitful conflict must start from unity, in the sense of an agreement about aims. On this basis, and only on this basis, can discussion, mutual criticism, and conflict be constructive, and lead to a new unity on a higher level. In any society experienced in democratic politics, this idea would be unremarkable. It is the absence in Chinese tradition of the expectation that conflict can be creative which gives it point. A platitude in the West, it was a liberating innovation in China.

The 'unity–criticism–unity' formula deals not only with the low expectations of the Chinese as to the value of conflict, but with the related problem of 'face'. Under this formula, a man need not lose face because he is criticised, since he knows that his critics accept that he loyally shares the common aims and that he will continue, in spite of having been criticised, to have an honourable place in the pursuit of these common aims. The vital need for this psychological change in China could be illustrated by Hu Han-min's description in the 1920s of the causes of inhibition of criticism within the Nationalist Party.

In Party councils, Mao has insisted not only that the Party must accept public criticism but must actively promote it. 'We must always set up an opposite', he says. In 1957 he argued that the issues facing China could only be made clear by encouraging public discussion. Through such discussion, the loyal majority would become conscious of their own beliefs and repudiate the irreconcilable minority. The main instrument of this discussion was the *da-zi bao*, in which protests, criticisms and suggestions were written by the individual or by a group and posted in a public place. Mao approved of these because, he declared, they were 'classless' (a remarkable statement from a Marxist!); anyone, whatever his position or opinions, had access to enough paper and ink to produce them. He advocated in 1957 that the writings of opponents should be republished, because people could not distinguish between good and bad ideas unless they were able to compare them. 'Everybody hates Chiang Kai-shek', said Mao, 'but very few people know what a bastard he is. We should republish Chiang's Collected Works so that they can learn.'[16] He proposed that the 'rightists' should be encouraged to hold public meetings and that they should have their own newspaper. His proposal to republish hostile works does not seem to have been accepted in 1957 (although later during the polemic against revisionism, works by Bernstein, Kautsky and Kardelj were actually reprinted). Nor was the creation of an opposition newspaper permitted. On the contrary, the Kuangming Daily, which had enjoyed a precarious independence as the organ of the social-democratic intellectuals, was put completely under Party control. It seems that the Party was less ready to accept conflict than its Chairman.

In this context, Mao's most striking defiance of tradition was his tolerance of disorder. During 1957 there were strikes, student riots, withdrawals from the collective farms and even, here and there, the appearance of explicitly anti-Communist organisations. The Party was alarmed and acted repressively. Mao condemned the repression and poured scorn on their fears. He insisted that protest could sometimes do a great deal of good. 'In XX', he said (the Red Guard source does not give the actual name of the place), 'they tried to control the slaughter of cattle among the Moslems. The Moslems beat up a few of the cadres and that solved the problem.'[17] Referring to the Shanghai strikes, he said, 'In 1000 factories in Shanghai only one worker in ten thousand caused trouble. It would have been better if it had been one in a hundred – that would have been the end of bureaucracy.'[18] Perhaps his most revealing statement was a remark about the troubles in Eastern Europe: 'A real statesman could have made something out of these situations in Poznan and Hungary.'

In 1966, he deliberately courted such a situation of disorder; he publicly approved Nieh Yuan-tzu's *da-zi bao* attacking the Party administration of Peking University; he sent a congratulatory letter to the pupils of the middle school attached to Tsinghua University on their creation of the Red Guards; and he wrote and posted his own *da-zi bao*, 'Bombard the Headquarters', which changed the target of attack from publicists to political leaders.

Mao has dealt with the problem of hierarchy in two contexts: decentralisation and democratic centralism. It is probable that his general attitude is like that of Lenin in *State and Revolution*: that while it is impossible to 'get rid of subordination' immediately, yet the revolution will provide an opportunity for building new forms of administration which, while involving subordination, will bear within them the seeds of its dissolution. The sequel in Soviet Russia has scarcely borne out Lenin's prediction, and Mao has a theory as to why that prediction was not fulfilled: the Soviet party, by accepting centralised control and by instituting one-man management, in essence preserved the 'bourgeois state'; and under Stalin, by minimising the importance of human relationships as opposed to the importance of technology and investment, the Soviet Union left itself no alternative to bureaucratic methods. So far from creating a system which could dissolve away into full participating democracy and workers' control, it created a system in which technocratic vested interests spontaneously increased in strength.

In applying his ideas to the problems of decentralisation, Mao was also dealing, as we have suggested, with an age-old and fundamental contradiction in Chinese government, and attempting to redefine the relationship between central government and local community. From

1956 onwards, this problem is one of his constant concerns. Briefly, Mao took the view that this relationship should be a dynamic one, one of mutual stimulus. This required a considerable degree of local autonomy: 'localities should fight for their rights', he said at one point; and as he explicitly stated, the relationship should be one of 'consultation'. He minimised the role of the Centre: 'our job is simply to produce ideas and employ cadres' – a definition of government which, *mutatis mutandis*, would have been acceptable to the Ch'ien Lung Emperor.

The definition of democratic centralism is another of Mao's abiding concerns. In origins democratic centralism was simply an insistence, necessary for revolutionary parties born in rebellion, that decisions once democratically agreed should then be binding on all. We take it for granted, but Lenin could not, nor can Mao. His definition is, as one would expect, a dialectical one. He does not regard it as a compromise between discipline and freedom, but as a 'unity of opposites', in which democratic decision-making strengthens the capacity for united action, while central discipline guarantees the implementation of democratic decisions. It is, in a Marxist form, an elaboration of Sun Yat-sen's insistence that government must be strong but that only democratic government *can* be strong.

Mao has made constant attacks on the authoritarianism of tradition, and on the authority of rank and office, of experts, teachers and elders. He has done everything possible to destroy the symbols of rank and office. The insignia of rank in the People's Liberation Army have been done away with. Cadres are made to spend a part of their time working side-by-side with those they rule. In the new education system an attempt is being made to break down the traditional authoritarianism, to give students the confidence to criticise their teachers, to substitute discussion for lectures, and to involve students in the writing of the syllabus. Anyone who has taught Chinese students is well aware of the difficulty they have in challenging the authority of the teacher, and will not be likely to think that Mao's policies in this respect are unrealistically extreme; and if the changes in education have been made in rather melodramatic ways, this may have been psychologically necessary.

Mao's attacks on the authority of experts have been supposed in the West to represent ideological interference in technical matters. There has always been plenty of evidence, however, that this was not what was intended, and in one of Mao's confidential speeches he is quite explicit as to what he means. His main point is the simple and familiar one that expert advisers should not be allowed to usurp the authority of political leaders to make decisions which have political implications. Yet there is more to it than this. Mao is shrewd enough to see that highly qualified experts are not always the most successful innovators, that innovation more commonly comes from somewhere nearer the shop-floor, and that the top experts must not be permitted to monopolise the responsibility for innovation. In particular, his strategy of localised development depends to a unique extent on the creation of intermediate technologies by adaptive innovation in response to local conditions. The experts must help this process and not inhibit it.

Yet though Mao's suspicion of the expert is defensible on practical grounds, it clearly echoes the traditional dictum that the last word on policy must be with the moral élite, and that experts are no more than the servants of the morally-trained policy makers.

The authority of age has been traditionally very great in China, and it hardly needs stressing that gerontocracy is an unsuitable instrument for the promotion of change. Again and again Mao returns to the idea that it is youth that is creative, and presents to the Politburo or some other high Party conference an interminable string of illustrations from world history and Chinese history.

These main elements in Mao's thought clearly represent a direct and conscious attack on elements of the traditional political culture. Yet in spite of this Mao has inherited a great deal from the Chinese past. Perhaps he is less conscious of the elements he has inherited than of the elements he has opposed. Mao believes, as Confucians always have, that man is essentially good. Repeatedly he has insisted not only that 90 per cent of the people are good, but that 90 per cent even of his opponents are good, at least in the sense (the good Confucian sense) that they are capable of being changed by education. He believes, as Confucians did (and as any Communist does, in spite of the theoretical ammorality of Communism) that government is legitimised by its representation of a higher morality; but like Confucians, and unlike other Communists, he accepts that the test of the moral legitimacy is pragmatic; that if a Communist Party is not successful in the eyes of the mass of the population in serving their aspirations then the Communist government will fall and should fall, though he believes that in the logic of history it would be replaced eventually by another and better Communist government. He accepts the totalitarian implications of the concept that government should represent moral ideals, and although he has deplored attempts to intervene in family life as impractical, he has set no limits to the scope of government control; the slogan 'politics in command' certainly does not imply limited government. At the same time, the harshness of his dictatorship of the proletariat is softened by his refusal to go to extremes, his insistence on leaving a way out for everyone but the most recalcitrant, and his interpretation of the unity of opposites to mean that the truth is never all on one side; the golden mean tradition has not been without its influence.

One might even suggest that in terms of the Confucian tradition, Mao leans to the Taoist side. His anti-authoritarianism, his scorn for élitist pretensions, his indifference to institutions, his hostility towards the apparatus of the state, and his sympathy for the life of the autonomous local community all have Taoist precedents.

Mao's views of political culture imply a 'new man'. The characteristics of this new socialist citizen are clear. He is both co-operative and critical. On the one hand, he is conscious of the interdependence and mutual responsibility of citizens from the village level to the national level, appreciating that his own interests are inseparable from the interests of the whole. On the other hand, he can stand up to higher authority; he does not suffer from neurotic anxieties about the social and political pecking order, and seeks neither patrons nor clients: he is at ease with limited and legitimised conflict and knows the rules; he can be critical of persons, policies and techniques, and he can accept criticism in return; he can experiment, improvise and innovate; he can perform the functions of supervision and accounting, as Lenin predicted. He is a farmer, a worker and a soldier. He is a politically active citizen and an articulate debater.

In power, he adopts no airs and graces and issues no commands. He listens to all opinions, 'seeks truth from facts' and submits his conclusions to the judgement of the community, though if necessary he will argue and organise stubbornly to win a majority for his views. He conscientiously maintains contact with manual labour and labourers.

The 'new man' is not an abstract ideological myth. He is the sort of citizen necessary to run China's new community-based system, and the sort of citizen which the system, if successful, will itself tend to produce.

### DISSONANCE BETWEEN THE OLD CULTURE AND THE NEW: OPPOSITION TO MAOISM

The Maoists describe the values and behaviour which prejudice the achievement of cultural revolution as 'bourgeois', and claim that the various groups involved are all linked.

The groups are said to include 'petty bourgeois' elements in the countryside (identified with the former rich peasants), remnants of the former capitalist class still employed in managerial positions, the old intellectuals, Communist intellectuals who have adopted 'bourgeois' attitudes, cadres who rule by force and command instead of by persuasion, cadres who act in collusion with members of the former upper classes, and some of the new élite of managers, technicians and bureaucrats.

Analysis of accusations made during the Cultural Revolution show that the attitudes which these groups are said to share include: the minimisation of conflict; élitist views of political, economic and educa-

tional policy; and the use of administrative orders and coercion to replace political organisation – all, it is claimed, in order to consolidate
their own power.

At this stage in our argument, it will scarcely be necessary to emphasise that these are precisely the attitudes which one would expect to
persist from the traditional political culture. And there is enough substance in the accusations made during the Cultural Revolution to confirm that these attitudes were indeed prevalent. Liu Shao-ch'i, for
example, leaned in every policy choice he made towards the élitist, the
centralist and the bureaucratic. This is not to argue that his choices
were wrong, but simply that they are all consistent with the view that
he was strongly influenced by the old political culture. At the same
time, he deplored and sought to minimise conflict; yet when conflict
occurred he dealt with it, as in the Socialist Education Movement and
the Cultural Revolution, by drastic administrative means, and in this
respect also he was behaving in the tradition.

Many others were accused of similar attitudes. There is some truth
in the Maoist belief that all those of like mind were involved in a
political bloc. The shock of the disastrous failure of the Great Leap and
the unpopularity of the dismissal of P'eng Teh-huai moulded the
opposition elements into a sort of unity, and in a common retreat
towards what they regarded as normal administration, which meant
(as in Liu Shao-ch'i's case) towards what was more compatible with
traditional practices and expectations.

There was, however, another side to Confucianism – its ideals of
'benevolence and righteousness' in government. The Great Leap had
been planned as a democratic mass movement, but had become a
monstrous tyranny. The opposition appealed to Confucian tradition
against it. The most direct appeal was a pilgrimage by a group of old
intellectuals in 1962 to the birthplace of Confucius,[19] where speeches
were made which attacked the Maoists obliquely by reasserting the continuing importance of Confucianism. They declared that Confucianism
represented the permanent values of the Chinese nation, which put
justice and humanity above class conflict. They equated the message
of Confucius with liberal democratic ideals.

From 1959 to 1963, when Mao's influence was at an ebb, the same
Confucian values were reasserted in literature and in historical writing.
There was a long controversy over the question of the possibility of
inheriting from the morality of feudalism. There was a similar controversy over whether or not the reforming officials of imperial China
had been 'progressive'. In both cases, the opposition authors implied
that there were permanent human values in politics, values above class.
In late 1959 a spate of historical plays began, with great figures from the
past used as parables of the present. Of these figures, the most important was Hai Jui. It is not generally realised that Wu Han's play, *The*

*Dismissal of Hai Jui*[20] (which ran only for five days in Peking), was part of a national movement. It was not the first Hai Jui play nor the last. There were many of them persistently appearing all over China until 1963. And there were as many more plays about similar heroes. The 'liberal' opposition in China thus identified themselves with the great remonstrating officials of the past, and through them reasserted Confucian values. They did so with the patronage of sections of the Party – P'eng Chen and the Peking Municipal Committee, Chou Yang and the propaganda ministry, and many of the provincial administrations – and they were tolerated, if not actually encouraged, by Liu Shao-ch'i and his government.

Mao Tse-tung himself did not at this time draw a connection between the opposition and the Confucian past, although many critics in the Cultural Revolution accused members of the opposition (including Liu Shao-ch'i) of appealing in their writings to the old values. The connection which was emphasised was that between the ideas of the opposition and those of the Soviet Union since Khrushchev – they were accused of revisionism, not Confucianism. Khrushchev's theory of 'a Party of the whole people' gave an authoritative Communist rationale for minimising conflict, very welcome to the right wing of China, while the normalisation of administration in Russia and in Eastern Europe provided similar authority for élitism and bureaucratism which Mao believed were being reasserted in China.

In 1973, however, an explicitly anti-Confucian campaign was launched in association with the posthumous condemnation of Lin Piao. Towards the end of the Cultural Revolution, which Lin Piao had helped to launch, he had appealed for moderation, and supported his appeal by quoting Confucius: 'Restore the proprieties and practise self-restraint'. This became the text of the anti-Confucius campaign – or more properly the campaign to 'tear up the roots of Lin Piao and Confucius'.

POLITICAL KNOWLEDGE

The Chinese people are accustomed to the restriction of information by the government. No Chinese in the past felt any obligation to defend the right to publish and propagate dissenting views or information which supported dissenting views. In practice, there was a good deal more freedom than these statements would imply, but the idea of freedom of thought and publication came to China only with the influx of Western ideas. And it remained an idea associated with a relatively small handful of Westernised liberal journalists, teachers and politicians. It was accepted in principle by the Nationalist party and government, but this did not prevent the continued exercise of censorship limited only by the general incompetence of the Nationalist régime and by its inadequate hold on the provinces of China.

Consequently the control of the news media and of publication under the present régime meets the expectations of most of the Chinese people. It is true that there was considerable protest in 1957 over the denial of civil freedoms, but these protests came almost entirely from the Westernised liberal minority. It is unlikely that any strong movement against censorship will arise in China unless and until large sections of the Chinese population have specific, shared grievances the expression of which is frustrated by censorship. Then possibly the principle of freedom of publication may become a matter of concern to the majority.

The control of the dissemination of information by the Party and the government in China is obvious. More than that, the systematic positive use of the channels of publication to inculcate a single point of view favoured by the régime is just as obvious. Nevertheless, there is in China in many respects much fuller dissemination of information and much more effective presentation of alternatives (even if only to condemn them) than in most other countries which profess or practise totalitarian rule. We have seen Mao Tse-tung's own insistence on the necessity for open debate, and on the need to 'set up an opposite'. Although it cannot be said that this idea has been fully honoured, nevertheless a great deal of China's official publicity does take the form of presenting readers with a choice of views; and even if the choice is preordained yet the debate which precedes it undoubtedly adds to political knowledge.

In so far as the development process in China has been decentralised and localised, there is a constant need for what the Chinese refer to as 'the generalisation of experience', that is, the reporting of local initiatives and their results as prescriptive examples for the whole nation. These too, because of the infinite variety of local conditions in China, often involve choice – this time real choice – and information on which choice can be based. More generally, the dependence of so much of Chinese planning and development on the authorities at county level and commune level of necessity demands a very full flow of public information concerning possibilities and problems.

From time to time in the course of major critical campaigns such as the Rectification Campaign of 1957 and the Cultural Revolution of 1966–9, a quite extraordinary degree of frankness has been shown in printing the opinions and criticisms of opponents. If western observers are able to build up from these revelations a picture of the alternatives with which China has been faced and of people inside and outside the Chinese party who supported them, many Chinese readers must be quite capable of doing the same for themselves.

One could add to this the consequence of an educational system which, within the general constraints of the ideology, is emphatically and successfully problem-solving, backed by two of Mao's important aphorisms, 'seek the truth from the facts' and 'no investigation, no right to speak'.

POLITICAL SOCIALISATION

While Mao depends primarily on the process of mass-line development to create and inculcate the new political culture, at the same time every possible direct means of socialisation is employed in relation to that process.

The traditional influence of the family is offset by the constant involvement of children from an early age in public activities, through the Little Red Soldiers, the Red Guards and the Youth League. These are composed of children chosen for their ready response, representing something of an élite though elected by their fellow pupils or students. The school population generally is involved through systematic political study, combined with participation in production as part of regular education. Teaching is geared to production and political problems. Children and the young are constantly involved not only in production but in social tasks (anti-litter campaigns, taking care of the old, tree-planting, and so on).

The whole egalitarian ethic of the schools, and the stress on discussion in place of lectures, on student participation in writing the syllabus, and on limiting the authority of the teachers, form an important part of the socialisation process.

In the work-place, management is carried on by committees which include workers, administrators and technicians (the committees are also carefully balanced as among age groups). All managers, technicians and members of Party committees participate in work on the shop-floor – the shop manager supervises from behind his own machine. It is stressed that experience has shown that workers will only accept a place in the boardroom if managers accept a place on the shop-floor.[21] This management ethic is taught in 7 May Cadre Schools, at courses of five or six months in which managerial personnel work on a farm, do their own chores and pursue political studies related to the new ethic.

There are also constant campaigns of which currently the anti-Confucius campaign is the greatest, in which social criticism is applied by everyone, individually or in his school, work-place or political group, to the practical problems of his own social relationships. This is done with near-religious intensity.

POLITICAL CULTURE AND POLITICAL CHANGE

In the introduction, it was stated that it is too soon to attempt to measure how far the new official 'Maoist' political culture has been internalised, and that no attempt at measurement would be made here. However, experience during a recent visit to China (June 1975) has provided the opportunity at least to make some comments based on observation, and to raise some further questions.

The concluding section will therefore be purely impressionistic. It was impossible to see more than perhaps fifty institutions in China, and impossible to talk to more than a few hundred people. Moreover, as China admits visitors only in groups, the places visited must have facilities to offer hospitality to groups; the same places thus tend to be regularly visited, and the proceedings become somewhat ritualised. Even if these institutions were not chosen in the first place as models of their kind, and therefore atypical, they are bound quickly to become atypical in the practised ability of those who represent them to participate in discussion with foreigners. In other words, the situation is one which will tend to maximise, in these particular institutions, the political articulateness and political knowledge of their members.

The first characteristic noted was that the rhetoric of the new political culture seemed to be universal. All questions, theoretical, practical or factual, were answered in the appropriate terms. There has been a sweeping change in the political language of China, and this perhaps indicates at least some degree of internalisation. It is difficult to imagine that mere conformity could produce a situation in which so many people applied this new language to their own affairs with such a sharp and intelligent sense of relevance – whether one agreed with this application or not. Yet at the same time, one could not but be conscious of an element of ritual incantation.

The second characteristic observed was that the Maoist social process, which is intended among other things to transform political consciousness, is well under way and should be expected to begin to yield results. This, however, was more obvious in the towns than in the countryside. There, agriculture, operating in conditions of general prosperity, threatens to bring total peasant incomes in the more favoured areas to levels above those of average industrial earnings, and on a partly individualist basis. On the other hand, much of this prosperity is the consequence of the collective creation of new resources, new forms of employment, and new social overheads, so that the total effect on peasant attitudes must be uncertain.

The third characteristic was that the institutional changes associated with the new political culture have proceeded apace – workers' management, revolutionary committees, the abolition of bonuses and piece-rates, the use of *da-zi bao* as a major means of protest and criticism, work-study education, and popular management of schools. There is, nevertheless, still significant opposition; for example, there were serious labour troubles in Wuhan in 1974 in which managerial opposition to the new industrial dispensation seems to have played a part.

However, the most striking contradiction in the new political culture, which is supposed to rid China of the traits of dependence, is the dependence of the whole movement on the personal authority of Mao Tse-tung. Two days in Ch'angsha were devoted by our hosts on our behalf to visiting places associated with Mao, places which have become shrines, and our hosts showed no signs of appreciating that we were not all as passionately interested in this as they themselves. In general, every speech referred to a Maoist text, and to quote Mao in return would bring instant and serious attention.

Mao did not create the cult of himself, but after 1960 when his influence in the Central Committee was seriously weakened, he permitted Lin Piao to create it. However, he has always insisted that it is his works which matter, not his person, and that even his works are not entirely personal – 'most of what are called my works', he said, 'are not my own; they were written in the blood of the Chinese people.' It is probable that it is easier to project the image of a personal leader out to half a million villages than to project some political abstraction like the state. Mao remarked to Edgar Snow that perhaps a little of the cult of personality would do no harm; he may have had in mind that the complete depersonalisation of Chinese leadership would be premature. It should also be remembered that the propagation of loyalty to Mao scarcely exceeds in intensity the simultaneous propagation of loyalty to the nation and to revolution.

There are other ambiguities in Maoism which might well inhibit the transformation of political culture for which Mao hopes. While it is emphasised that the Party should lead only by its moral authority, it is equally emphasised that the Party leads, and enjoys a unique and dominant role among all social organisations. What this means in practice in the context of 'democratic conflict' is far from clear.

While it is stressed that coercion and command are last resorts, and are to be applied only to those who practice actual physical resistance to the régime, nevertheless the elements of dictatorial suppression are present: ambiguous definitions of political crime, the admitted necessity of 'making a few examples' to encourage the others, and a theory of reform through labour which can be exploited for economic purposes. Gulag extends to China, even if there it is very thinly populated.

We must finally therefore ask what the effects will be on Mao's passionately hoped for evolution of democratic values, expectations and responses of a cult which makes criticism of his own person something near to blasphemy; of a Party which still determines all rewards and punishments; and of the constant threat, however discreetly hidden, of exile in the countryside or worse. Under Mao, as under the Emperors, how can the subject demand, or expect, or educate himself in the rights of a citizen, against a governing élite which claims to represent a morality higher than his own?

On the other hand, Mao may be realistic in insisting that too much freedom for the educated, articulate, well-connected élite might prove a worse inhibition of the development of democratic capacities among the ignorant and scattered peasant majority, than the limits of freedom which he sets. And we must recall that Mao's hopes of the transformation of the political culture depend upon a complex of economic and social policies which many of the new élite, at the height of their power in 1960–2, were determined to reject. Perhaps, as we used to be taught, freedom is indivisible; but this is an aphorism easier for us to preach than for Mao to practise at the risk of so many hopes.*

NOTES

* Mao Tse-tung died on 9 September 1976, after this book had gone to press. His death raises the question whether his attempt to create a new political culture will survive him. Perhaps the process of economic and social change which he promoted, and which he hoped would transform the political culture, has already reached the point of self-sustained growth; but Mao himself expressed no optimistic opinions on this possibility. He seems to have believed to the end that unless the Communist Party continued to hold the ring the process might peter out. It remains to be seen how far his successors will be willing and able to ensure its continuation.

1 While almost anything written on Chinese society and its history must refer constantly, if only obliquely, to matters relevant to the Chinese political culture, there has been little special writing on the subject. The most comprehensive and successful study is Richard H. Solomon, *Mao's Revolution and the Chinese Political Culture* (London, 1971). For other materials, the reader may refer to Solomon's excellent bibliography. The correctness of his stress on the importance of the problems of the handling of conflict in China has been confirmed by the appearance of 'Long Live the Thought of Mao Tse-Tung' (n. 10 below).

2 *The Water Margin* was translated by Pearl Buck under the title *All Men Are Brothers*. Arthur Waley's translation of *Monkey* was reprinted by Penguin Books in 1960; and Penguin also published, in 1973, David Hawkes' translation of the first part of 'The Dream of Red Pavilions', under one of its many possible titles, *The Story of the Stone*.

3 See Mark Elvin, 'The Gentry Democracy in Chinese Shanghai, 1905–1914' in Jack Gray (ed.), *Modern China's Search for a Political Form* (London, 1969) pp. 41–65.

4 See Jean Chesneaux, 'The Federalist Movement in China, 1920–3' in Gray, ibid., pp. 96–137.

5   Liang Ch'i-ch'ao, *Yin-p'ing Shih Ho-chi*, vol. 32, pp. 1 ff.
6   Hu Han-min, *Ko-ming Li-lun yü Ko-ming Kung-tso.*
7   Edgar Snow, *Scorched Earth*, 2 vols (London, 1942) *passim.*
8   See Mao Tse-tung's study of the Border Region economy, *Ching-chi Wen-t'i yü Ts'ai-cheng Wen-t'i.* A translation by Andrew Watson is forthcoming.
9   See Hsin-hua Pan-yueh-k'an, late 1957, *passim.*
10  Mao Tse-tung, Speech at the Chengchow Conference, 5 March 1959, in *Mao Tse-tung Ssu-hsiang Wan Sui* (Long Live the Thought of Mao Tse-tung') 1967, p. 44. This title covers two collections of confidential speeches and papers of Mao Tse-tung, the first published in 1967 and the second in 1969. Some of the documents are translated in Stuart Schram, *Mao Unrehearsed* (Penguin Books, 1974); the remainder were translated as *Miscellany of Mao Tse-tung Thought*, Parts 1 & 2, by the Joint Publication Research Service (Arlington, Virginia, 1974). Hereafter referred to as *Wan Sui*, 1967, and *Wan Sui*, 1969.
11  Mao Tse-tung, 'Comments on [Stalin's] Reply to Comrades Sanina and Venzher'. *Wan Sui*, 1967, p. 121.
12  Mao Tse-tung, 'Speech at the Hankow Conference, 6th April, 1958' in *Wan Sui*, 1969, p. 183.
13  Mao Tse-tung, 'Comments on Stalin's "Economic Problems of Socialism in the USSR" ', *Wan Sui*, 1967, p. 156.
14  J. Gray, 'La teoria del gran balzo in avanti', in *l'Est* (Milan, 1972); translated in H. Bernstein, *Underdevelopment and Development* (Penguin Books, 1973).
15  Mao Tse-tung, 'Concluding speech at the Conference of Provincial and Municipal Secretaries', January 1957, in *Wan Sui*, 1969, p. 85.
16  Ibid.
17  Mao Tse-tung, 'Interjections at a Conference of Provincial and Municipal Secretaries', January 1957, ibid.
18  Mao Tse-tung, 'Talk at the Hangchow Conference of the Shanghai Bureau', April 1957, in *Wan Sui*, 1969, p. 104.
19  See 'Forum on Confucius', by Chingkangshan Combat Group of Red Guards for the Study of Mao Tse-tung's Thought, Peking Normal University. Reprinted in *People's Daily*, 10 January 1967.
20  See J. R. Pusey, *Wu Han: Attacking the Present Through the Past* (Cambridge, Mass., 1969).
21  This was strongly emphasised by the Chairman of the Revolutionary Committee of the Shihchiachuang 7 May Cadre School in an interview in June 1975.

# 8 Cuba: Communist State or Personal Dictatorship?

## FRANCIS LAMBERT

In any study of the impact of the Communist system on political culture Cuba occupies a special place. It is (so far) the only Iberian Communist state, and this chapter therefore devotes a certain amount of space to considering Iberian political culture. It is one of the Communist states which does not have a land frontier with the Soviet Union. It is also the first Communist state in the non-Asiatic 'Third World'. All these factors contribute to the feeling that Cuba represents a third centre in the Communist world perhaps as significant as Moscow and Peking.[1] It is, however, very difficult to describe Cuban political culture with any degree of certainty. Cuba has only been a Communist state for fifteen years, and it is still evolving; it would have been very difficult to predict the present situation of the Soviet Union in 1932 or of China in 1964. Nevertheless Cuba seems to be developing as an interesting hybrid – a Communist state led by a charismatic leader and his loyal followers, most of whom have had little training in Marxism and were not Communists before taking power. It is therefore interesting as an interaction between the rigid Soviet model of government and an unusual political culture.[2]

All political cultures are conditioned by the past political experience of the nations in which they exist (or rather by what the majority of adults can remember of their past). In Cuba this past experience is especially complex, since it falls into two parts – the experience that Cuba shares with the rest of Spanish America and the experience peculiar to the island itself. The political experience of Latin America is much too lengthy a subject to go into here,[3] but it is marked by the contrast between a revolutionary, unstable political tradition and a conservative, stable society. It is of course true that this society has seen major changes in the present century. But these changes have been evolutionary rather than revolutionary; the landowning élite has come to terms with new economic and social forces in the same way as the British ruling classes did in the nineteenth and twentieth centuries. The rural élites have moved into positions of control in business, either as the civil servants running nationalised industries or as the local executives of foreign companies. New members of the bourgeoisie, whether foreign immigrants or (increasingly) rising members of the lower middle classes, imitate the landowning élite and attempt to join it by marriage or the purchase of land. Landowners control the new mass electorates of the cities by an expanded and modernised version of the patron-client relationship familiar in traditional society, a relationship which also occurred in the United States. Even the skilled working classes have been drawn into the system through government-run trade unions, and aspire in their turn to find a patron who will elevate them to the middle classes. Thus all the more vocal groups of society are co-opted into support for the existing structure, and social change has not overthrown the basic fabric of society. Perhaps the most sophisticated version of this development has appeared in Mexico, where the revolutionary leadership has organised the various sectors of the nation by co-opting their leaders and providing benefits in return for loyalty to the Revolution – an odd kind of corporate state.

It is a truism to say that Latin America is always having revolutions, but it helps outside observers to remember that many of the conservative features characteristic of European, Asian and even African societies are unusual or entirely lacking in Latin America. The only successful monarchy collapsed in Brazil nearly a century ago; most nations have never had a titled aristocracy or a social system characterised by caste as against class. Other features of traditional society, such as tribalism and national minorities, are also largely absent. Latin America is thus less weighed down by the past than many societies in Eastern Europe and Asia.

This built-in tendency to instability is reinforced by the political history of the continent. As in large areas of Eastern Europe, the states of Latin America originated in revolution and devastating wars of national liberation.[4] This had two major effects. One was to create a tradition of respectable revolutionary activity which has persisted almost to the present day, particularly among such privileged sectors of youth as students and young army officers, and which contrasts with traditions of reverence for authority found in Eastern Europe.[5] The other result has been to make the armed forces (which remained as irregular and 'revolutionary' armies until well into the 1890s) the traditional arbiters of national destiny. The armed forces created the independence of the nation; it is now their duty to intervene to save the nation from the politicians and to moderate the conflicts between different classes and parties in a Bonapartist manner. Even under normal 'constitutional' government the armed forces take a much more active role in running the administration and the economy than is normal in more developed countries.[6] The result is a tradition of revolutionary and military activity as a permanent part of the political culture.

But this political instability coexists almost everywhere with a very considerable degree of social stability. Since independence the basic

social institutions have survived and adapted to changed circumstances with remarkable facility. The division between Conservatives
and Liberals, established in the first years after independence, is still
important even in such politically relatively advanced countries as
Colombia and Uruguay.[7] The Roman Catholic Church is still an
important force even in Mexico, where the collapse of the colonial
social structure took place over a century ago.[8] But the most important
conservative factor is the survival of the *latifundio*, the great landed
estate. The *latifundio* has kept most of the rural population docile under
the traditional social control of the owner, and has thus prevented the
appearance of peasant revolts. It has also provided the backing for a
traditional élite which has always held the best political and bureaucratic positions. This élite has adapted very well to urbanisation and
industrialisation by diversifying into industrial management and organ-
ising the urban voters, who are often looking for the type of patron-
client relationship which existed in the countryside.[9]

Pre-Castro Cuba had most of the features of instability common to
the rest of Latin America and very few of the features of stability.
The island had become independent seventy years after the rest of
Latin America, and failed to develop any of the major stabilising institutions.[10] Even before independence the *latifundio* had disappeared, to be
replaced by plantations owned by United States corporations.[11] Large
businesses were owned by North Americans, small ones by Spaniards.
The Roman Catholic Church had little influence or control.[12] As a
whole Cuban society was in an unstable and fluid situation; even the
army did not provide an element of stability.[13] Under these circumstances it is not surprising that Cuban political culture was unstable
and fluctuating to a degree only paralleled in the smaller republics
round the Caribbean.[14] Political parties rapidly rose and collapsed, and
the class system was too fragmented for more stable forces to emerge.
The best way of looking at Cuban politics between independence in
1902 and the rise of Castro in 1959 is in terms of generations. The rulers
of Cuba until the radical revolution of 1933 had all been prominent
figures in the wars of independence; between 1933 and 1959 the island
was controlled by the leaders of the coalition of students and army
sergeants who had seized power from the previous generation. The
pattern of generational leadership has continued under Castro.

CUBANS' PERCEPTION OF THEIR HISTORY

It is relatively easy to point out the major features of a country's objective political experience; it is much more difficult (especially for a
foreigner) to say how that experience appears to the mass of the people.
Literature is helpful, but may only give the views of intellectuals;

surveys of public opinion are rare in most Communist countries.[15] None the less the evidence that exists shows that there was a widespread feeling of disillusion with independence, coupled with a feeling that the ideals of the independence movement had been betrayed. The symbol of the idealism of the Cuban war of independence was José Martí, the founder of the revolutionary movement of 1895, who occupied a prominent place in the official mythology of the nation as 'The Apostle of Liberty'.[16] Martí had great advantages as a symbol (he died young and his ideas were at once beautifully expressed and totally vague) and he has been used as such throughout Cuba's independent history. Every Cuban government has encouraged this cult, and the comments of ordinary Cubans show that Martí is a major symbol of an ideal republic with which the corruption of pre-revolutionary Cuba could always be unfavourably contrasted.[17]

Independent Cuba was (perhaps inevitably) a sad contrast with Martí's dreams. The corruption and confusion of politics was a permanent feature from 1902 to 1959; every politician promised reforms, honesty and adherence to the ideals of Martí and then consumed the spoils of office with even greater energy. From 1902 to 1933 Cuba was ruled by the surviving leaders of the independence struggle. Of these Estrada Palma (1902–6) was financially honest, but was overthrown for scandalous attempts at election rigging; José Miguel Gomez (1909–13) was known as 'the shark' because of his rapacity; and Menocal (1913–1921) and Zayas (1921–5) both refused to accept bills because they had not been bribed to do so. The façade of constitutionalism finally collapsed under Machado (1925–33), who bribed Congress to grant him an extension of his term of office. The leaders of the 1933 revolution, which aimed at regeneration, rapidly conformed to the same pattern. Batista's corruption may be excused by his poverty-stricken origins, but the same cannot be said for Grau and Prio, who destroyed any possibility of social democracy by their corruption and incapacity. This dismal record created a contempt for democracy among both intellectuals and the mass of the people.[18]

As we have seen, a consistent feature of Cuban political experience has been a feeling that the revolution has been betrayed. What are the fundamental values of the average Cuban when thinking about politics? A central belief is in independence. Cuba came into existence after a heroic and exhausting struggle only just passing out of living memory.[19] The war created the belief that independence could only be attained by conflict and revolution, and this feeling has been maintained by hostility to the United States, which has remained a constant feature of Cuban politics. Ever since the beginning of Cuban political life before independence the United States has been 'the Colossus of the North', controlling Cuba's economy, constantly interfering in Cuba's politics, and responsible for everything that is wrong in Cuba.[20] The myth of the Cuban wars of independence is that of a struggle backed by the intellectuals, represented by José Martí, but also by the common people, led by the mulatto guerrillas Antonio Maceo and Máximo Gomez, which had almost won independence from Spain when the United States intervened and destroyed the possibility of a 'true' republic.[21] Thus emphasis on independence always goes with hostility to the United States, a posture assumed (at least in theory) by every Cuban government.

Another feature of the Cuban belief in independence was its moral aspect. Martí had promised that independence in Cuba would produce a society different from the 'decaying and corrupt republics of America';[22] he wanted to free Cuba from North American economic domination and to end her dependence on sugar. These aims had a wide appeal which was reinforced by the failures of social radicalism which it might otherwise not have had. The ideas of Martí remained popular among progressive students, and were the foundation of the student movement which remained active from the 1920s until the triumph of the Castro revolution. One of the major achievements of Castro has been to fuse this native tradition with his own movement: 'if [our generation] took an example from anyone it was from men like Guiteras, Mella, Martí, Maceo, Agramonte'.[23] As a result the Cuban revolution had derived a utopian dimension from the nation's political culture which has influenced some of its more unusual features, such as its hostility to money and its abolition of most private property in 1968.

### VALUES AND FUNDAMENTAL POLITICAL BELIEFS

Another fundamental question in looking at political culture is that of the value placed upon political liberty. On this we have the evidence of Maurice Zeitlin's survey of Cuban workers in 1962.[24] He found that 70 per cent were in favour of free speech and 27 per cent opposed (when dealing with the opponents of the revolution). The main variable was education; only 30 per cent of those who had completed no grades at school were in favour of freedom, as against 82 per cent of those who had completed seven grades. Zeitlin outlines several possible reasons for this. He points out that Fidel, Che, and other revolutionary leaders encouraged (ostensibly at least) freedom of speech and expression, and that the Cuban revolution was one that fostered participation and discussion.[25] Perhaps more realistically, he points out that Cuba was unusual in that the old order had largely collapsed without a fight. There was no real military threat internally; the island was relatively developed, with few social cleavages; and the economy was wrongly developed rather than underdeveloped. Thus the revolution could afford to be 'generous' (as Castro put it)[26] to its opponents in a manner impossible to most other revolutions. But it seems doubtful whether freedom is a major value of either the élite or mass post-revolutionary political culture.

Since the Revolution there has been a great change in Cuban political attitudes towards individualism and collectivism. Before the Revolution Cuban political culture was very individual; the collapse of traditional society had destroyed many of the old institutions which supported the basic structure of other Latin American societies. Since the Revolution the government has attempted to change the political culture in the direction of the 'new man'. The leadership has recognised that this will be very difficult, but it is determined to promote this change. To quote the official newspaper *Granma* on the sixth anniversary of the Revolution:

> The construction of Communism demands, as its fundamental ele-
> ment, the struggle for the formation of the new man; and it will not
> terminate until this job has been completed. ... The struggle to
> make spiritual and social sentiments predominate over narrow,
> limited, and individual feelings ought to be the centre of our effort
> to forge the new man. ... We see him in the classrooms studying and
> becoming interested in technology, science, and production. We see
> him in the trenches of our Revolutionary Armed Forces.[27]

As Fagen shows, a concern for the 'new man' has been behind some of the major innovations of the Cuban Revolution, the Committees for the Defence of the Revolution (CDRs) and the Schools for Revolutionary Instruction (EIRs).[28] This was also one of the aims of the campaign to eradicate illiteracy; the Castro régime has great faith in the benefits of sending urban youth to the countryside (and vice versa).[29] Again it is difficult to say how far this is successful. There is some evidence that these campaigns created a great deal of enthusiasm in the early days of the Revolution, but it is difficult to believe that this has lasted for fifteen years. Certainly the Cuban government complains about 'vagrants' and 'loafers' in a manner familiar in Eastern Europe, and observers like Barry Reckord report an atmosphere of apathy and cynicism among some (but not all) sections of the population.

FOCI OF IDENTIFICATION AND LOYALTY

One of the more remarkable features of Cuban Communism is the degree to which it has continued to use the myths of the previous régime – largely because they are firmly revolutionary, though non-Communist. Ever since the nineteenth century Cuban nationalism had (inevitably) been directed against the United States. Cuba's wars of independence had created a tradition of armed struggle of which the heroes were the common people – the *guajiro* or peasant and the *mambi* or negro. The ideas of Martí, and still more of the revolution of 1933, had given a large section of Cuban youth a belief in 'a strange mixture of anti-imperialism (and) trigger happy anarchism'.[30] Indeed the revolutionary struggles of the past century have created a political culture in which all groups must at least claim to be attempting a revolution.[31] Under these circumstances it is both inevitable and easy for the Castro Revolution to use as foci of identification figures of the Wars of Independence, like Martí and Maceo, or of the 1933 revolution, notably Antonio Guiteras and Eduardo Chibas. These figures give the revolution legitimacy by linking it to the heroic past, and, at least in the case of the heroes of 1933, they have been in a very real sense the inspiration of the present revolutionary leaders, to a far greater degree than Marx and Lenin. This general cult of the past links very well with the particular cult of the guerrilla phase of the revolution, from the attack on Moncada in 1953 to the triumphant entry to Havana in 1959. The heroic struggle is emphasised for two reasons. It establishes Castro as a gallant and successful *caudillo*, and it lays stress on the idea of continuous struggle, which is a notable feature of the Cuban version of Communism.[32]

Another instance of the way in which the Cuban Revolution has made use of traditional nationalist sentiment is in the continuity of Cuban symbolism. The flag remains the same, though the 'Internationale' has largely replaced the national anthem; the wars of independence continue to be constantly referred to as a source of inspiration. Indeed it may be argued that Castro has deliberately tried to create a feeling of continuity between his own revolution and previous struggles. This is made easier by the fact that very little rewriting is necessary in order to present Cuban history as a series of revolutions that failed but whose failure has been redeemed by the success of Castro himself. The Cuban leader has often specifically appealed to the memory of previous revolutions:

Ours ... is the best generation that the country has had ... but the coming generation will be better than ours. It will be inspired not only by the generations of 1868 and 1895 [the first and second wars of independence] but by the generation of 1953 [the attack on the Moncada barracks].[33]

This emphasis on traditions of nationalist revolution rather than of Communism is of course a reflection of the coalition of forces within the Cuban polity, but it is carried a good deal further than in other Communist states.[34]

The political experience and expectations of the Cuban people pulled them in two different directions. On the one hand Cuba had had a formally democratic political system ever since independence; only Czechoslovakia could rival her in this among Communist states. On the other hand the corruption and gangsterism which marked constitutional government in practice had produced widespread disillusion with the system. This is shown by Castro's contemptuous denunciations of the *lumpenbourgeoisie*, and also by Zeitlin's survey, which showed that only 44 of his representatives wanted elections 'soon' (in 1962) with 136 against. Both groups regarded wanting elections as a sign of opposition to the revolution (and vice versa). Those supporting the revolution claimed that elections were unnecessary because 'those who are now leaders of our country are the true representatives of the people', 'politics in Cuba only produce benefits for a few, while with the revolution benefits are equal for all.'[35] At the same time it must be remembered that Cuba is increasingly becoming a Communist state on the Soviet model, even if it has been until recently the dictatorship of a *caudillo* rather than a party.[36] Castro is in fact Cuba's first *caudillo*. He attracted a group of followers by his personal appeal; he fought his way into power with their aid; he now uses them in his government and distributes benefits to his loyal followers in return for their support. The essential point about the power of a *caudillo* is that it is a personal dictatorship, depending on the appeal of the leader much more than on the power of institutions. At the beginning this was very much the case with Castro, who filled the government with his friends and relatives and attempted to govern through improvisation and a series of mass meetings.[37] Since the failure of the ten million-ton harvest in 1970, however, this has changed and Castro seems to have adopted a model of government much more on Soviet lines with an emphasis on strong institutions and a move towards an economy based on material incentives.[38] But Castro continues to exercise overriding control over the system and to maintain a close contact with the masses which makes his régime more direct and approachable than the remote bureaucracies of other Communist states.

THE NEW OFFICIAL POLITICAL CULTURE

Cuba has seen an attempt to change her political culture unparalleled in scope except perhaps in China.[39] In a number of ways the official political culture differs from that of the Soviet Union; Castro has never been happy with the compromises characteristic of bureaucratic socialism, and his aims are much more utopian than those generally pursued in Eastern Europe. (This divergence is also shown in the manner in which Castro largely ignores Marx and rarely quotes him, a result of Castro's lack of training in an orthodox Communist Party.) Two distinctive features of Cuba's present official political culture are its emphasis on struggle and its pursuit of the millennium. Castro has constantly emphasised the need for war against both external and internal enemies. Externally he has the advantage that Cuba is very much isolated from the rest of the Communist bloc and has always faced a potential threat from the United States; this had led to a continual need for military mobilisation which can in turn be used for further measures of socialism. Thus the Committees for the Defence of the Revolution, one of the chief mass organisations, originated as a 'home guard' against counter-revolutionary attacks. The North American threat is also the reason for maintaining an enormous army which is increasingly used for civilian purposes like cutting the cane harvest or improving industrial production. Castro has maintained his emphasis on the military in spite of the lack of a serious internal counter-revolutionary movement and the tacit recognition of his position in 1962 by the United States; it has obvious advantages in order to maintain national unity. In the last few years, however, he has been increasingly ready to resume friendly relations with other Latin American countries, including not only 'Socialist' or 'progressive' governments like Chile (under Allende) and Peru, but also Argentina and Panama. Another means of maintaining an atmosphere of open military crisis is intervention in wars of national liberation in other parts of the Third World, notably Angola and support for North Vietnam. These international military operations are useful in three ways. They maintain an atmosphere of militant revolutionary struggle (especially among the young); they provide the Cuban army with experience of real fighting; and they provide the Soviet Union with some return for its massive investment in Cuba.

But mobilisation and struggle are also directed to internal ends. Thus the Committees for the Defence of the Revolution were assigned new tasks in 1963, when the need for military vigilance had lessened. These included education, public health administration, urban reform rationing, voluntary work, propaganda and sport.[40] The military metaphors have also been used for other major campaigns; thus the campaign against illiteracy between July and December 1961 was carried out by 'brigades' of volunteers in semi-military uniform in the 'élite corps' of the 'army of education' and inspired by revolutionary martyrs.[41] Militarisation, indeed, has become more and more characteristic of the Revolution; it was very much in evidence in the campaign for a ten million-ton harvest in 1970, and it seems to be seen increasingly as the answer to failures in production. There appear to be two major reasons for this emphasis, practical and ideological. On a practical level, militarisation produces relatively effective work without the need to provide material incentives (which the régime opposes as counter-revolutionary and cannot produce anyway). On an ideological level it creates participation in the régime by all citizens and gives the revolution a continuous momentum by presenting a series of crises which can only be overcome by great effort.[42]

The utopian nature of the new official political culture can be seen most clearly in its determination to sweep away every vestige of the old Cuba. The old Cuba was dominated economically, culturally, and politically by the United States; the new Cuba must be independent of outside powers. The Old Cuba had great extremes of wealth and poverty; therefore the new Cuba must be characterised by absolute social equality and crack down on any possibility of a new ruling class of administrators. In old Cuba Havana flourished while the countryside was neglected; now Havana is neglected while the Revolution makes every effort to bring good living conditions to the countryside. The old Cuba was formally democratic but in fact riddled by corruption; the new Cuba will be built by the willing participation of all. There are other more specific signs of utopian socialism in some of the official aims. The Revolutionary leaders have dabbled with the old idea of abolishing money, 'that bitter and transitory instrument of exchange and distribution'.[43] As Castro put it in 1968, the year of the abolition of most private businesses and landholdings:

> We hope to achieve the Communist society in absolutely all ways some day. Just as books are distributed today to those who need them, just as medicine and medical services are distributed to those who need them, and education to those who need it, so we are approaching the day when food, clothing and shoes will be distributed as necessary to those who need them. We certainly aspire to a way of life apparently utopian for many – in which man will not need money to satisfy his essential needs for food, clothing and recreation, just as today no one needs money for medical attention or education.[44]

Between 1965 and 1970 this campaign reached its height under the influence of the memory of Che Guevara. The last few years however have shown Castro undertaking a more pragmatic policy in foreign affairs, and internally there have been signs of a growing Sovietisation which may indicate that Cuba is on the way to becoming a more orthodox Communist state.

The aim of the Cuban Revolution is to combine two processes, the creation of the new 'Socialist' man and the development of the resources of the nation. As Castro put it on the fifteenth anniversary of the Revolution:

People aspiring to live under Communism must do what we are doing. They must emerge from underdevelopment; they must develop their forces of production ... The problem from our point of view is that Communist consciousness must be developed at the same rate as the forces of production.[45]

The aim, then, of both technical and political change must be the creation of a new type of personality:

The concept of Socialism and Communism, the concept of a higher society, implies a man devoid of those feelings (of selfishness), a man who has overcome such instincts at any cost, placing above everything else his sense of the solidarity and brotherhood of man.[46]

Castro has little sympathy with most Eastern European Communist states, although he is tied to the Soviet Union in order to survive.[47] He is influenced by the revolutionary tradition which has existed in Cuba ever since the wars of independence, and which was particularly prominent at Havana University during Castro's education.[48] For Castro, and to a greater extent, Che Guevara, the basic aims of their revolution have been anti-Americanism, utopian ultra-revolution, the belief in violence and 'the propaganda of the deed', and a mystical faith in the 'new man'.[49] These ideas mark Cuba off from the other Communist states, and many can be derived from Cuba's past experience.

The revolutionary leaders are, nevertheless, extremely conscious of the difficulties of implanting these ideas in Cuba, where the influence of traditional patterns of behaviour, both Latin American and North American, is still very strong. The chief means of implanting the new culture, apart from the usual Communist youth and women's movements, are the militia and the Committees for the Defence of the Revolution.[50] In the past the militia has played an important role in defence and organisation, but its role became redundant as the revolution settled down to the creation of permanent institutions. Similar problems arise with the Committees for the Defence of the Revolution. These are intended to be the mass movement of the Revolution, while the Communist Party remains confined to the élite, and they have a continuous programme of campaigns and activities. It is difficult to say how far the enthusiasm and purpose which were a marked feature of the Committees in their early years have survived the recent years of siege economy and of 'Socialism in one country' as far as Latin America is concerned.

## POLITICAL SUB-CULTURES

Cuba has a relatively homogeneous society. There are no minority cultures based on religion;[51] the organisation of Cuban agriculture has created an agricultural proletariat rather than a peasantry with its own culture;[52] and political parties have been too unstable to develop established loyalties.[53] The only significant minority group is the negroes, between 20 and 30 per cent of the population. But the negroes were fairly well integrated into the dominant society even before the Revolution. Admittedly they occupied a disproportionate number of lower-class jobs and tended to be unemployed or underemployed, but many negroes none the less succeeded in reaching high positions. Batista was of mixed origins (probably Afro-Chinese) and many of his army officers were negroes; by contrast Castro's supporters tend to be white and middle-class. Such opinion polls as are available show that negroes were marginally less pro-Communist before the Revolution than whites, but that they now tend to be more in favour of the Revolution, while still having reservations about the old-guard Communist leadership.[54] There is also as yet relatively little sign of an 'opposition' or 'dissident' political culture; this can be attributed to the general popularity of the régime and the emigration of most of those who might otherwise have formed the nucleus of an internal opposition.

### SOCIO-ECONOMIC FACTORS AND POLITICAL CULTURE

We have already seen that the way was prepared for the Cuban Revolution by the weakness of the political and social structure of the island. The Revolution has also been influenced by the curious stage which Cuba's development had reached. By the standards of Latin America, and even more of the Third World in general, Cuba was not underdeveloped.[55] In general the island was as developed as southern Europe, with (significantly) extremely efficient communications. Population growth was relatively low, under 2 per cent per year; the gross national product was roughly on the level of Romania; illiteracy was on a level with such moderately developed countries as Yugoslavia or Portugal; over half the population lived in the towns; Cuba had proportionately as many doctors as Sweden and more television sets than France. The country had a reasonable climate and no problem of over-population; it also had an integrated society, without divisions of religion or community and without an unintegrated indigenous population. (Even before Castro, Cuba had more of the characteristics of a modern society than Mexico after forty years of 'institutional Revolution'.) These factors, combined with the close links of Cuba with the international economy, created a relatively open political system, free from the traditional constraints which face Communist states in Europe and Asia.

But if Cuba was developed she was developed very unevenly. In common with the rest of Latin America, facilities and services were concentrated in the towns, while very little was done for the country-side.[56] This imbalance was intensified in Cuba, where the economy was dependent on sugar, which was exposed to great fluctuations in price and was in any case dependent on the United States. Other sectors were also dominated by North American interests. The situation was worsened by previous attempts at reform; the trade union movement was well organised, but neglected the rural workers while it achieved considerable advances in the cities.[57] The result of this combination of circumstances was to create a feeling that Cuba suffered from under-development, but also that she could be liberated from underdevelop-ment by a sustained national effort. It was precisely the fact that Cuba was on the verge of the affluent world that made her position un-bearable. Her position was not as hopeless as that of India, Bangladesh, or China before the revolution. Castro could claim that utopia could easily be reached.[58]

The Cuban economy has also given the régime opportunities for political mobilisation. The sugar crop has to be harvested in a single spectacular burst, and this provides a pretext for revolutionary action by the whole population in a way impossible in an industrial (or a more diversified agricultural) economy. 'The Battle for the Cane', which culminated in the attempt to cut ten million tons in 1970, is of signifi-cance in keeping up the spirit of struggle and sacrifice which Castro regards as an important factor in changing the traditional individualism and hedonism of Cuban political culture.

POLITICAL CULTURE AND POLITICAL CHANGE

Much of what has hitherto been said about the attempted transforma-tion of Cuban political culture applies to the period before 1970. Since then two trends have become increasingly apparent. One is the degree to which the Revolution is becoming institutionalised, culminating in the publication of the Cuban Constitution and the holding of the first Party Congress in 1975. As we shall see, the emphasis is shifting towards the creation of permanent institutions, the end to charismatic leader-ship, and the reorganisation of the economy. As Edward Gonzalez has pointed out, the government seems to be moving towards a more bureaucratic system (although he is incorrect in claiming that this means a return to influence of the pre-1959 Communist leadership).[59] The armed forces, and especially that sector of the army associated with Raul Castro, are becoming increasingly important in providing technical and administrative expertise, and the Armed Forces and Interior ministries are taking over more and more of the duties of mobilisation. The public ceremonies of the Revolution are turning increasingly into formal military parades, and the role of the regular army is being promoted while that of the militia and the Committees for the Defence of the Revolution diminishes.

But at the same time an attempt seems to be being made to combine a growing emphasis on efficiency and regimentation on the Soviet model with some elements of popular participation. This can be seen in the new Constitution, which provides for a degree of free election in contrast to the usual single party list offered in most Communist countries.[60] The proposed electoral system, which was tried out in Matanzas province in June 1974, consists of the election of delegates to municipal councils, which in turn elect regional assemblies.[61] These will then elect a 'National Assembly of Popular Power' for five years under the new Constitution. The councils and assemblies will be under strict control by their executive committees, and all candidates will have to be approved by a Party branch or one of the mass organisations, but the voters are given a choice of candidates (there must always be two for each seat, and in some cases there have been as many as fifteen) and there appears to have been a free vote for everyone over 16.[62] This seems to represent an attempt to put into practice one of Castro's new aims – the 'democratisation' of the revolution. Since 1970 he has encouraged 'dialogue' with the masses: 'it is we who must go to the factories, where the workers are, to learn lessons in consciousness from them, not to teach them lessons in consciousness.'[63]

Another major theme in the recent pronouncements of the Cuban leadership has been the international role of the revolution. Cuban foreign policy has passed through three stages since the revolution; the first, of support for guerrilla movements throughout Latin America, lasted until the failure of Guevara's expedition to Bolivia in 1967, and was then replaced by a policy of 'socialism in one country' and an attempt to make allies with constitutional Marxist governments like Chile, progressive military régimes like Peru and Panama, and even nationalist governments like Argentina. Now this seems to have been abandoned and replaced by a renewed and aggressive military policy, but now directed outside Latin America. Cuba had been involved in Algeria and Vietnam from the start of the Revolution, but the real extension of her activities outside Latin America came with the development of the war in the Portuguese African territories. By 1970 Cuba was heavily engaged in Guinea Bissau,[64] and in 1975 she had what amounted to expeditionary forces serving in Syria and Angola.[65]

These three trends – institutionalisation, popular participation, and armed struggle outside Latin America – were all stressed by Castro at the first Congress of the Cuban Communist party.[66] The Cuban leader emphasised the need for a constitution:

We are already entering a period of institutionalisation of the revolutionary process, a phase of security, a phase of great guarantees, because guarantees are no longer given by men but by institutions. And we men are frail; we disappear and fade away over little things, indigestion or a car accident, not to speak of the truculent and shadowy assassination plans of the CIA.

He also praised the armed forces, the main administrative agency:

The Rebel Army was the soul of the Revolution ... In the days when there was still no integration of all the revolutionary forces nor the party which was to be born later, the army was the element unifying the people, guaranteeing power for the workers and the existence of the revolution.

The National Assembly of Popular Power was approved by one of the main resolutions of the Congress,[67] and the main portion of Fidel's speech to the rally after the Congress was devoted to the export of revolution. Cuban foreign policy is 'subordinate to the international needs of the struggle for socialism and the national liberation of peoples', and the intervention in Angola was justified on the ground that 'Cubans are not only Latin Americans but also Latin Africans'. Thus Cuba seems to have entered a period of Sovietisation, with increased technocracy and a foreign policy dominated by Soviet Russia.[68] But certain other features – the position of Fidel and his followers, the role of the army, and the emphasis on popular participation – continue to set Cuba apart from most other Communist states.

NOTES

1 Cuba has made two major attempts to assert herself as an international Communist force. In the 1960s guerrilla movements were encouraged throughout Latin America, a policy whose complete failure was symbolised by the death of Che Guevara in Bolivia in 1967. Since then Cuba has tried to achieve a *rapprochement* with 'nationalist' or 'popular' régimes like Chile (until 1973), Peru, Panama and Argentina, but continues to attempt to export revolution, notably to Portugal and the former Portuguese colonies. Cuba seems to be having some success in establishing herself as the centre of Third World militancy.

2 The fifteenth anniversary of the Cuban Revolution produced a series of reassessments of the régime; Lowry Nelson, *Cuba: The Measure of a Revolution* (Minneapolis, 1972) and Jaime Suchlicki (ed), *Cuba, Castro and Revolution* (Coral Cables, 1974). There is little opinion poll material on Cuba since the Revolution; Maurice Zeitlin, *Revolutionary Politics and the Cuban Working Class* (Princeton, 1970), was based on a sample of 210 industrial workers in 1962; and Richard R. Fagen, *The Transformation of Political Culture in Cuba* (Stanford, 1969), examines three means of transformation – the campaign against illiteracy, the Committees for the Defence of the Revolution, and the Schools of Revolutionary Instruction. Travel books can also be used to some extent; Jose Yglesias,

*In the Fist of the Revolution* (London, 1969), and Barry Reckord, *Does Fidel Eat More than Your Father?* (London, 1971), are interesting.

3 The best single study of Latin America is probably Jacques Lambert, *Latin America: Social Structures and Political Institutions*, trans. H. Delpar (Stamford, USA, 1969). Other treatments of the general theme can be found in two volumes edited by Claudio Veliz: *Obstacles to Change in Latin America* (London, 1965), and *The Politics of Conformity in Latin America* (London, 1967).

4 The Latin American wars of independence were political rather than social in aim, but they had a considerable effect in opening up the rigid society of the colonial period, which was based on caste divisions and privileged corporations. The abolition of slavery and the admission of the Indians to legal equality, in particular, made it easier for talented members of the lower classes to rise to positions of influence, a development which was assisted by the rise of the mainly middle- and lower-class military as a factor in politics. See John Lynch, *The Spanish American Revolutions* (London, 1971).

5 In some ways this is comparable with Eastern Europe between independence and 1944, but the extent of instability in Latin America was much greater and the conservative elements in politics less powerful. For the revolutionary tradition in Latin America see Hugh Hamill, *Dictatorship in Latin America* (New York, 1969).

6 This situation can, of course, be paralleled in other underdeveloped countries, but Latin America is unusual in the degree to which the military is involved in administration. Brian Pollitt is engaged on work which will show how Batista ran Cuba between 1938 and 1944 through a coalition based on the army and the Communists. See Hugh Thomas, *Cuba* (London, 1971) pp. 706–16.

7 For a brief and generally reliable survey of the Latin American political parties see the Pelican Latin American Library, *Guide to the Political Parties of South America* (London, 1973).

8 The conservative side of Mexican history has been neglected until recently, but for a survey of the Mexican church see Robert E. Quirk, *Mexico and the Catholic Church* (Albuquerque, 1970).

9 There are many discussions of landowners' influence, especially in Brazil; see Victor Nunes Leal, *Coronelismo, enxada e voto* (Rio de Janeiro, 1948). For a survey in detail of landowning influence on the 1967 elections in Brazil see *Revista Brasileira de estudos politicos*, July 1967/January 1968.

10 It has been argued recently that certain elements of Cuban society, notably the national bourgeoisie, were more stable and more powerful than has generally been believed. But their governmental system, established in the Constitution of 1940, was destroyed with contemptuous ease by Batista in 1952; it had also been undermined by the corruption and gangsterism characteristic of the presidencies of Grau and Prio. They also failed to offer any effective resistance to Castro (Robin Blackburn, *New Left Review*, October–December 1963, p. 361). This indicates that the Cuban bourgeoisie did not have the capacity to resist change found in Brazil in 1964, and, most notably, in Chile in 1972–3.

11    For the economic transformation of Cuba see Roland T. Ely, *When Sugar was King* (New York, 1963). The Cuban landowning class in the nineteenth century was so unstable that families usually went through their fortunes in twenty years.

12    See Leslie Dewart, *Cuba, Church and Crisis* (New York, 1964). Gwendolyn Midlo Hall, *Social Control and Slave Plantation Society* (Baltimore, 1971) indicates the failure of the church to make much impact with the slaves of the nineteenth century.

13    The Cuban army was never very efficient and never had an aristocratic officer corps. In 1933 the army was taken over by sergeants, a unique event in Latin America, and their rivalries contributed greatly to Batista's military inefficiency against Castro. See Thomas, *Cuba*, pp. 490, 1032–41.

14    All the presidents of Cuba between 1902 and 1933 had been leading figures (four out of six of them generals) in the second war of independence. Of the leading figures between 1933 and 1959 Grau had been president of the revolutionary government, Prio had been a student leader, Batista was leader of the sergeants, and others like Chibas were also prominent in the 1933 revolution. Castro's government has been very much a 'band of brothers', composed of those who were with him at the attack on the Moncada garrison in 1953 and the landing in Cuba from *Granma* in 1956. See Bonachea and Valdes, *Revolutionary Struggle* (Boston, 1972) p. 2, n. 2.

15    There were opinion polls in pre-revolutionary Cuba but they give little guidance to underlying political beliefs. Zeitlin provides the best data published since the Revolution, *Revolutionary Politics and the Cuban Working Class.*

16    There is no really satisfactory biography of Martí; the best is probably Jorge Manach, *Martí*, Havana, 1950. Martí is best seen as the Mazzini of Cuba, combining an intensely moral republicanism with a very vague belief in social justice and a very definite dislike of the United States, which makes him the ideal source of ideas (and quotations) for any Cuban government. Martí's *Obras Completas* were published in 1931. See also Richard Butler Gray, *José Martí, Cuban Patriot* (Gainesville, 1962).

17    This feeling was reinforced by the relatively late date of independence; in 1960 an eighty-year-old would have personal memories of the struggle for liberty. Until the 1940s the veterans of the war of independence were a major political force. One of Castro's earliest political activities was an expedition with some of these veterans to seize the bell which had announced the 1895 rising and take it to Havana University as a symbol of liberty. (Roland Bonachea and Nelson Valdes, *Revolutionary Struggle: Selected Writings of Fidel Castro* (Boston, 1972) p. 136.)

18    Grau was so corrupt that a fountain he built in Havana was nicknamed 'Paulina's bidet' after his mistress (and secretary). Revolutionary propaganda has constantly emphasised the honesty of the revolutionary government in contrast to its predecessors and this seems to be generally accepted. A former agricultural labourer told Zeitlin: 'These men are one hundred per cent better than before. I have known governments from Menocal till Batista left three years ago, and I have never seen any like this government.' Other comments: 'They are honest hardworking men',

'They are people of high and untouchable morality' (Zeitlin, *Revolutionary Politics and the Cuban Working Class*, pp. 37–8, also pp. 25–8). This attitude may have changed with the decline of revolutionary zeal and the persistence of shortages.

19  Approximately 300,000 out of a population of 1,800,000 died in the second war of independence, largely of disease and starvation.

20  This is partly myth rather than history, but it has been believed by most Cubans. In particular the United States has been blamed for the existence of gambling and prostitution in pre-revolutionary Cuba. It is perhaps inevitable that Cuba should treat the United States as a convenient scapegoat for all the defects in her society, since American influence in pre-Communist Cuba was very considerable and the image of the interfering large neighbour could only be bolstered by episodes such as the abortive Bay of Pigs invasion.

21  Again this does not fully square with reality: the Cuban guerrilla movement might well have been defeated without United States aid. But it is true that the Cuban war of independence was more of a popular movement than its equivalents elsewhere in Latin America, owing to the collapse of the landowner class. It is also true that the revolutionary war brought about greater equality between whites and blacks.

22  Manifesto of Montecristi, 1895, in Guerra y Sánchez, ed., *Historia de la nación cubana* (Havana, 1950–6).

23  *Guia del pensamiento político-económico de Fidel* (Havana 1959) p. 44. Guiteras was the leading left-winger in Grau's revolutionary government in 1933; Mella was a student leader and founder of the Cuban Communist party in the 1920s; Maceo was one of the chief generals in the second war of independence, killed in action by the Spaniards; Agramonte was one of the heroes of the first war of independence (1868–78). The manifesto published before Castro's attack on the Moncada barracks in 1953 refers to 'the revolution of Cespedes, Agramonte, Maceo and Martí, Mella, Trejo and Chibas – the true revolution that has not yet ended' and claims that the revolutionaries have 'no other interest than the desire to honour the unrealized dream of Martí with sacrifice'. 'The revolution identifies with the roots of Cuba's national being, the teachings of its greatest men, and embraces the national flag' (*13 documentos de la Revolución* (Havana 1959) pp. 19–21).

24  Maurice Zeitlin, *Revolutionary Politics and the Cuban Working Class*, Chapter 10, 'Revolutionary Workers and Individual Liberties', pp. 242–277, also pp. 17–21. Zeitlin was particularly concerned to point out that those who had been Communists before the Revolution (or militant after it) were especially in favour of civil liberties.

25  It is difficult to say how far this attitude has survived the fading of the original revolutionary enthusiasm. Certainly later observers like Barry Reckord indicated a growing degree of regimentation, even if people were still willing to make anti-revolutionary comments.

26  Richard R. Fagen, *Transformation of Political Culture in Cuba*, p. 116. See also Zeitlin's new preface written after a visit in 1969 for the Harper Torch Book edition.

27  *Granma*, 27 September 1966.

28   *The Transformation of Political Culture in Cuba*, op. cit., pp. 13–17.

29   The literacy campaign 'put the youth of Cuba in daily contact ... with the peasants and mountain people, the poorest and most isolated in the island. Almost 100,000 teachers and students, aided by more than 170,000 adult volunteers, have launched a true movement of national fusion' (Dr Max Figueroa, *Escuela y Revolución en Cuba*. February–March, 1963.)

30   Bonachea and Valdes, *Revolutionary Struggle*, p. 17.

31   An anti-Communist worker told Zeitlin: 'The Cuban people knew nothing of Marx and Lenin, but only of Martí. We should be ruled in accordance with his doctrine, but now we have a Marxian doctrine' (Zeitlin, *Revolutionary Politics and the Cuban Working Class*, p. 293). Even anti-Castro exiles share this attitude. Juana Castro told a North American interviewer that Cuba needed 'a true revolution' and one 'which owes nothing to the past or the present'.

32   The guerrilla past is also invoked to justify the growing militarisation of the Revolution, a development closely associated with the group round Raul Castro. Areas of concern, such as rationing or sports, are designated *frentes* (military fronts), (José Matar, head of the Committees for the Defence of the Revolution, in *Revolución*, 27 September, 1962). Working groups are called *centurias*, *brigadas*, and similar military epithets.

33   *Pensamiento político-económico de Fidel*, p. 44.

34   Cuba today is a personal dictatorship, supported by an alliance of pre-1959 Communists and of military leaders who fought beside Castro. The latter group predominates on the Central Committee and is in total control of the armed forces; the 'old Communists' are rather in eclipse among the leadership but are important in the party machinery and the trade unions. See Hugh Thomas, *Cuba*, pp. 1488–91, and Zeitlin, *Revolutionary Politics and the Cuban Working Class*, pp. viii–ix.

35   Maurice Zeitlin, *Revolutionary Politics and the Cuban Working Class*, pp. 38–43. Political corruption was probably at its worst in the early years of the Republic and also under the ex-revolutionaries Grau and Prio (1944–52).

36   For *caudillismo* see Jacques Lambert, *Latin America*, pp. 149–67.

37   Castro's government has a strong family flavour. His deputy and successor is his brother Raul; Raul's wife, Vilma Espin, is head of the Union of Cuban Women; and there are several other married couples in the leadership (Armando Hart, and Haydee Santamaria, for example). For Castro's explanation of this situation, see his speech to the final rally of the first party congress (*Granma Weekly Review*, 26 December 1975).

38   For a valuable summary of the trend towards institutionalisation see Carmelo Mesa-Lago, *Cuba in the 1970s* (Albuquerque, New Mexico, 1974).

39   For a major discussion of this problem, see Richard R. Fagen, *Transformation of Political Culture in Cuba*, ch. 1, 'Toward a New Political Culture', especially pp. 10–18. Fagen specifically points out the comparison with China (n. 13 to ch. 1).

40   José Matar, *Revolución*, 26 September 1962. Over-enthusiastic members of Committees seem to have had a field day in the spirit of 'Dad's Army'.

Children's Committees 'have been a very good idea for improving the behaviour of the kids', while a man proposed a new revolutionary slogan: 'Death to hot-plates between six and ten in the evening' (Richard Fagen, *Transformation of the Political Culture*, pp. 85, 93).

41  See, for example, Castro's speech to departing volunteers, 14 May 1961: 'There are two armies in our nation: one armed with rifles and cannon to defend the work of the Revolution, and one armed with books to advance the Revolution; one army to combat foreign enemies, traitors, and those who would destroy what we have accomplished, and another army to combat lack of culture and illiteracy. The revolution needs both these armies; neither can do anything without the other. The militiamen and soldiers can do nothing without you; and without the support of the soldiers and militiamen you cannot carry on in this campaign.' (R. Fagen, ibid., Appendix B, pp. 180–92). Conrado Benitez, a volunteer who was allegedly murdered by counter-revolutionaries, has been commemorated as one of the chief martyrs of the revolution.

42  This is not to deny that political mobilisation and compulsory membership of organisations is characteristic of all Communist (and all totalitarian) régimes; but the Cuban régime is surely unusual in the emphasis which it places on the army and on military symbolism. This is a reflection of the fact that in Cuba the Revolutionary Army directs the party and the state, an exact reversal of the normal Communist model.

43  Castro's speech at the University of Havana, 13 March 1968, in *Granma Weekly Review*, 24 March 1968.

44  *Granma Weekly Review*, 24 July 1968. This is not to say that all these aims have been achieved, but such quotations indicate the type of values that the leaders of the Cuban Revolution wish to inculcate. The violence of their attacks on traditional values shows the strength of the latter. Between 1965 and 1970 this campaign reached its height under the influence of the memory of Che Guevara. The last few years, however, have shown Castro undertaking a more pragmatic policy in foreign affairs, and internally there have been signs of a growing Sovietisation of internal policy which may indicate that Cuba is on the way to becoming a more orthodox Communist state.

45  *Granma Weekly Review*, 26 July 1968.

46  *Granma*, 27 September 1966. Castro attacked man under capitalism as 'the man of the Jungle', inspired by 'the wolf instinct, the beast instinct'.

47  One of the reasons given by Castro to justify his support of the Soviet Union's invasion of Czechoslovakia was that it was merely an extreme example of deviations from socialism. The Communist state most consistently admired by the Cuban leadership is North Vietnam, which parallels their emphasis on anti-Americanism and revolutionary struggle.

48  For student politics see Rolando Bonachea and Nelson Valdes (eds), *Revolutionary struggle; Selected Writings of Fidel Castro*, pp. 16–19, introduction to vol. 1. Also Jaime Suchlicki, *University Students and Revolution, 1920–68* (University of Florida, 1972). For ideas of the 1933 Revolution and their influence on the present leadership see Luis Aguilar, *Prelude to Revolution: Cuba 1933* (Albuquerque, 1974).

49  Guevara's vision is summarised in 'Man and Socialism in Cuba'. 'We will

make the man of the twenty-first century; we ourselves. We will be tempered in daily actions, creating a new human being with a new technology. The personality plays the role of mobilisation and leadership in so far as it incorporates the highest values and aspirations of the people and does not become diverted. The road is opened up by the vanguard group, the best among the good, the party. The basic raw material of our work is youth. In it we place our hope and we are preparing it to take the flag from our hands.' (In John Gerassi, ed., *Venceremos: the speeches and writings of Ernesto Che Guevara* (London, 1968) pp. 387–400, n. 5 to para. 21.)

50  The literature on socialisation into the new political culture is good, especially for the early years of the Revolution. See Richard R. Fagen, *Transformation of the Political Culture*, Chapter 4, 'The Committees for the Defence of the Revolution', pp. 69–104, and Castro's speech on their first anniversary, Appendix B, pp. 193–211.

51  Cuba has a small but militant group of evangelical Protestants, who seem to have taken a part in the Revolution disproportionate to their numbers. But in general religion has been unimportant in Cuban history and the Roman Catholic church has had little political influence. See Leslie Dewart, *Cuba, Church and Crisis* (London 1964).

52  The sugar industry employed two groups of workers, a highly skilled group of industrial workers in the mills and a floating mass of agricultural labourers who were only employed during the sugar harvest. Neither group had the deep attachment to a personal plot of land characteristic of peasant societies.

53  Maurice Zeitlin, 'Race Relations in Politics', in *Revolutionary Politics and the Cuban Working Class*, pp. 66–89. Negroes in Zeitlin's sample complained of pre-revolutionary discrimination, but mainly in expensive tourist spots; some white poor complained that discrimination was against the poor in general (ibid., p. 174).

54  In the early years of the Revolution intellectuals were allowed artistic (though not political) freedom under the principle 'everything within the revolution–nothing against the revolution'. This was abruptly ended by the Chinese style 'revolutionary offensive' of 1968, which led to persecution of intellectuals like Herberto Padilla. See Gemma del Duca, 'The Cultural Dimension in the New Cuba', in Jaime Suchlicki, ed., *Cuba, Castro, and the Revolution*, pp. 114–17, and the *Times Literary Supplement*, 11 July, 22 August, 19 November 1968. For a recent summary see Carmelo Mesa-Lago, *Cuba in the 1970s*, op. cit., pp. 97–102.

55  For a general survey of pre-revolutionary Cuba see Wyatt McGaffey and Clifford R. Barnett, *Cuba: Its People, its Society, its Culture* (New Haven, 1962), and Dudley Seers *et al.*, *Cuba: the Economic and Social Revolution* (Chapel Hill 1964). A good summary can be found in Hugh Thomas, *Cuba*, 'Old Cuba at sunset', pp. 1093–193.

56  This can be seen in the statistics on education. The illiteracy rate was around 20 per cent, a creditable figure when compared with most of the Third World; but in the rural areas 45 per cent had never been to school and 90 per cent had never got beyond the third grade.

57  The Cuban trade union federation, the CTC, was established under

Communist control in 1939, and formed a kind of 'popular front' with Batista during the Second War. The federation was taken over by the anti-Communist Eusebio Mujal during the cold war. Although it was very corrupt, it achieved major benefits for its members; the port workers of Havana were so well paid that they practically put the port out of business (although like the sugar workers, they suffered seasonal unemployment).

58   As Castro said in his 'History Will Absolve Me' speech: 'Cuba could easily provide for a population three times as great as it now has. What is inconceivable is that there are men going hungry while one square inch of ground remains uncultivated' (*La historia me absolverá* (Havana, 1961) p. 68).

59   Edward Gonzalez, *Cuba under Castro: the Limits of Charisma* (Boston, 1974) pp. 226–30. It can, however, be argued that a new *apparatchik* leadership, trained since the creation of the Cuban Communist party in 1965, is gradually taking over positions from veteran *fidelistas*. For the increasing militarisation of the party's public image see (among many others) *Granma Weekly Review* for 26 July celebrations in 1974. For a detailed discussion of the institutional and economic changes since 1970 see Carmelo Mesa-Lago, *Cuba in the 1970s*, especially pp. 61–107 for the structure of government.

60   In this the new system possibly compares with the limited choice offered for the Polish parliament since 1956.

61   This important reform was only quietly announced by Raul Castro on Bulgarian television, and then appeared in the Cuban news agency *Prensa Latina* (*Latin American Review*, 16 June 1974).

62   For the description of an election at a high school see *Granma*, 21 June 1974. For Castro's generally approving report on the Matanzas experiment, see his 26 July speech at Matanzas in the same year (*Granma*, 28 July 1974).

63   *Granma*, 20 September 1970.

64   The first member of the new Central Committee to be singled out for praise by Castro at the first Party Congress was Pedro Rodriguez Peralta, who had been captured in Guinea Bissau in 1969 and only released by the Portuguese revolution of 1974 (*Granma*, 4 January 1976).

65   The expeditionary force in Syria was small, and may have been withdrawn to go to Angola. In early 1975 Cuba had as many as 12,000 men in Angola.

66   *Granma*, 28 December 1975, 4 January, 11 January 1976.

67   *Granma*, 21 December 1975. Castro also produced a curious idea that 'genius is not within men ... genius is within the masses ... when the masses have the opportunity to study, differences disappear and there is a collective genius' (*Granma*, 11 January 1976).

68   There were only brief references to Che (usually among other dead revolutionary heroes), and China was implicitly condemned: 'Cuba rejects all efforts to destroy the unity of the Communist forces on a world level and to slander or diminish the role that the Communist Party of the USSR has played in contemporary history' (*Granma*, 11 January 1976).

# 9 Conclusions

## JACK GRAY

The main premise of this book is that certain political factors were constant at the point of origin of the Communist régimes with which we have been concerned, in so far as these countries shared a common ideology and common institutions. Cuba, however, is to some extent an exception in that the adoption of this common ideology and these common institutions occurred only after the revolution and gradually, and is not complete even today.

With these things fairly constant, it is a reasonable hypothesis that the divergences which have occurred in Communist states are due to national variables. Among these variables are the political values, expectations, etc., which, as a consequence of their unique national history, the different nations impose upon the operative interpretation of the ideology and upon the working of the institutions. In a word, differences of national political culture may have played a significant – perhaps even a decisive – part in the divergences in political behaviour which have occurred.

An obvious objection to this is that these divergences might be more satisfactorily explained by differences in the socio-economic levels among these countries. The participants in our symposium, however, found it impossible to accept either that there was a simple correlation between political culture and socio-economic level, or that socio-economic development could be regarded as providing an independent and alternative explanation. Certainly, the idea that demands for a pluralistic political system are directly related to high average incomes is untenable.

It is possible, however, that although absolute levels of income and welfare cannot be shown to have an unambiguous influence on political culture, other economic factors may be important. Gaps between the promises and the performance of a régime, conflict between the ambitions of the state and the ambitions of the citizen, and questions of relative incomes among different sections of the community are certainly among the principal issues of politics in most parts of the world, especially in countries in which the state plays a major role in controlling the economy. However, the fact that much of the content of political conflict in such countries is concerned with the distribution of economic resources does not mean that, in the study of politics, we must replace political explanations with economic explanations. Economic demands are processed through the political system (to the extent that they are not left to the operation of market forces) and our evidence suggests that the functioning of the political system is significantly influenced by the nature of political culture.

Explanations of political change in terms of economic levels or economic demands do not therefore offer a form of explanation which excludes or renders superficial or historically meaningless explanations in terms of political culture. They explain different things. The first provides data mainly on the content, or part of the content, of political inputs; the second explains the subjective attitude of citizens as to how these and other inputs ought to be handled or are expected to be handled.

A further objection to resort to explanations in terms of political culture would be that the politics of the countries concerned are subject in varying degrees to the effects of an international situation dominated by Russian and American power, perhaps to the extent that different degrees of divergence from the original Soviet model may be considered to have been determined almost entirely by the nature and extent of Russian or American influence. This is so obviously true that the point need hardly be laboured, but our evidence suggests that although a particular country's international position may inhibit or permit or encourage divergence, it does not determine the nature of the divergences which have been sought or which have occurred. There is still a great deal left which can perhaps only be explained in terms of the national political culture.

Political culture itself, however, still leaves us with a formidable number of variables. This is so much so that, even if we could use fully and freely the questionnaire techniques appropriate to the study of subjective political attitudes in these Communist countries – even if we could choose our questions and ask the same questions throughout them all – it is doubtful if the results would be satisfactory. To depend wholly on questionnaire techniques can very easily lead the investigator straight into the Baconian trap. 'Hypothesis is the general and facts are the soldiers' in the social sciences as in all others.

The two main sources of hypotheses are the observation of history and the observation of actual political behaviour. The relations between the study of political behaviour and the study of political culture give rise to a methodological problem with which the authors of this book have been very much concerned. If the purpose of our analysis is to explain political behaviour by political culture, then to turn around and explain political culture by political behaviour seems to be a form of circular argument. Yet this is not so. On the one hand, as Archie Brown pointed out in Chapter 1 (p. 4), the time dimension is of critical importance here. On the other hand, the final test of the reality of a political culture must lie in its demonstration in behaviour. In so far as a hypothesis concerning political culture has any predictive value, it lies in its ability to predict behaviour. If it fails adequately to predict behaviour, then this failure becomes a datum to be used for the modification and improvement of the original hypothesis.

The use of historical analysis in the study of political culture is also desirable and necessary. Such analysis enables us to identify views consistently held over long periods, or in varying contexts, or both. It can also enable us to explain the occurrence of such attitudes from the circumstances in which they arose, and thus to postulate the changed circumstances in which one might expect these attitudes to change. The historical method too, however, can be used unintelligently to produce circular arguments. Moreover, Europeans in interpreting European history have in mind certain broad hypotheses which are not easy to test in individual cases, but which nevertheless often form the unspoken assumptions behind historical interpretation. Some of these are relevant to the present purpose. They must be brought into the light of day.

The first such assumption is that differing religious experience, especially differing concepts of the relations between church and state, have played a fundamental part in the formation of European political cultures. The Orthodox church accepted that the state should enforce spiritual as well as secular control. In the Catholic states, while in the spirit of Augustine's City of God the spiritual and secular aspects of society were in the same way seen as two sides of a single coin, the state was nevertheless confined to a secular role. Although this judgement demands many qualifications, no historian would challenge the fact that European theories of the right of resistance to the state arose largely from the belief that the church represented a higher morality and claimed a higher loyalty. With the Reformation, religion in the Protestant countries increasingly became a question of individual conviction, and morality a question for the individual conscience. The pluralistic implications of this interpretation of religion for politics have always been obvious, not least to the kings who attempted to crush religious dissent, in the belief that it was inevitably the forerunner of political and social dissent.

The second historical assumption is that the idea of limited government was in the first place a feudal idea, which began from the limited powers which the king enjoyed over his tenants-in-chief, and they in turn over their sub-feudatories. The process by which European democratic constitutional government was created consisted essentially of the transformation of feudal privileges into popular rights. One would expect therefore that, other things remaining equal, those countries where feudal privileges were most marked and feudal contracts most explicit would be those in which there would be expressed the strongest attachment to the idea of limited government.

A third hypothesis would be that European states varied with respect to the effectiveness of executive government (whether autocratic or subject to popular control), with consequently different attitudes and expectations towards executive power in the different societies.

These general ideas may be valid; but they do not provide a basis on which we could range the European countries included in the present study. As a consequence of the turbulent past of central Europe, the frequency of conquests and partitions, the insecurity of national life, the conflicting pressures and influences of East and West, and the creation of a multiplicity of small nations with profound differences of historical experience, a very great effort of research would be required in order to analyse their religious beliefs and organisation, the role of their feudal aristocracies, and their experience of executive government, to the point where systematic comparisons could be made. Some of the material in this volume may point the way towards such an effort, but our present information does not make it possible to examine these historical generalisations fully.

The historical picture is also complicated by the fact that, for all its national and religious divisions, the culture of Europe has an underlying unity. Ideas which may arise in the particular circumstances of one European state can spread across frontiers and have an appeal on the basis of that cultural unity. The most influential case of course was the spread of French revolutionary ideas across Europe – even, though with greatly weakened force, as far east as Russia. If we forget how much that sense of unity meant, we might recall that when the Republicans in Paris in 1848 seized the Hotel de Ville, they ran up the flag of Poland beside the Tricolor.

As this incident reminds us, a new concept of nationalism spread with the revolutionary armies of France and into the countries of central and eastern Europe with their broken national histories. Indeed the ideas of the French Revolution were interpreted in the east of Europe in such a way as to subordinate all else to nationalism. A sense of national insecurity is, in one way or another, an important factor in the political culture in these countries. Poland looks back over centuries of domination and division, and over further centuries of a precarious national existence, to a period of wealth and of great-power status and cultural leadership. Hungary looks back over centuries of the defence of Magyar autonomy against the Habsburgs to a comparable period of near-Imperial splendour. The submergence of Bohemia having been almost complete from the Battle of the White Mountain until at least 1848, the Czechs cannot look back like the Poles and the Hungarians to a period of great national strength, but they revere and identify with the national and religious hero, Jan Hus, whose career was of European significance. In Yugoslavia, however, there are no such unifying historical memories: the idea of a fully integrated nation state of south Slavs is still largely an aspiration.

The most general consequence of continued national insecurity under Russian dominance is probably a willingness among the population to tolerate behaviour on the part of their governments which in other circumstances would be rejected as out of harmony with the political culture, because people believe that the government represents the best deal they are likely to get from the point of view of the maintenance of some degree of independence from the Soviet Union.

The orthodox tradition of Communism itself, however, represents not only an ideology and a set of institutions but also a political culture. We have, potentially at least, in Communist countries a situation with respect to political culture quite different from the normal expectation of a consensus more or less shared by government and society, though with differences of emphasis. In Communist-ruled societies the official Communist political culture and the dominant culture are not identical, but, on the contrary, are to a greater or lesser extent mutually antagonistic.

Perhaps indeed Communist parties in power represent two political cultures, the first being the values and expectations of the perspective of the transition to full Communism, and the second the values and expectations developed through the actual exercise of one-party dictatorship.

We are dealing with countries in rapid social and economic transition. If, as must always to *some* extent be the case, there are significant differences in the political sub-cultures of different classes and social groups, then it is clear that when, for example, peasants as a proportion of the population are falling, urban workers increasing, and the number of educated functionaries doubling every few years, there could be significant and even decisive shifts in the balance of the political culture as a whole, even if the opinions held within each of these social categories were not changed.

Also of great potential significance is the change from a situation in which the majority of the population have reached maturity before the Communist government was established to one in which the majority have been educated under Communism.

Finally, there is another complication with which it is methodologically very difficult to deal. The content of political culture being, as it is, an unsystematic accumulation of ideas derived only partly from deliberate processes of socialisation, it is inevitably full of inconsistencies and of alternatives. Poland, for example, has a tradition of adaptability to foreign domination, and at the same time a romantic tradition of desperate *sans-peur-et-sans-espoir* revolt; which of these equally valid Polish traditions will determine behaviour depends on circumstances. In the case of China, the contradictions within the political inheritance have been enumerated in Chapter 7, but by no means exhaustively. The problem is that the alternative views within a single tradition do not always represent orthodoxy versus dissent, but express two contrasting possibilities, each equally validated by the tradition. Therefore the alternative will not always appear in the answers given to an attitude survey, in the form of a majority of answers favouring one and a minority favouring the other; the alternative may not figure at all unless particular circumstances have called it forth.

THE SOVIET MODEL

Except for Cuba, which may represent a case of convergence towards Communist orthodoxy rather than divergence from it, all the Communist régimes began by imposing Soviet ideology and institutions, on the grounds – no doubt accepted with complete sincerity – that this political framework had been created by socialism and for socialism, that it owed nothing to a particular national past, that it was equally valid in all countries, and that there was no socialist alternative to it.

In fact, it is perfectly clear that the traditional Russian political culture was historically peculiar in European terms, not to speak of world terms. Russia was Orthodox, and therefore the state was given power to control the moral as well as the material welfare of the people; the classical struggle between church and state in Catholic Europe scarcely affected the Orthodox world. In Russia, feudal and corporate privilege was never allowed to rival the rights of the state; the Russian administration showed consistently over many centuries a remarkable vigilance against any institutionalisation of consultation or consent or of any form of judicial independence which would limit the freedom of the autocracy to interpret the national interest. In all these respects, Russia occupied a position at one extreme of the political spectrum of Europe, the polar opposite of the ideas of pluralistic politics and limited government associated most closely with the British tradition, but influential in varying degrees throughout Europe. The close analogy between Russian political tradition and the practice of the Soviet Union is very obvious.

On the other hand, Marxist theory gave no unambiguous warrant for the development of the political practices which we now associate with Soviet Russia. Indeed, Marx and Engels had very little to say about the future socialist state. Only literal-minded and fundamentalist self-professed followers of Marx could wrest his phrase 'the dictatorship of the proletariat' out of its context, and take it for anything but the deliberate paradox which it so patently was. 'The dictatorship of the proletariat' simply meant the effective rule of the majority; a majority which would be, Marx mistakenly supposed, increasingly composed of property-less industrial workers, as the course of industrial development proceeded. Marx's use of the term did not exclude the possibility that the rule of the proletarian majority could be exercised through a parliamentary system. He did not predict or demand the suppression of individual freedom – indeed his passionate hatred of the spiritually crippling effects of exploitation on the individual, caught up in a system he could neither understand nor control, was the emotional starting point of his work. His 'new man' was a good deal more in the image of a citizen of nineteenth-century America than in the image of the Soviet citizen of today. His call for the destruction of the bourgeois state was an attack on the militarism and bureaucratism of the Continental autocracies. Marx's ideas on politics can indeed be regarded as one possible logical conclusion of nineteenth-century liberalism, rather than as a theoretical basis for Soviet politics as shaped by Lenin and Stalin.

Nor does Lenin's prediction of the nature of the socialist state, expressed in *State and Revolution* and based on Marx's *Civil War in France*, imply the political culture and the political system which we now associate with the Soviet state and party. The main characteristics of Lenin's socialist state all suggest a kind of direct democracy; although his pamphlet was directed partly against the anarchists, its implications were anarchistic rather than statist. Government was to be based on local communities with a Paris-Commune type of organisation. These communities would be 'voluntarily associated for the defence of the whole'. Popular support for the revolution would, Lenin supposed, be so overwhelming that 'no special apparatus' would be needed for the suppression of enemy classes. With a loyal people armed, there would be no need for a standing army. Believing that the workers could supervise and keep accounts, Lenin assumed that they could control industry fully and directly.

The conditions created by the socialist revolution would create in turn new habits. A new socialist man would be produced who would find no contradiction between individualism and collectivism, but who would co-operate and participate in a sort of freedom of necessity; and this same voluntary yet inevitable co-operation would re-create and maintain the state through the enlightened self-interest of the autonomous local communities.

There is, however, another Leninist tradition represented by *What Is To Be Done?*, which stressed the necessity for the vanguard role of the Party. No doubt in Lenin's mind there was no contradiction between the highly disciplined and centralised organisation demanded in *What Is To Be Done?* and the spontaneous re-creation of society in *State and Revolution*. The first applied to pre-revolutionary organisation in the Tsarist police state, the second to the situation succeeding the seizure of power by the masses. It is often argued that *State and Revolution* is less typical of Lenin's thought than *What Is To Be Done?* Yet from the point of view of the formation of the official Soviet political culture, it remains a most significant work, representing (broadly) the political aspirations and expectations of the transition to Communism. Indeed the unresolved conflict, already alluded to, between this aspect of the official political culture and that which has grown out of the practice of one-party domination in the context of Russian tradition goes back to Lenin's own ambivalence.

In the event, however, Soviet politics developed in the spirit of *What Is To Be Done?* and not in the spirit of *State and Revolution.* In the circumstances which succeeded the seizure of power in 1917, Lenin himself, while continuing to be committed to the democratic alternative, chose at every critical point the authoritarian alternative. Under Stalin the authoritarian preference of the leader became unambiguous.

At each successive crisis – whether the grain crisis during the Civil War or the industrialisation debate at the end of NEP – there was a choice, and in each case the preferred solution was that which more nearly approximated to Tsarist practices, while the feebleness of the opposition in the New Course debate – in which the one word 'fraction' was enough to emasculate the opposition's demands for intra-Party democracy – suggests that the Russian political culture provided no effective barriers to the re-creation of an autocracy prepared to control the thought of citizens, maintain power through a system of secret police and brook no rival power in society.

Until the condemnation of Stalin by Khrushchev in February 1956, the Soviet political model was accepted throughout the Communist world (except in Yugoslavia after 1953), although it was based largely on traditional Russian values and expectations. There was bound to be, to a greater or lesser degree, dissonance between the Russian-derived political system and the various national traditions.

At the same time, the Soviet model itself embodied profound contradictions. At the risk of oversimplification, one could suggest that there are two Communist Party political cultures. The first is represented by the long-term aspirations and expectations grouped round the idea of 'new socialist man'. The second is the operational code of the hierarchical, self-perpetuating party enjoying a monopoly of political power. The relationship between the two could be analysed at length. It is sufficient for our purpose here, however, to point out that neither of those political cultures shows any interest in the legitimisation of conflict, the central problem of politics in the Western sense.

### NEW SOCIALIST MAN

The operative political culture of the Communist countries is a 'subject culture'. Nevertheless, the ideals remain those of a 'civic culture'. New socialist man is still seen very much as portrayed in *State and Revolution.* His characteristics are: full acceptance of the idea that his individual interests are best served through the pursuit of collective interests; acceptance of an egalitarian ethic; acceptance of a high level of voluntary participation in all decision-making processes, both economic and political; and a socialist view of both past and future. It also appears to be a general assumption that new socialist man will have no motive for social conflict and therefore no interest in maintaining freedom of choice in policies or parties; no interest, in fact, in the legitimation of conflict. His view of politics will be partly expressed by identification with a new set of symbols.

These characteristics, if they are indeed in the process of evolution in Communist countries, should be easy enough to investigate, especially where there have been surveys conducted by persons who regard as important the creation of the new political culture which socialist man represents.

Among the countries studied, Poland has provided the most interesting range of relevant surveys. The results, however, scarcely suggest that a new type of socialist citizen is emerging in Poland. If one takes the evidence on attitudes to history, it is clear that the Polish view of the national past has shifted very little in the direction of the Marxist preoccupations which new socialist man would be expected to display. Most Poles still look on their history in familiar terms of national insecurity and national subjugation. They still tend to identify themselves with the familiar figures of pre-war historiography – Casimir the Great, Kosçiusko – rather than with the figures of the Polish working-class movement. The 3 May Constitution still symbolises political aspirations. Identification with the USSR is extremely weak.

Surveys of student opinion showed that only a minority of students considered themselves to be Marxist, and the difference between students from intellectual families and students from working-class families was not significant. Only a bare majority thought that the world should head for socialism, but as socialism was not defined, even this means very little.

Students in surveys both in 1958 and 1973 showed fairly strong egalitarian tendencies, with almost half advocating the abolition of income differentials; this apparent radicalism among students, however, was not echoed by those who had passed into employment, among whom attitudes to differentials were related primarily to the differential which the respondent himself actually enjoyed.

Other surveys showed that interest in participation in politics appears to be very low; at the same it increases substantially with education and with professional status.

The student surveys of 1958 and 1973 showed a pronounced commitment to civil freedoms and the toleration of opponents. This commitment, shared by students regardless of their class origin, indicates both an expectation of conflict and an interest in its legitimation.

There is little enthusiasm for workers' control in industry.

One is forced to accept the conclusion of George Kolankiewicz and Ray Taras that the pattern of responses could reflect that of any industrial society. There is little sign here of the creation of new socialist man.

The evidence from other East European Communist states is for the most part less direct and less detailed, but all of it points in a similar direction. In Hungary during the revolution of 1956 the main demands were for parliamentary democracy and a multi-party system, and the members of the new Hungarian proletariat identified themselves with these demands. The new symbols of socialism – its coat of arms, its red stars, its military uniforms – were attacked. Although workers' councils played a prominent part in the insurrection, little interest has since been shown in them as a means for industrial management. Egalitarianism would seem to be advocated only by the lowest paid who would directly benefit from it. There seems to be a general acceptance of individual and material self-interest and a widespread distaste for participation in public life.

In Czechoslovakia the political changes of 1968, the significance of which is confirmed in detail by the surveys of that year, also produced no sign of a new man in the Leninist mould. Views of Czechs on their history, documented in the survey of 1946, not only bore a definite resemblance to their views in 1968, but after twenty years of Communist rule Czechs showed an even stronger attachment to symbols of social democracy than before. The only major change was in the vastly increased popularity of the pre-war democratic republic and of its personification in Masaryk. The Czech working class were almost as strongly identified with these views (so far removed from the interpretation of Czech history which the party had officially been purveying for almost twenty years) as the intellectuals, and such a perception of Czech history was almost as widely shared inside the Party as outside it. Identification with the USSR following the Soviet invasion became as weak as in Poland, in spite of the Czechoslovak tradition of friendship with Russia. There was little sign of any strong commitment to egalitarianism; on the contrary, there was a powerful reaction against the rigidly egalitarian policies which in Czechoslovakia had characterised the whole Communist period before 1968. The chief political demand was for the legitimation of pluralism. Here, as in Poland and Hungary, the new man of official Communist political culture was conspicuously absent. In so far as the Prague Spring foreshadowed, before the intervention of the Russian tanks, a new type of citizen, he was very much in the image of the Czech social democrat of the pre-war democratic republic.

When we turn from the Soviet-dominated Communist countries to the three societies which produced unambiguously indigenous revolutions – Yugoslavia, China and Cuba – we might expect that the new socialist man would have a better chance to emerge.

In Yugoslavia since 1953 there has gradually been developed a decentralised system based on the idea of self-management in all aspects of life, including workers' ownership (legally, usufruct) of industry at shop-floor level. This system should, one might suppose, maximise the citizens' opportunities for the development of a high and rewarding level of voluntary participation in decision-making which would seem to be, in practical terms, the most essential precondition for the evolution of the new socialist citizen. Yet the results are very ambiguous. It is true that self-management is valued in principle, but it does not seem to rouse high expectations of success. We find evidence that the communes are dominated by 10–15 per cent of their population, and that those who dominate are either those with high education or skills or members of the League of Communists. In industry, a survey found that only 18 per cent of workers believed that they, the workers, really made the decisions. In 1964, of respondents who were asked what they liked best in Yugoslav society, only 6.8 per cent said self-management; the commonest answers were freedom, democracy and equality, thus suggesting that these values were not identified in the public mind with the self-management system. There is evidence that the power which is offered to workers through their control of industry, in so far as it has been exercised at all, has been exercised simply to increase wages to the point of contributing to serious inflation.

As far as Yugoslav attitudes to history are concerned, one would expect new socialist man to interpret the past in terms of a Yugoslav identity. In fact, however, attitudes to history seem to have remained firmly fixed upon the separate identities of the country's different nationalities.

One survey shows a stronger attachment to Marxism in Yugoslavia than in Poland, with twice as large a proportion of Yugoslav as of Polish students claiming to be Marxist; but as another survey shows that 70 per cent of young respondents could not name the founder of Marxism, the significance of this commitment is in some doubt. It is difficult to resist the conclusion that the Yugoslav self-management system has not been significantly more successful in promoting the development of socialist man than the centralised bureaucratic system in Poland, Hungary and Czechoslovakia.

In China the situation is more complex, while our information is poorer, but the starting point of any discussion of the new man in China must be the fact that the Maoist group have made a far more conscious and strenuous effort to create him than has been made elsewhere, even in Yugoslavia. Whether or not this effort has been successful is still unknown. The significance of China in the present comparison is that the Chinese have launched, and so far sustained, an elaborate process of economic and social change which is explicitly intended to create such a man, a process which its authors believe with some justice to be a fresh start within the Communist world towards the creation of a new socialist political culture. This political culture they see in terms of the strongest possible contrast with the social process and cultural norms of the Soviet Union and East Europe.

Cuba is a particularly interesting case in this respect. The partisan origins of the revolution, the smallness of the country and (related to this) the directness of relations between the population and its partisan-hero leaders, and the informality of organisation which these circumstances make possible, have certainly produced every appearance of a high level of participation through which the régime has sought consciously to transform political attitudes. Yet recent years have seen an increasing resort to more normal bureaucratic methods of organisation, precisely of that kind which one must associate with the failure of the new socialist man to appear in other Communist countries; so we cannot with confidence assume that Cuba will prove an exception in the long run.

When we turn to the 'homeland of socialism', the Soviet Union, we find no evidence to suggest that the new socialist man is more likely to appear there than elsewhere. The available Soviet surveys are concerned only with participation in socio-political activities; we have no quantified information about attitudes to history. Because of the nature of the Russian political tradition, however, there is little sign (even among refugees) of interest in pluralism or in the limitation of the rights and responsibilities of government. The extent and effectiveness of participation in socio-political activities provide one possible index to the development of the new man, especially in the Soviet Union whose revolution is now at the stage when the vast majority of the population have received their education and their socialisation under the régime and have no personal memories of an alternative system, and where at the same time the effectiveness of political and social controls is far greater and meets less resistance.

It is striking, therefore, that the results of surveys of socio-political activity from the Soviet Union point in the same direction as those from the Communist countries of East Europe. It is true that a higher proportion of the Soviet population in general report that they participate in such activities, but this apparent superiority disappears in the face of the evidence from other Soviet surveys that much of this participation is obligatory and that much of it is formalistic. For the rest, the position in the Soviet Union is the same as elsewhere: participation in social and political activities is largely a middle-class habit. As Stephen White remarks in Chapter 2: 'Soviet society, in fact, emerges as a society which is stratified politically in a manner very similar to that of other developed (but capitalist) societies . . .'

## HOW FAR HAVE THE TRADITIONAL POLITICAL CULTURES CHANGED?

One would suppose that a generation or more of exposure to Communist governments, enjoying formally at least a monopoly control over education and socialisation, would produce some change in the political culture of the countries concerned. Yet there is little evidence that this has taken place.

The evidence of historical attitudes, which we referred to in dealing with the question of the new man, is relevant here also. There has been little or no disposition among the population generally to rewrite the past from the point of view of a Marxist present, or to replace old historical symbols with new. This is clear in the case of Poland and of Czechoslovakia, where it is shown in the results of surveys. It seems clear in Hungary in the rejection of Communist symbols and the restoration of old nationalist symbols in 1956. In Yugoslavia, it is evident in official concern with the bias towards historical views which contribute to the maintenance of strong and separate national consciousness within the society. In China, the old and essentially anti-Marxist interpretation of the national history surfaced again with the stream of writing between 1959 and 1961, of which the play *the Dismissal of Hai Jui* is the best-known example. In all of these cases there is an evident dissonance between what is valued in the past and what is being imposed at the present.

In Czechoslovakia, we find that experience under Communism served not to weaken but to strengthen attachment to the values of pre-war Czech democracy. That this should be so in the only one of the countries studied with a record of successful democratic government is to be expected. More surprising, however, is the strong assertion of the same values in Poland and Hungary, whose immediate pre-war experience was not of parliamentary democracy but of quasi-fascist semi-autocracy. The powerful demand expressed by all classes in Hungary in 1956 for the creation of a parliamentary system, and the persistent and increasingly successful pressure towards pluralist politics and limited government exercised by the Poles, are impressive. It could well be argued that the strength of this attachment to Western liberal democratic values has gone beyond anything which the history or the experience of these populations would lead one to expect. If their political cultures have been changed by the experience of Communism, it has been a change in the opposite direction from a totalitarian Communist model.

Whether this change is a permanent one – whether the increased attachment to liberal values is irreversible – can at present only be guessed.

At the same time, there appears to be in these countries a general acceptance of socialist aims which might be considered a change in the political culture. In the available surveys, however, socialism is not defined, and therefore we do not know what the significance of this commitment is.

In Yugoslavia, the experience of Stalinist autocracy was very brief. For the most part, what the Yugoslavs have experienced under Communism is a form of political and social organisation which has given room for much more variety and flexibility, and in which the suppression of dissent, though not negligible, has been sporadic and less severe. A substantial part of the population has shown itself prepared to identify their government with the values of freedom and equality; and apart from the nationalities question, there seems to be far less dissonance between the values and expectations of the peoples of Yugoslavia and the practices of its government than in the other societies with which we have been concerned. It may be that in a country where historically there has been little experience of strong centralised government, in which there are powerful traditions, and indeed myths, of local self-sufficiency in the political sense, and where such strong political discontent as exists seems to be almost entirely the consequence of differences of nationality and related differences in socio-economic levels, the present system of institutionalised conflict – not so much among parties as among communities and localities – may be in a more harmonious relationship with the traditional political culture.

We have suggested that in China the inappropriateness of so much of the traditional political culture to the needs of modernisation has played a very large part in the divergence of the Chinese from the orthodox Soviet model, while there are, nevertheless, other elements of the traditional culture which can be exploited in a Communist-led modernisation process. How far these efforts to transform some parts of the political culture and to revive others have succeeded it is too soon to say. Certainly, the visitor to China tends to conclude that there has been an enormous change; that the old Confucian-based élitism has been broken down; that through the localisation of a large part of economic development, the strength of local loyalties has been paradoxically but successfully harnessed (as Liang Ch'i-ch'ao proposed sixty years ago) to the creation of a new sense of national loyalty, and that in this way the sense of a moral community wider than the village, once felt mainly by the mandarinate, is rapidly becoming part of the popular consciousness; and that the mass-line idea of leadership is now universally valued in principle, though it may halt a good deal in practice and can still be subject to a very great degree of manipulation. The student of China, however, cannot but be aware, if only from the official press itself, that opposition to the new culture is still very powerful, both from the bureaucratically minded and from those who, on the grounds of Confucian tradition, demand that government should

be above class. It is clear too that some of the opposition have assimilated liberal values into their interpretation of Confucianism.

In the case of Russia itself, we have noted that as the new official
political culture is in so many important respects a revival of the old,
in these particular respects there has been little conflict and little pressure for change.

From the broadest point of view, our general conclusion must be that
the results of political change so far in the Communist countries have
been consonant with what we know of their previous political experience and political culture. The Hungarians seem to have settled, *faute
de mieux*, for a system in which parliament, the courts and the press
have much the same ambiguous but not ineffective role as they had be-
for the Second World War. The Poles have used their traditional alter-
nation of adaptation and insurrection to limit the rights and responsibilities of government to a level not dissimilar to that which Polish
governments enjoyed between 1919 and 1939. The Yugoslav system
seems to satisfy very well the political expectations of a society in
conditions in which the only experience of centralised government,
being associated with one nationality, the Serbs, suffers discredit from
this association. The *caudillo* element in Cuban socialism is obvious,
and in this respect Cuban government is probably very much what the
Cubans expect good government to be. In China there has as yet been
no settlement of a *modus vivendi* between the old and the new, but the
issues involved could well be expressed, as far as values are concerned,
entirely in the language of the traditional political culture – and frequently are, even by the great iconoclast Mao Tse-tung himself. In the
Soviet Union, the relative lack of change since the death of Stalin expresses the consonance of Russian tradition and Soviet practice; such
change as there has been might be described as the relinquishment of
Stalinist excesses in order to return to the normal Tsarist level of
authoritarianism.

### EFFECTS ON THE OFFICIAL POLITICAL CULTURE

This section can only be speculative; Communist leaders do not answer
questionnaires. The political changes which have occurred in Poland and
Hungary have been achieved by pressure from below. Such concessions
as have been made have usually been given reluctantly and have frequently been withdrawn. In all the European Communist states, including Russia, though to some extent excluding Czechoslovakia, there has
been a pattern of alternating thaw and freeze. If one could be confident
that recent concessions (where they have been made) were irreversible,
then it might be possible to argue that they represented a change of
attitude on the part of Communist leaders. But one can have no such
confidence.

Such a judgement, however, is too crude. Undoubtedly, some members of the Communist Parties in Poland and Hungary have come to share values, attitudes and expectations prevalent outside the Party, and to share these with conviction. A study of the internal history of the Communist Parties, if undertaken explicitly with this question in mind, would almost certainly reveal a degree of continuity between the opinions held by the public at large and those held within the Party. The cathartic shock of the condemnation of Stalin in February 1956 first brought this relationship to the surface. Such few references as we have to opinion within the Party in the surveys available to us point in this direction. The Hungarian revolution of 1956 was Communist-led. So were the reforms of the Prague Spring. In Yugoslavia and in China, the divergence from Soviet orthodoxy has been promoted by the Party leaders themselves, Tito and Mao Tse-tung. In China in particular, the Party and the Party leadership have been responsive to the conflicting demands of the Chinese political culture, and controversies within the Party have reflected conflicts of opinion among the population as a whole.

The conclusion seems obvious – but perhaps, nevertheless, worth stating: ruling Communist Parties have been strongly influenced by the national political culture and have shown themselves to be capable of a creative response in terms of that culture, except where Russian force has dictated the lines and the limits of change.

### DOMINANT POLITICAL CULTURE AND SUB-CULTURES

So far in this summing-up we have discussed the national political cultures as if they were homogeneous. In fact, however, we must always be alert to the possible existence of sub-cultures. First, there is the possibility of cultural division by class – briefly, the differences of attitudes as among peasants, workers and those of high education, high skills or managerial experience. There is a vast literature on the social and political idiosyncrasies of peasant communities, but in the concrete evidence available to the authors of this book there is almost nothing which would enable us to delineate for any country a peasant political sub-culture. However, as the peasants are a rapidly dwindling class in all of these countries except China, this perhaps matters less. As far as the workers are concerned, a good deal of our survey material has measured their attitudes and to some extent distinguished them from the attitudes of the intelligentsia, but this material would certainly give us no justification for postulating the existence in any of these countries of a distinctive working-class political culture. In all of these societies the only difference that can be shown is that a somewhat lower proportion of working-class respondents are committed to certain values and

aspirations expressed by the intelligentsia. This difference is so slight as
to throw into serious doubt the whole idea, fundamental to the political
expectations of the Communist Party élites, that there is a difference
between working-class consciousness and 'middle-class' consciousness as
far as politics is concerned, at least during the period in which socialism
is being built. True, in Communist theory there should be no such
difference within the socialist state; this however, assumes a shared
'socialist' consciousness in which the distinction between worker and
functionary disappears in the creation of new socialist man. When,
however, this shared consciousness expresses dissonance from the official
political culture, and an attachment to pre-Communist values and
symbols, the virtual identity of views between workers and 'middle-
class' elements takes on a different meaning.

Having found it possible to distinguish among different national
political cultures, we are also able to make distinctions among the
cultures of national groups within the same state. The two most obvious
and interesting cases are Czechoslovakia, with the significant differences
between Czech and Slovak, and Yugoslavia with its mixture of nationalities and religions and the sharply contrasting historical experience of
these different groups.

The 1968 surveys conducted in Czechoslovakia provide an opportunity to examine whether or not there is a separate Slovak political
culture. On the question of identification with foreign countries, while
both Czechs and Slovaks (expressing no doubt a conviction that the
Yugoslav system offered far greater freedom within socialism than any
other Communist country) voted overwhelmingly for Yugoslavia, their
subsequent choices (see Chapter 6) showed substantial differences.

The Slovaks were much less ready than the Czechs to identify with
the pre-war democratic Republic and with Masaryk (although he was
half-Slovak), and generally speaking they showed significantly less
commitment to liberal values and a significantly greater tolerance of
authoritarian systems. The Czechs' commitment to pluralist democracy
may be largely attributed to their distinctive pre-1918 political experience and to the fact that they were better prepared than the Slovaks
to take advantage of the possibilities offered by the First Republic. It
may also be associated with the strong tradition of religious dissent in
Czechoslovakia and to the disproportionate influence of the Protestant
minority on Czech values. Conversely, the different values in Slovakia
may in some measure be due to the traditional overwhelming predominance of Catholicism in Slovakia.

The political differences should not be overstressed. Both communities, in the circumstances of 1968 at least, showed a high level of
identification with liberal, pluralist values. Even then, however, a major
concern of Slovaks was with righting what they perceived as their
specifically *national* grievances. And the political cultural differences

are probably sufficiently great to be exploited by a government or a foreign power which saw advantages in a policy of divide and rule – a situation which some observers would see in Czechoslovakia today.

In Yugoslavia, tensions among the different nationalities tend to mask any differences there might be with respect to political culture. Yet in a country which includes Orthodox, Catholic and Muslim communities, and in which there are obvious historical differences in experience of the state, which was for some the Habsburg bureaucratic autocracy and for others the local *begs* of a remote Turkish despotism (and for others little except their own local and tribal customs), there must be profound differences. Indeed, as far as Yugoslavia is concerned, to think in terms of a dominant culture and sub-cultures is inappropriate, because no national group has a majority and each group has – potentially at least – its own political culture. Until recently, the confrontation between Serbs and non-Serbs in a centralised multinational state has tended to obscure positive differences in political cultures. Federalism and *samoupravljanji* may now give freer rein to such differences, and may at the same time provide the answer to the question whether the new decentralised system has in fact been, partly at least, the consequence of these differences. Present existing survey material does not provide a rounded picture of each political culture; but it suggests what differences there might be. What one can say with confidence, however, is that no national group within Yugoslavia, except for the Serbs (and they are probably only a partial exception) holds high expectations of centralised bureaucracy. Croat habits of self-government, Slovene peasant distaste for officialdom, Macedonian ambivalence towards the state, Montenegrin and South Serbian 'Dinaric man' attitudes, all in different (and perhaps conflicting) ways tend to support decentralisation and local autonomy.

Although the information available to us is far less systematic and satisfactory from the point of view of comparisons than we would wish, it is nevertheless possible to reach some tentative comparative conclusion, if only as a basis for further work.

It is quite clear that national political cultures have played some part in the political changes which have taken place throughout the Communist world. In particular, where pluralist, parliamentary aspirations have been a part of the national tradition, if only a subordinate part, these aspirations have been strengthened rather than weakened in reaction to the experience of one-party Communist rule.

The attempt to create a new socialist man, the end product of the official political culture, has been on the whole a depressing failure; the authoritarian, bureaucratic practice of most of these régimes (as opposed to the long-term ideal) has quite clearly scotched the development of the sort of participatory democracy through which the new socialist citizen must be created if he is to be created at all. Indeed the effort to create him has visibly slackened as the acceptance of 'legal consciousness', expressed obliquely in Kadar's 'He who is not against us is for us', has spread. Almost, everywhere apathy, privatism and 'economism' are prevalent and tolerated and sometimes even encouraged. Only China and perhaps Cuba (although bureaucratism is growing apace there too) still pay more than lip service to the idea; and only in China has there been a consistent and vigorous attempt to create a new kind of social and political organisation which will (it is hoped) provide a milieu in which the new man can grow.

There has been little sign of much penetration of the national political cultures by the official culture, except in the form of a vague general commitment to socialism, undefined.

There is a substantial and significant contrast between those countries in which Russian influence puts sharp limits on the possibility of change, and those countries (China, Cuba and Yugoslavia) which are independent. The degree of divergence in these countries is very great. Cuba may be a case merely of incomplete *con*vergence, but in the other two countries free of Russian dominance the Communist system has been wholly remodelled in ways powerfully influenced by national tradition.

In general, many aspects of political culture in the Communist world suggest that modernisation and industrialisation tend to produce significant similarities notwithstanding differences of ideology between East and West; but again it is worth noting that the two socialist countries which have most clearly broken away from Soviet orthodoxy have both, though in very different ways, revolutionised industrial organisation and management in a deliberate attempt to avoid the apparently universal political and social consequences of orthodox industrialisation.

Perhaps the most striking implication of our study is the relative failure of Communist processes of socialisation and education, in spite of the enjoyment of all the institutional powers which a Communist political system bestows.

Amid all the variety of values, attitudes, expectations and attachments which our study of seven Communist countries has revealed, there is one persistent theme – the question of the handling of conflict.

The Yugoslav author quoted by David Dyker, who criticised Yugoslav education on the grounds that it taught the young to expect a conflict-free world and that it was therefore an inappropriate preparation for participation in self-management, touched on a theme which is central to the problems of Communist politics.

One of the main premises of Mao Tse-tung's criticisms of the Soviet Union (both under Stalin and his successors) was that the Russians asserted that there were no grounds for conflict in socialist society. Mao on the contrary accepts that conflict is both inevitable and healthy, and in his theory the question of how best to handle conflict occupies a prominent place. Richard Solomon was able to write a revealing narrative of Chinese political history in the early sixties, based on the hypothesis that the controversies of the time were all about how to handle conflict; and while no such one-factor explanation will explain everything it is remarkable how much this one factor does explain.

Economists have pointed out that the idea of marginal utility is missing from Marxist economics. In the same way, and in a close psychological relationship, the idea of legitimate conflict and competition is missing from Marxist politics. The market place, whether for goods or ideas, is irrational and dangerous.

Perhaps the most important conclusion which this book suggests is that in countries where there has in the past been experience of the fruitful play of competing ideas and competing interests, experience of Communist government has not weakened but actually strengthened the conviction among the population that political freedom brings both greater justice and greater efficiency.

# Index

Bruegel, J. W., 191
Brus, W., xii
Brzezinski, Z. K., 129
Buchanan, Sir George, 29
Buck, P., 229
Bulgaria, 15
Burlatsky, F. M., 58
Buzek, A., 128

Čapek, Karel, 193
Carter, April, xii
Casimir (the Great), 101, 261
Castro, Fidel, 236, 242, 248
  coming to power, 233, 235, 245, 246, 247
  political beliefs, 239, 240–1, 243, 244, 252
  style of leadership, 237, 238, 249, 250
Castro, Juana, 249
Castro, Raul, 243, 249, 252
Cavendish, Patrick, viii
censorship
  China, 224–5
  Czechoslovakia, 184, 185, 193
  Hungary, 150
  Poland, 102, 115, 128
  USSR, 33, 62
  Yugoslavia, 82
Cespedes, C. M., 248
Četnici, 75, 76, 88
Chalidze, V., 62
Charles IV, King, 164, 165, 166, 179, 180
Chermensky, E. D., 60
Cherniavsky, M., 59, 60
Chesneaux, J., 229
Chiang Kai-shek, 218
Chibas, E., 237, 247, 248
Ch'ien Lung, Emperor, 220
Chikin, V., 62
Chile, 239, 244, 245
Ch'in dynasty, 201
China, 1, 188, 197–230, 231, 243, 257, 265, 266, 267, 268, 271
  cultural revolution, 211, 216, 222–3, 224, 225
  Great Leap Forward, 213, 214, 216, 233

legalism, 199, 201
paucity of data, 10, 11, 15, 19, 263
People's Liberation Army, 220
political trials, 228
Taiping rebellion, 208, 210
Taipings, 209, 210
Taoism, 199, 201, 222
Chinese Communist Party, 205, 210, 218–19, 224–5, 228, 229
Chodak, S., 128
Chou Yang, 224
Chulanov, Yu. G., 55, 64
Cieplak, T., 129
Cimić, E., 99
'civic culture', 12–13, 260
Clementis, V., 179, 180, 186
Colombia, 233
Colotka, P., 175
Comenius, J. A., 179, 180
communism (full), 35, 214, 217, 240–241
comparative Communism, xi, 13–16, 20, 22–3
Confucianism, 1, 197, 199, 200, 201, 202, 203, 204, 205, 223, 224, 266, 267
Confucius, 197, 223, 224
Connor, W. D., 62
Copernicus, N., 103
CPSU (Communist Party of the Soviet Union), 14, 41, 182
  Programme, 35
  Twentieth Congress, 184, 185–6
  Twenty-second Congress, 184, 185–186
  Twenty-third Congress, 46
  Twenty-fourth Congress, 37, 46
Critchley, W. Harriet, 23
Croatia, 67, 68, 69, 72, 75, 79, 89
  nationalism, 93–4, 95, 97
Cuba, 1, 15, 231–52, 253, 258, 263, 264, 271
  armed forces, 243, 244, 245
  Constitution, 244
  paucity of data, 11, 19
  and USA, 234–5, 237, 239, 240, 243
  and USSR, 238, 239, 241
Cuban Communist Party, 239, 243–4